CHAPTER 21

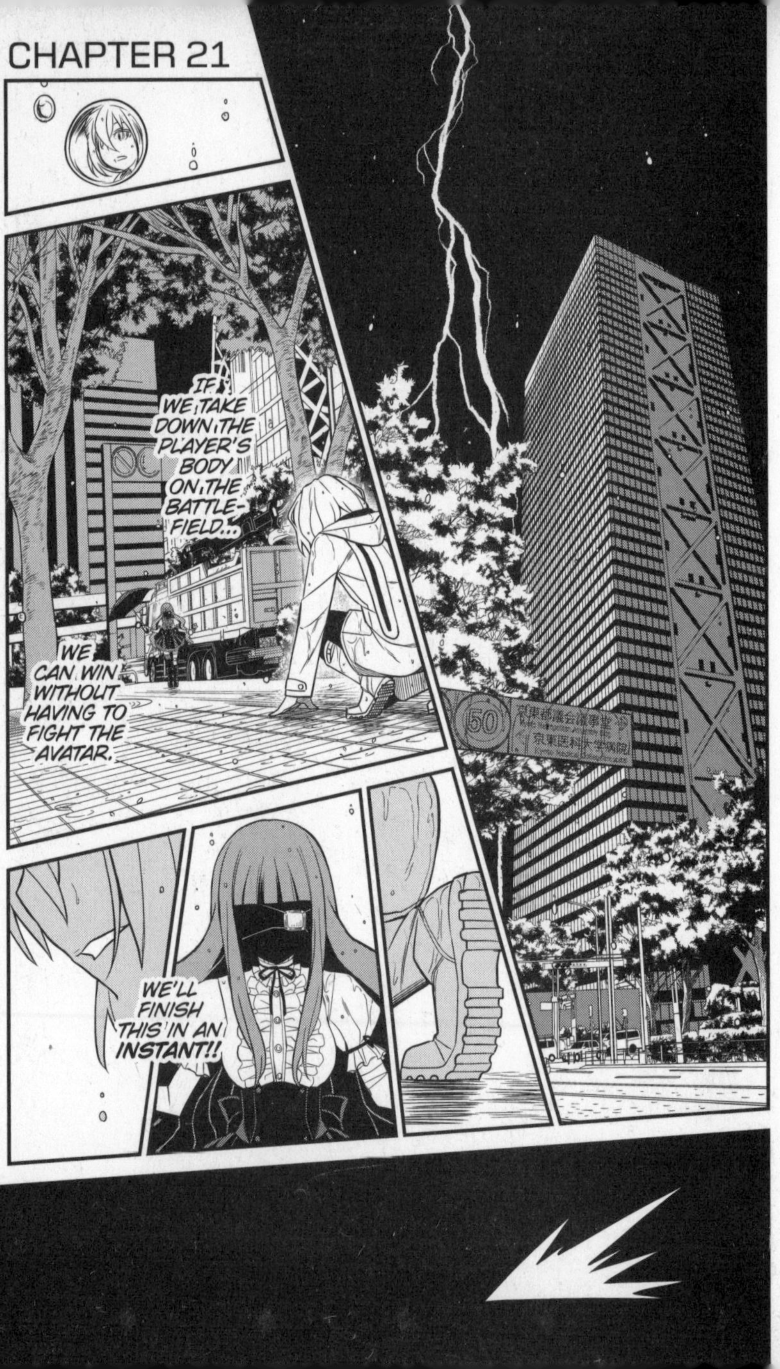
IF WE TAKE DOWN THE PLAYER'S BODY ON THE BATTLEFIELD...
WE CAN WIN WITHOUT HAVING TO FIGHT THE AVATAR.
WE'LL FINISH THIS IN AN INSTANT!!

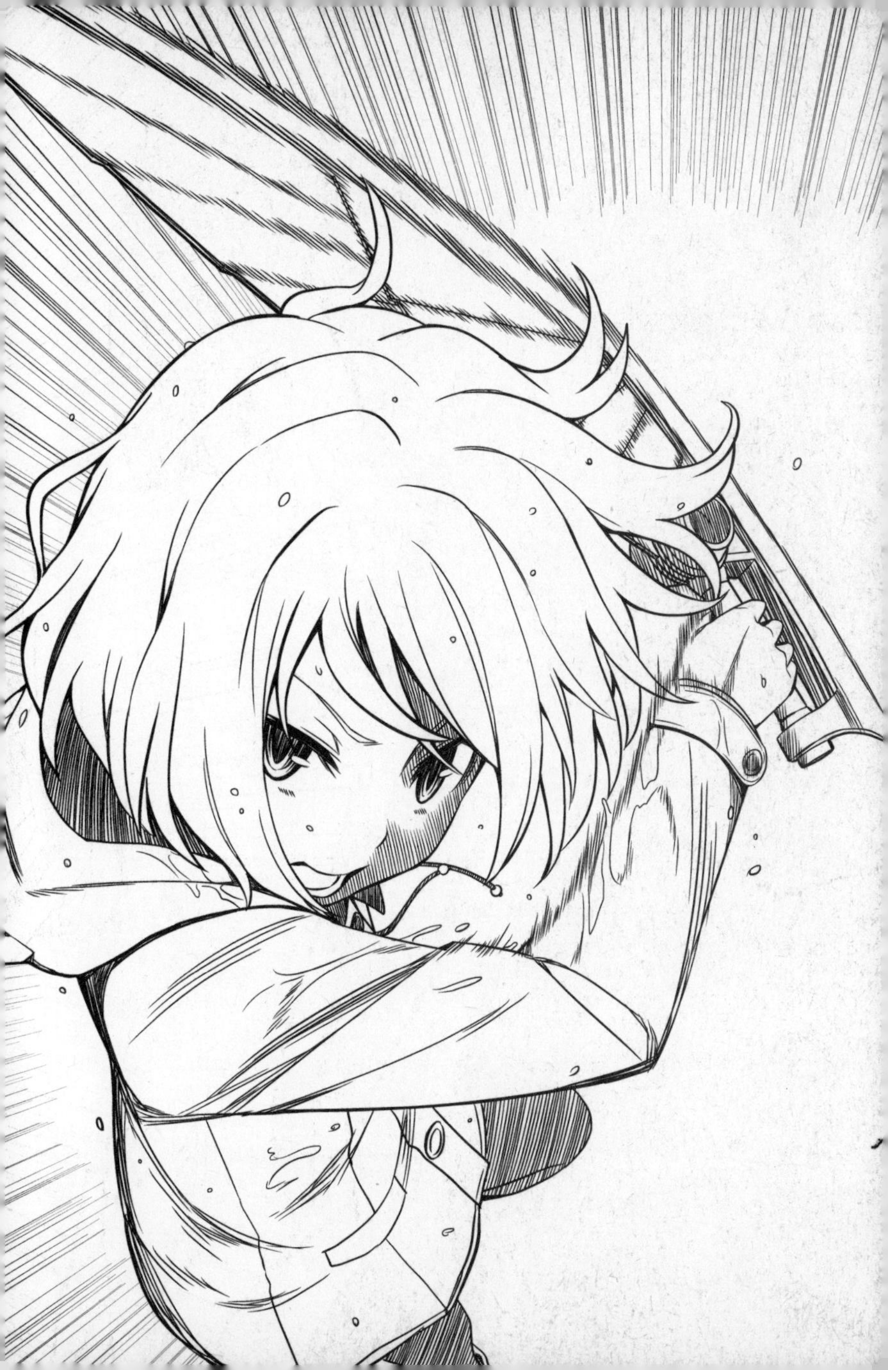

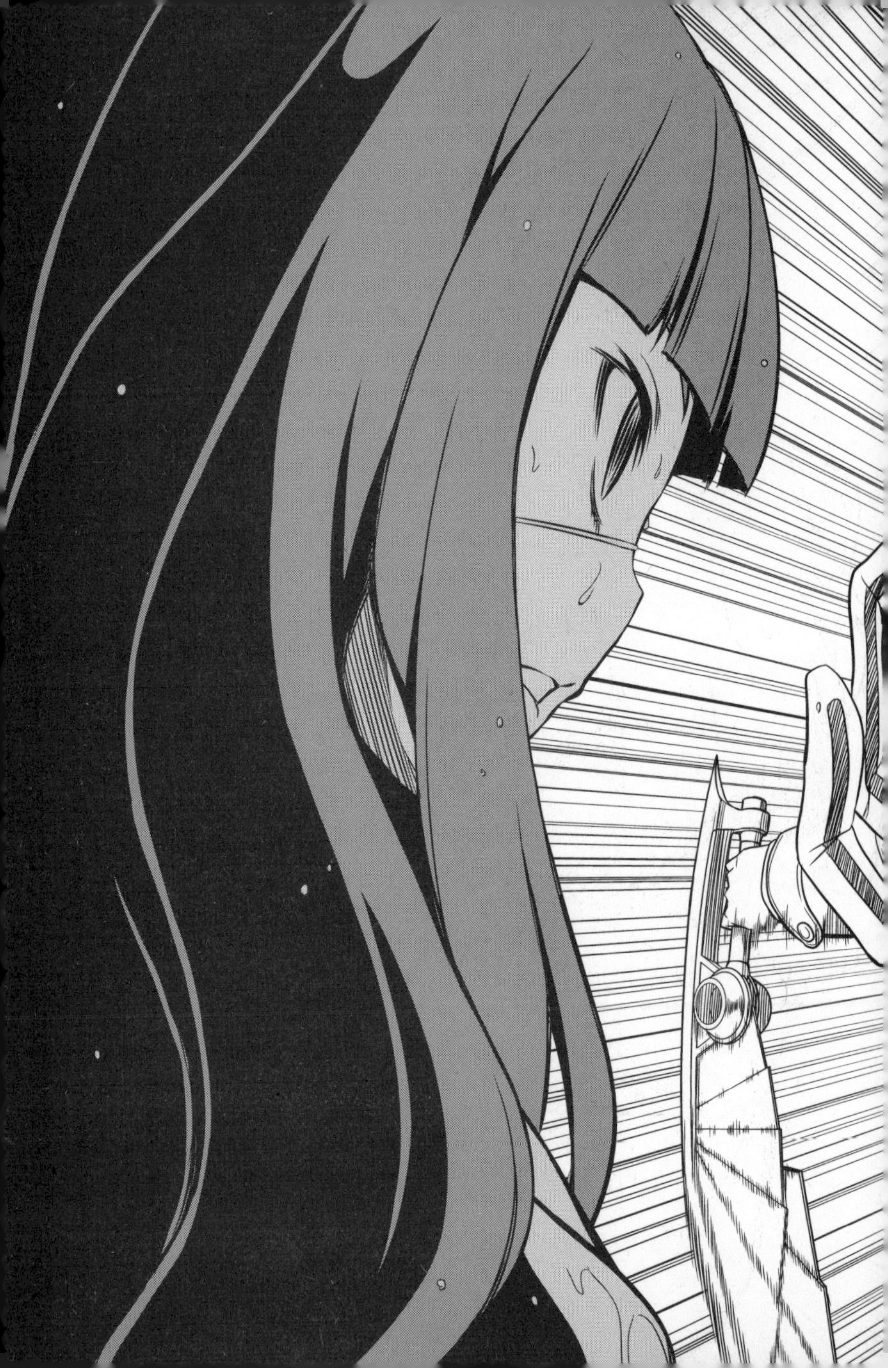

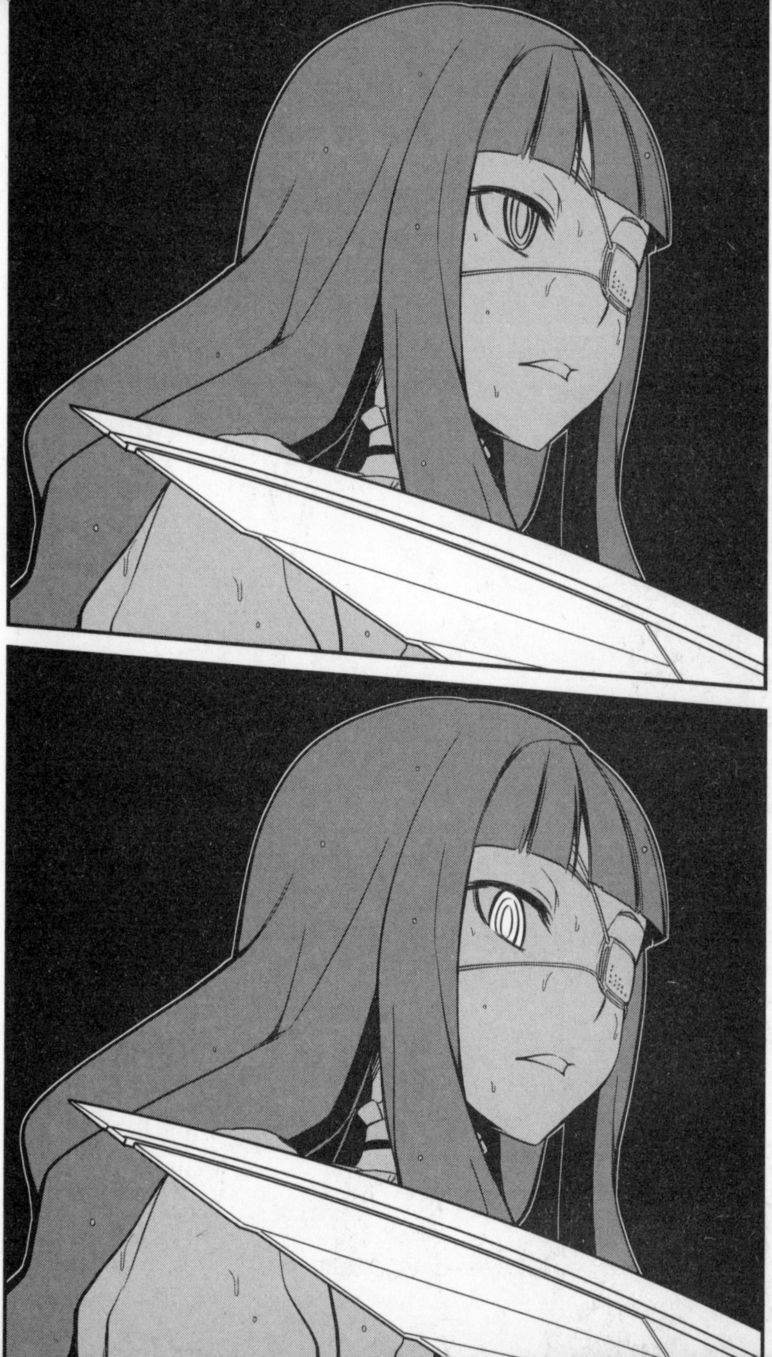

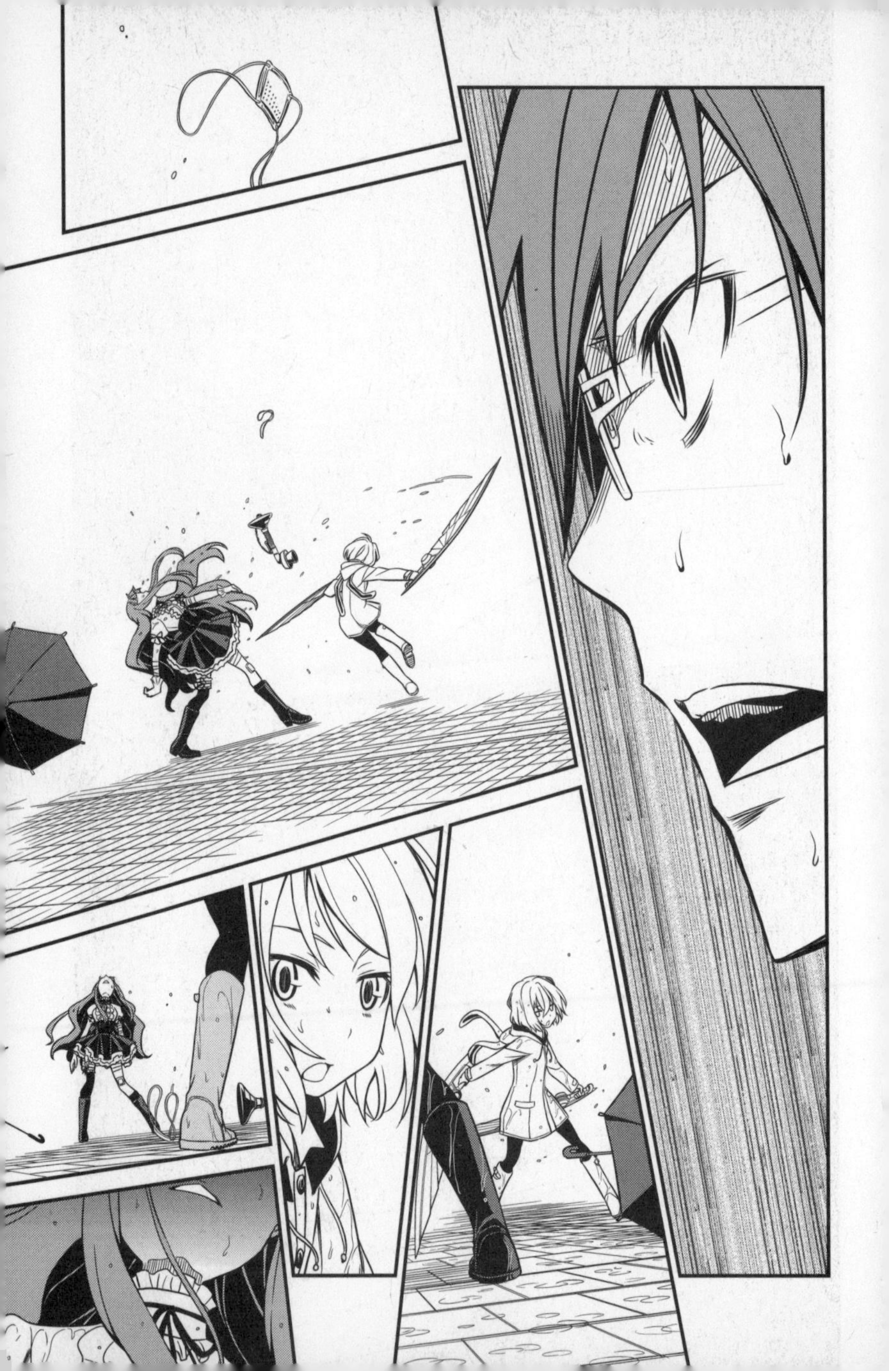

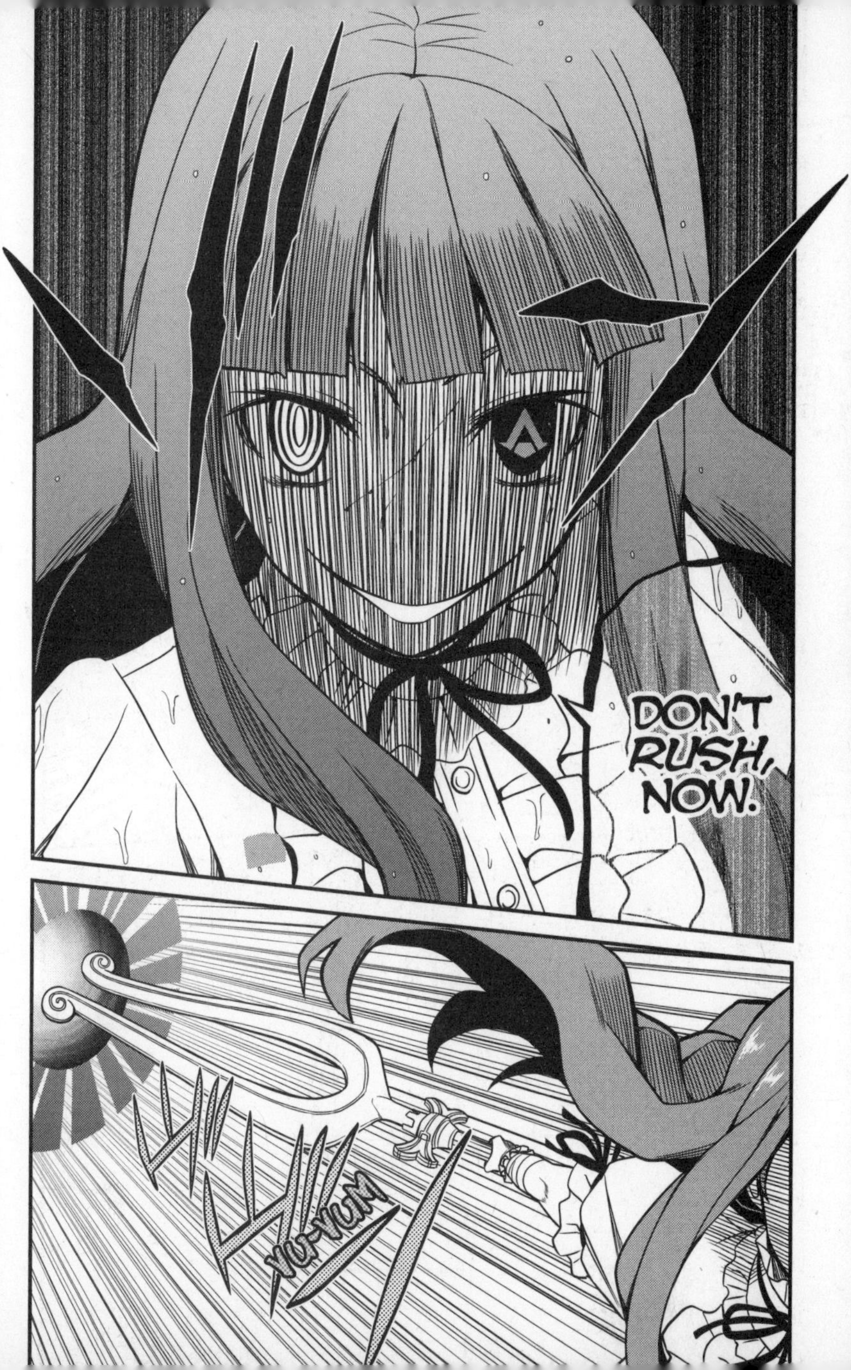
DON'T RUSH, NOW.
VU-VUM

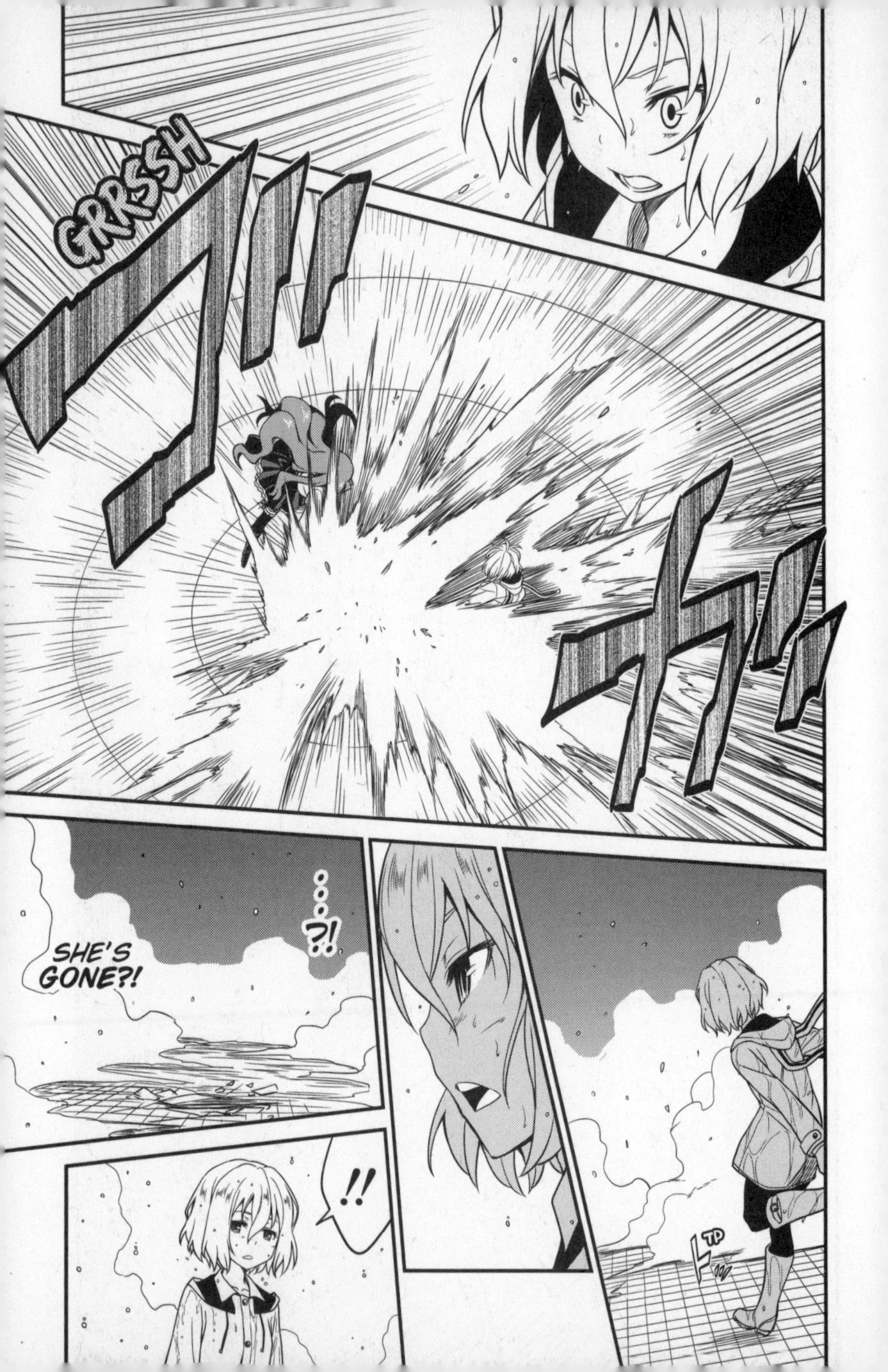
GRRSSH
TP
...?!
SHE'S GONE?!
!!

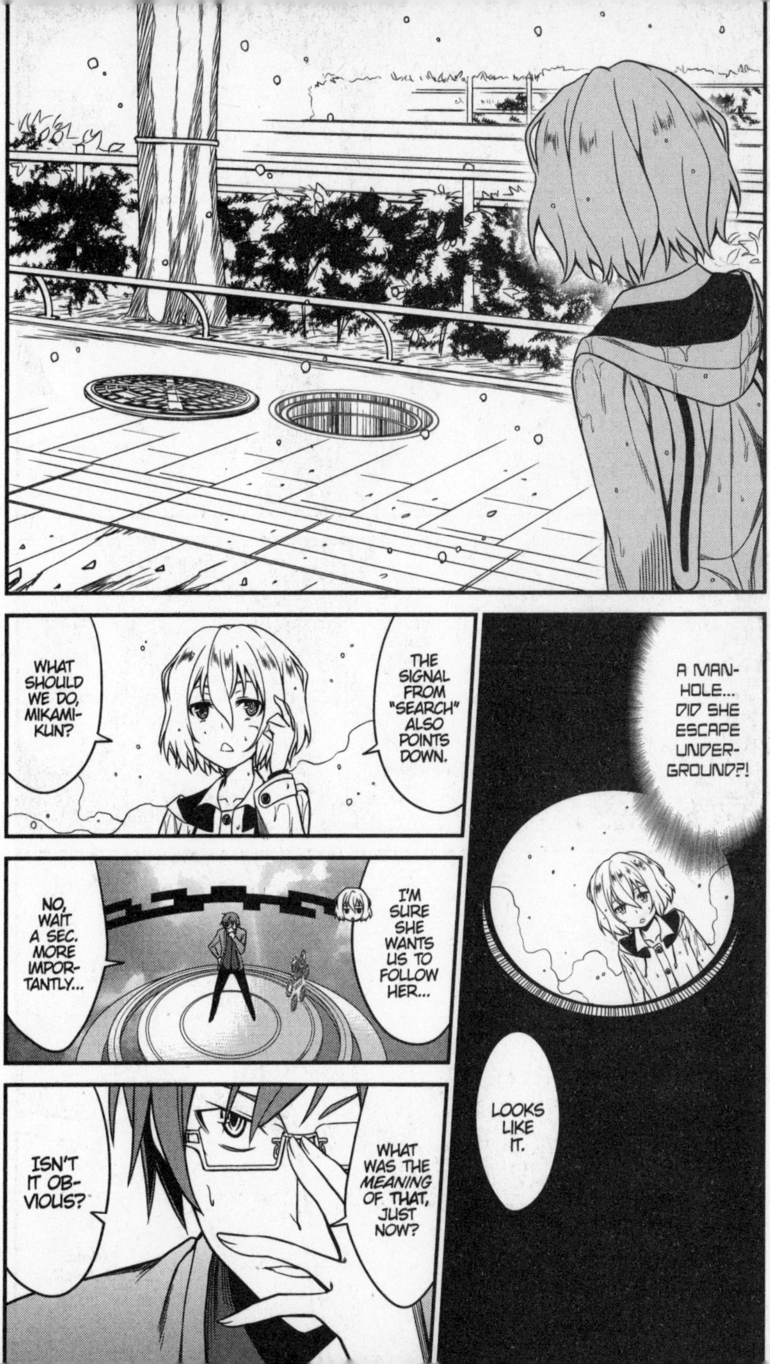
A MAN-HOLE... DID SHE ESCAPE UNDER-GROUND?!
LOOKS LIKE IT.
THE SIGNAL FROM "SEARCH" ALSO POINTS DOWN.
WHAT SHOULD WE DO, MIKAMI-KUN?
I'M SURE SHE WANTS US TO FOLLOW HER...
NO, WAIT A SEC. MORE IMPORTANTLY...
WHAT WAS THE *MEANING* OF THAT, JUST NOW?
ISN'T IT OBVIOUS?

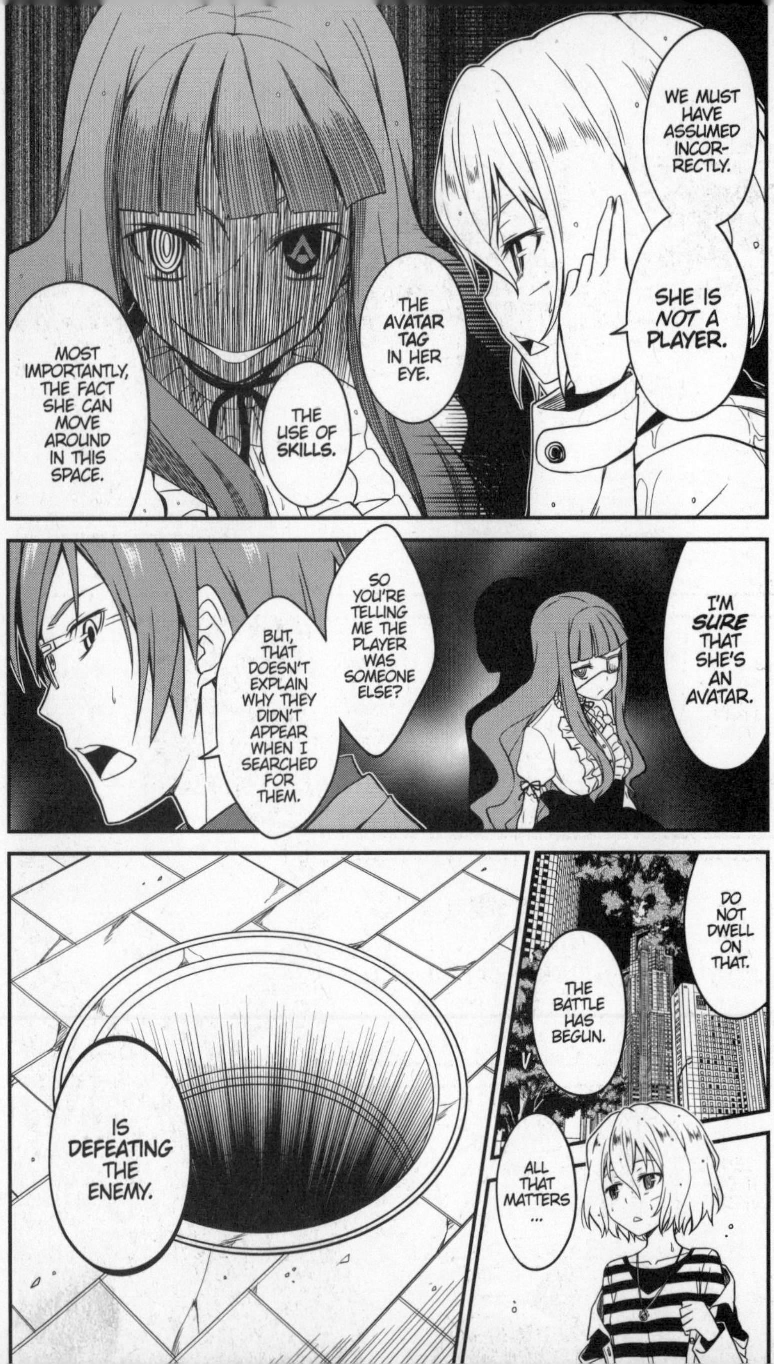
WE MUST HAVE ASSUMED INCORRECTLY.
SHE IS *NOT* A PLAYER.
THE AVATAR TAG IN HER EYE.
THE USE OF SKILLS.
MOST IMPORTANTLY, THE FACT SHE CAN MOVE AROUND IN THIS SPACE.
I'M *SURE* THAT SHE'S AN AVATAR.
SO YOU'RE TELLING ME THE PLAYER WAS SOMEONE ELSE?
BUT, THAT DOESN'T EXPLAIN WHY THEY DIDN'T APPEAR WHEN I SEARCHED FOR THEM.
DO NOT DWELL ON THAT.
THE BATTLE HAS BEGUN.
ALL THAT MATTERS...
IS DEFEATING THE ENEMY.

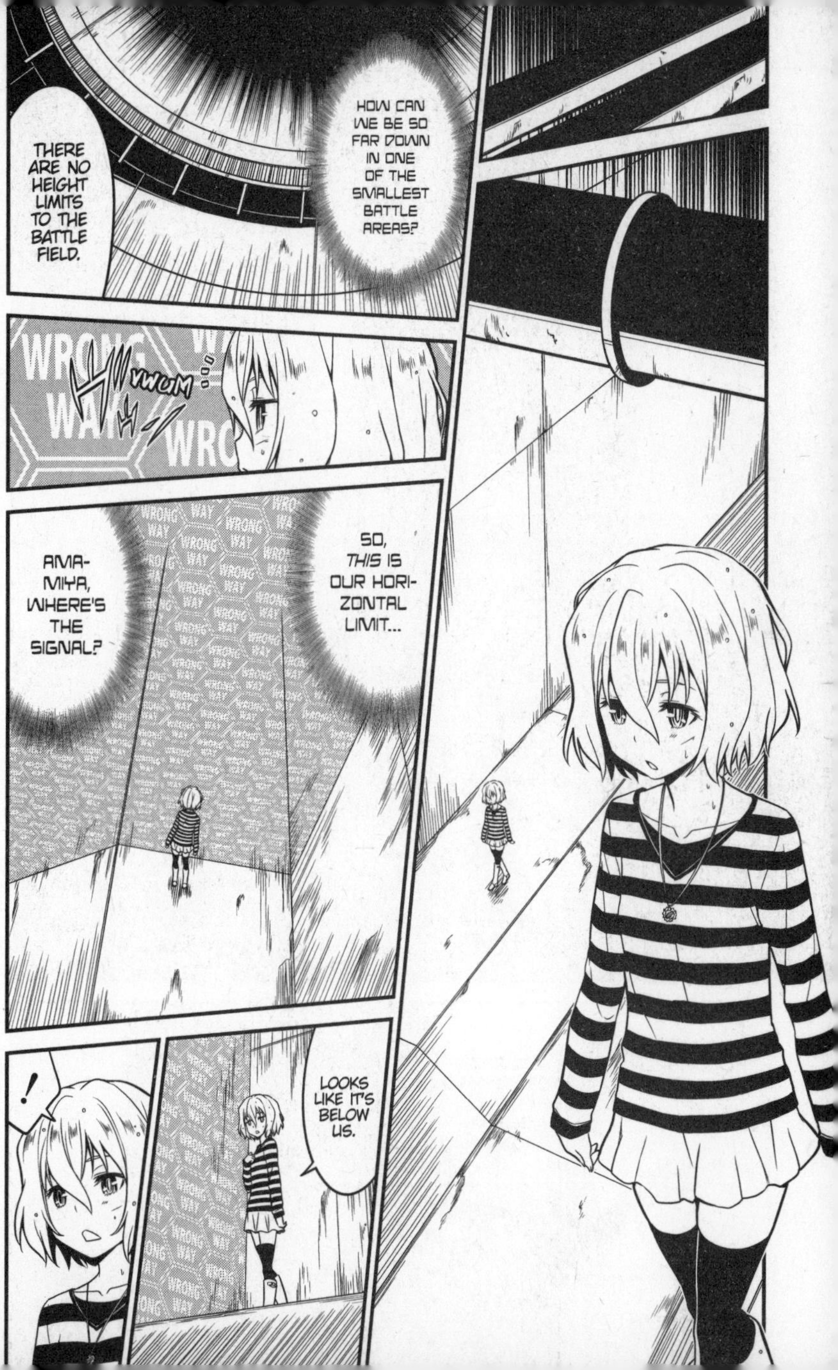
HOW CAN WE BE SO FAR DOWN IN ONE OF THE SMALLEST BATTLE AREAS?
THERE ARE NO HEIGHT LIMITS TO THE BATTLE FIELD.
WRONG WAY
VWUM
SO, *THIS* IS OUR HORI-ZONTAL LIMIT...
AMA-MIYA, WHERE'S THE SIGNAL?
LOOKS LIKE IT'S BELOW US.
!

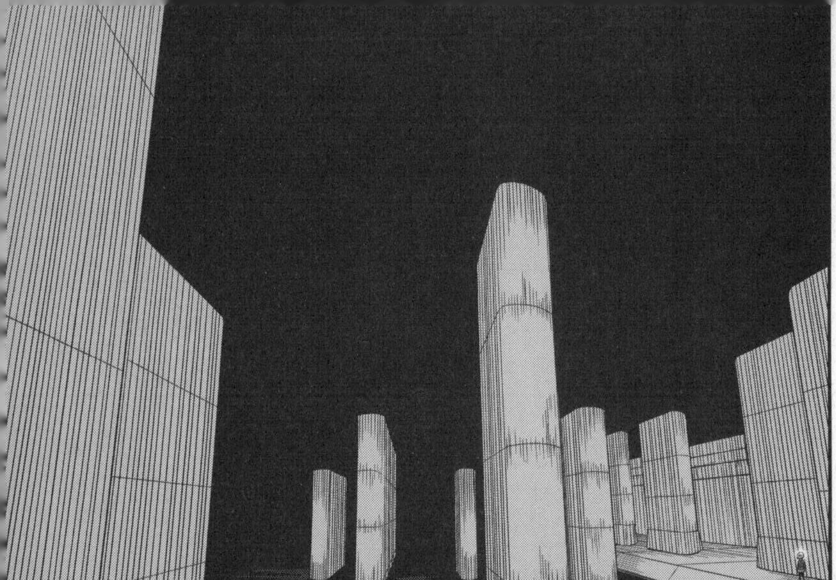

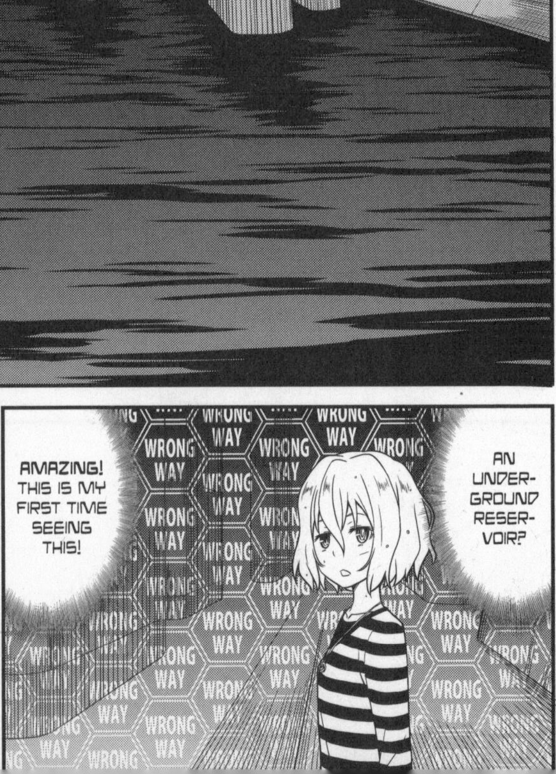
AN UNDER-GROUND RESER-VOIR?
AMAZING! THIS IS MY FIRST TIME SEEING THIS!

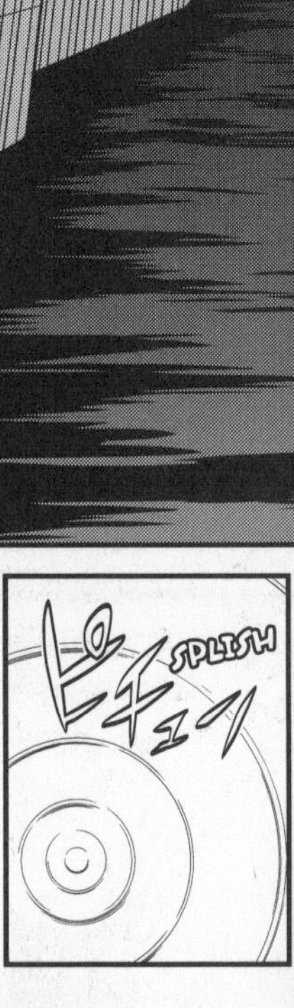
SPLISH

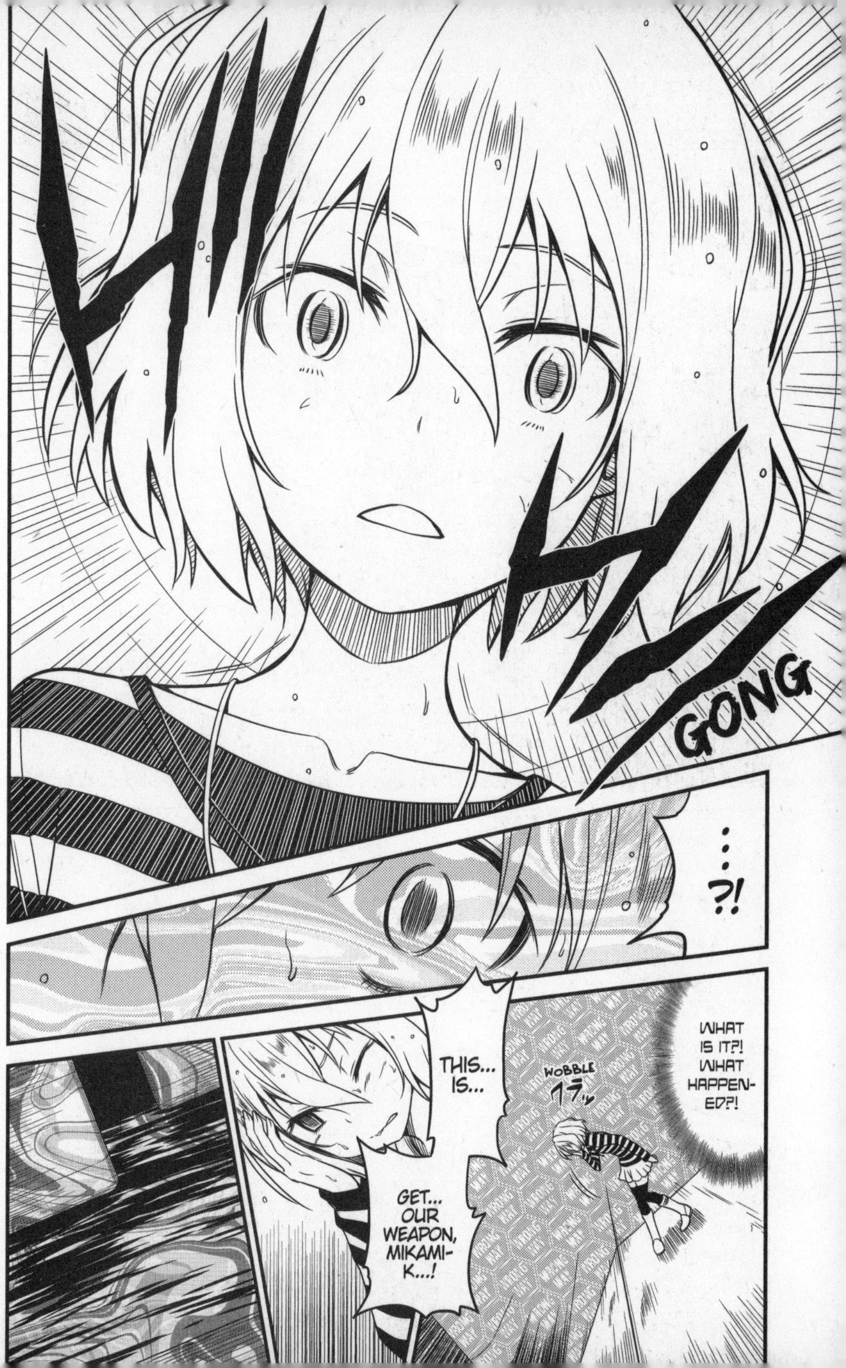
GONG
...
?!
WHAT IS IT?! WHAT HAPPEN-ED?!
WOBBLE
THIS... IS...
GET... OUR WEAPON, MIKAMI-K...!

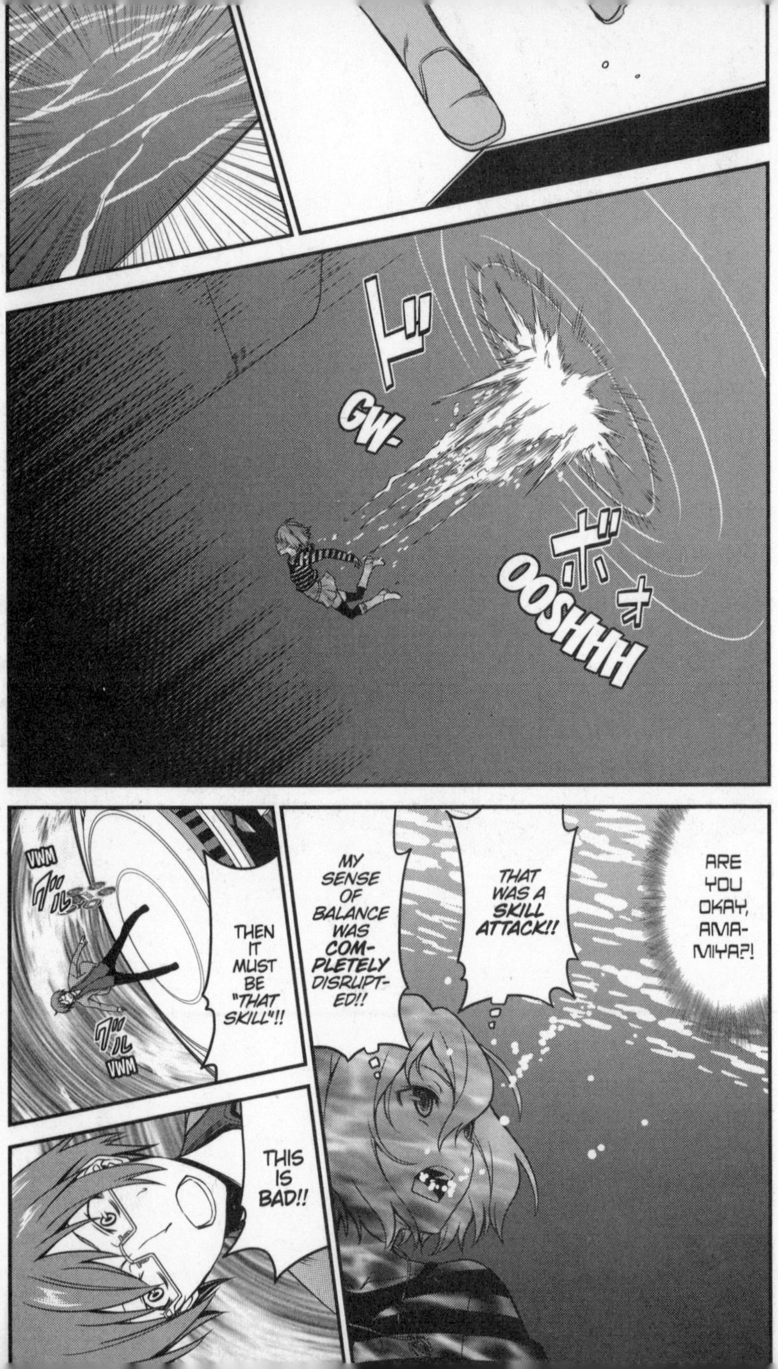
ドッ
GW-
ボォ
OOSHHHH
ARE YOU OKAY, AMA-MIYA?!
THAT WAS A SKILL ATTACK!!
MY SENSE OF BALANCE WAS COM-PLETELY DISRUPT-ED!!
VWM
グル
THEN IT MUST BE "THAT SKILL"!!
グル
VWM
THIS IS BAD!!

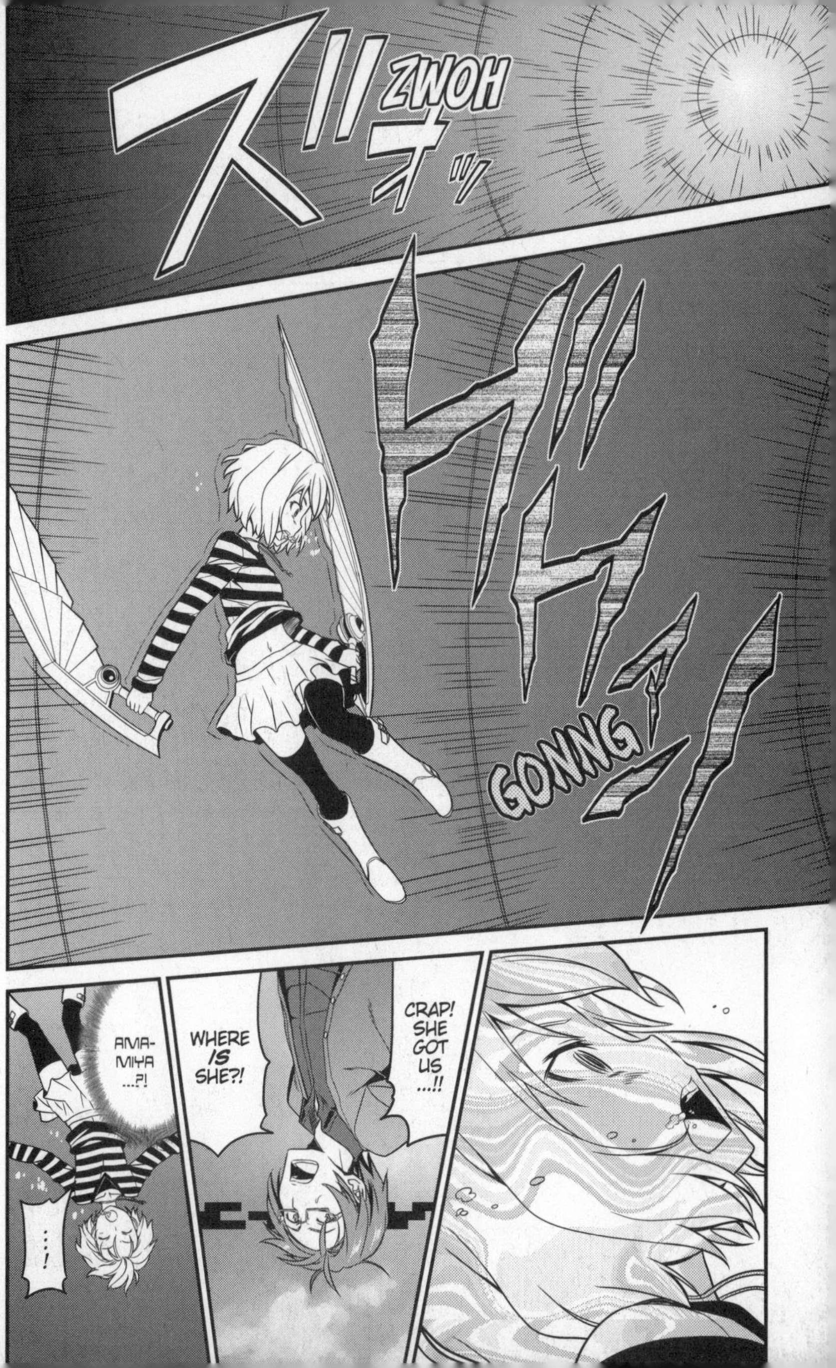
ZWOH
GONNG
CRAP! SHE GOT US ...!!
WHERE IS SHE?!
AMA-MIYA ...?!
...!

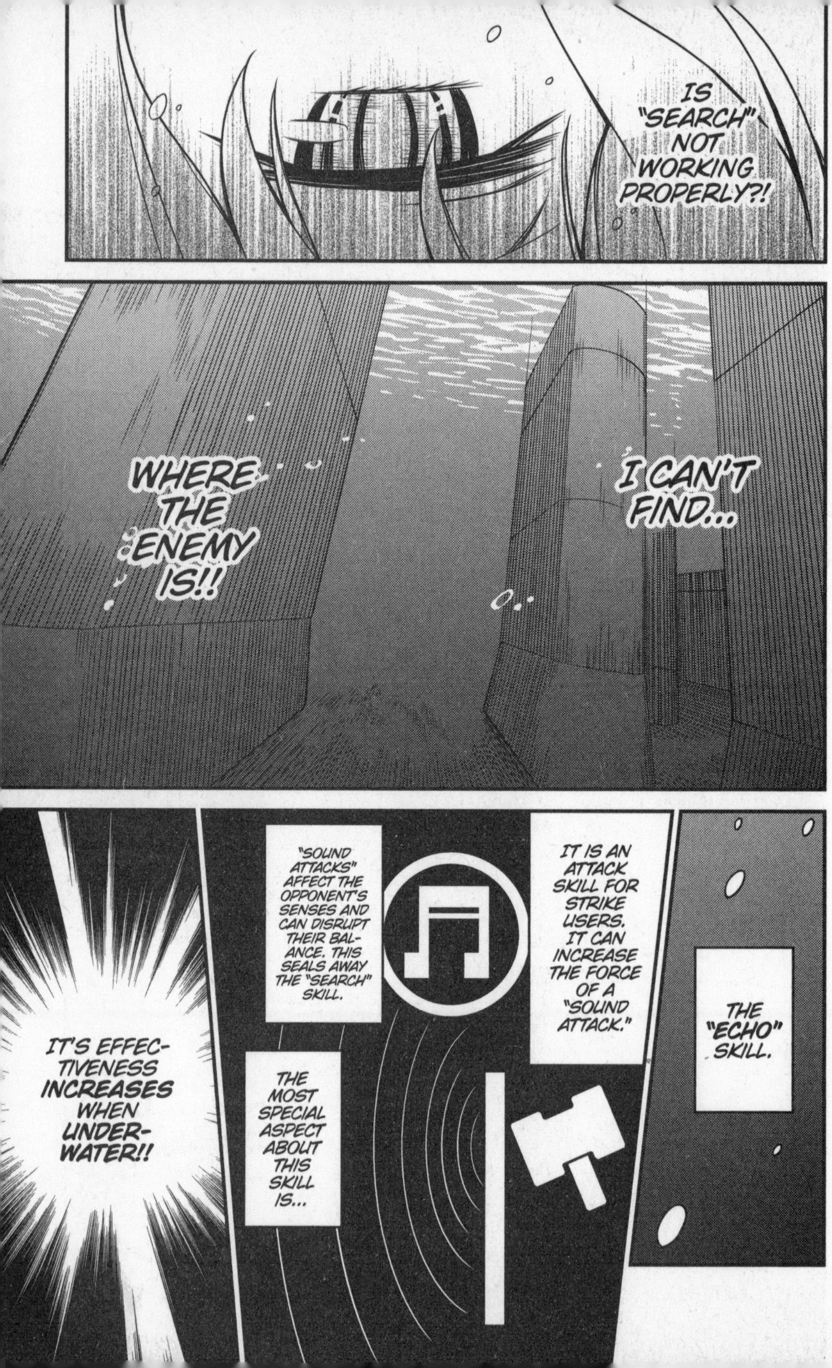
IS "SEARCH" NOT WORKING PROPERLY?!
I CAN'T FIND...
WHERE THE ENEMY IS!!
THE "ECHO" SKILL.
IT IS AN ATTACK SKILL FOR STRIKE USERS. IT CAN INCREASE THE FORCE OF A "SOUND ATTACK."
"SOUND ATTACKS" AFFECT THE OPPONENT'S SENSES AND CAN DISRUPT THEIR BAL-ANCE. THIS SEALS AWAY THE "SEARCH" SKILL.
THE MOST SPECIAL ASPECT ABOUT THIS SKILL IS...
IT'S EFFEC-TIVENESS INCREASES WHEN UNDER-WATER!!

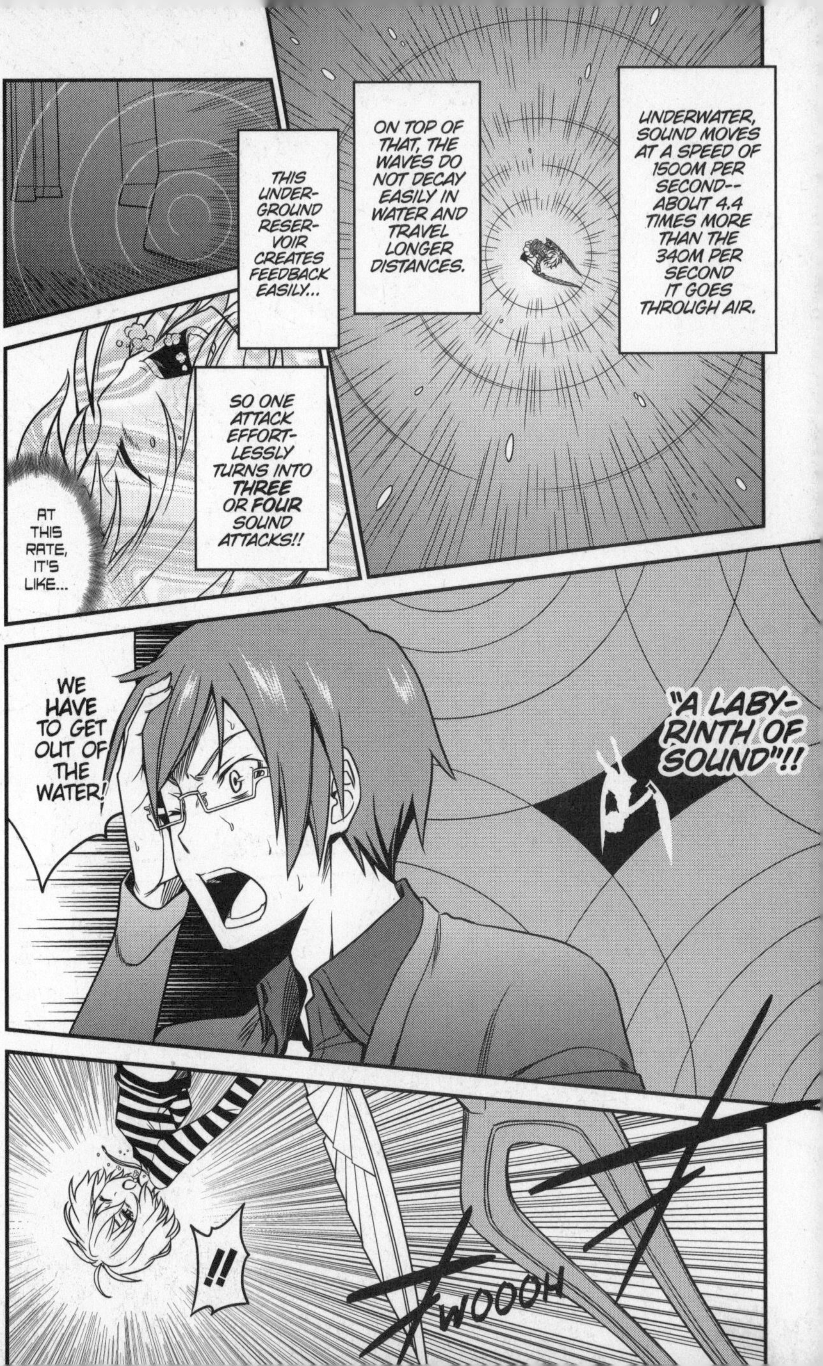
UNDERWATER, SOUND MOVES AT A SPEED OF 1500M PER SECOND--ABOUT 4.4 TIMES MORE THAN THE 340M PER SECOND IT GOES THROUGH AIR.
ON TOP OF THAT, THE WAVES DO NOT DECAY EASILY IN WATER AND TRAVEL LONGER DISTANCES.
THIS UNDER-GROUND RESER-VOIR CREATES FEEDBACK EASILY...
SO ONE ATTACK EFFORT-LESSLY TURNS INTO THREE OR FOUR SOUND ATTACKS!!
AT THIS RATE, IT'S LIKE...
"A LABY-RINTH OF SOUND"!!
WE HAVE TO GET OUT OF THE WATER!
WOOOH
!!

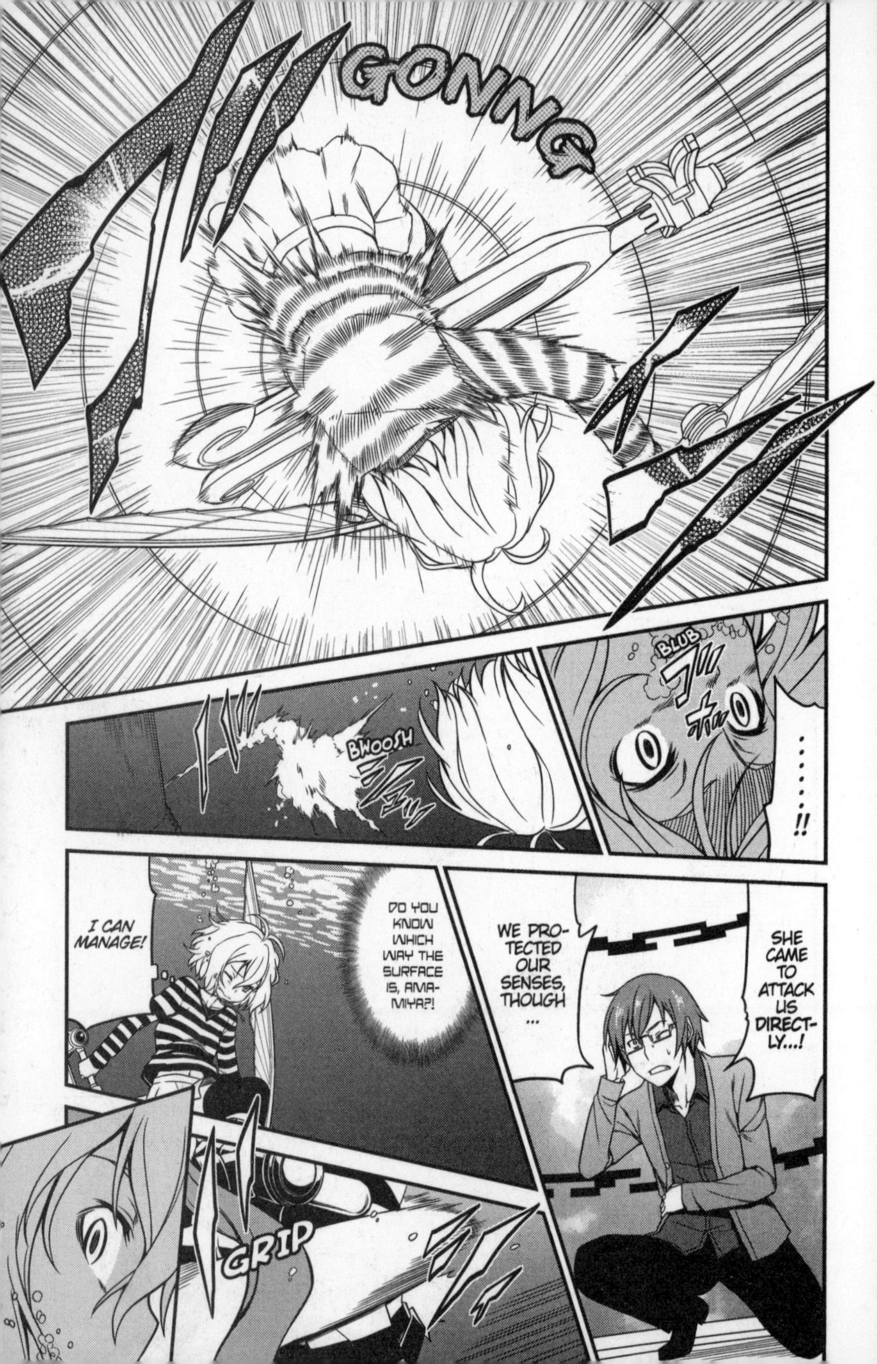
GONNG
BLUB
......!!
BWOOSH
SHE CAME TO ATTACK US DIRECTLY...!
WE PROTECTED OUR SENSES, THOUGH...
DO YOU KNOW WHICH WAY THE SURFACE IS, AMAMIYA?!
I CAN MANAGE!
GRIP

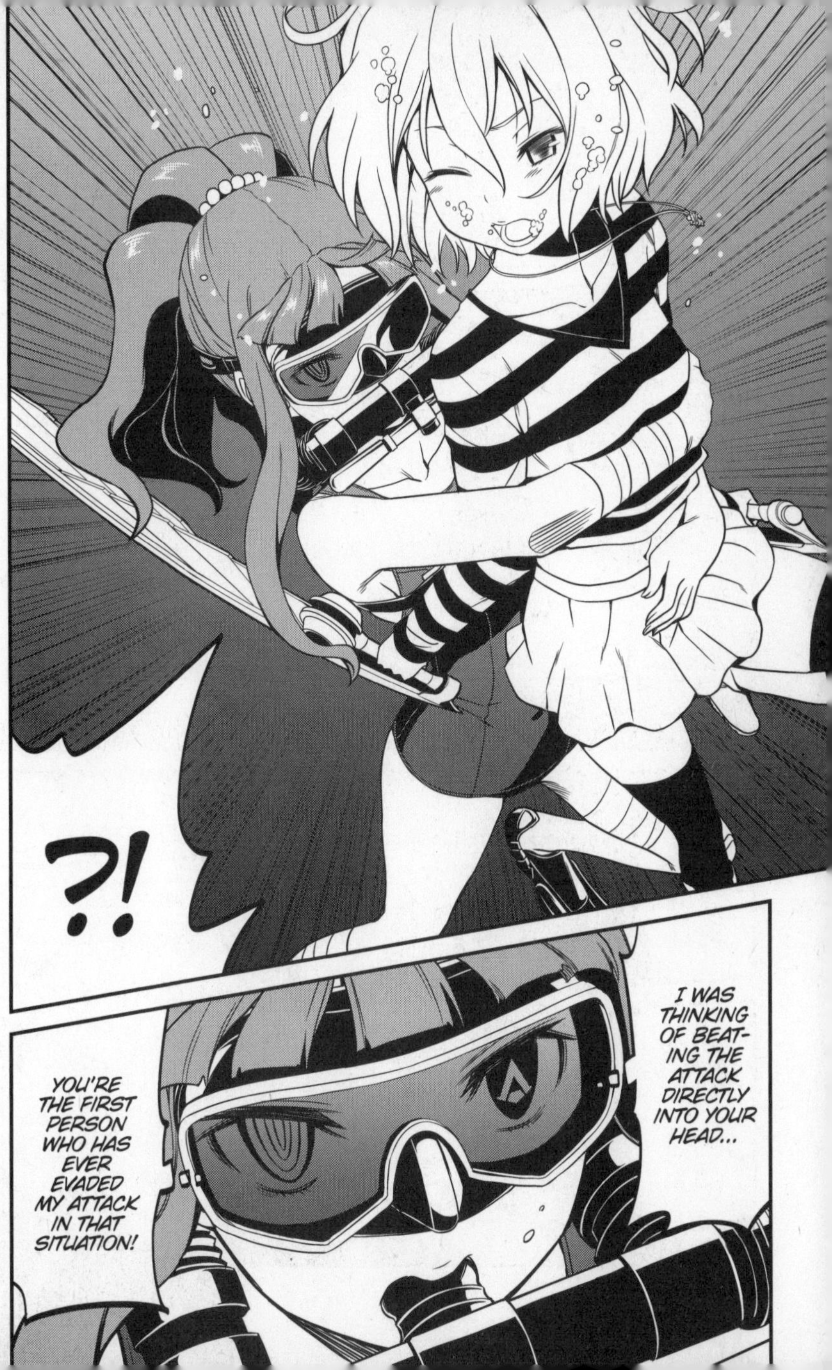
?!
I WAS THINKING OF BEAT-ING THE ATTACK DIRECTLY INTO YOUR HEAD...
YOU'RE THE FIRST PERSON WHO HAS EVER EVADED MY ATTACK IN THAT SITUATION!

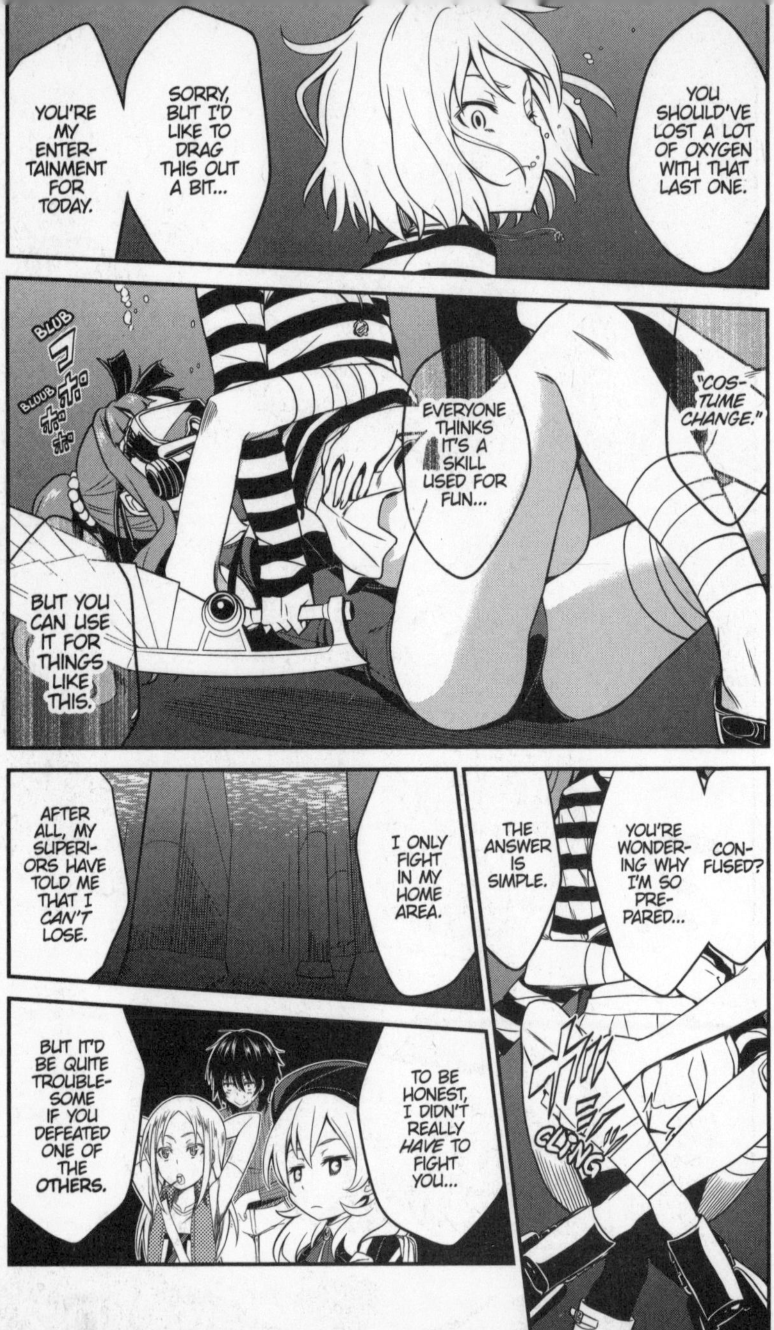
YOU SHOULD'VE LOST A LOT OF OXYGEN WITH THAT LAST ONE.
SORRY, BUT I'D LIKE TO DRAG THIS OUT A BIT...
YOU'RE MY ENTERTAINMENT FOR TODAY.
"COSTUME CHANGE."
EVERYONE THINKS IT'S A SKILL USED FOR FUN...
BLUB
BLUUB
BUT YOU CAN USE IT FOR THINGS LIKE THIS.
CONFUSED?
YOU'RE WONDERING WHY I'M SO PREPARED...
THE ANSWER IS SIMPLE.
GLING
I ONLY FIGHT IN MY HOME AREA.
AFTER ALL, MY SUPERIORS HAVE TOLD ME THAT I CAN'T LOSE.
TO BE HONEST, I DIDN'T REALLY HAVE TO FIGHT YOU...
BUT IT'D BE QUITE TROUBLESOME IF YOU DEFEATED ONE OF THE OTHERS.

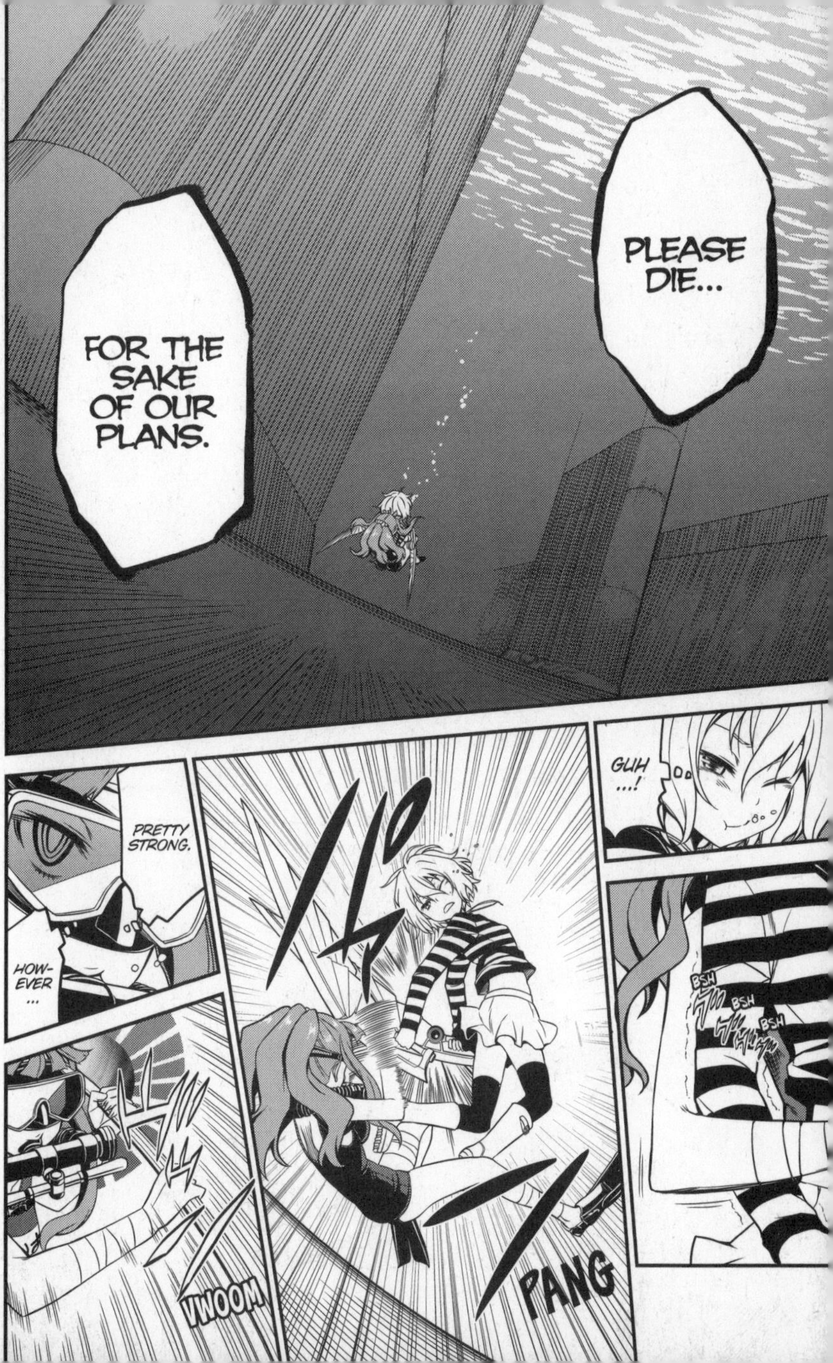
PLEASE DIE...
FOR THE SAKE OF OUR PLANS.
GUH ...!
BSH BSH BSH
PANG
PRETTY STRONG.
HOW-EVER...
VWOOM

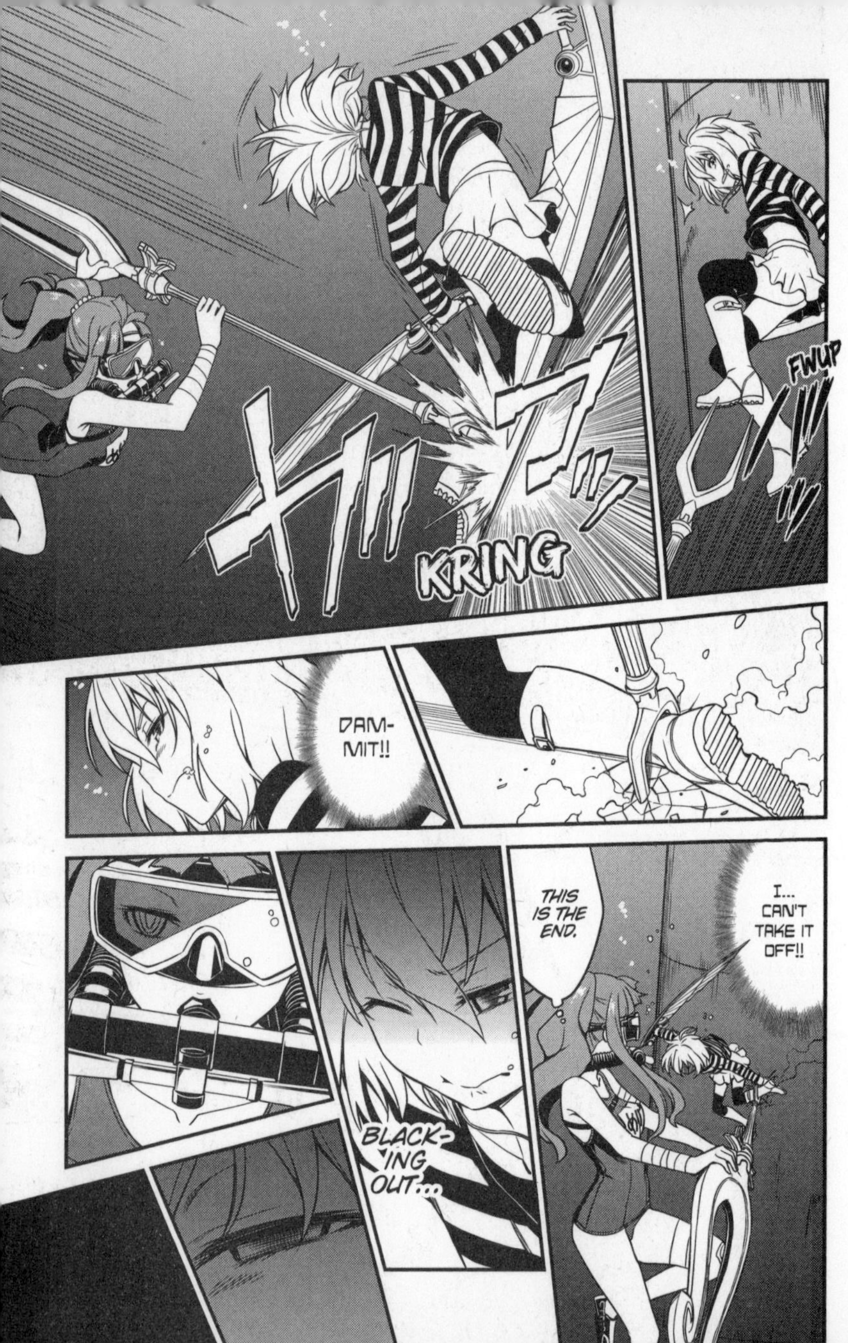
FWUP
KRING
DAM-MIT!!
I... CAN'T TAKE IT OFF!!
THIS IS THE END.
BLACK-ING OUT...

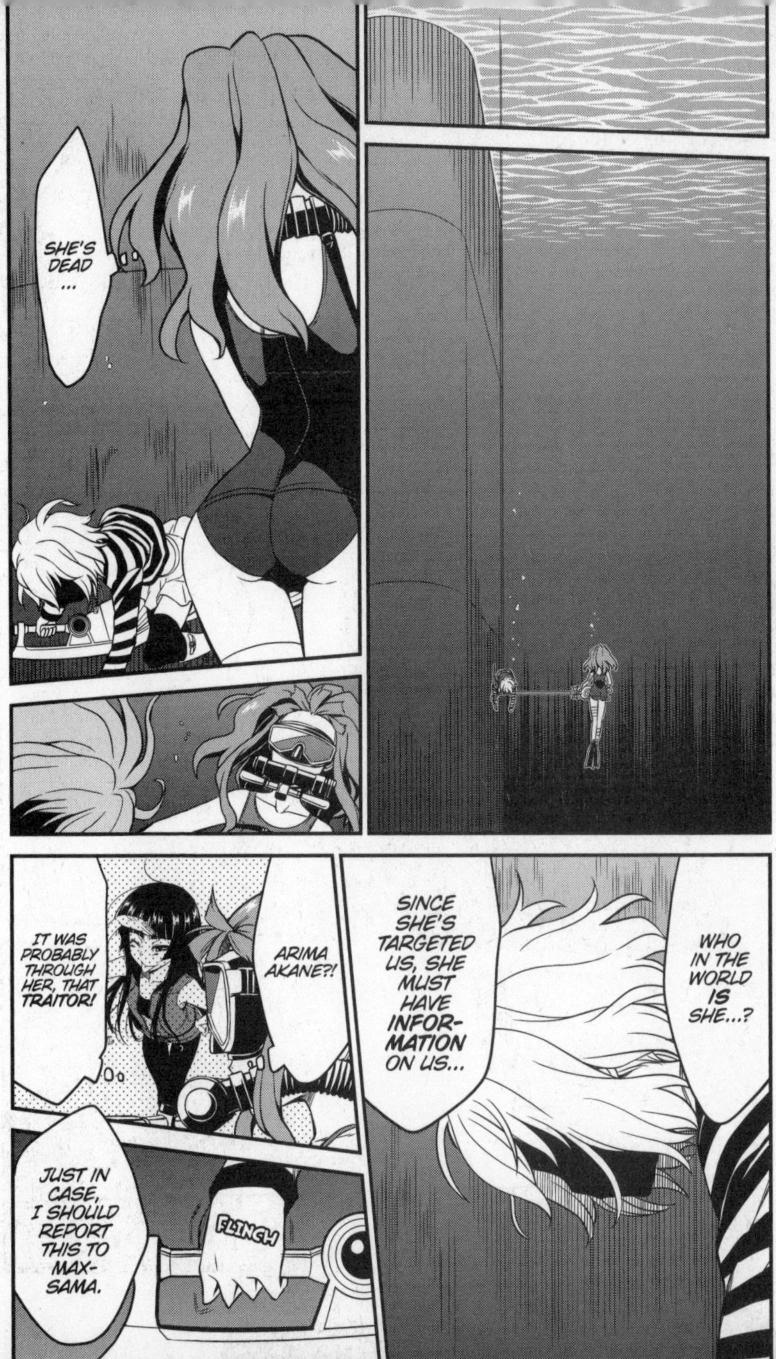
SHE'S DEAD ...
WHO IN THE WORLD IS SHE...?
SINCE SHE'S TARGETED US, SHE MUST HAVE INFORMATION ON US...
ARIMA AKANE?!
IT WAS PROBABLY THROUGH HER, THAT TRAITOR!
FLINCH
JUST IN CASE, I SHOULD REPORT THIS TO MAX-SAMA.

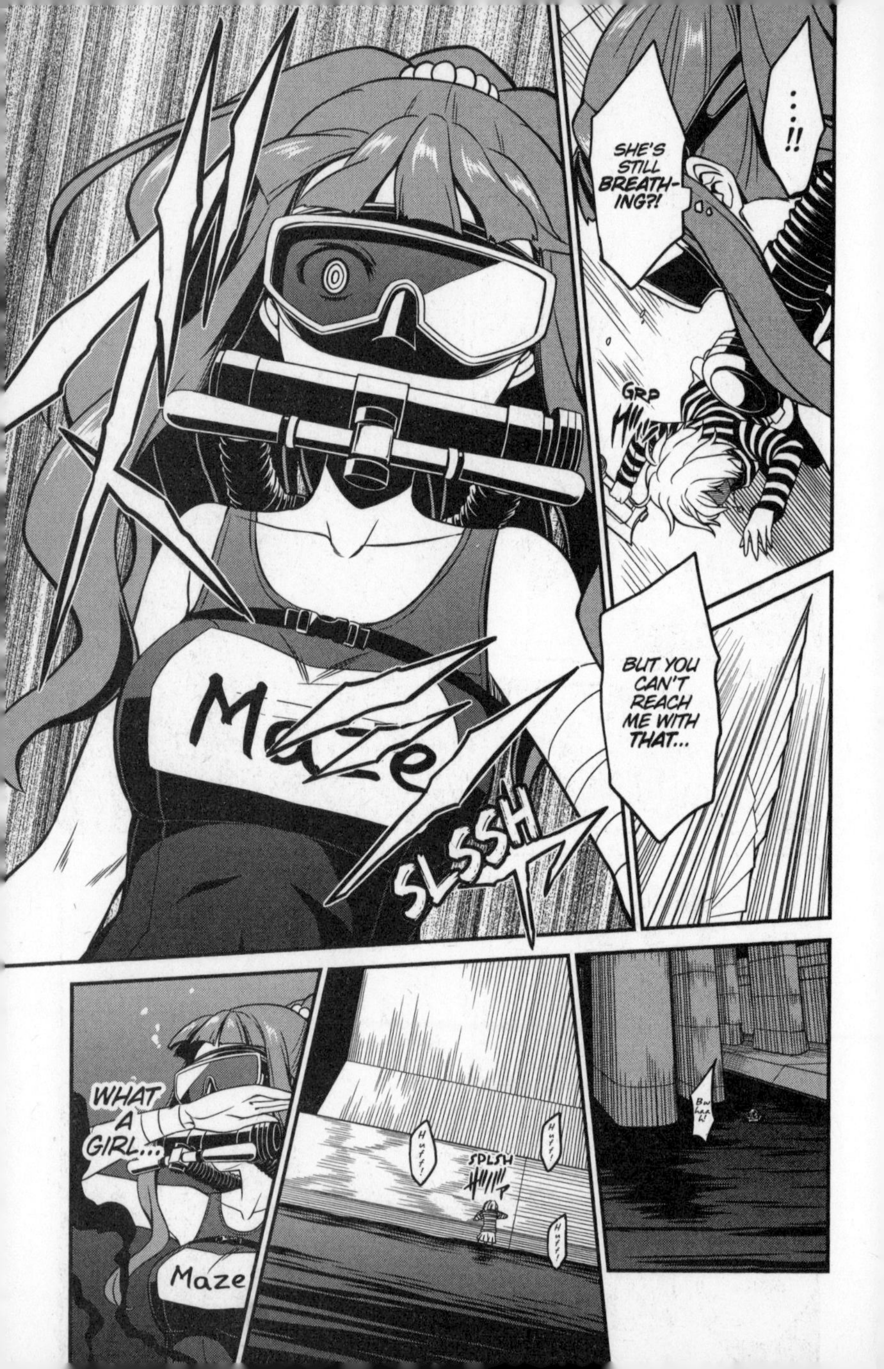
…!!
SHE'S STILL BREATHING?!
GRP
BUT YOU CAN'T REACH ME WITH THAT…
SLSSH
Maze
Bwhaah!
Huff!
Huff!
SPLSH
Huff!
WHAT A GIRL…
Maze

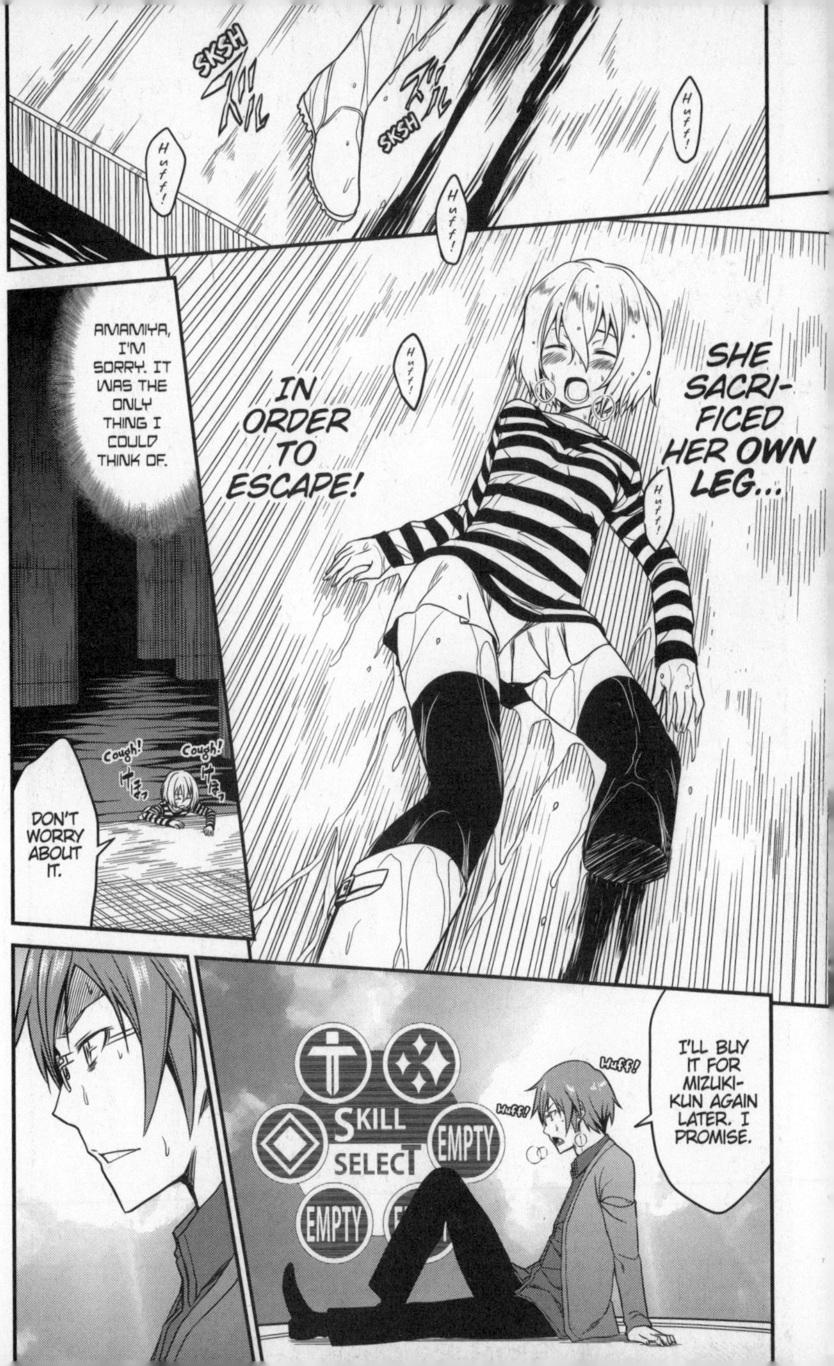
Huff!
SKSH
SKSH
Huff!
Huff!
SHE SACRI-FICED HER OWN LEG...
Huff!
IN ORDER TO ESCAPE!
Huff!
AMAMIYA, I'M SORRY. IT WAS THE ONLY THING I COULD THINK OF.
Cough!
Cough!
DON'T WORRY ABOUT IT.
I'LL BUY IT FOR MIZUKI-KUN AGAIN LATER. I PROMISE.
Huff!
Huff!
SKILL SELECT
EMPTY
EMPTY

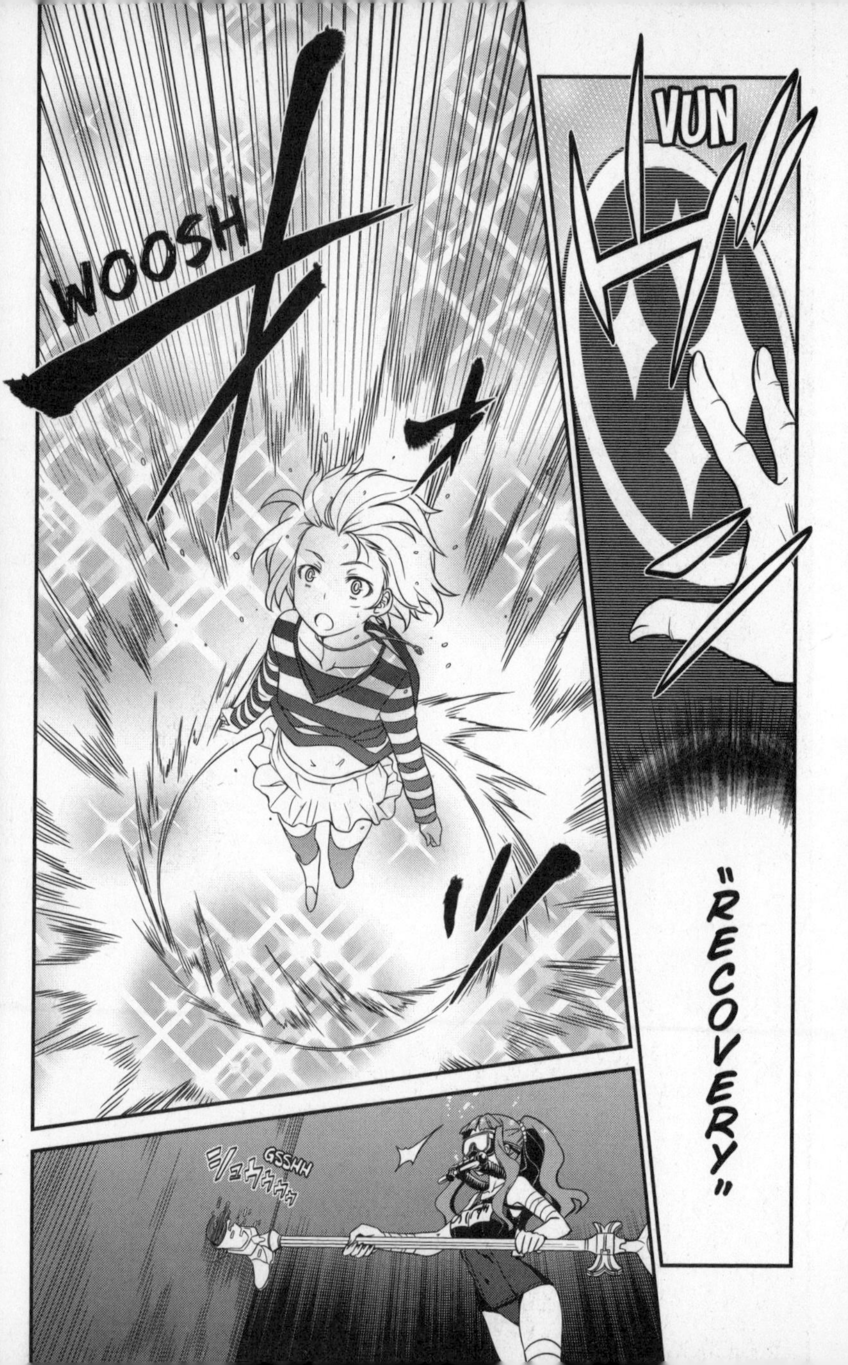
VUN
"RECOVERY"
WOOSH
GSSHH

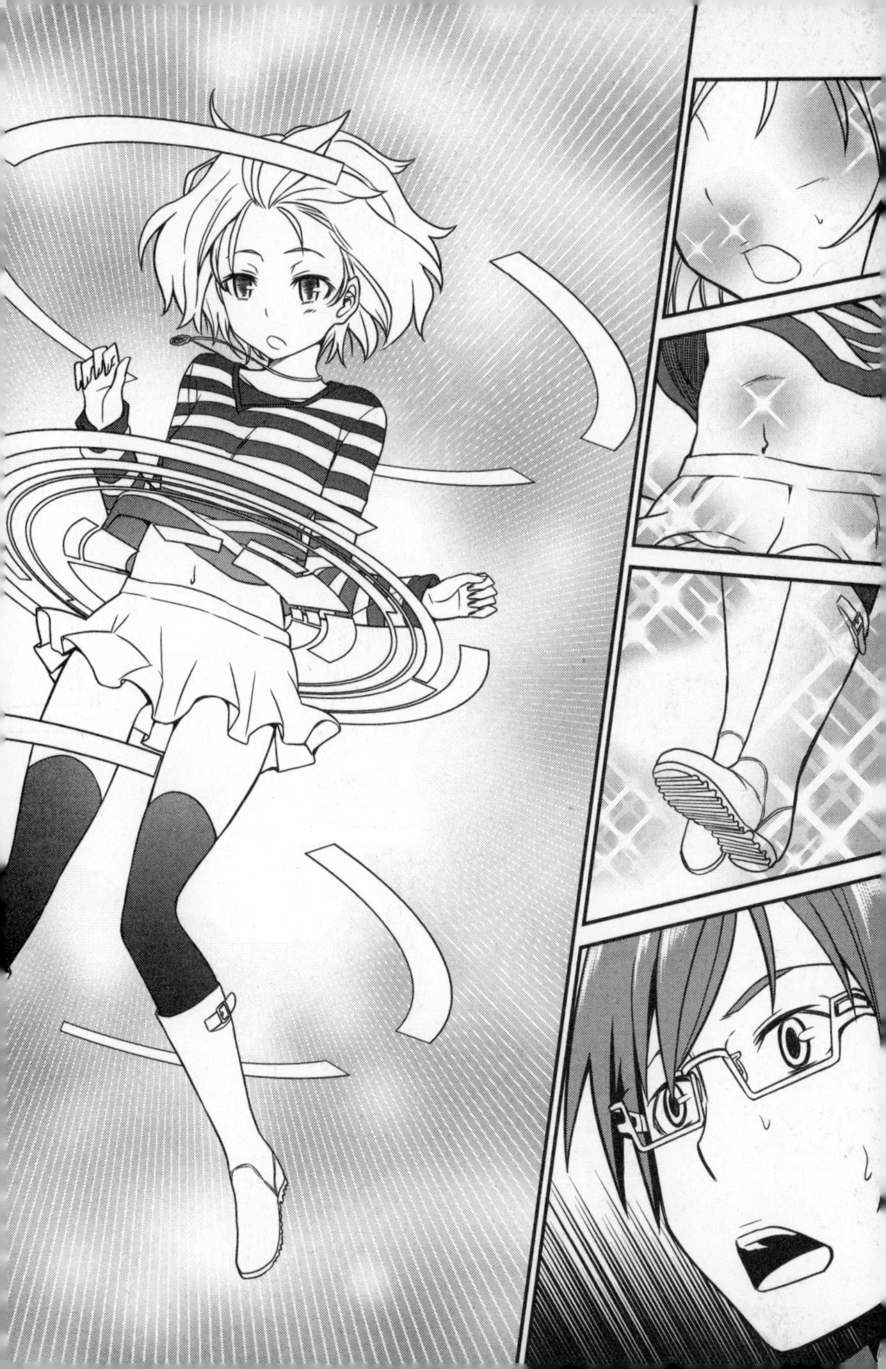

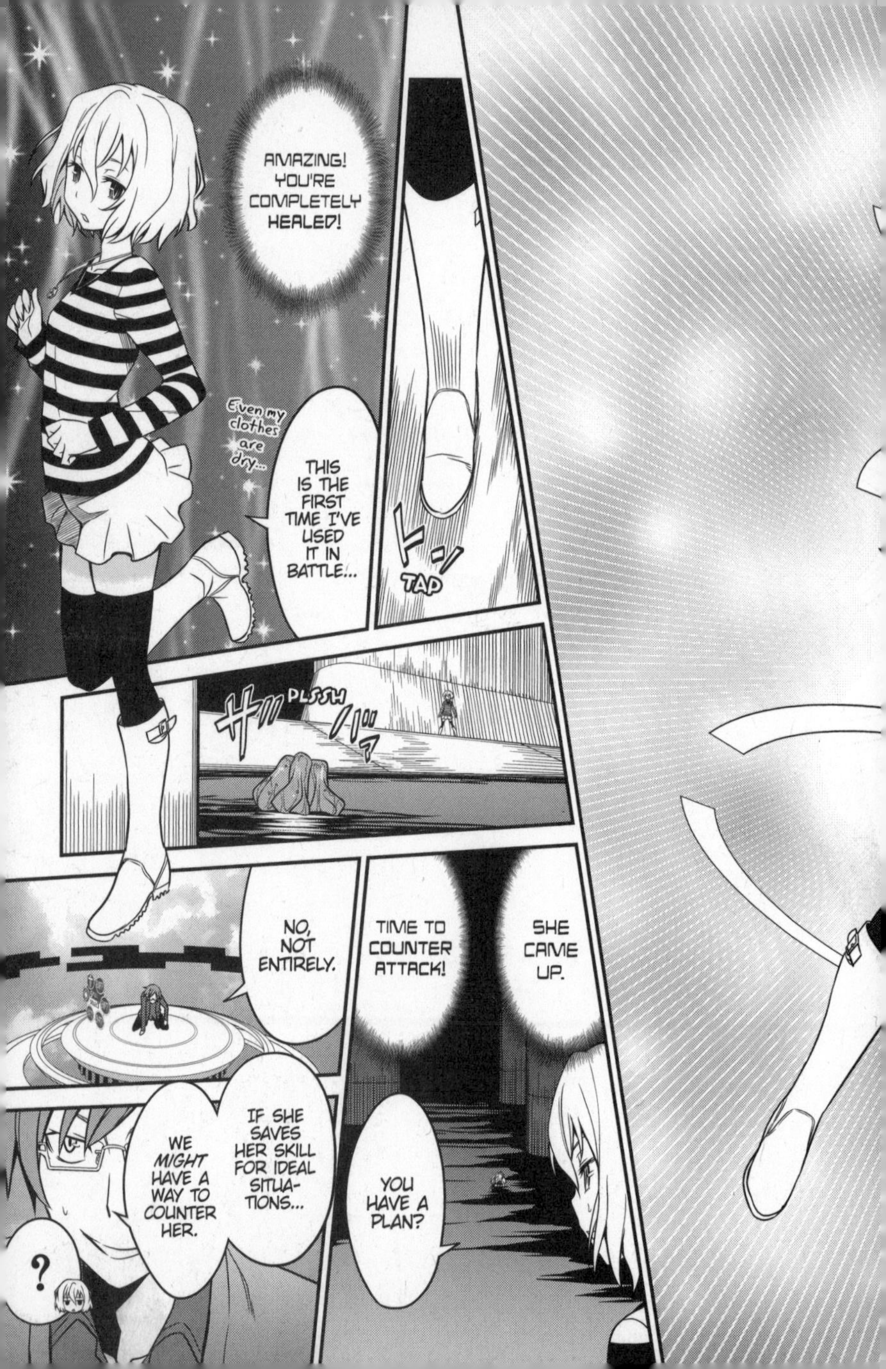
TAP
AMAZING! YOU'RE COMPLETELY HEALED!
THIS IS THE FIRST TIME I'VE USED IT IN BATTLE...
Even my clothes are dry...
PLSSH
SHE CAME UP.
TIME TO COUNTER ATTACK!
YOU HAVE A PLAN?
NO, NOT ENTIRELY.
IF SHE SAVES HER SKILL FOR IDEAL SITUA-TIONS...
WE *MIGHT* HAVE A WAY TO COUNTER HER.
?

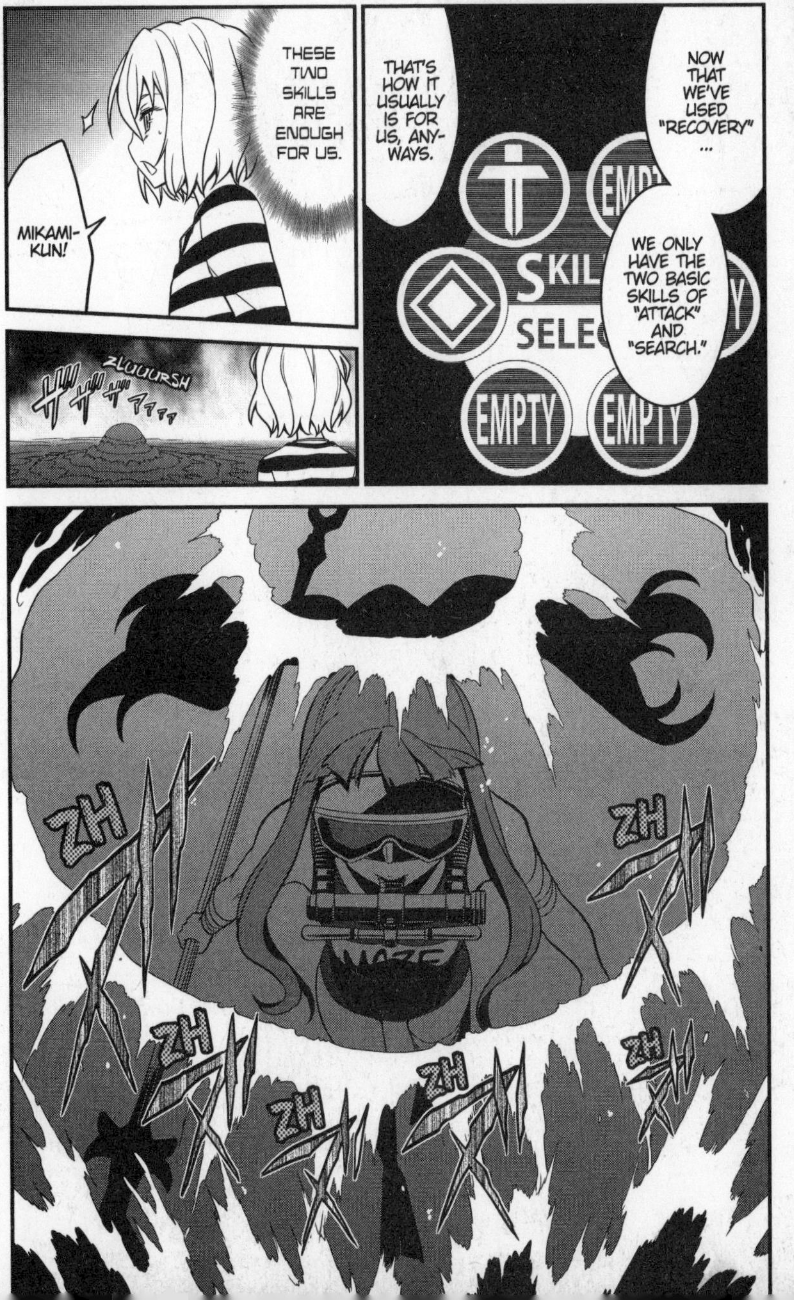
NOW THAT WE'VE USED "RECOVERY" ...
WE ONLY HAVE THE TWO BASIC SKILLS OF "ATTACK" AND "SEARCH."
THAT'S HOW IT USUALLY IS FOR US, ANYWAYS.
EMPTY
EMPTY
THESE TWO SKILLS ARE ENOUGH FOR US.
MIKAMI-KUN!
ザザザァァァ
ZLUUURSH
ZH
ZH
ZH
ZH
ZH
ZH

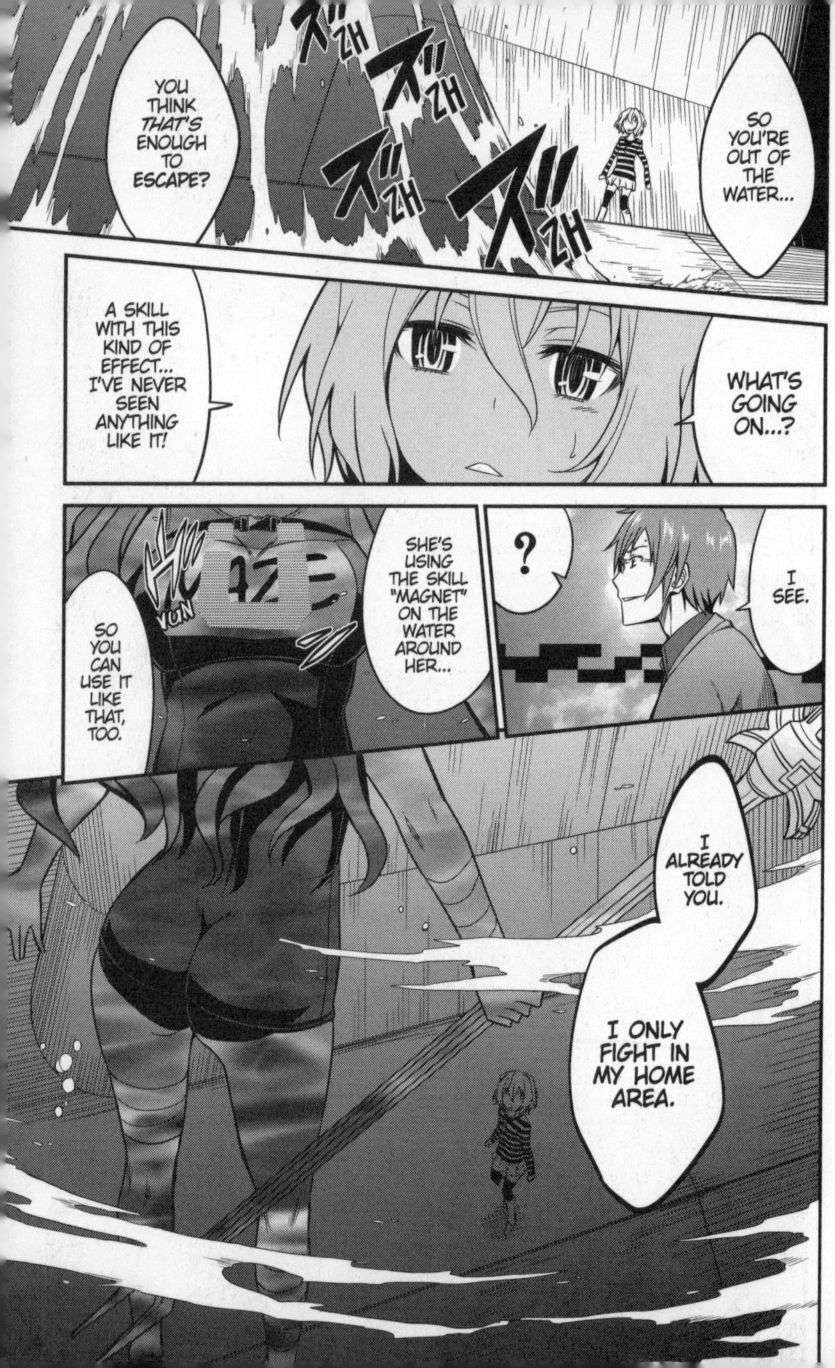
SO YOU'RE OUT OF THE WATER...
ズ ZH
ズ ZH
ズ ZH
ズ ZH
YOU THINK *THAT'S* ENOUGH TO ESCAPE?
WHAT'S GOING ON...?
A SKILL WITH THIS KIND OF EFFECT... I'VE NEVER SEEN ANYTHING LIKE IT!
I SEE.
?
SHE'S USING THE SKILL "MAGNET" ON THE WATER AROUND HER...
VUN
SO YOU CAN USE IT LIKE THAT, TOO.
I ALREADY TOLD YOU.
I ONLY FIGHT IN MY HOME AREA.

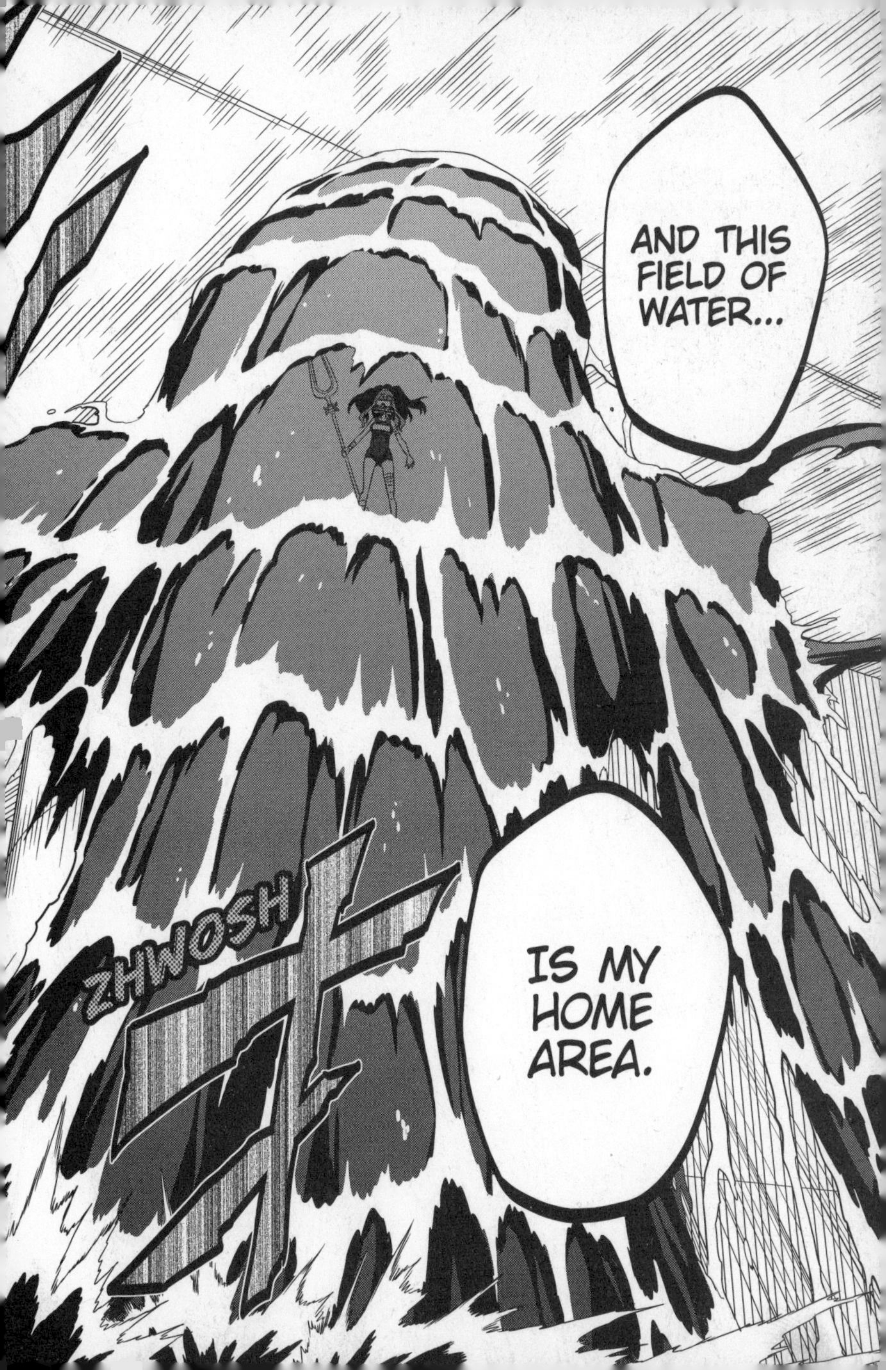
AND THIS FIELD OF WATER...
IS MY HOME AREA.
ZHWOSH

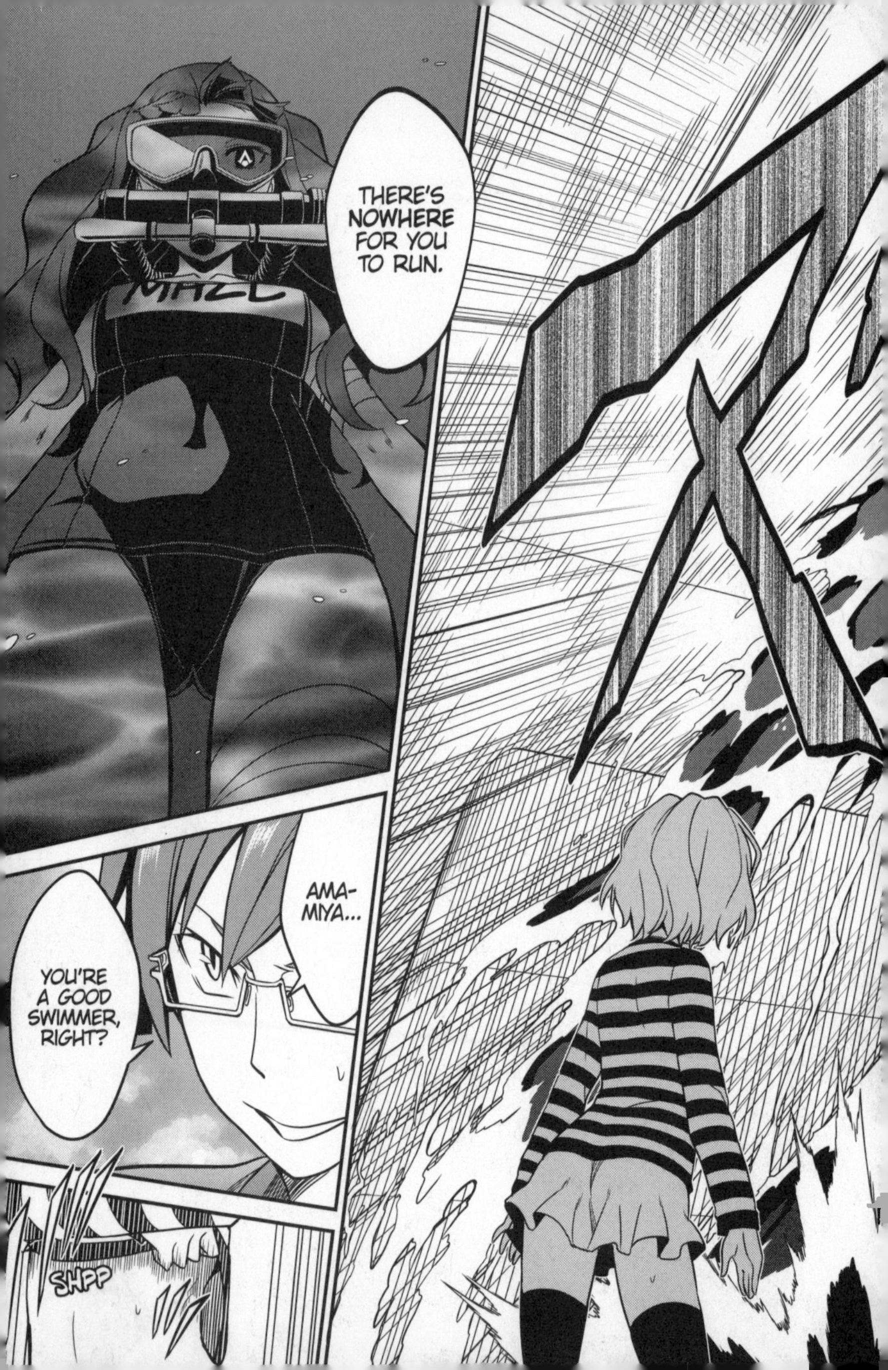
THERE'S NOWHERE FOR YOU TO RUN.
AMA-MIYA...
YOU'RE A GOOD SWIMMER, RIGHT?
SHPP

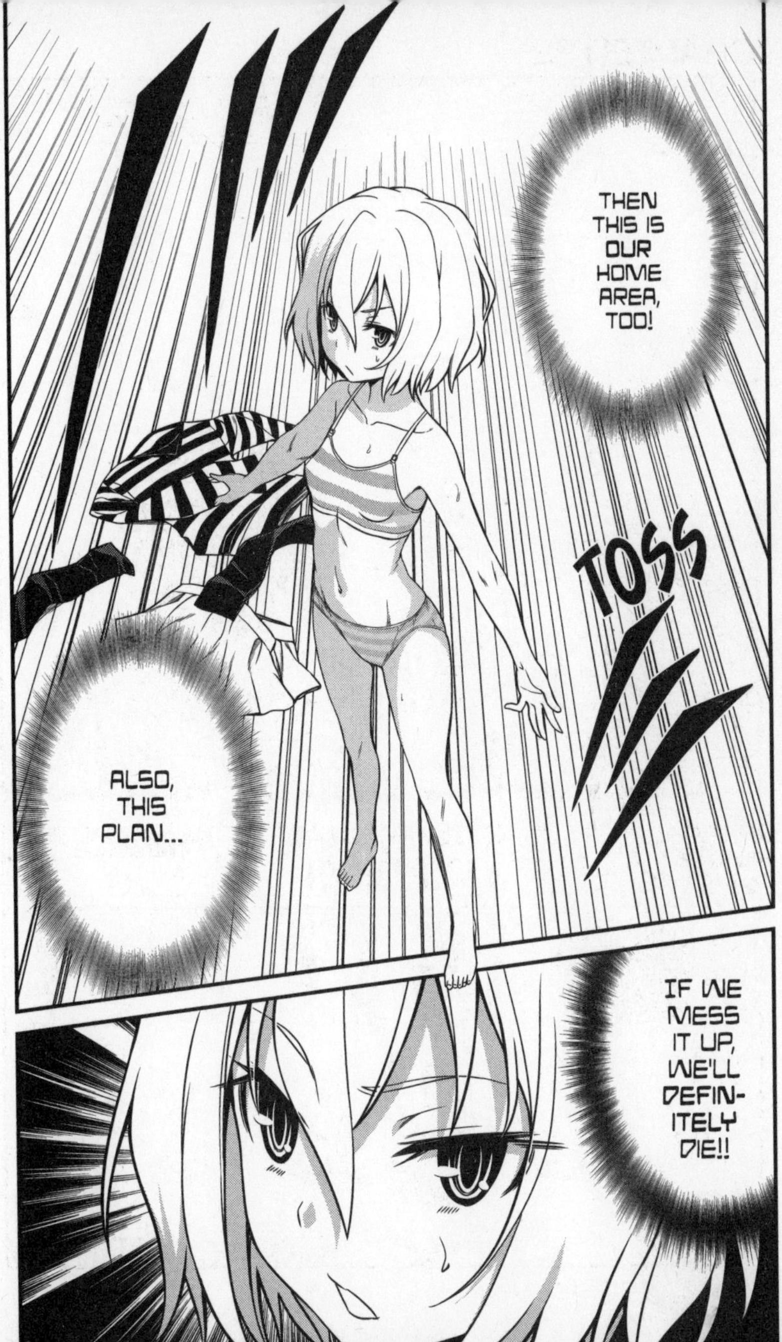
THEN THIS IS OUR HOME AREA, TOO!
TOSS
ALSO, THIS PLAN...
IF WE MESS IT UP, WE'LL DEFIN-ITELY DIE!!

CHAPTER 22

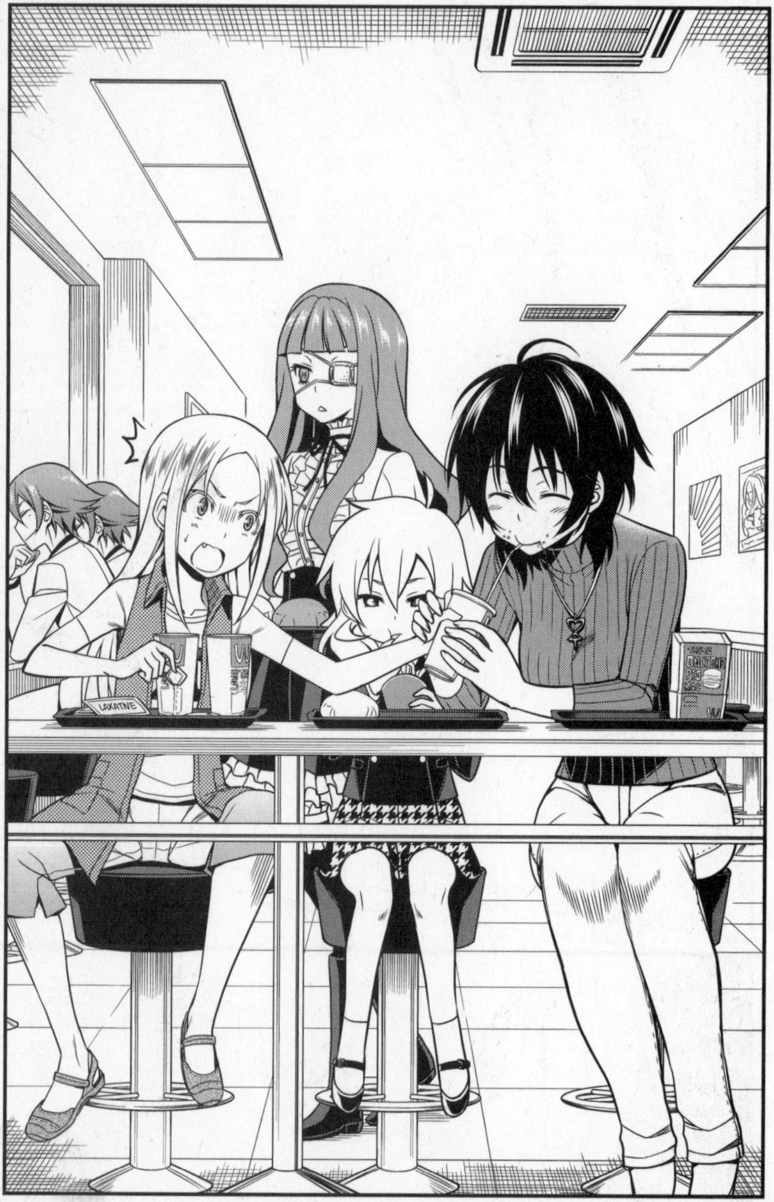
LAXATIVE

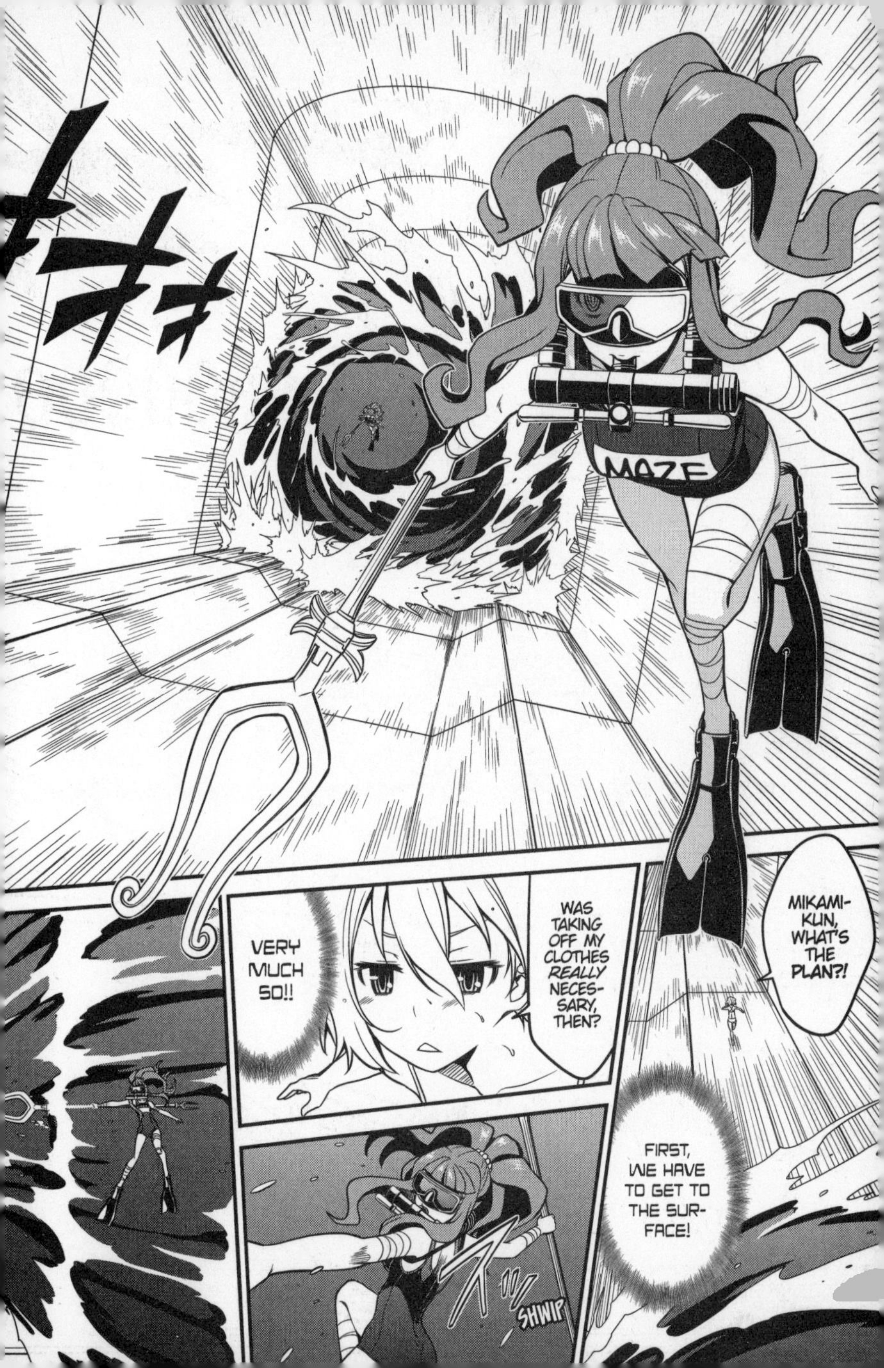
MAZE
MIKAMI-KUN, WHAT'S THE PLAN?!
WAS TAKING OFF MY CLOTHES REALLY NECESSARY, THEN?
VERY MUCH SO!!
FIRST, WE HAVE TO GET TO THE SURFACE!
SHWIP

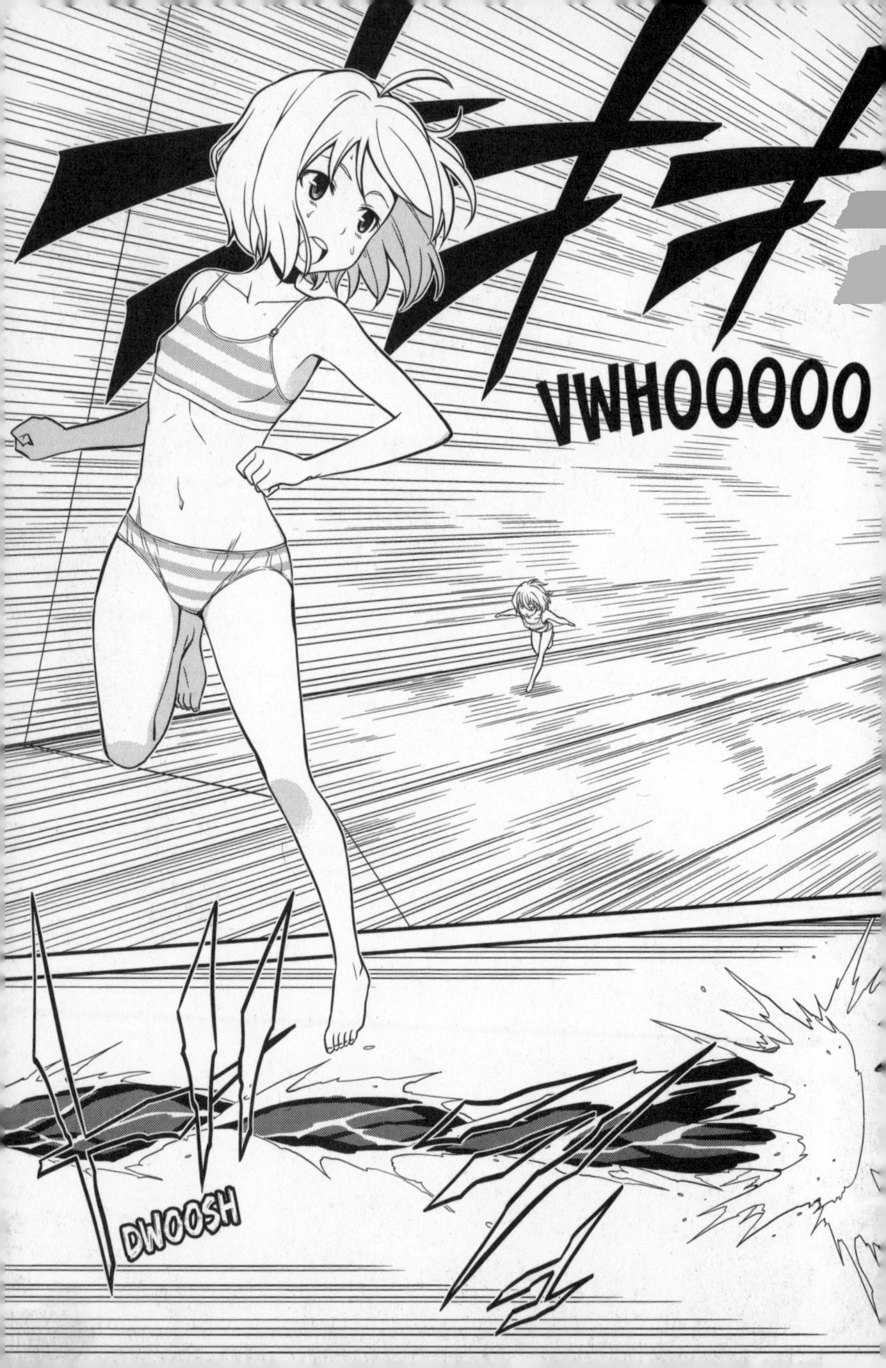
VWHOOOOO
DWOOSH

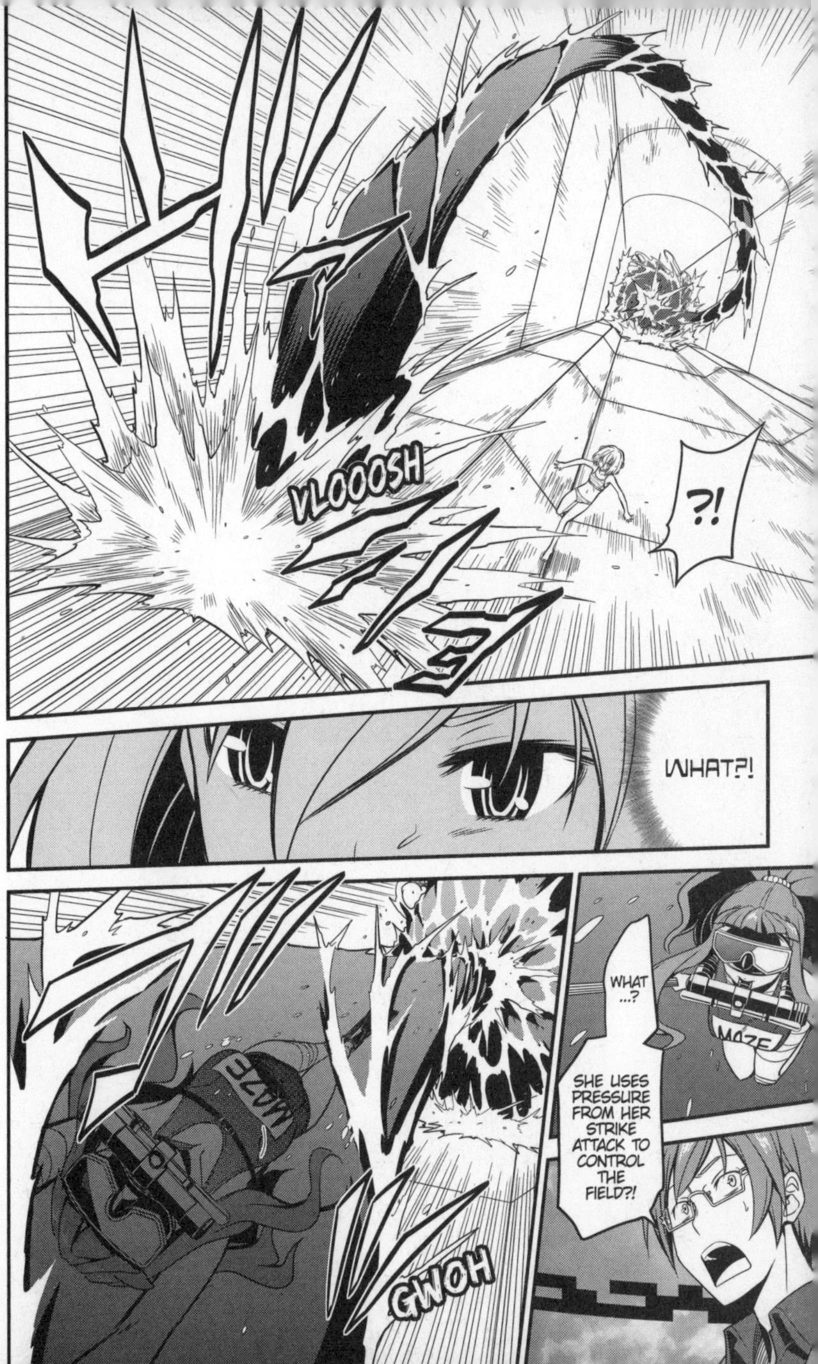
VLOOOSH
?!
WHAT?!
WHAT ...?
SHE USES PRESSURE FROM HER STRIKE ATTACK TO CONTROL THE FIELD?!
GWOH

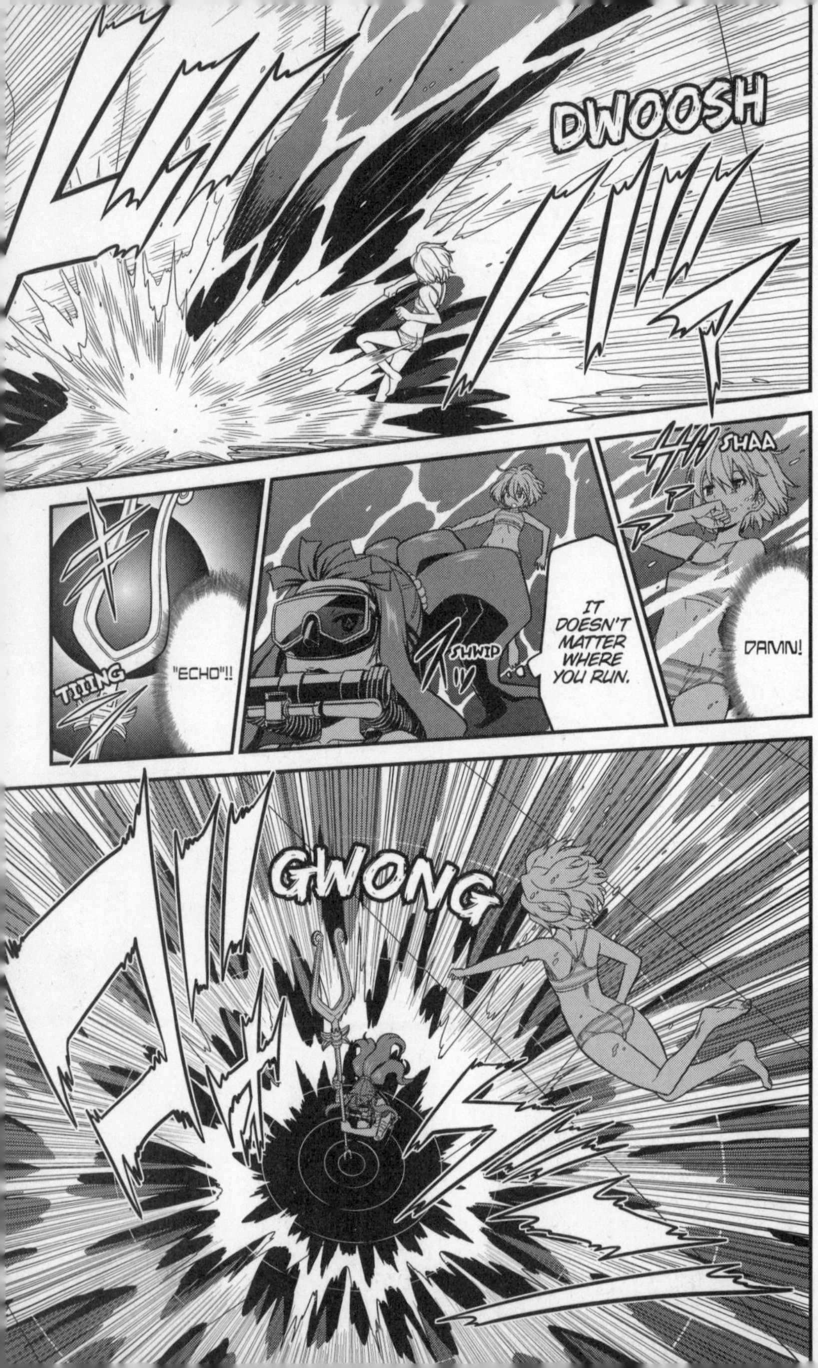
DWOOSH
SHAA
DAMN!
IT DOESN'T MATTER WHERE YOU RUN.
SHWIP
"ECHO"!!
TIIING
GWONG

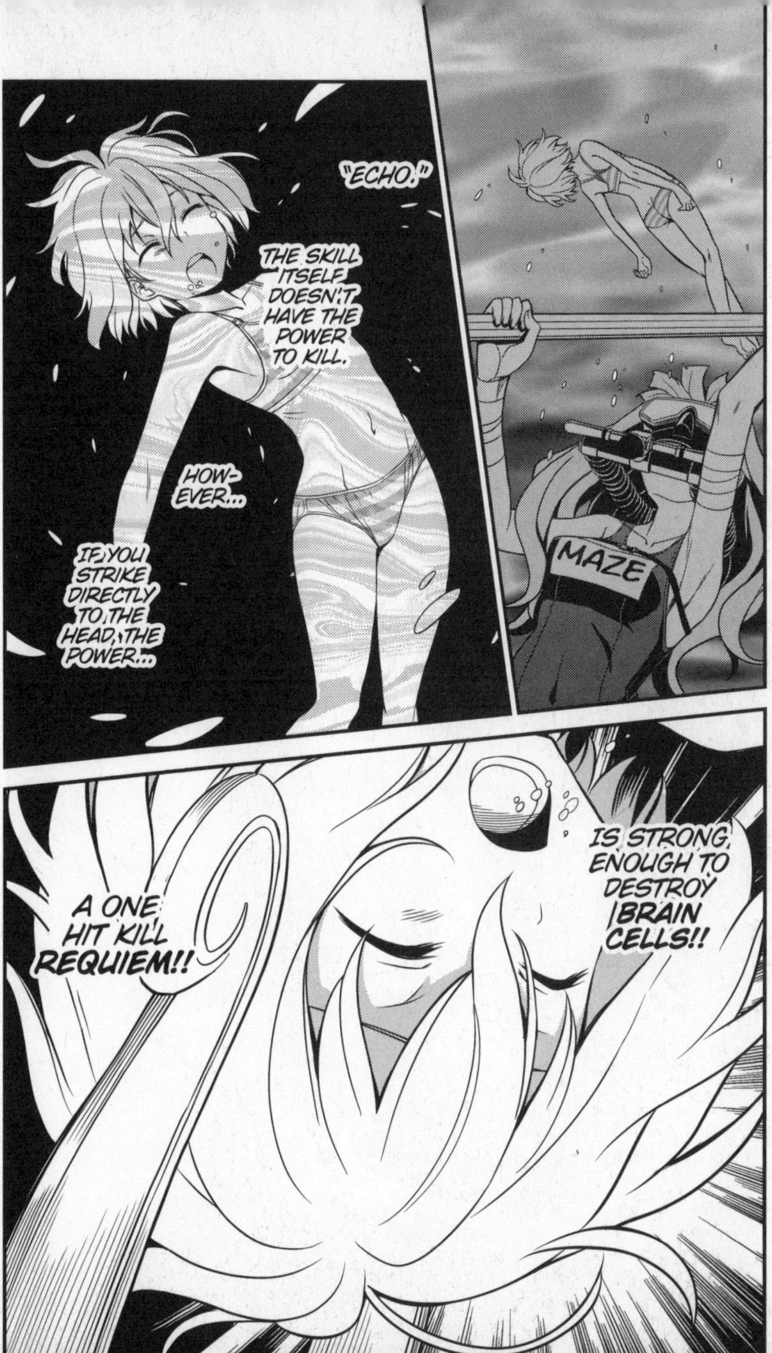
"ECHO."
THE SKILL ITSELF DOESN'T HAVE THE POWER TO KILL.
HOW-EVER...
IF YOU STRIKE DIRECTLY TO THE HEAD, THE POWER...
IS STRONG ENOUGH TO DESTROY BRAIN CELLS!!
A ONE HIT KILL REQUIEM!!

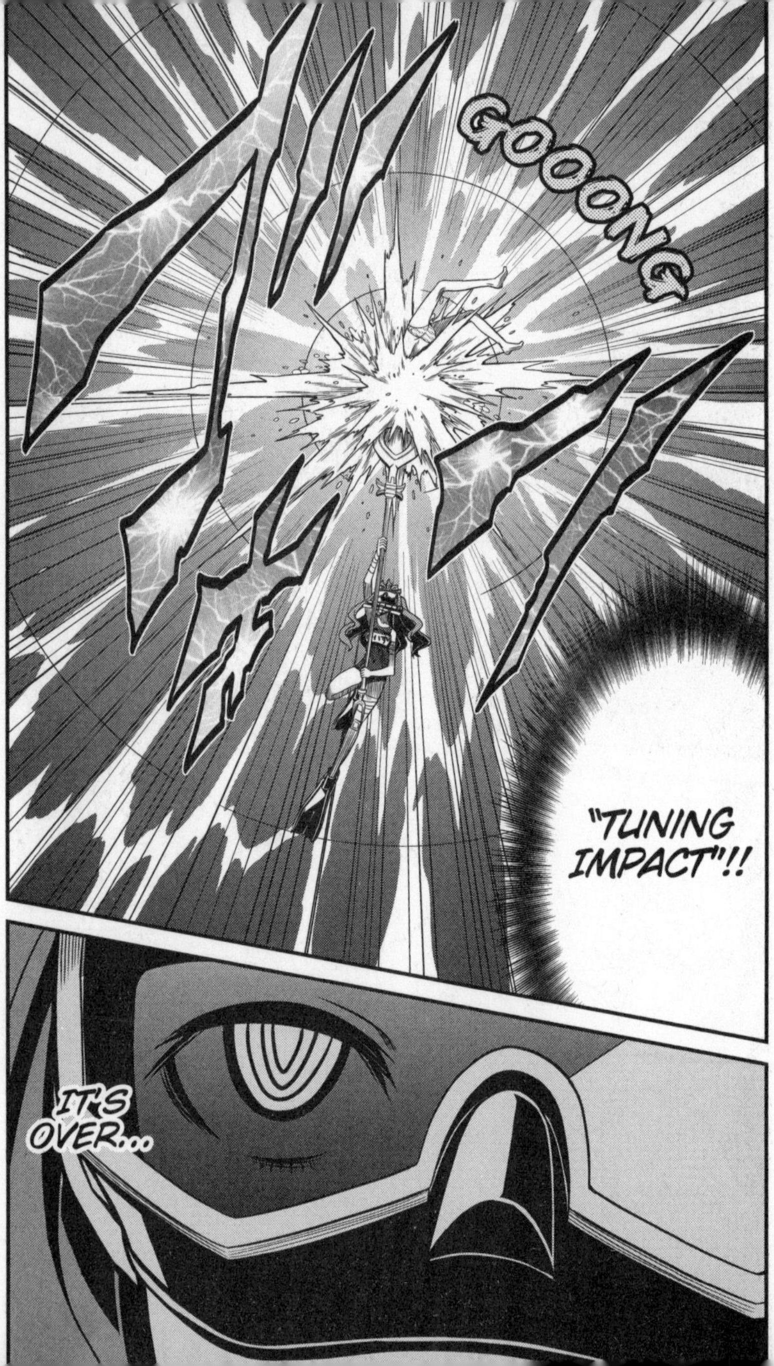
GOOONG
"TUNING IMPACT"!!
IT'S OVER...

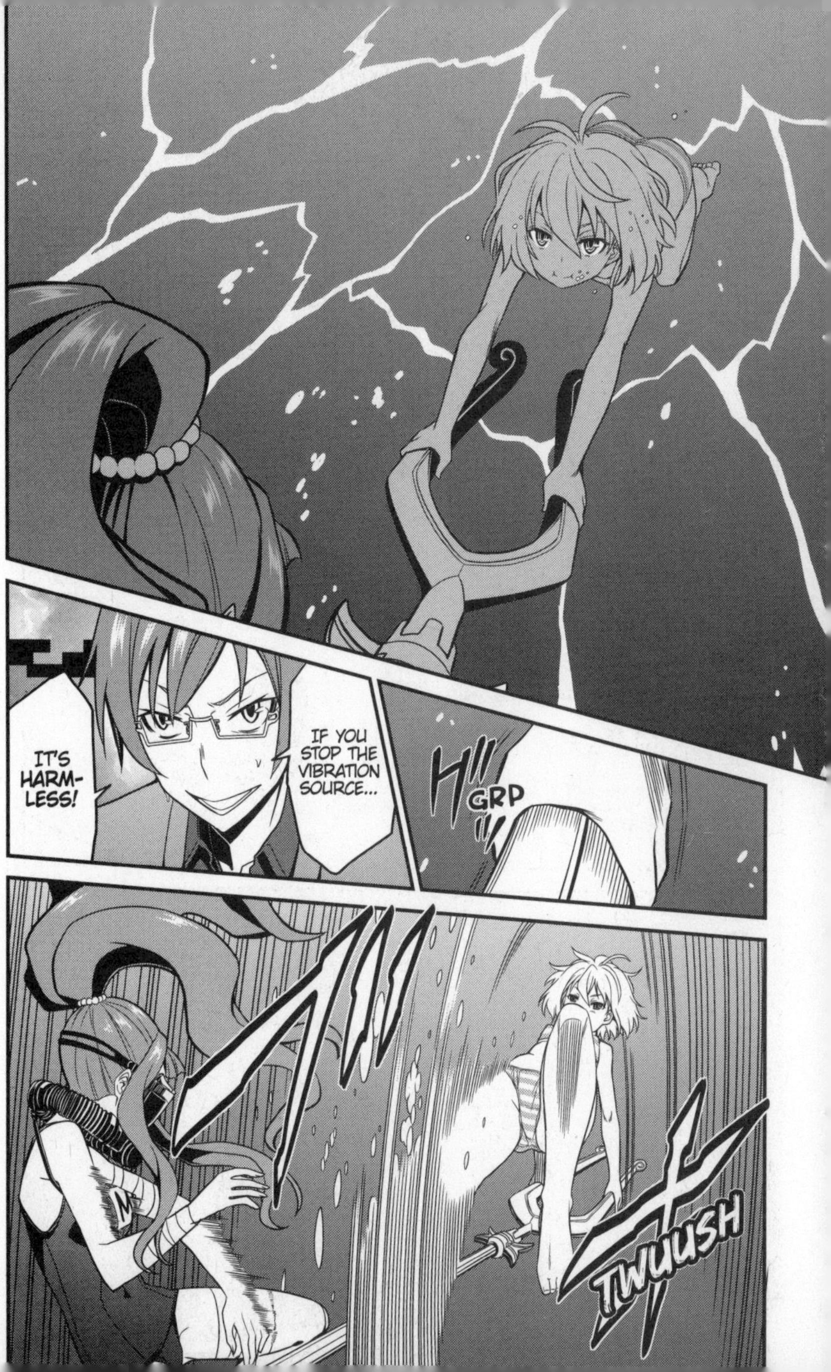
GRP
IF YOU STOP THE VIBRATION SOURCE...
IT'S HARMLESS!
TWUUSH

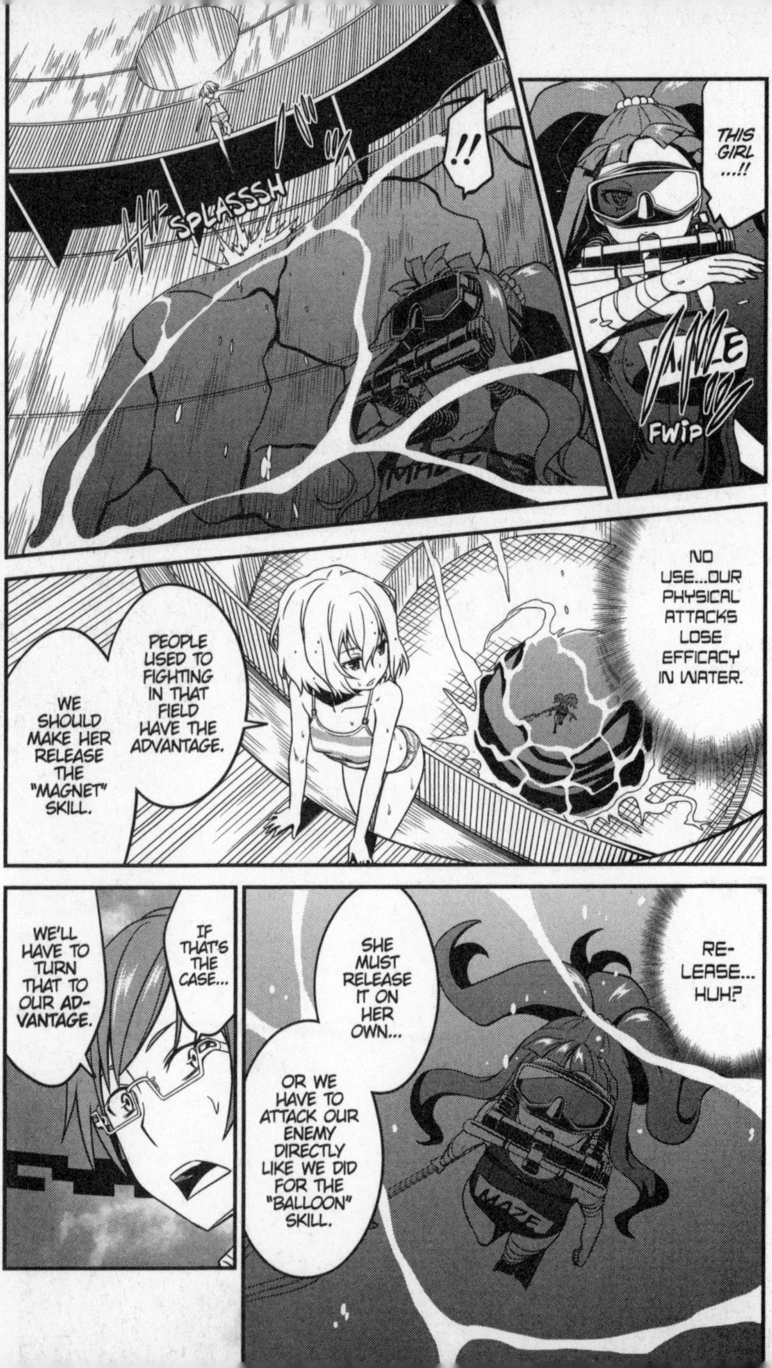

THIS GIRL ...!!
FWIP
!!
SPLASSSH
NO USE...OUR PHYSICAL ATTACKS LOSE EFFICACY IN WATER.
PEOPLE USED TO FIGHTING IN THAT FIELD HAVE THE ADVANTAGE.
WE SHOULD MAKE HER RELEASE THE "MAGNET" SKILL.
RE-LEASE... HUH?
SHE MUST RELEASE IT ON HER OWN...
OR WE HAVE TO ATTACK OUR ENEMY DIRECTLY LIKE WE DID FOR THE "BALLOON" SKILL.
IF THAT'S THE CASE...
WE'LL HAVE TO TURN THAT TO OUR AD-VANTAGE.

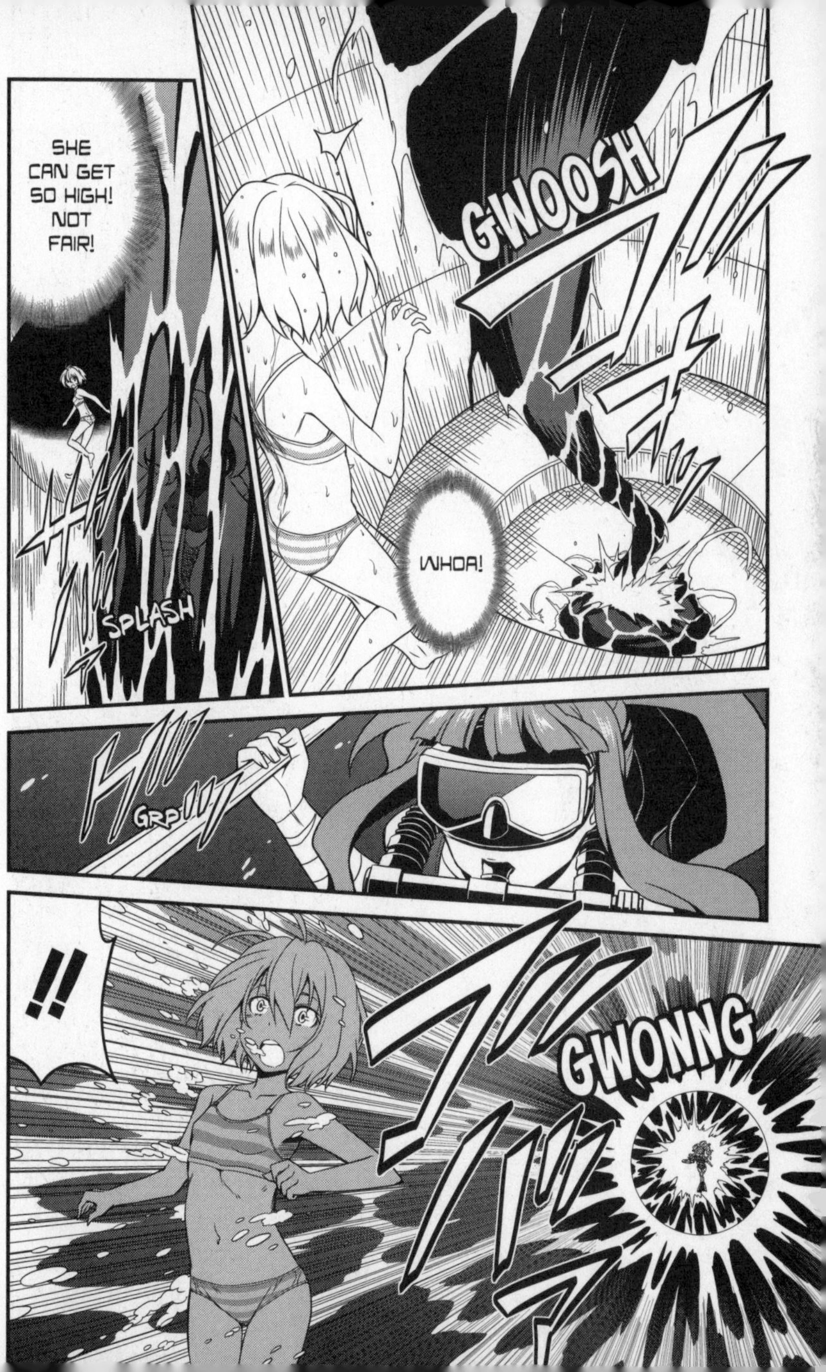
GWOOSH
WHOA!
SHE CAN GET SO HIGH! NOT FAIR!
SPLASH
GRP
!!
GWONNG

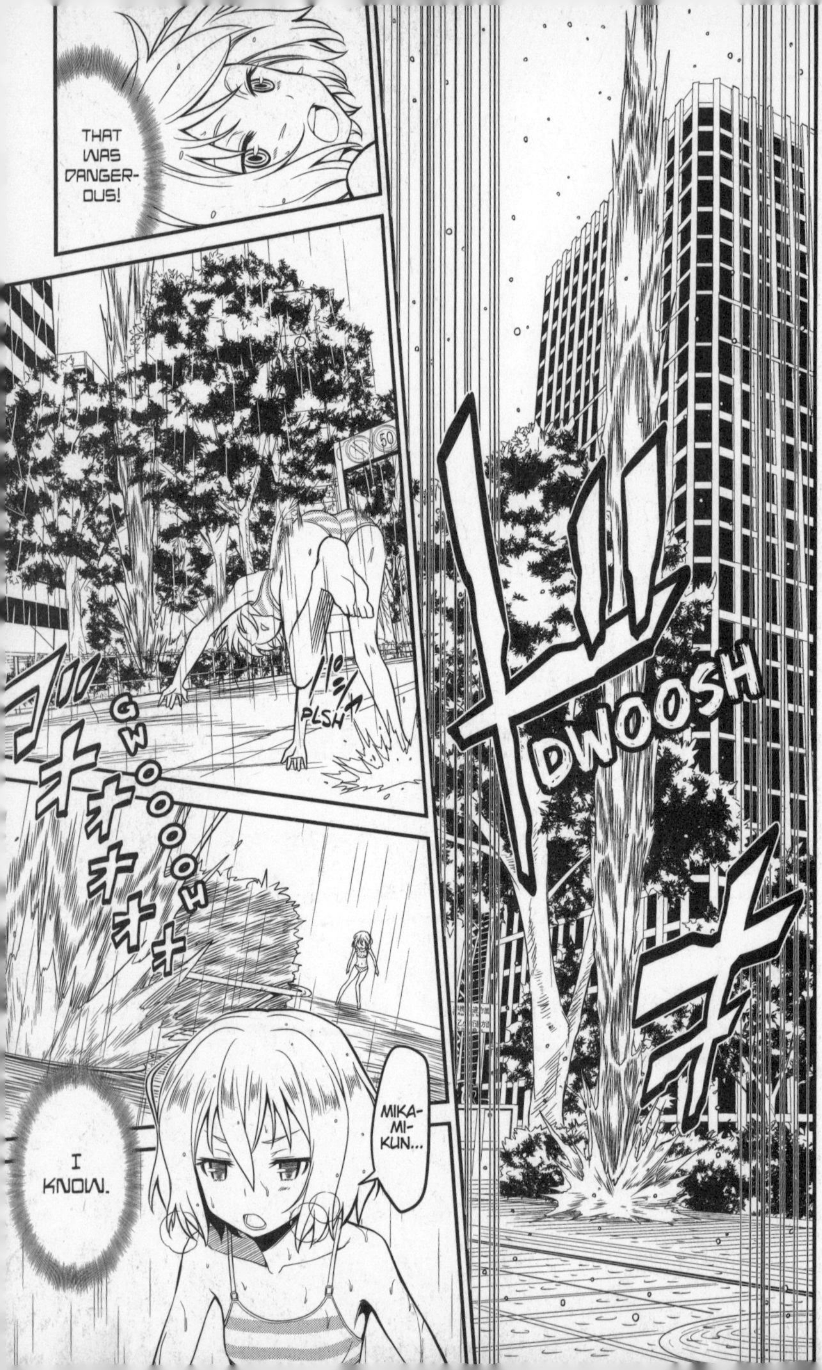
DWOOSH
THAT WAS DANGER-DOUS!
PLSH
GWOOOOOH
MIKA-MI-KUN...
I KNOW.

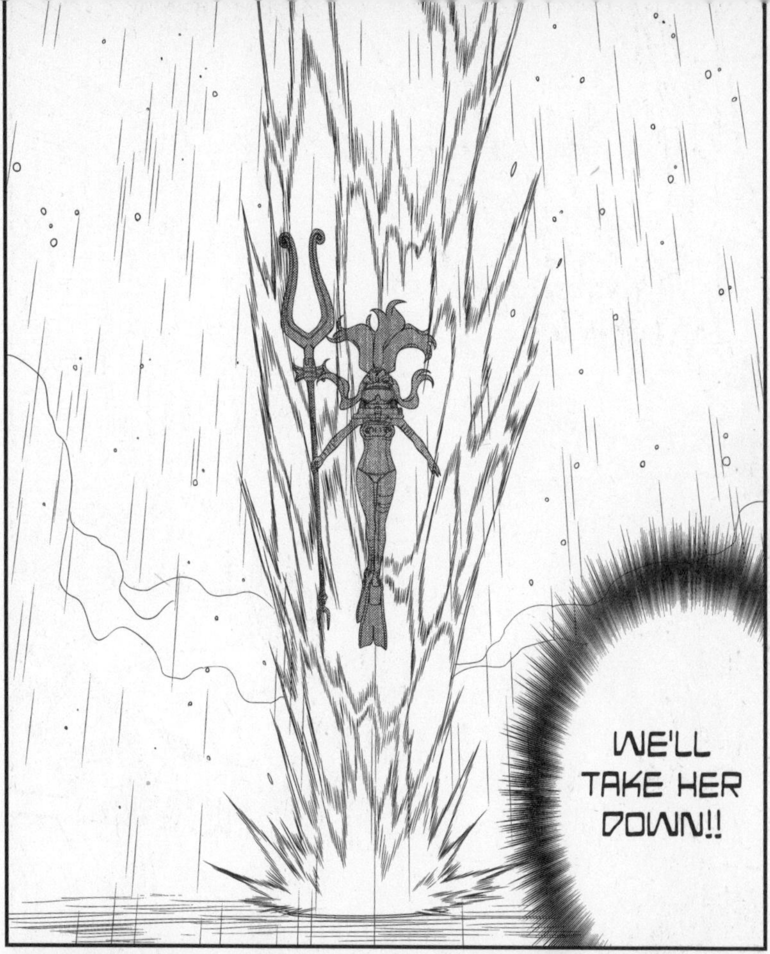
WE'LL TAKE HER DOWN!!
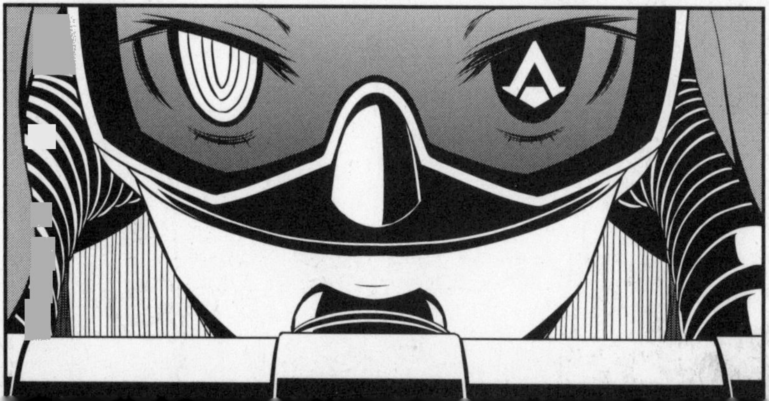

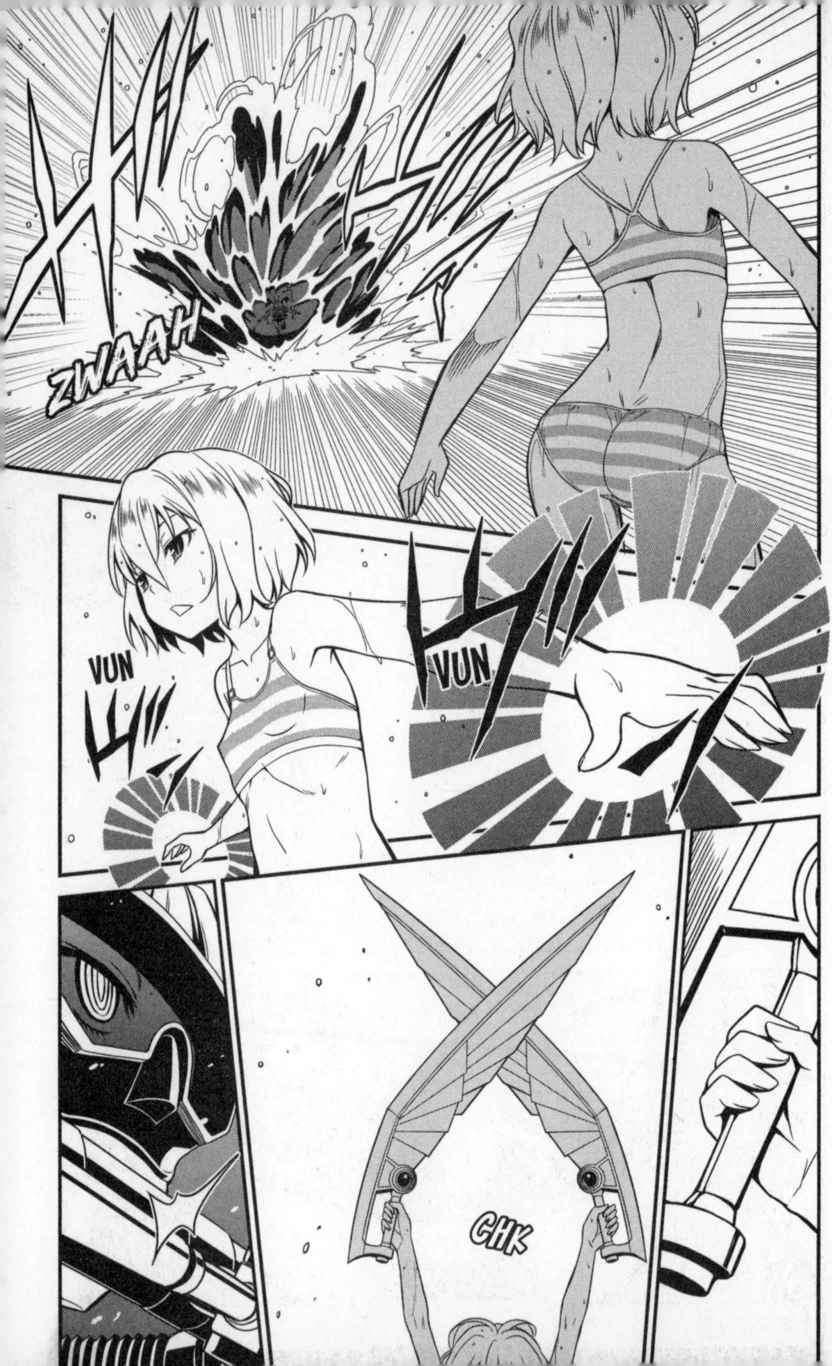
ZWAAH
VUN
VUN
CHK

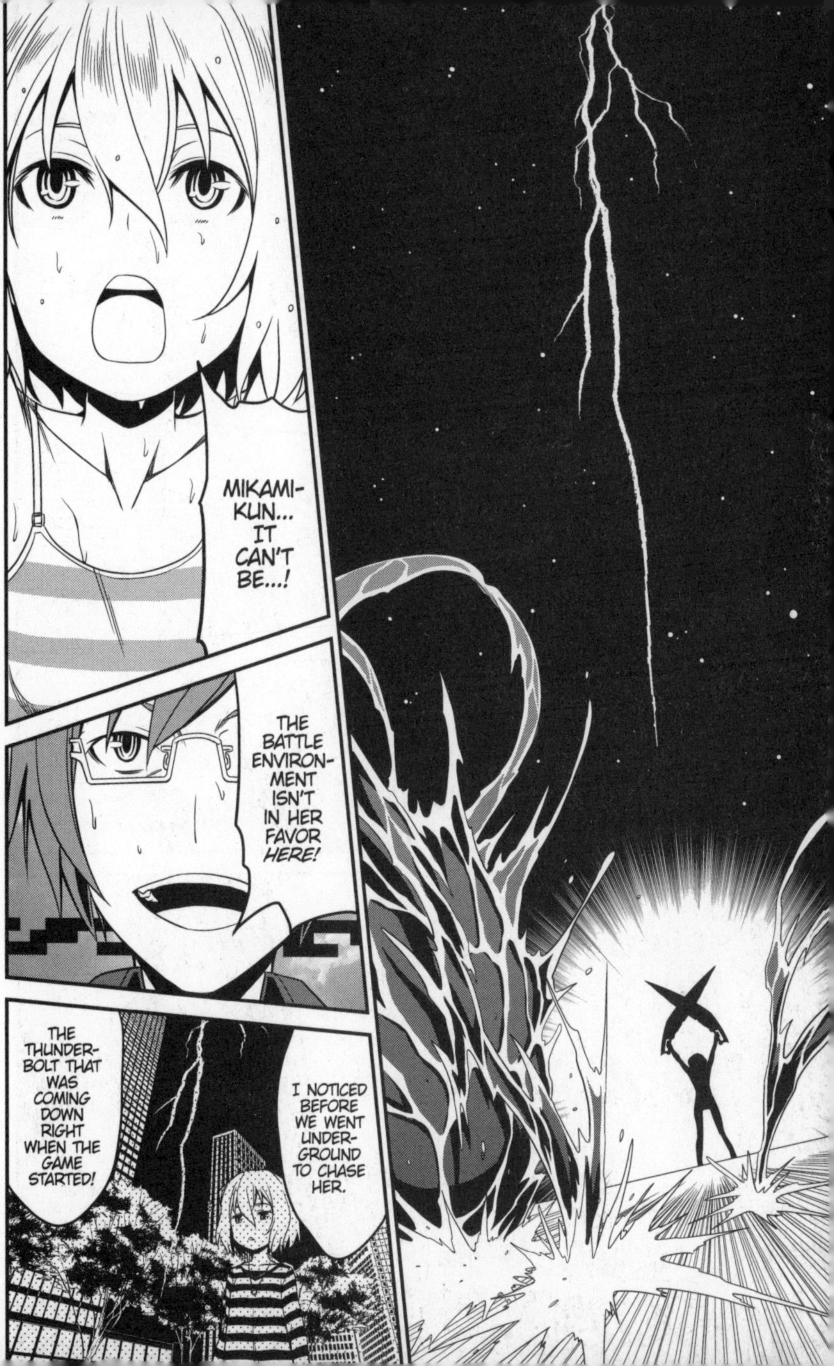
MIKAMI-KUN... IT CAN'T BE...!
THE BATTLE ENVIRONMENT ISN'T IN HER FAVOR HERE!
I NOTICED BEFORE WE WENT UNDERGROUND TO CHASE HER.
THE THUNDERBOLT THAT WAS COMING DOWN RIGHT WHEN THE GAME STARTED!

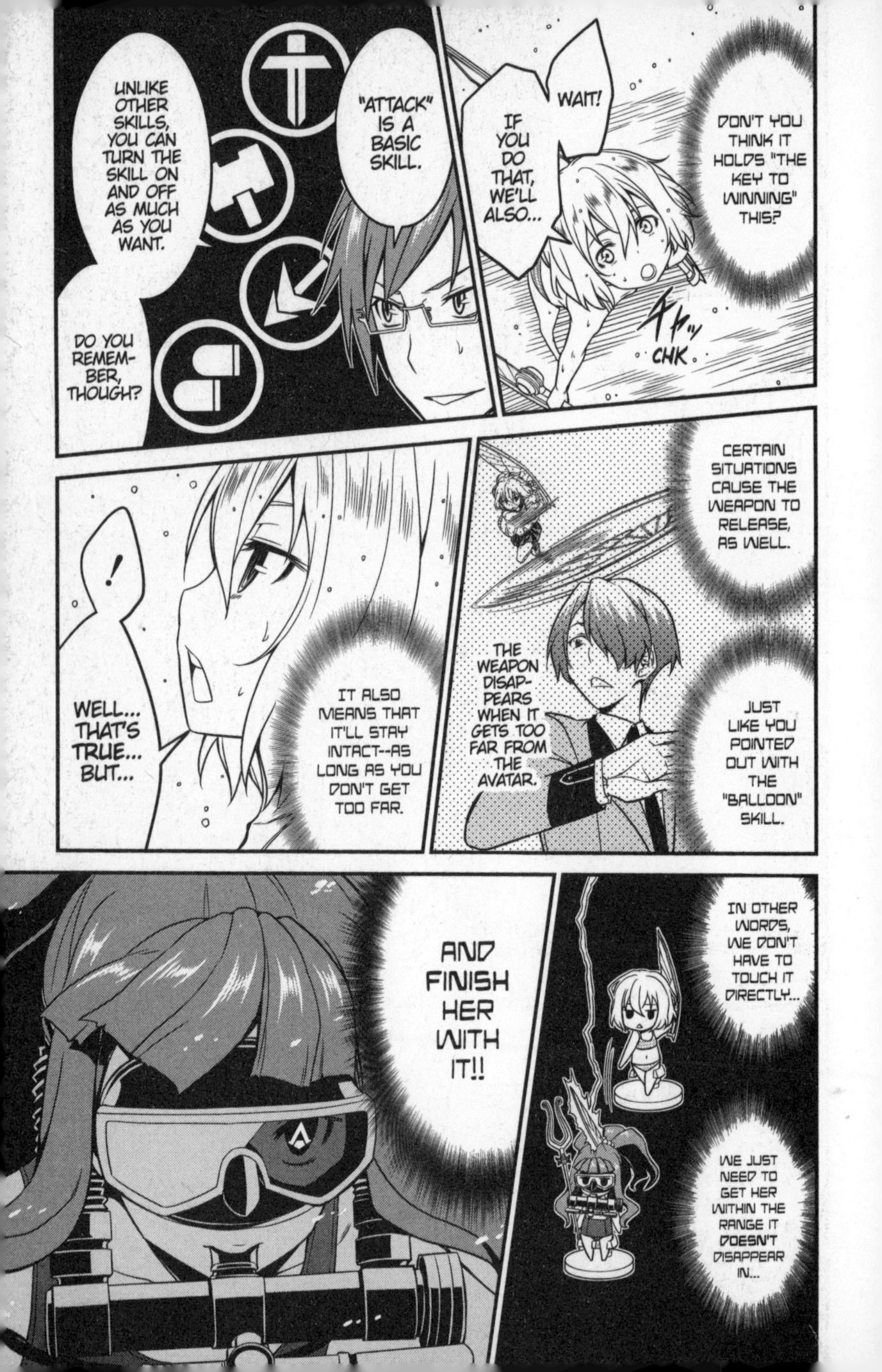
DON'T YOU THINK IT HOLDS "THE KEY TO WINNING" THIS?
WAIT!
IF YOU DO THAT, WE'LL ALSO...
CHK
"ATTACK" IS A BASIC SKILL.
UNLIKE OTHER SKILLS, YOU CAN TURN THE SKILL ON AND OFF AS MUCH AS YOU WANT.
DO YOU REMEMBER, THOUGH?
CERTAIN SITUATIONS CAUSE THE WEAPON TO RELEASE, AS WELL.
JUST LIKE YOU POINTED OUT WITH THE "BALLOON" SKILL.
THE WEAPON DISAPPEARS WHEN IT GETS TOO FAR FROM THE AVATAR.
IT ALSO MEANS THAT IT'LL STAY INTACT--AS LONG AS YOU DON'T GET TOO FAR.
!
WELL... THAT'S TRUE... BUT...
IN OTHER WORDS, WE DON'T HAVE TO TOUCH IT DIRECTLY...
WE JUST NEED TO GET HER WITHIN THE RANGE IT DOESN'T DISAPPEAR IN...
AND FINISH HER WITH IT!!

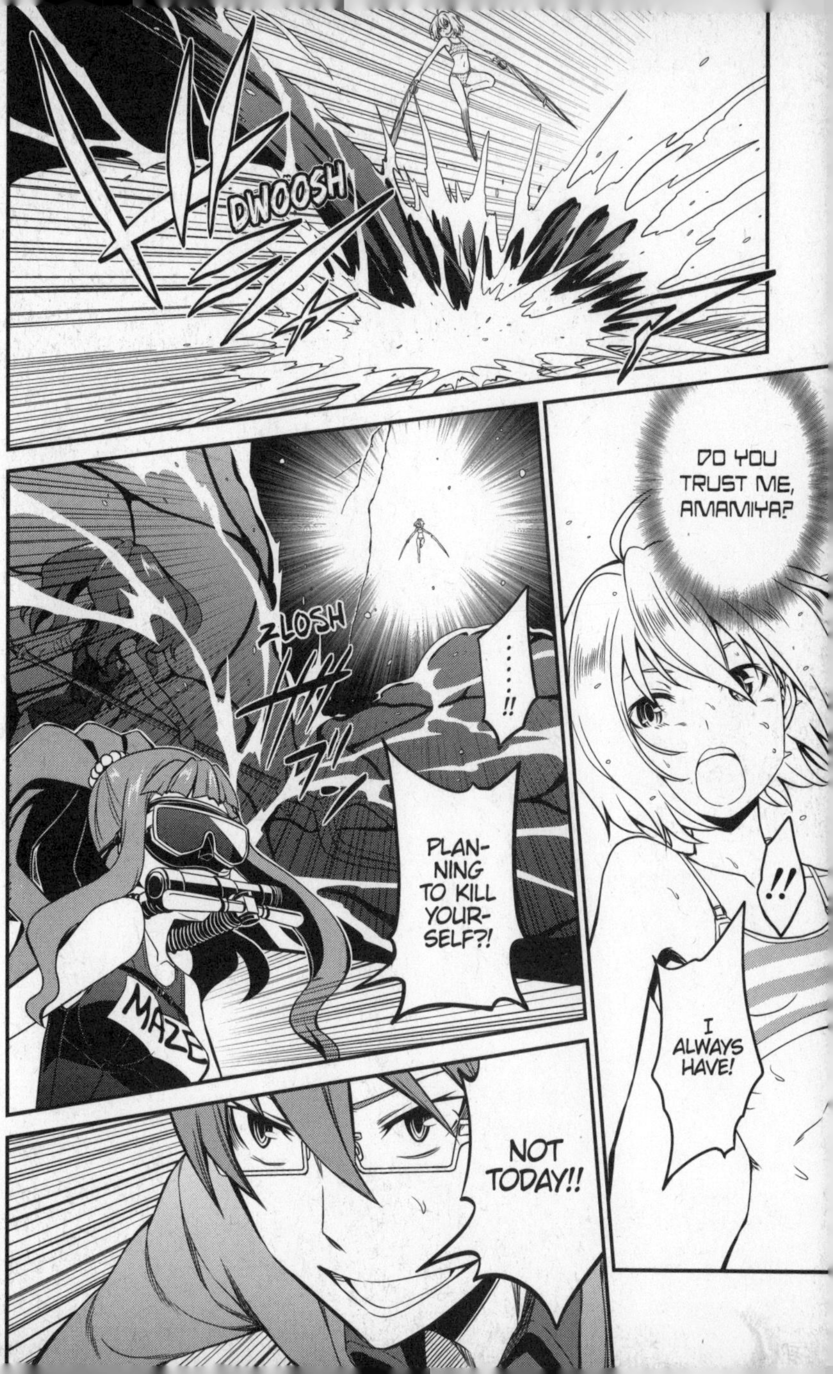
DWOOSH
DO YOU TRUST ME, AMAMIYA?
!!
I ALWAYS HAVE!
ZLOSH
......!!
PLAN-
NING
TO KILL
YOUR-
SELF?!
MAZE
NOT TODAY!!

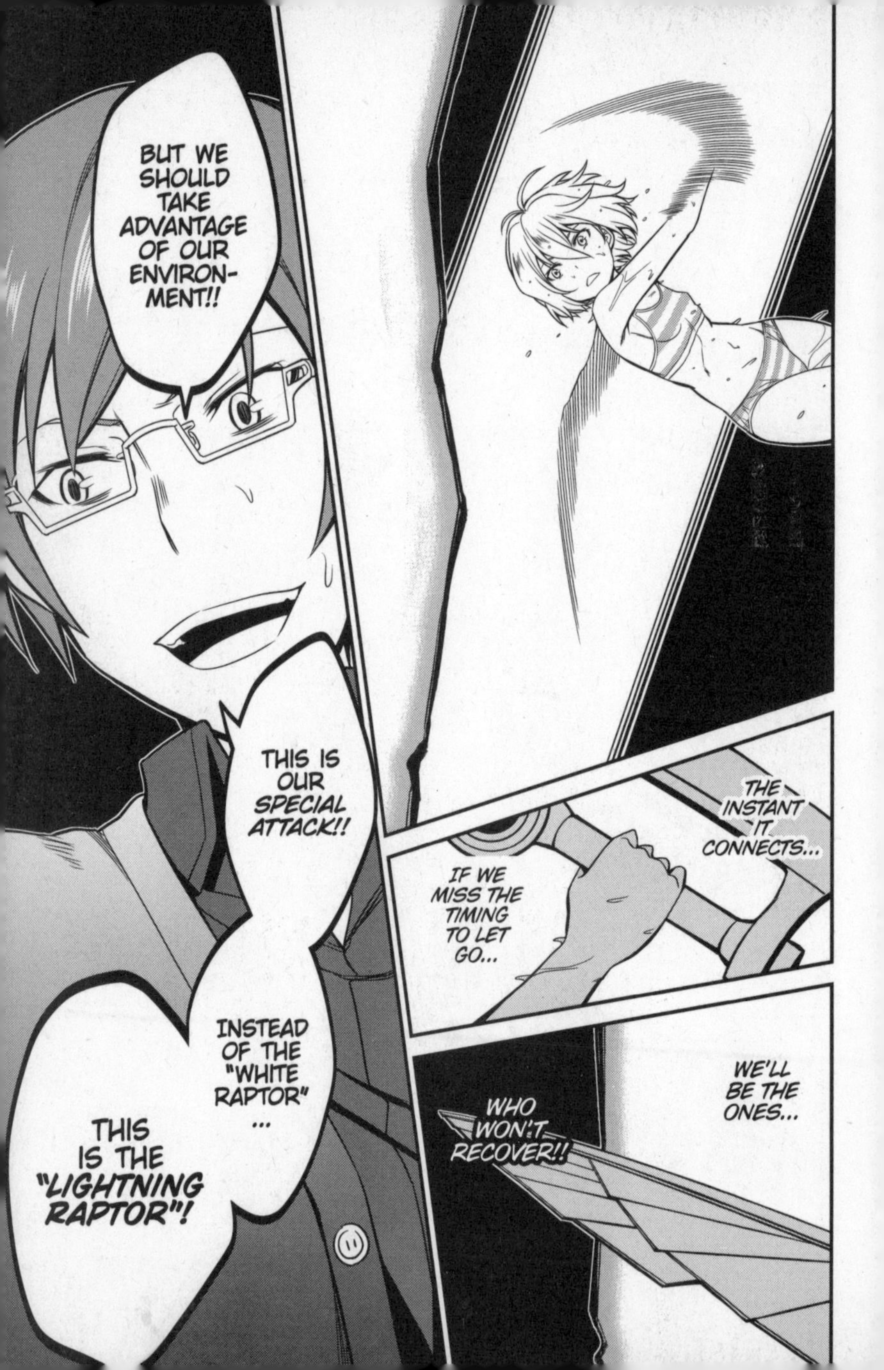
THE INSTANT IT CONNECTS...
IF WE MISS THE TIMING TO LET GO...
WE'LL BE THE ONES...
WHO WON'T RECOVER!!
BUT WE SHOULD TAKE ADVANTAGE OF OUR ENVIRON-MENT!!
THIS IS OUR SPECIAL ATTACK!!
INSTEAD OF THE "WHITE RAPTOR" ...
THIS IS THE "LIGHTNING RAPTOR"!

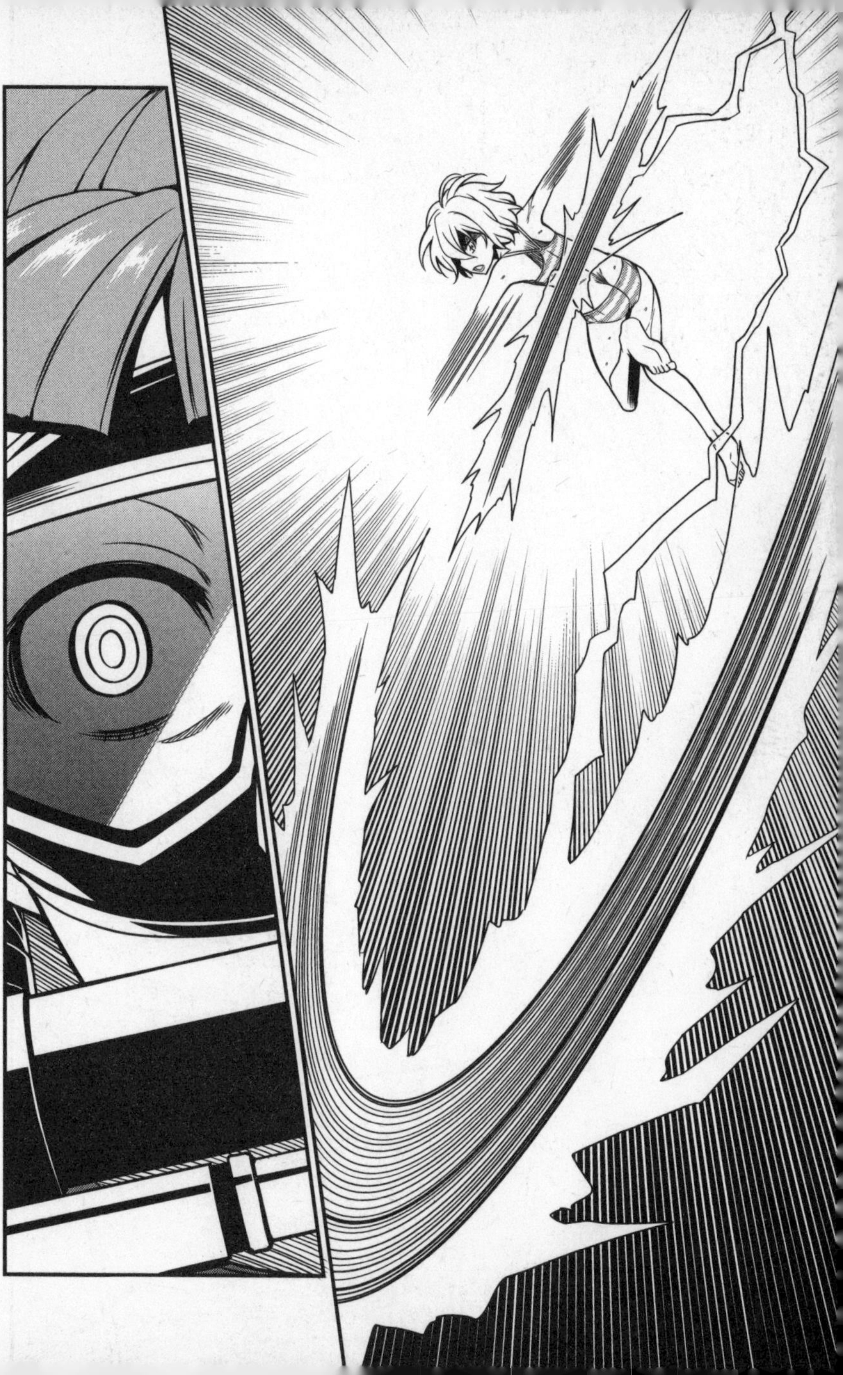

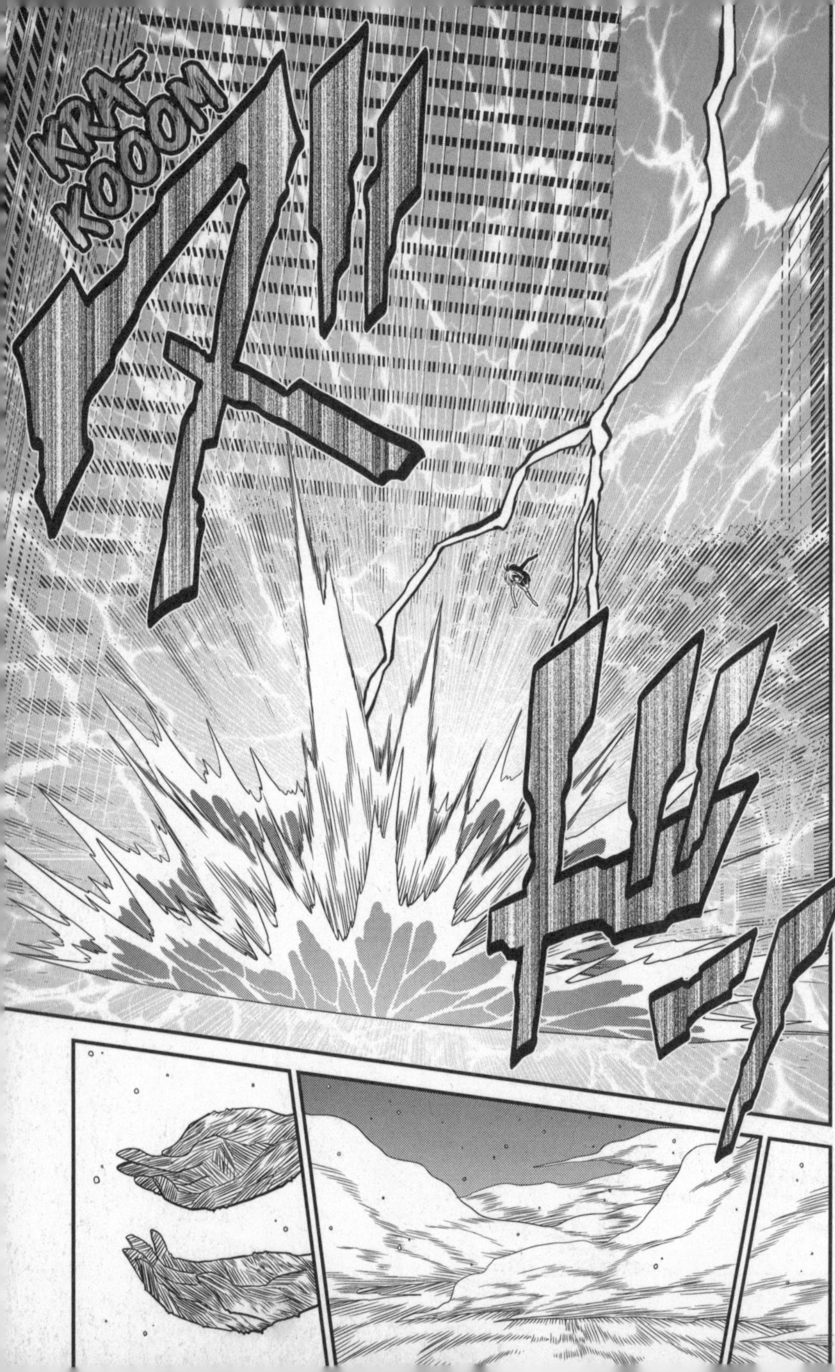
KRA-KOOOM

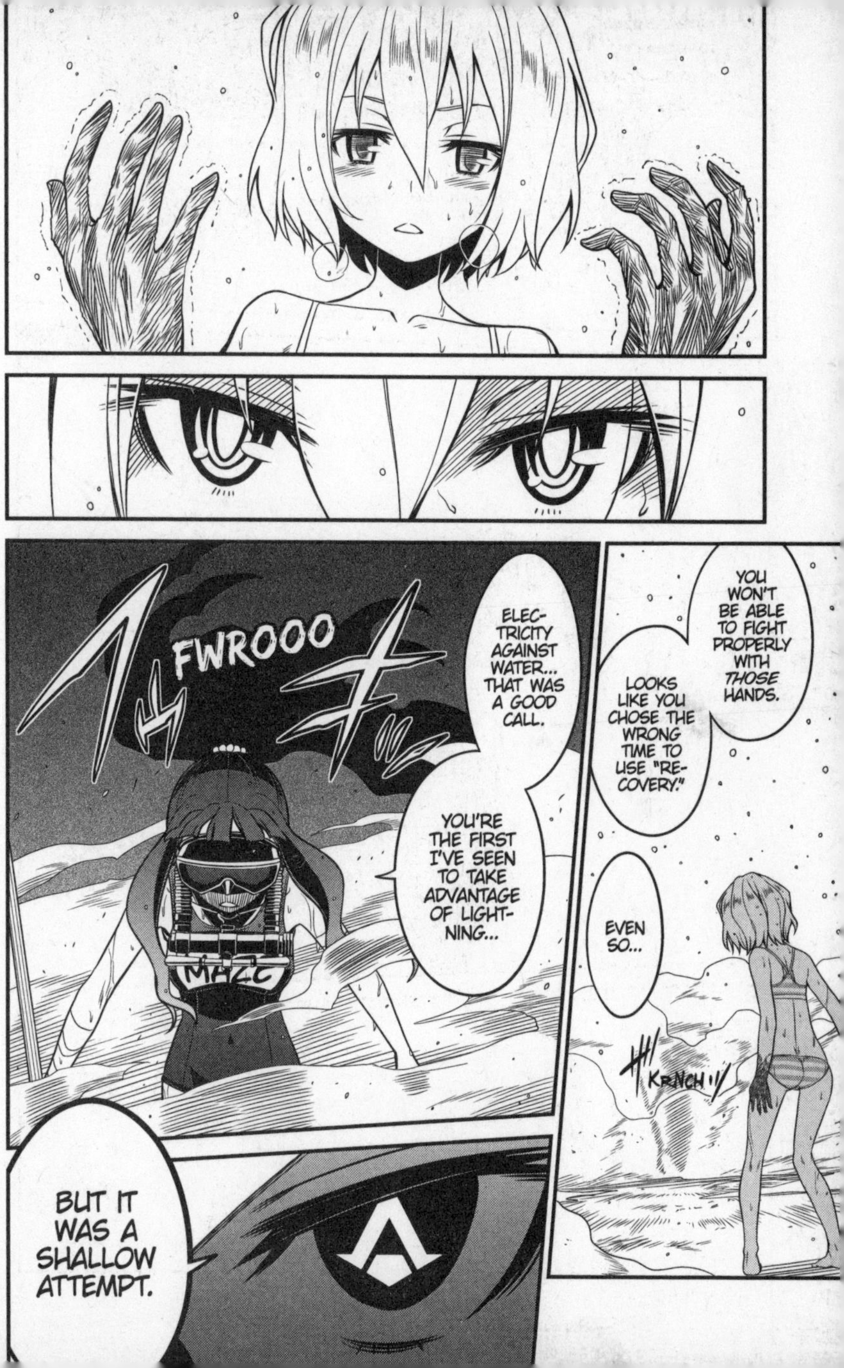
YOU WON'T BE ABLE TO FIGHT PROPERLY WITH *THOSE* HANDS.
LOOKS LIKE YOU CHOSE THE WRONG TIME TO USE "RECOVERY."
EVEN SO...
KRNCH
FWROOO
ELECTRICITY AGAINST WATER... THAT WAS A GOOD CALL.
YOU'RE THE FIRST I'VE SEEN TO TAKE ADVANTAGE OF LIGHTNING...
BUT IT WAS A SHALLOW ATTEMPT.

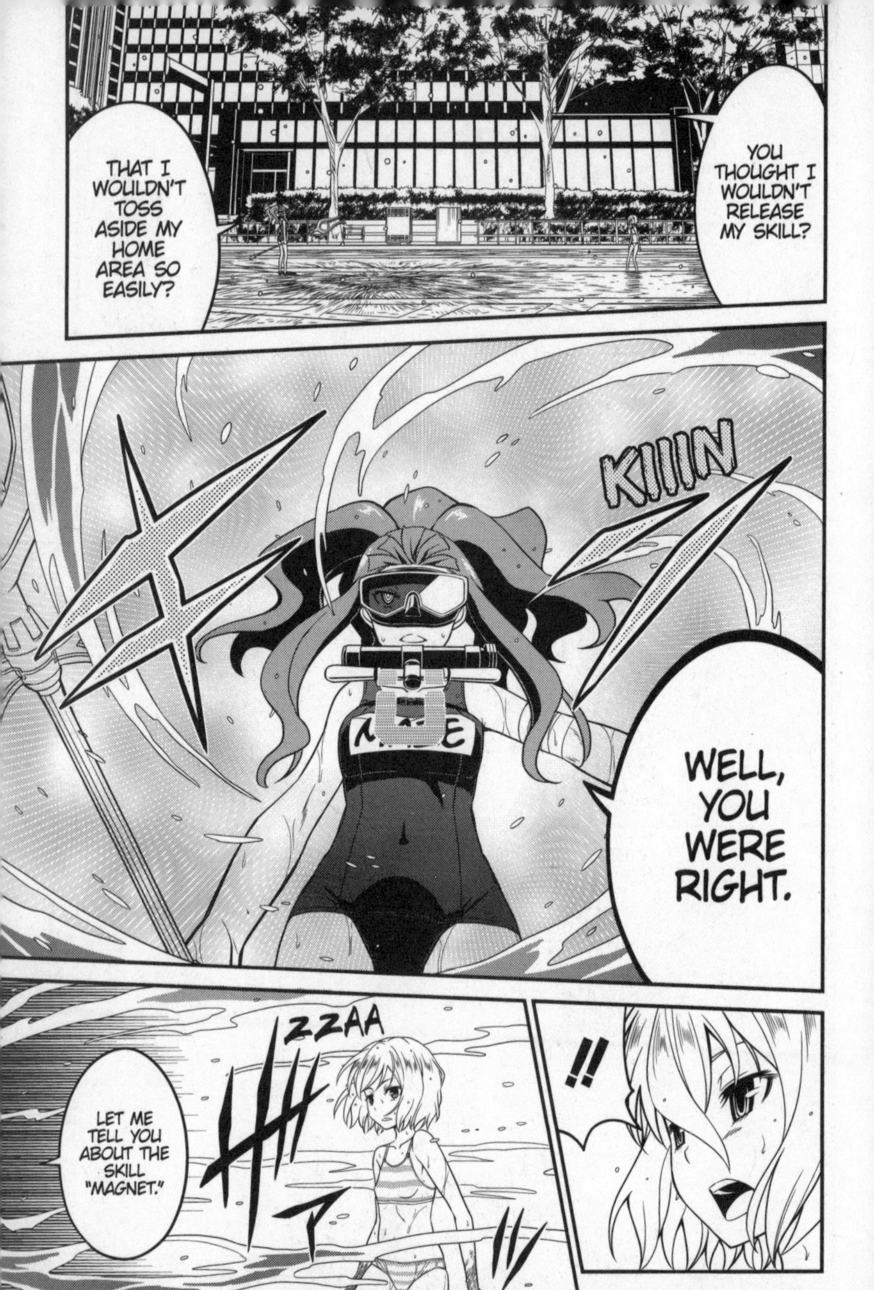
YOU THOUGHT I WOULDN'T RELEASE MY SKILL?
THAT I WOULDN'T TOSS ASIDE MY HOME AREA SO EASILY?
KIIIN
WELL, YOU WERE RIGHT.
!!
ZZAA
LET ME TELL YOU ABOUT THE SKILL "MAGNET."

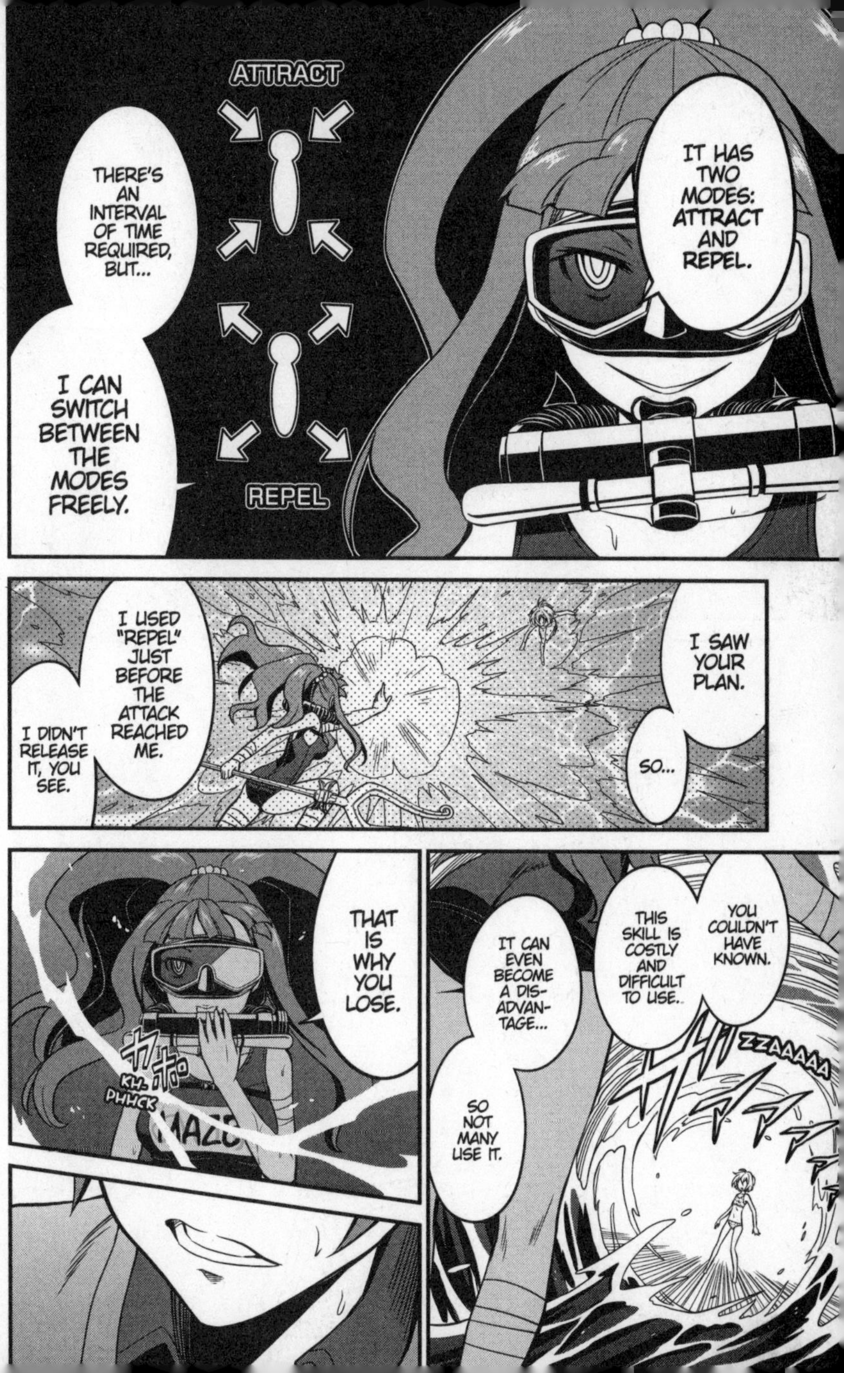
IT HAS TWO MODES: ATTRACT AND REPEL.
ATTRACT
REPEL
THERE'S AN INTERVAL OF TIME REQUIRED, BUT...
I CAN SWITCH BETWEEN THE MODES FREELY.
I SAW YOUR PLAN.
SO...
I USED "REPEL" JUST BEFORE THE ATTACK REACHED ME.
I DIDN'T RELEASE IT, YOU SEE.
YOU COULDN'T HAVE KNOWN.
THIS SKILL IS COSTLY AND DIFFICULT TO USE..
IT CAN EVEN BECOME A DIS-ADVANTAGE...
SO NOT MANY USE IT.
ZZAAAAA
THAT IS WHY YOU LOSE.
KH-PHHCK

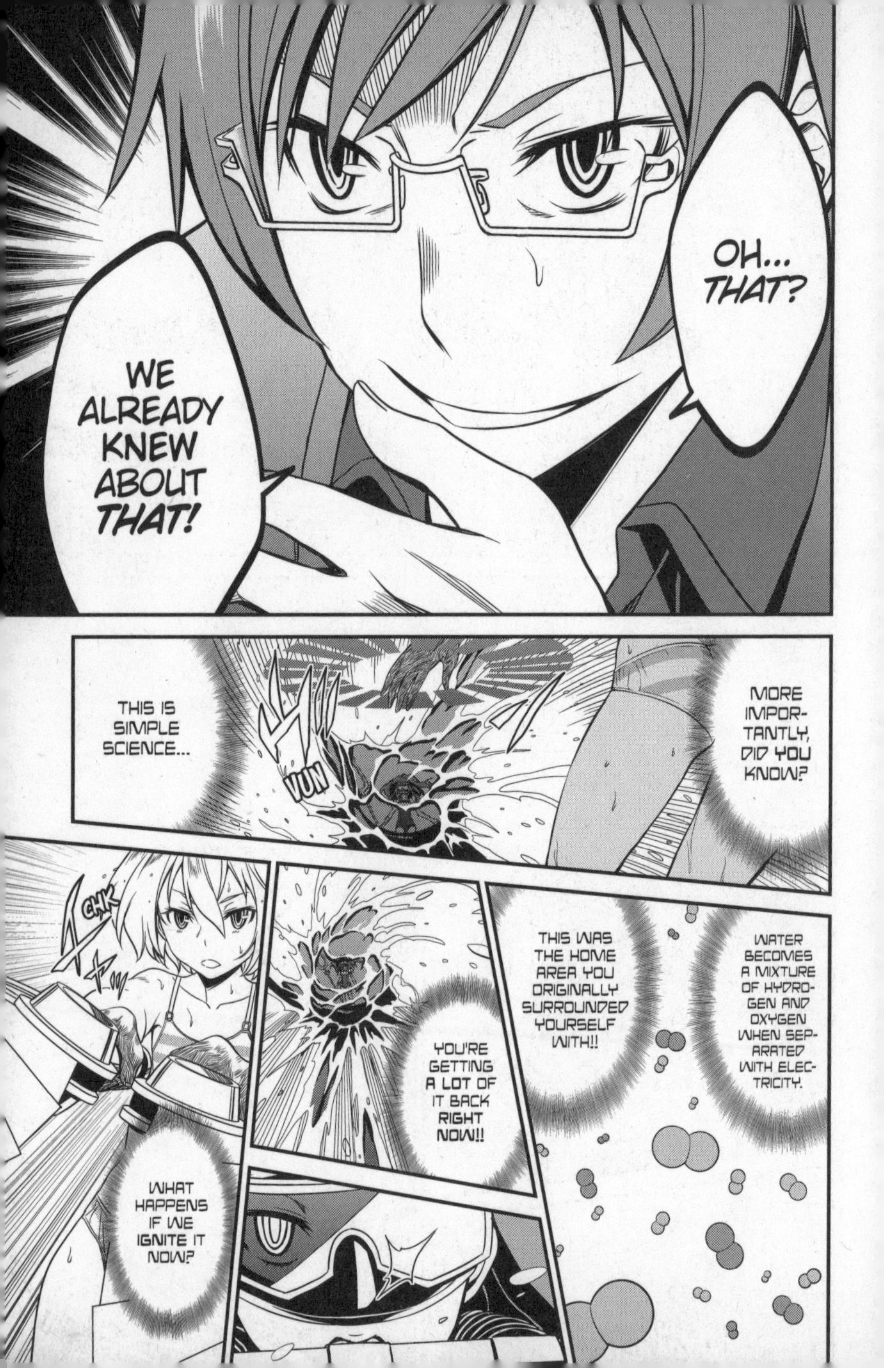
OH... THAT?
WE ALREADY KNEW ABOUT THAT!
MORE IMPORTANTLY, DID YOU KNOW?
VUN
THIS IS SIMPLE SCIENCE...
WATER BECOMES A MIXTURE OF HYDROGEN AND OXYGEN WHEN SEPARATED WITH ELECTRICITY.
THIS WAS THE HOME AREA YOU ORIGINALLY SURROUNDED YOURSELF WITH!!
YOU'RE GETTING A LOT OF IT BACK RIGHT NOW!!
CHK
WHAT HAPPENS IF WE IGNITE IT NOW?

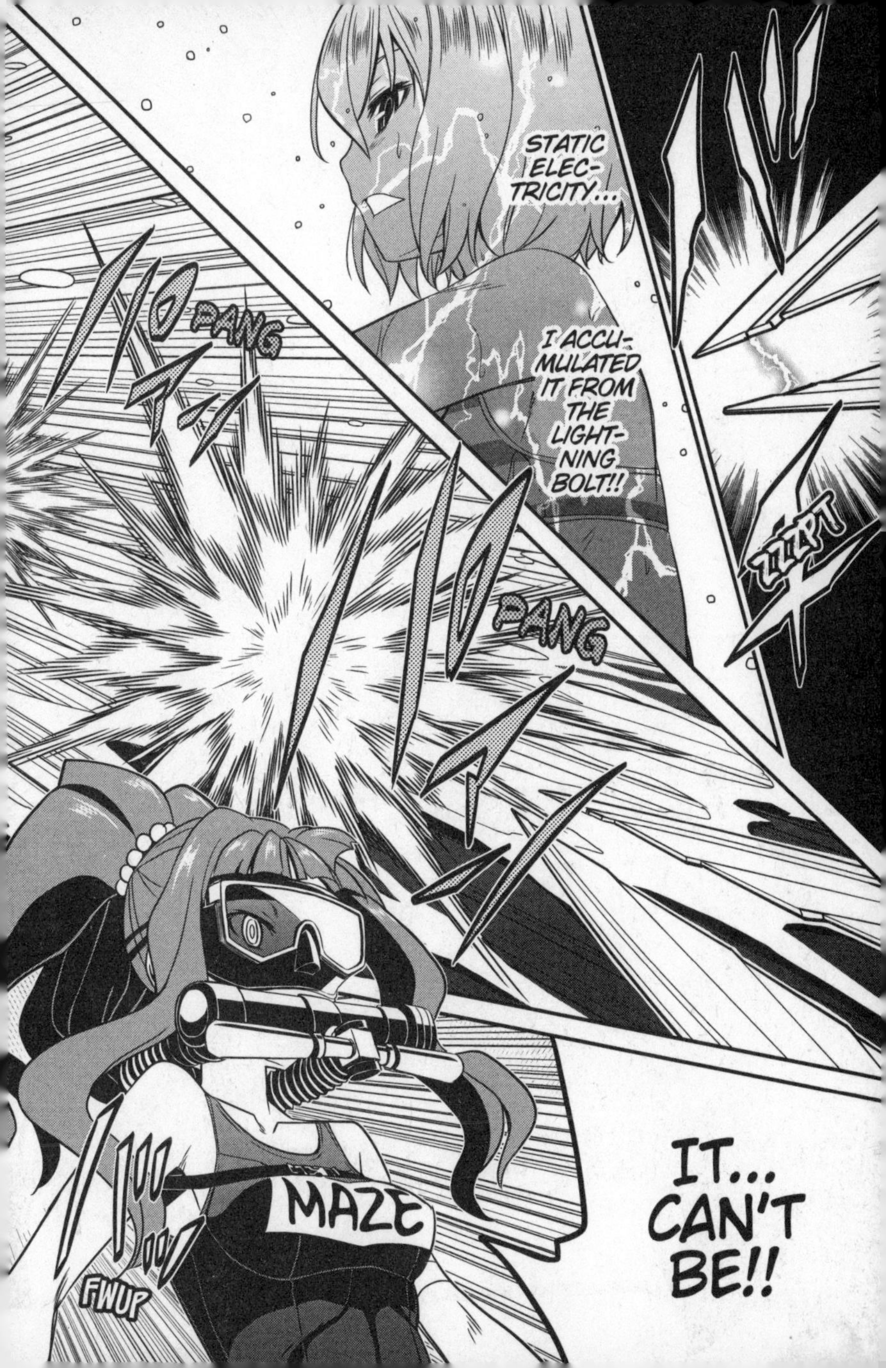
STATIC ELEC-TRICITY...
I ACCU-MULATED IT FROM THE LIGHT-NING BOLT!!
ZZZZPT
PANG
PANG
IT... CAN'T BE!!
MAZE
FWUP

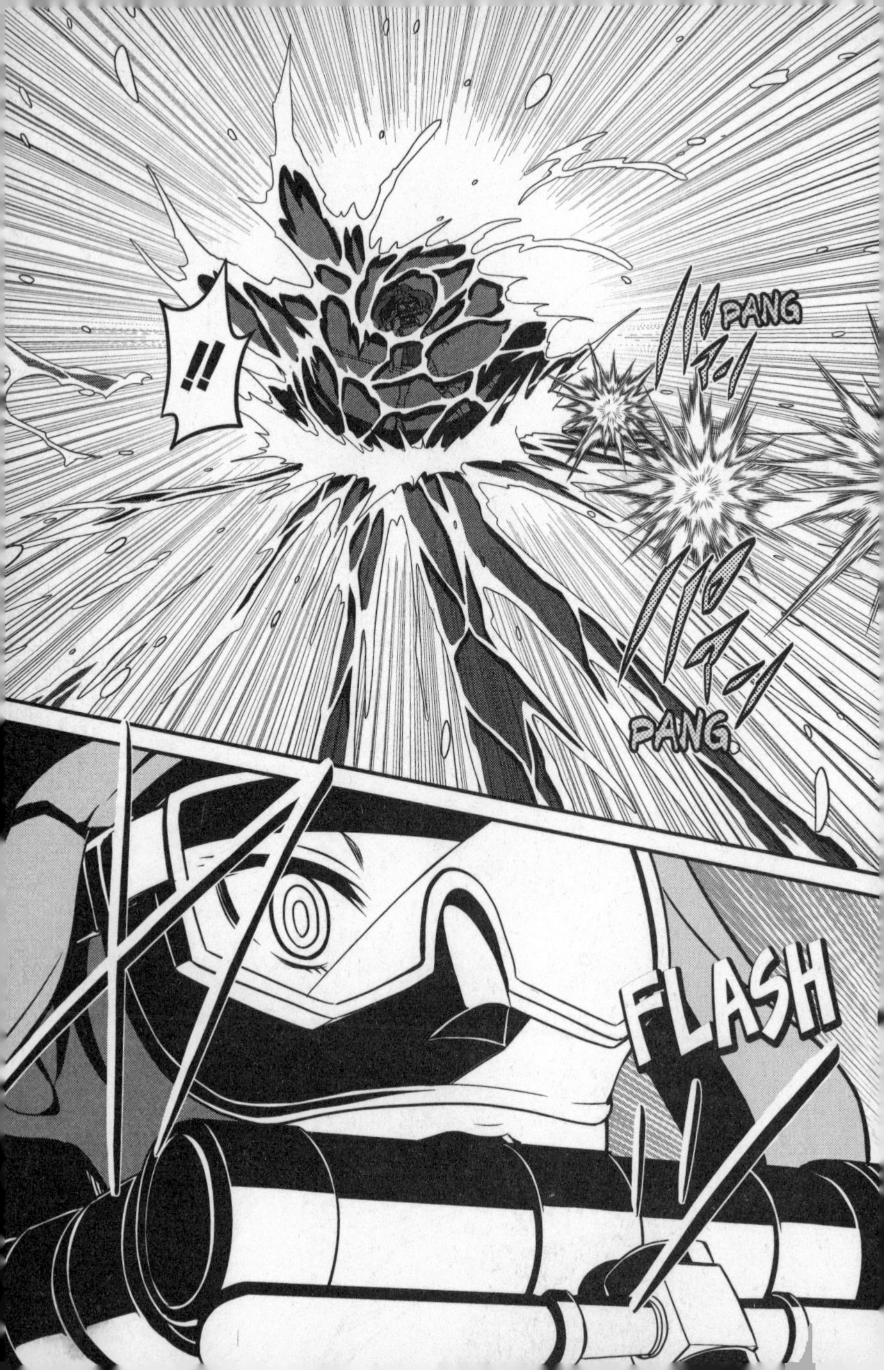
PANG
!!
PANG
FLASH

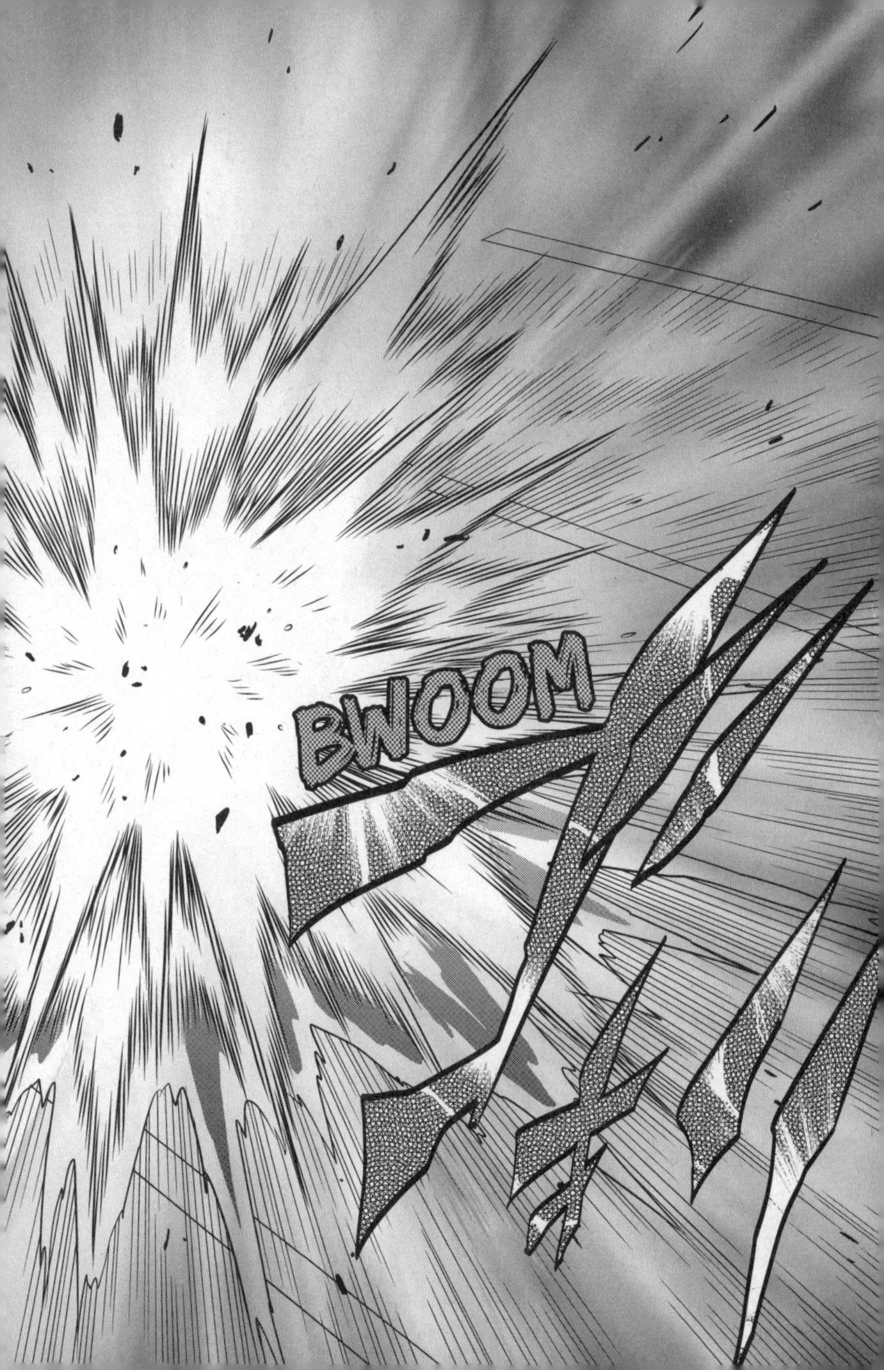
BWOOM

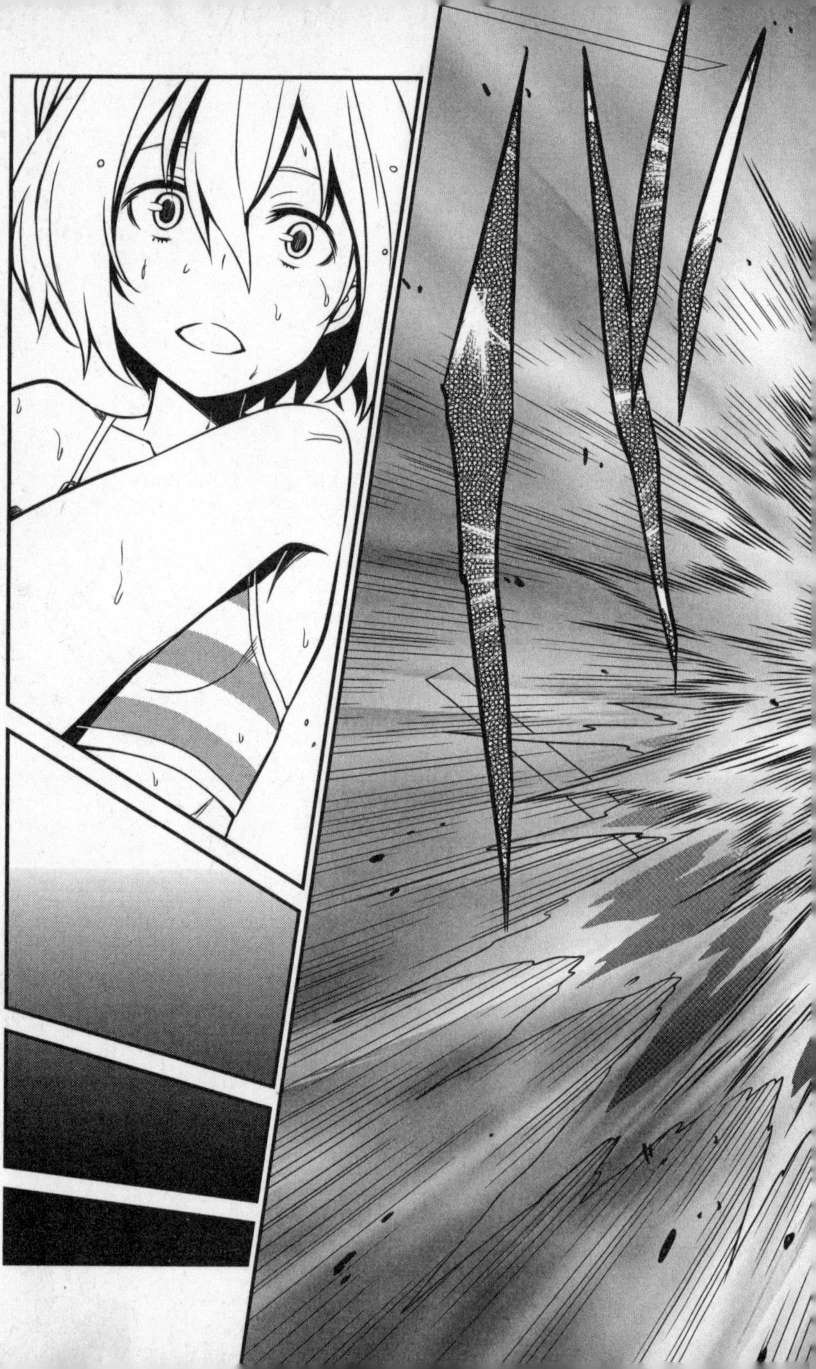

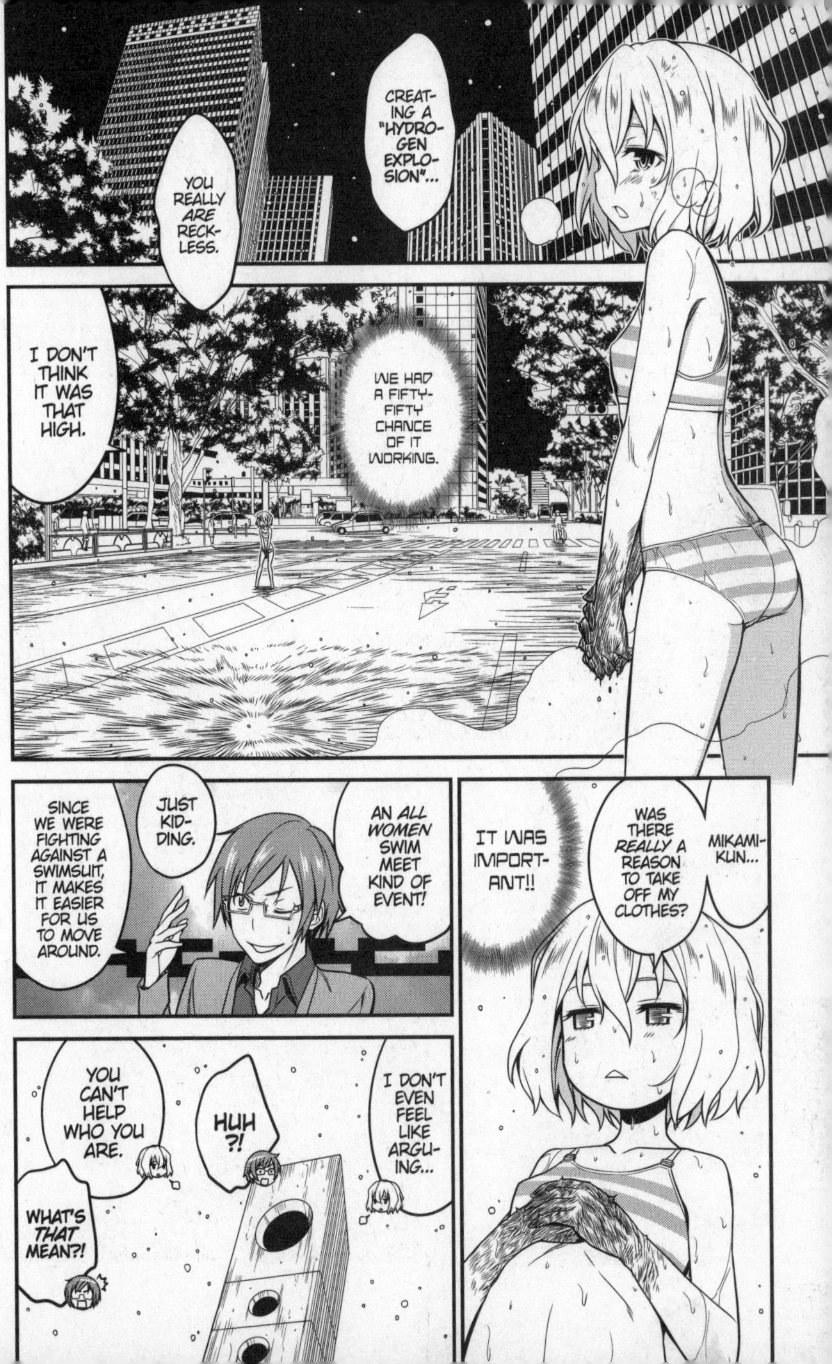
CREATING A "HYDROGEN EXPLOSION"...
YOU REALLY *ARE* RECKLESS.
WE HAD A FIFTY-FIFTY CHANCE OF IT WORKING.
I DON'T THINK IT WAS THAT HIGH.
MIKAMI-KUN...
WAS THERE *REALLY* A REASON TO TAKE OFF MY CLOTHES?
IT WAS IMPORTANT!!
AN *ALL WOMEN* SWIM MEET KIND OF EVENT!
JUST KIDDING.
SINCE WE WERE FIGHTING AGAINST A SWIMSUIT, IT MAKES IT EASIER FOR US TO MOVE AROUND.
I DON'T EVEN FEEL LIKE ARGUING...
HUH?!
YOU CAN'T HELP WHO YOU ARE.
WHAT'S *THAT* MEAN?!

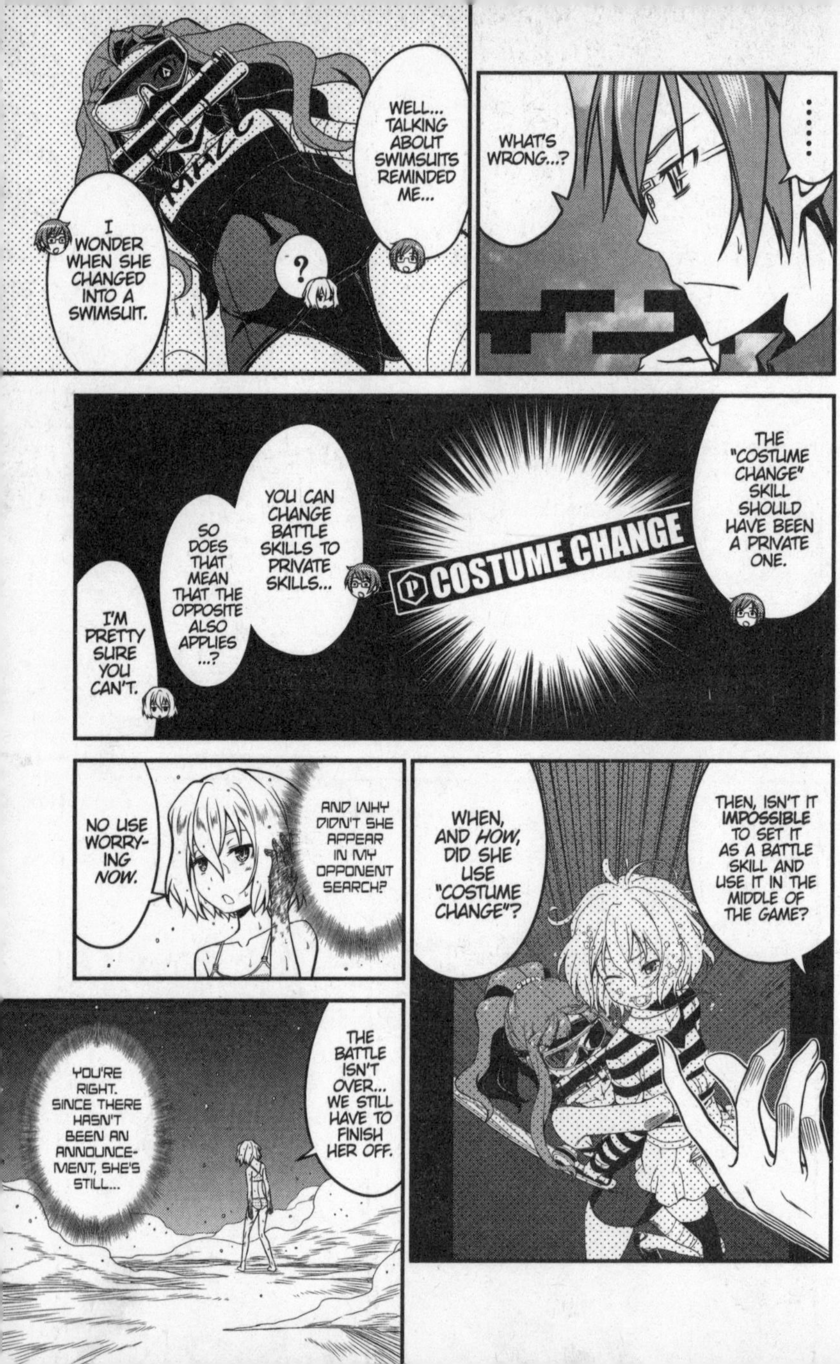
......
WHAT'S WRONG...?
WELL... TALKING ABOUT SWIMSUITS REMINDED ME...
?
I WONDER WHEN SHE CHANGED INTO A SWIMSUIT.
THE "COSTUME CHANGE" SKILL SHOULD HAVE BEEN A PRIVATE ONE.
P COSTUME CHANGE
YOU CAN CHANGE BATTLE SKILLS TO PRIVATE SKILLS...
SO DOES THAT MEAN THAT THE OPPOSITE ALSO APPLIES ...?
I'M PRETTY SURE YOU CAN'T.
THEN, ISN'T IT IMPOSSIBLE TO SET IT AS A BATTLE SKILL AND USE IT IN THE MIDDLE OF THE GAME?
WHEN, AND *HOW*, DID SHE USE "COSTUME CHANGE"?
AND WHY DIDN'T SHE APPEAR IN MY OPPONENT SEARCH?
NO USE WORRYING *NOW*.
THE BATTLE ISN'T OVER... WE STILL HAVE TO FINISH HER OFF.
YOU'RE RIGHT. SINCE THERE HASN'T BEEN AN ANNOUNCEMENT, SHE'S STILL...

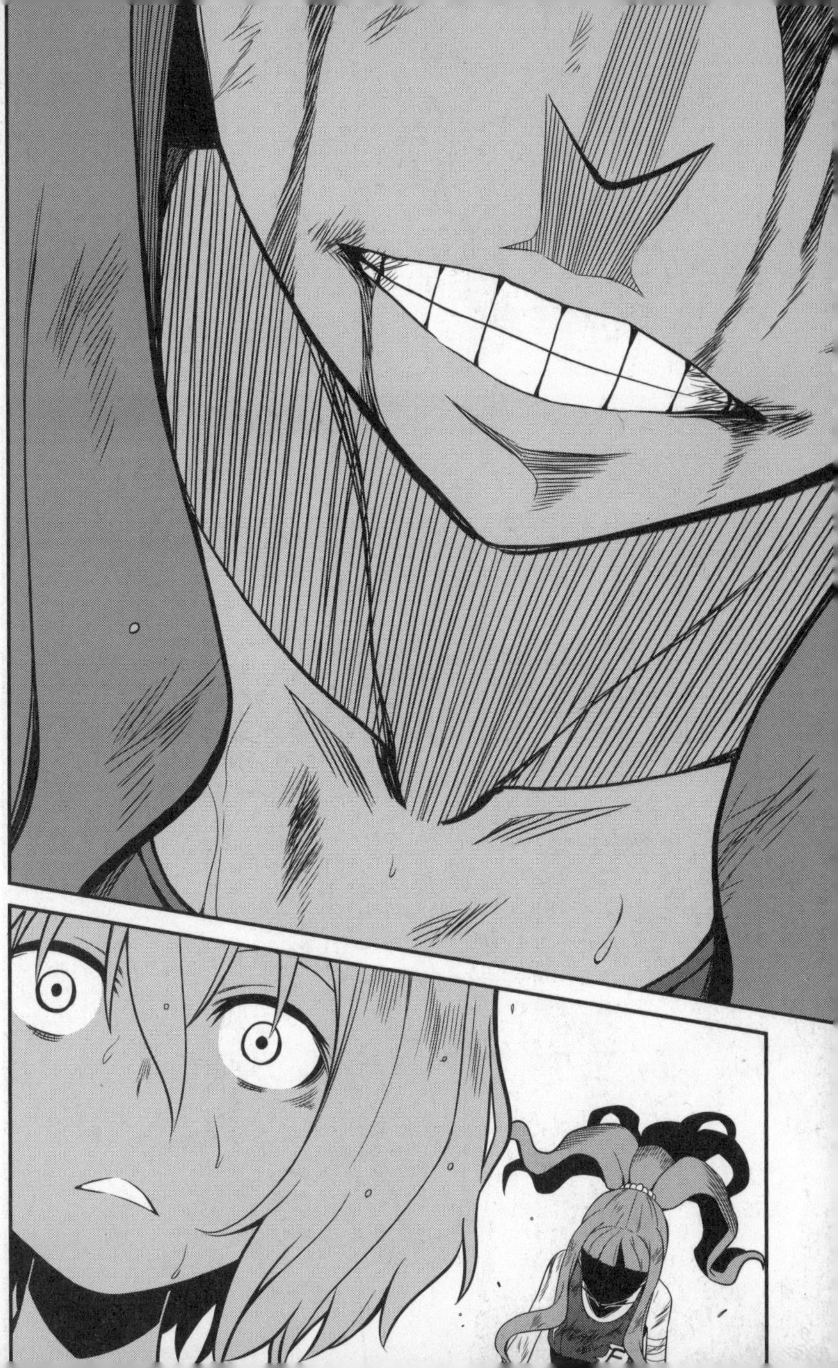

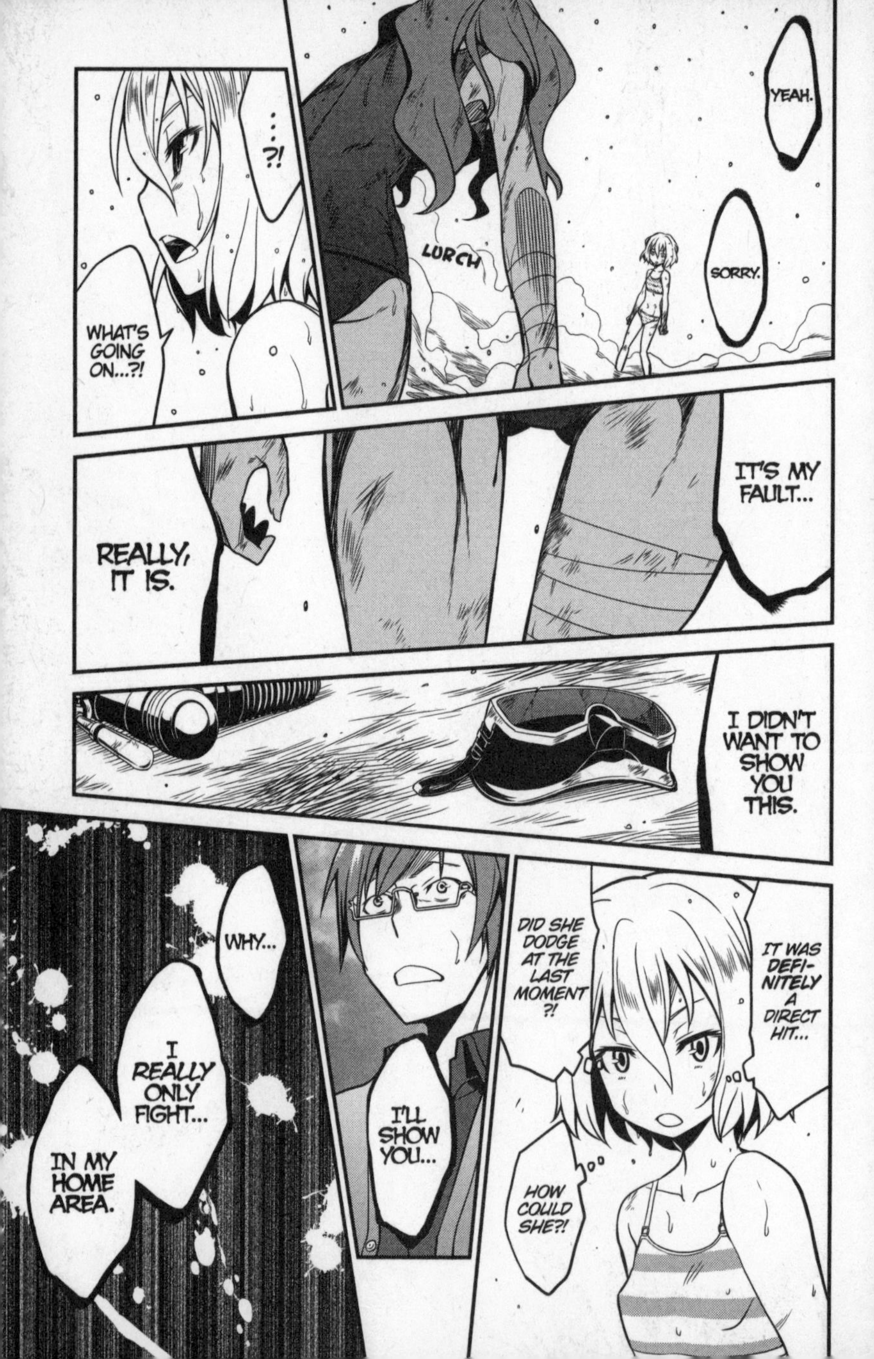
YEAH.
SORRY.
LURCH
...?!
WHAT'S GOING ON...?!
IT'S MY FAULT...
REALLY, IT IS.
I DIDN'T WANT TO SHOW YOU THIS.
IT WAS DEFINITELY A DIRECT HIT...
DID SHE DODGE AT THE LAST MOMENT?!
HOW COULD SHE?!
I'LL SHOW YOU...
WHY...
I REALLY ONLY FIGHT...
IN MY HOME AREA.

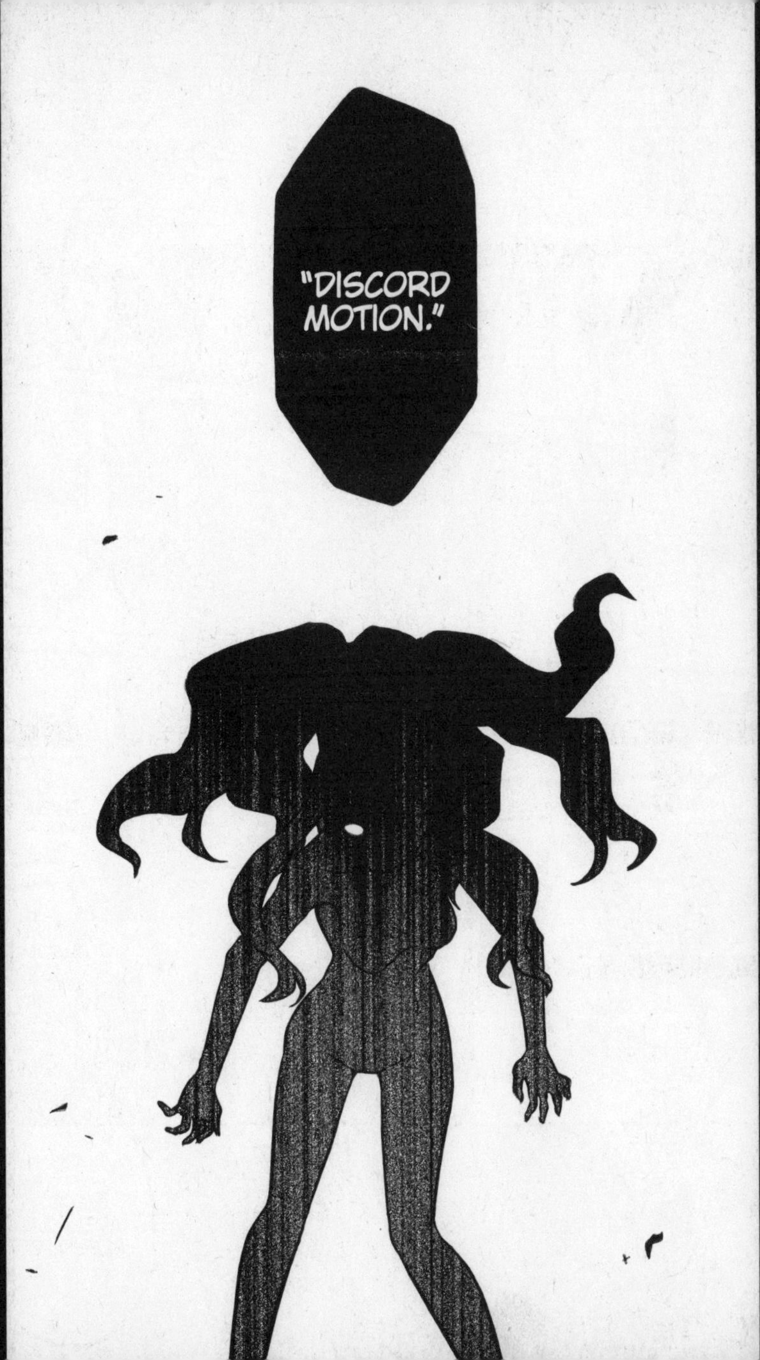
"DISCORD MOTION."

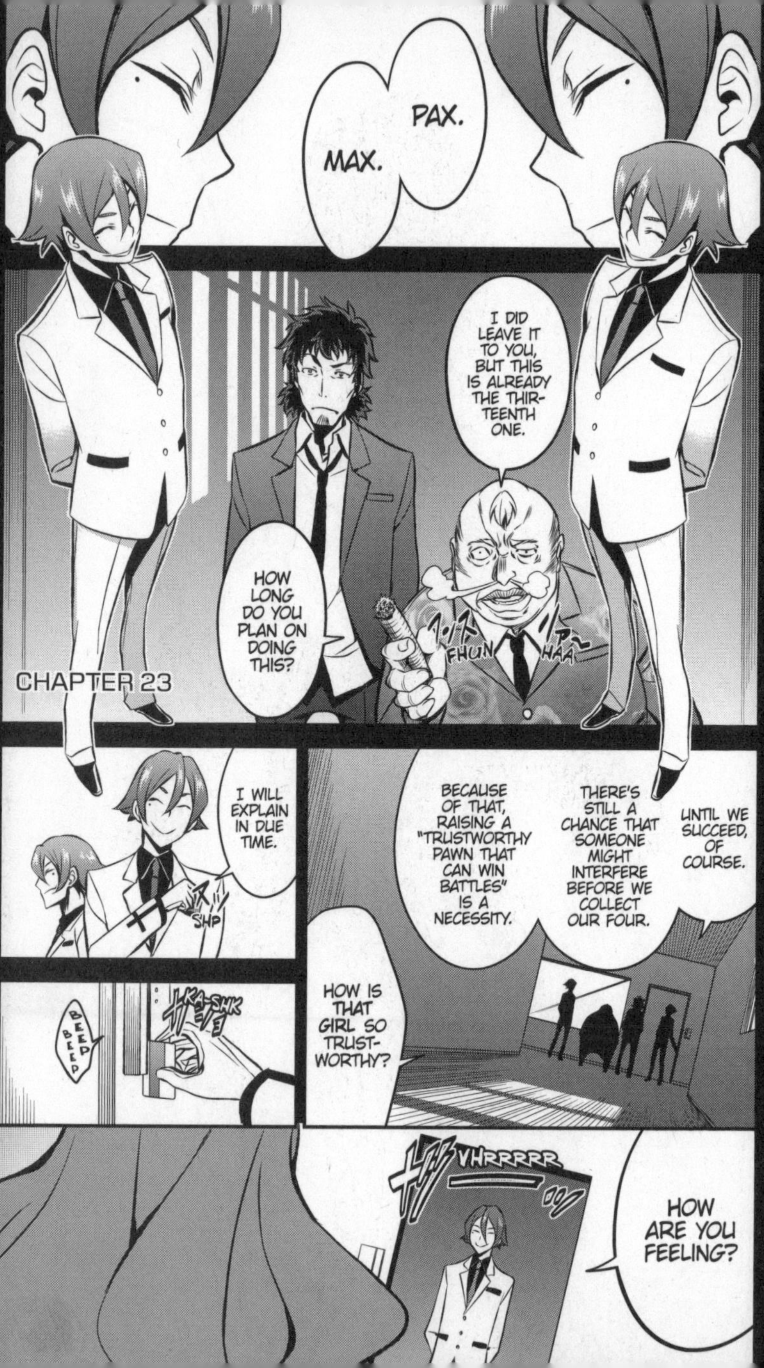
PAX.
MAX.
I DID LEAVE IT TO YOU, BUT THIS IS ALREADY THE THIRTEENTH ONE.
HOW LONG DO YOU PLAN ON DOING THIS?
HAA
FHUN
CHAPTER 23
UNTIL WE SUCCEED, OF COURSE.
THERE'S STILL A CHANCE THAT SOMEONE MIGHT INTERFERE BEFORE WE COLLECT OUR FOUR.
BECAUSE OF THAT, RAISING A "TRUSTWORTHY PAWN THAT CAN WIN BATTLES" IS A NECESSITY.
I WILL EXPLAIN IN DUE TIME.
SHP
HOW IS THAT GIRL SO TRUST-WORTHY?
KA-SHK
BEEP BEEP
HOW ARE YOU FEELING?
VHRRRRR

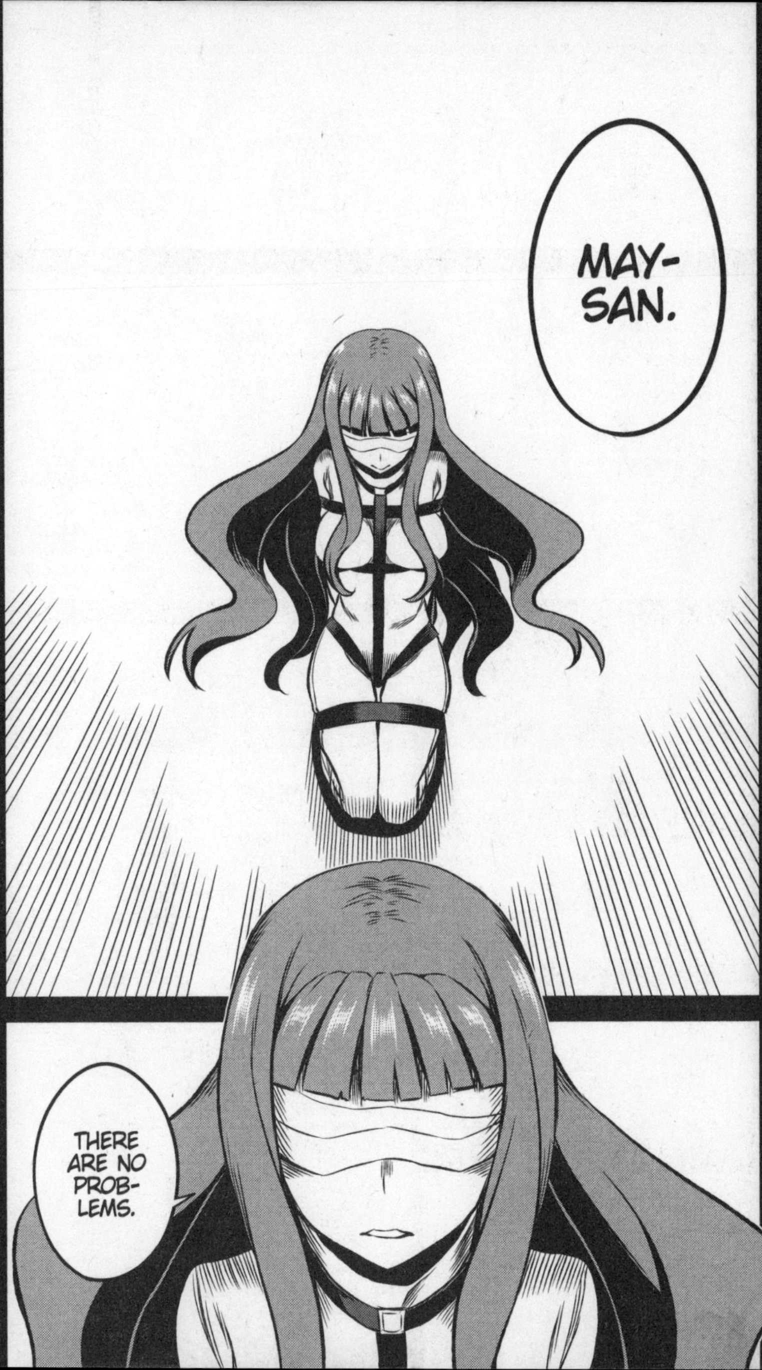
MAY-SAN.
THERE ARE NO PROB-LEMS.

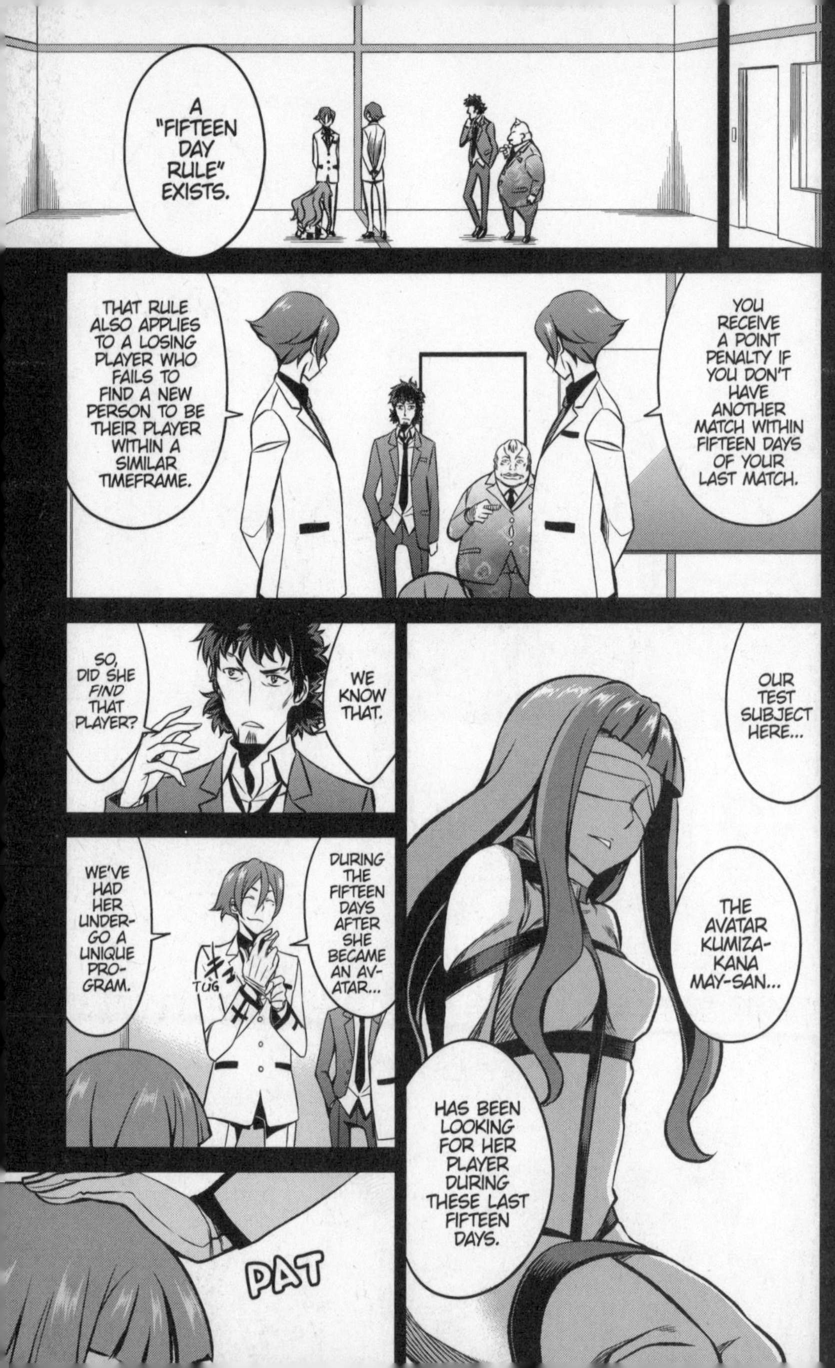
A "FIFTEEN DAY RULE" EXISTS.
YOU RECEIVE A POINT PENALTY IF YOU DON'T HAVE ANOTHER MATCH WITHIN FIFTEEN DAYS OF YOUR LAST MATCH.
THAT RULE ALSO APPLIES TO A LOSING PLAYER WHO FAILS TO FIND A NEW PERSON TO BE THEIR PLAYER WITHIN A SIMILAR TIMEFRAME.
OUR TEST SUBJECT HERE...
THE AVATAR KUMIZA-KANA MAY-SAN...
HAS BEEN LOOKING FOR HER PLAYER DURING THESE LAST FIFTEEN DAYS.
WE KNOW THAT.
SO, DID SHE *FIND* THAT PLAYER?
DURING THE FIFTEEN DAYS AFTER SHE BECAME AN AV-ATAR...
WE'VE HAD HER UNDER-GO A UNIQUE PRO-GRAM.
TUG
PAT

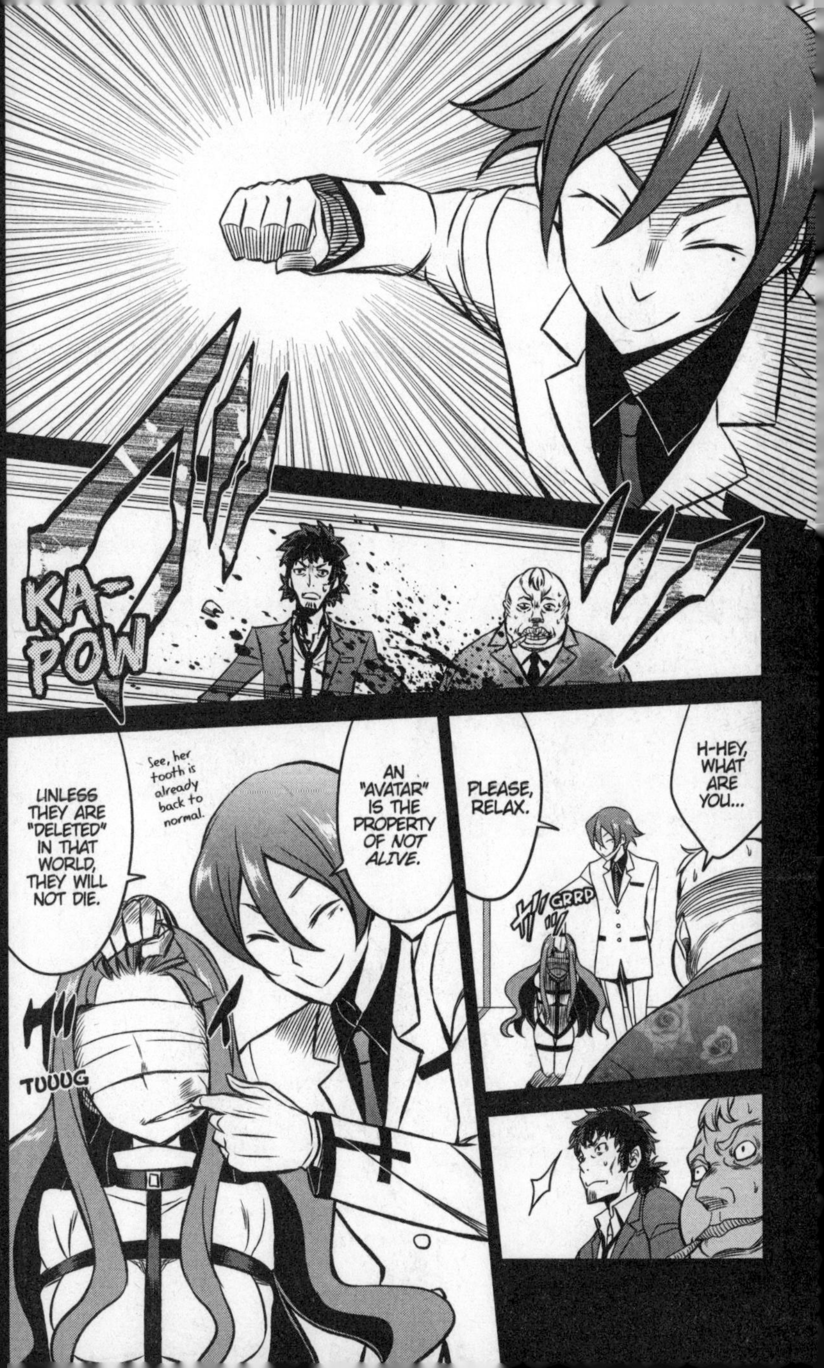

KA-POW
H-HEY, WHAT ARE YOU...
PLEASE, RELAX.
GRRP
AN "AVATAR" IS THE PROPERTY OF NOT ALIVE.
See, her tooth is already back to normal.
UNLESS THEY ARE "DELETED" IN THAT WORLD, THEY WILL NOT DIE.
TUUUG

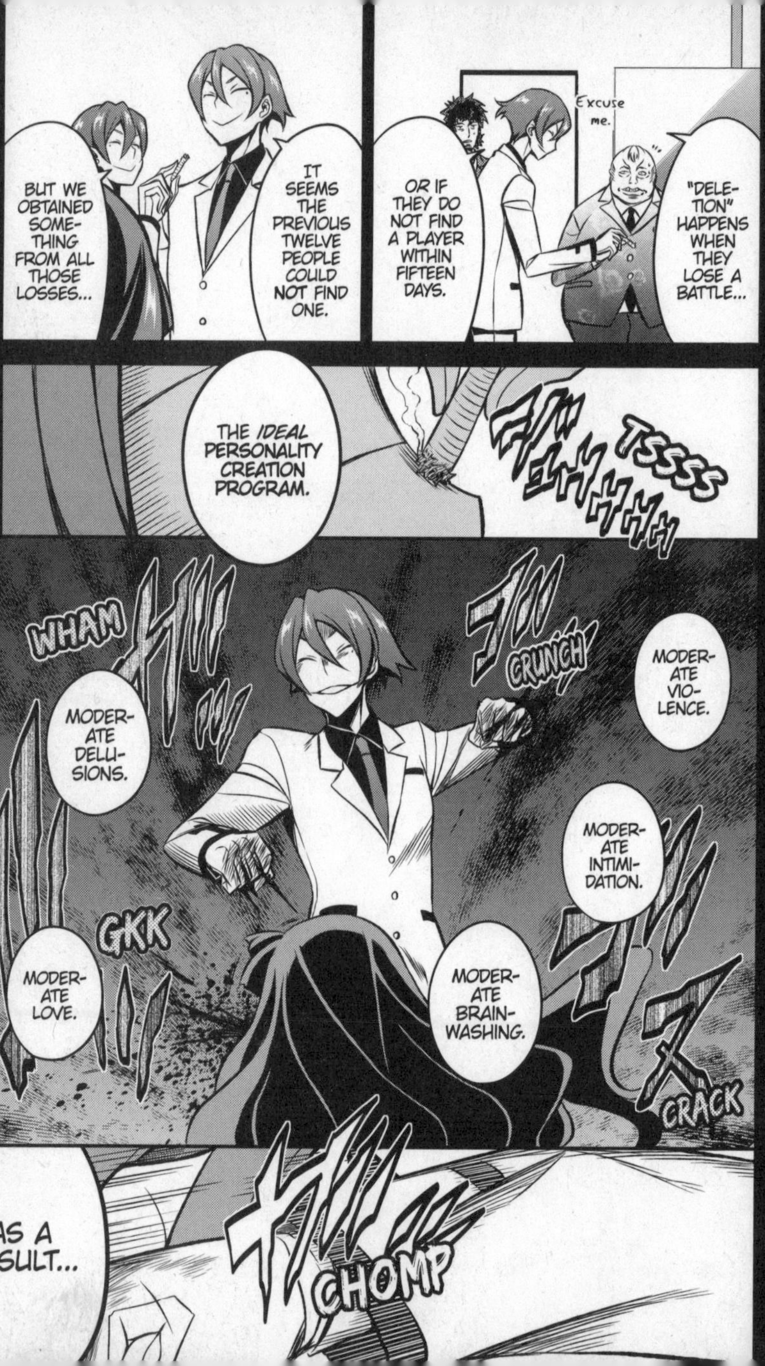
Excuse me.
"DELETION" HAPPENS WHEN THEY LOSE A BATTLE...
OR IF THEY DO NOT FIND A PLAYER WITHIN FIFTEEN DAYS.
IT SEEMS THE PREVIOUS TWELVE PEOPLE COULD NOT FIND ONE.
BUT WE OBTAINED SOMETHING FROM ALL THOSE LOSSES...
TSSSS
THE *IDEAL* PERSONALITY CREATION PROGRAM.
MODERATE VIOLENCE.
CRUNCH
WHAM
MODERATE DELUSIONS.
MODERATE INTIMIDATION.
GKK
MODERATE BRAINWASHING.
MODERATE LOVE.
CRACK
CHOMP
AS A RESULT...

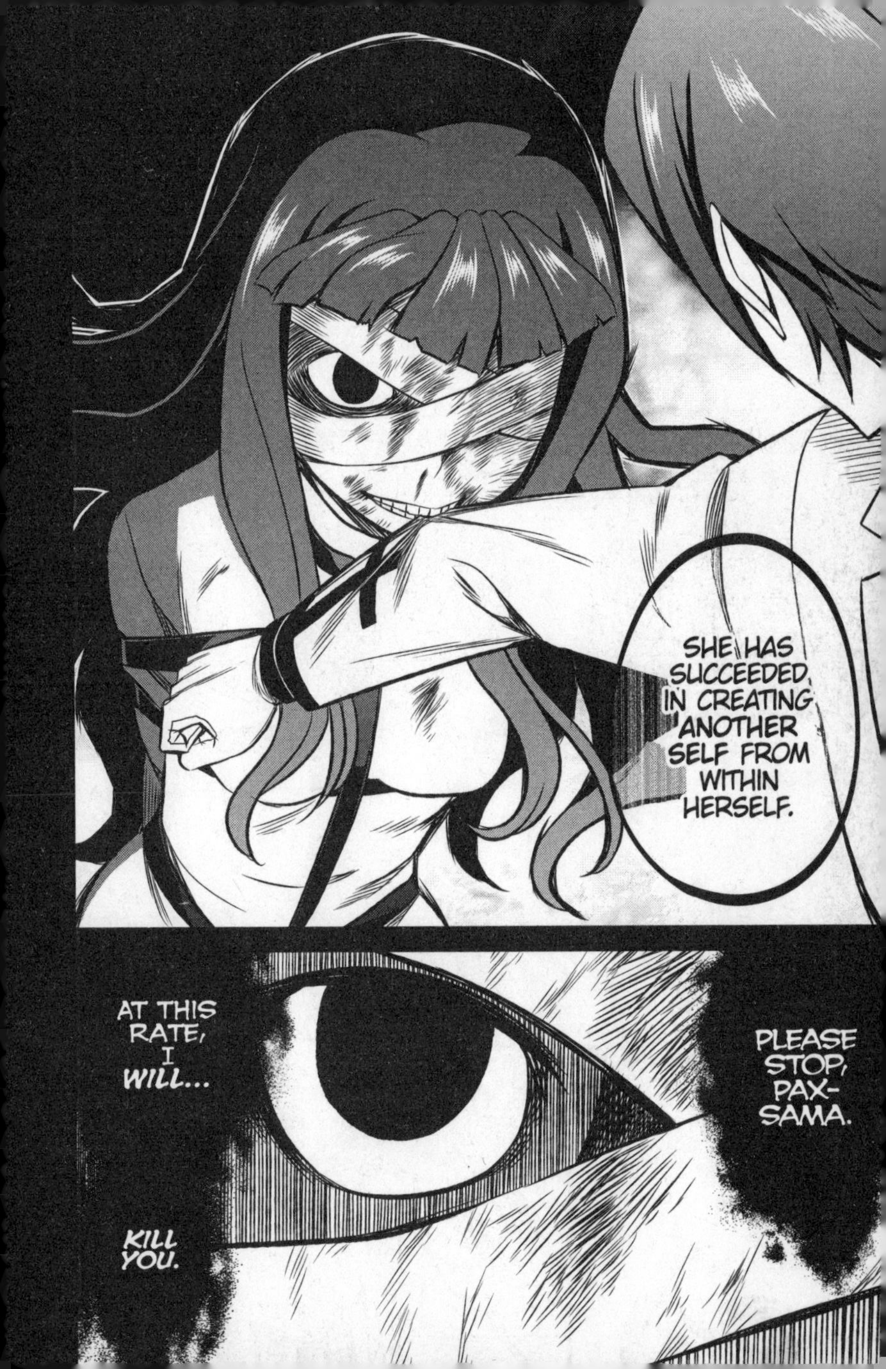
SHE HAS SUCCEEDED IN CREATING ANOTHER SELF FROM WITHIN HERSELF.
PLEASE STOP, PAX-SAMA.
AT THIS RATE, I *WILL...*
KILL YOU.

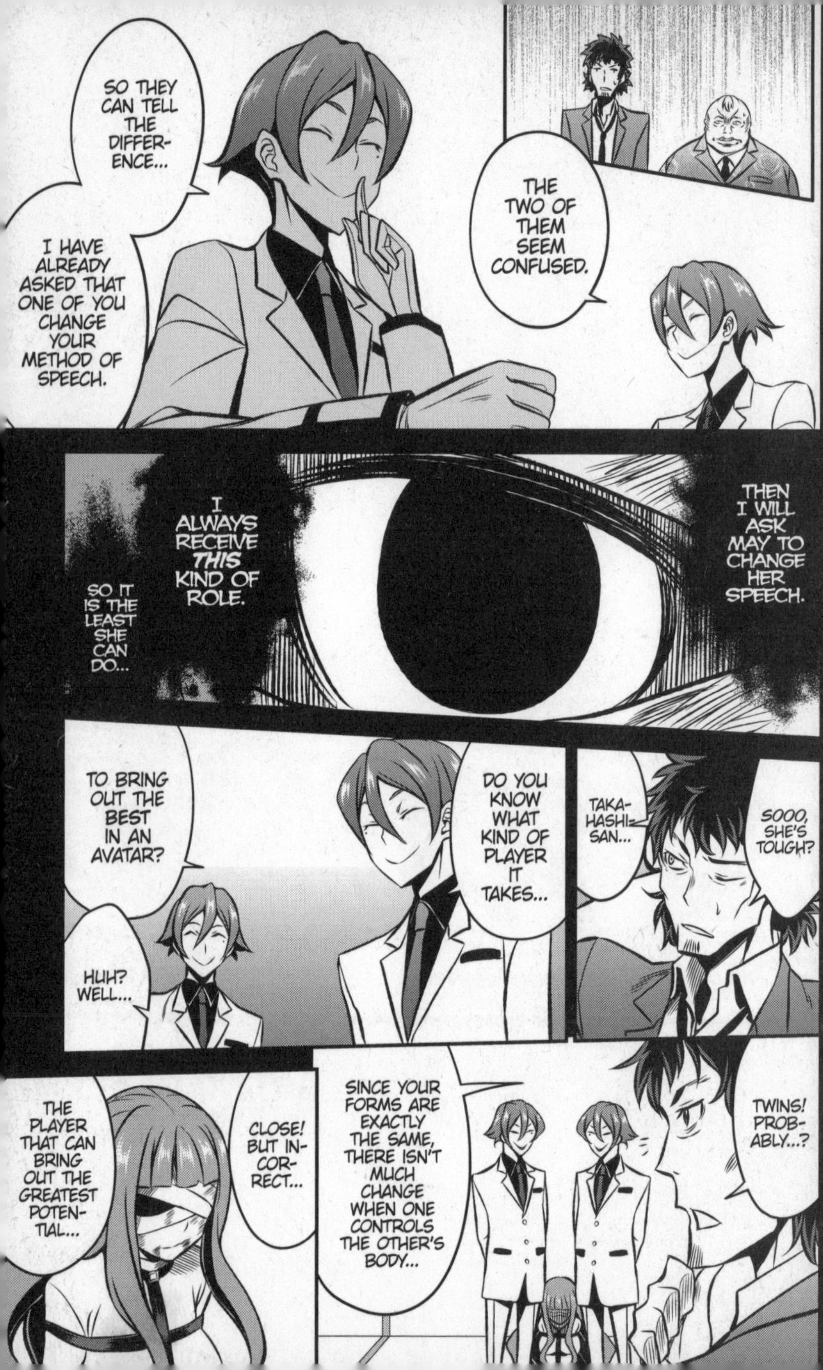

THE TWO OF THEM SEEM CONFUSED.
SO THEY CAN TELL THE DIFFERENCE...
I HAVE ALREADY ASKED THAT ONE OF YOU CHANGE YOUR METHOD OF SPEECH.
THEN I WILL ASK MAY TO CHANGE HER SPEECH.
I ALWAYS RECEIVE *THIS* KIND OF ROLE.
SO IT IS THE LEAST SHE CAN DO...
SOOO, SHE'S TOUGH?
TAKAHASHI-SAN...
DO YOU KNOW WHAT KIND OF PLAYER IT TAKES...
TO BRING OUT THE BEST IN AN AVATAR?
HUH? WELL...
TWINS! PROBABLY...?
SINCE YOUR FORMS ARE EXACTLY THE SAME, THERE ISN'T MUCH CHANGE WHEN ONE CONTROLS THE OTHER'S BODY...
CLOSE! BUT INCORRECT...
THE PLAYER THAT CAN BRING OUT THE GREATEST POTENTIAL...

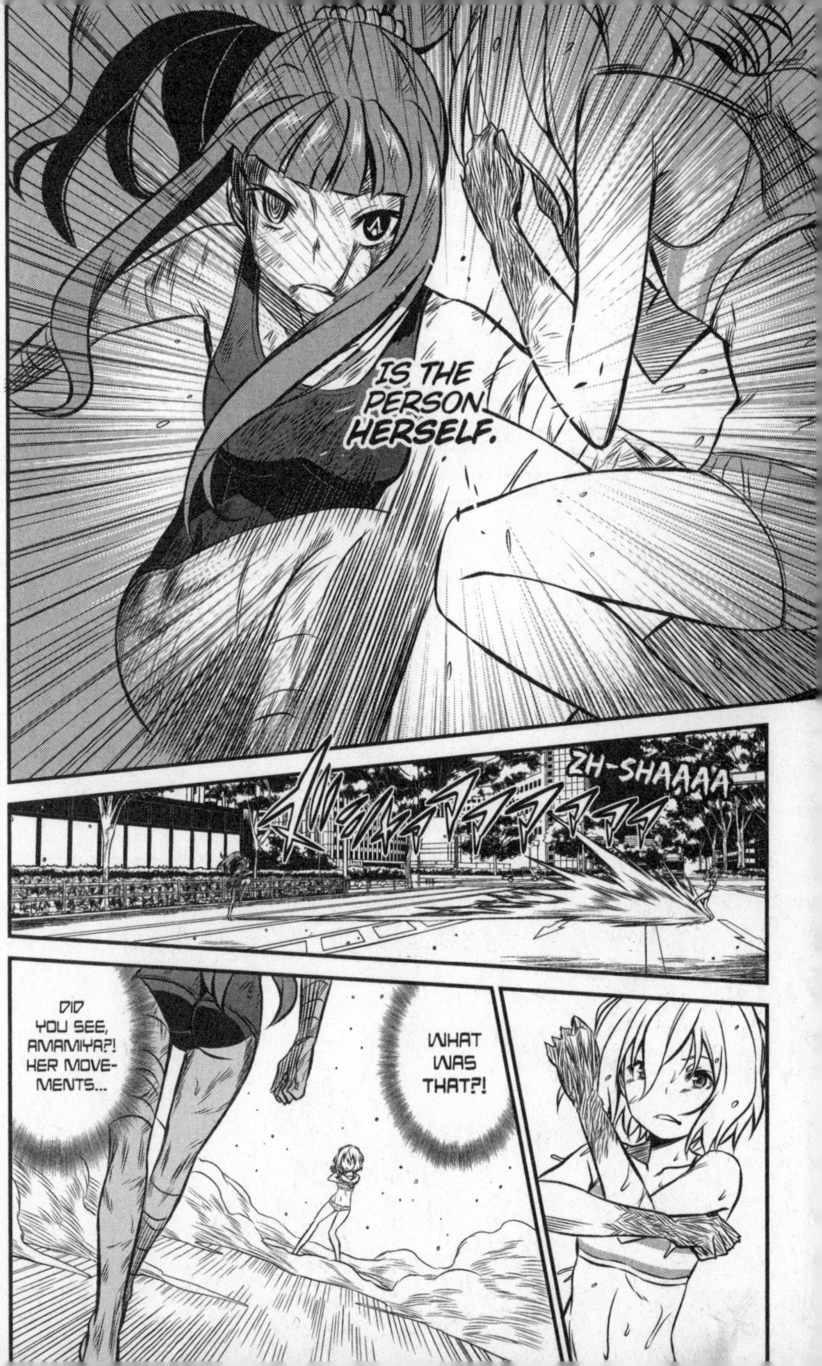
IS THE PERSON HERSELF.
ZH-SHAAAA
WHAT WAS THAT?!
DID YOU SEE, AMAMIYA?! HER MOVEMENTS...

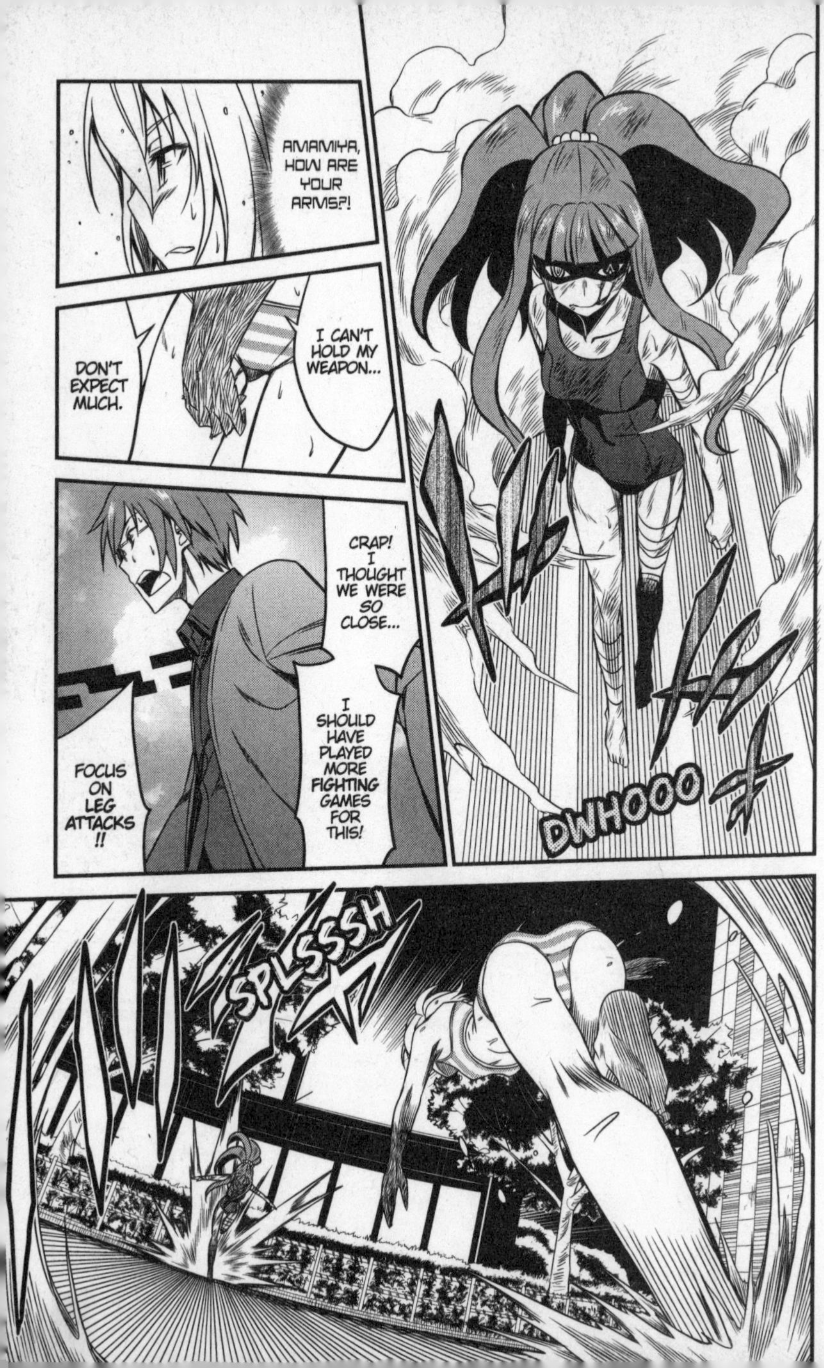
DWHOOO
AMAMIYA, HOW ARE YOUR ARMS?!
I CAN'T HOLD MY WEAPON...
DON'T EXPECT MUCH.
CRAP! I THOUGHT WE WERE SO CLOSE...
I SHOULD HAVE PLAYED MORE FIGHTING GAMES FOR THIS!
FOCUS ON LEG ATTACKS!!
SPLSSSH

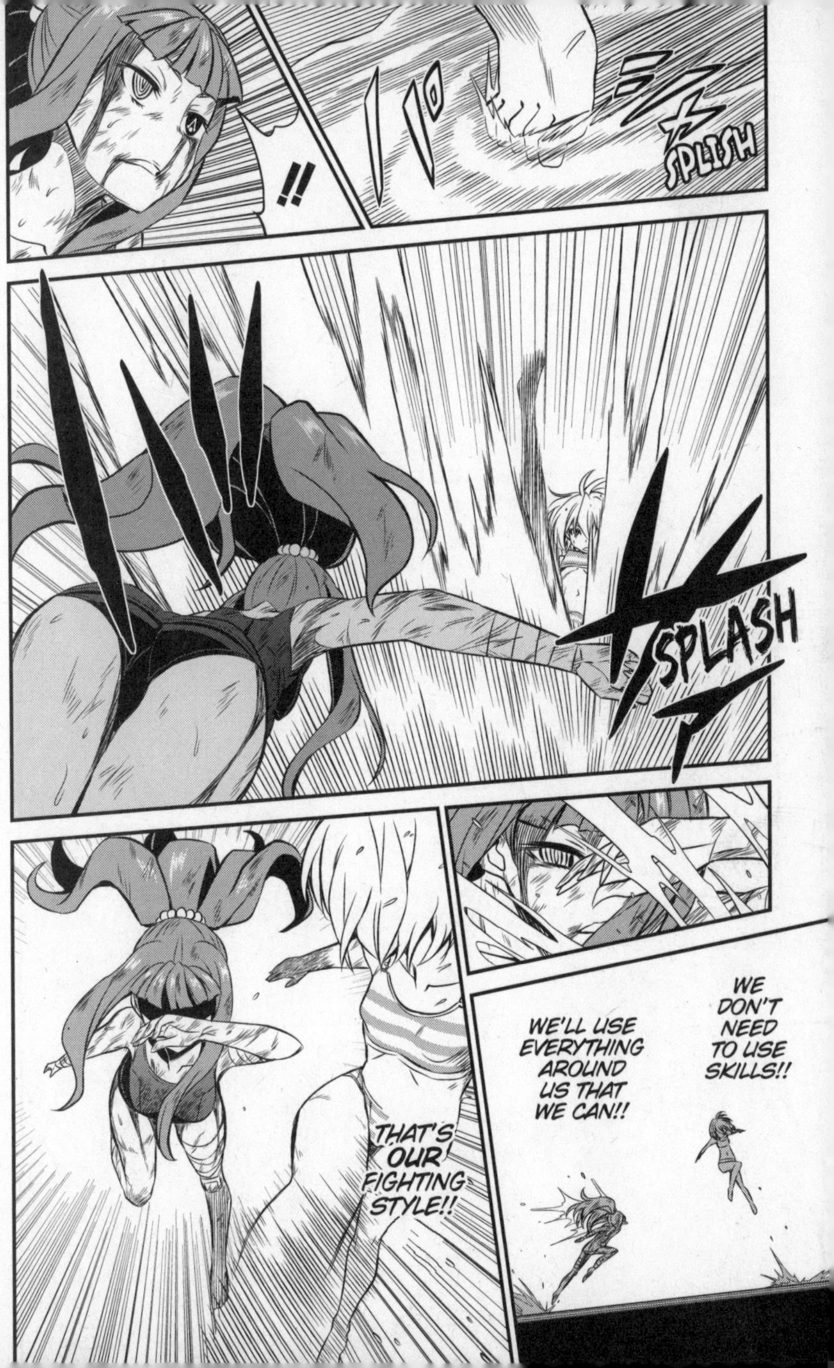
SPLISH
!!
SPLASH
WE DON'T NEED TO USE SKILLS!!
WE'LL USE EVERYTHING AROUND US THAT WE CAN!!
THAT'S OUR FIGHTING STYLE!!

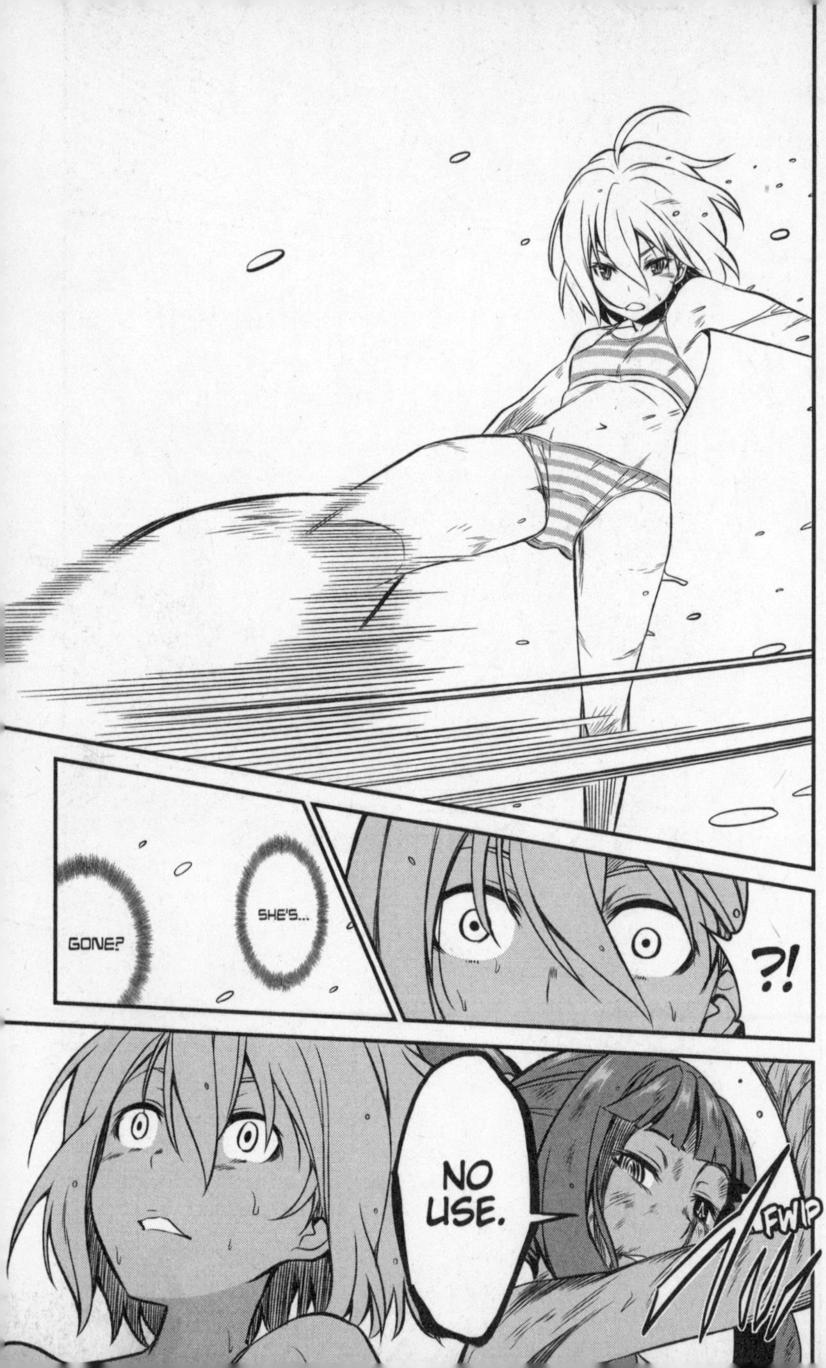
?!
SHE'S...
GONE?
NO USE.
FWIP

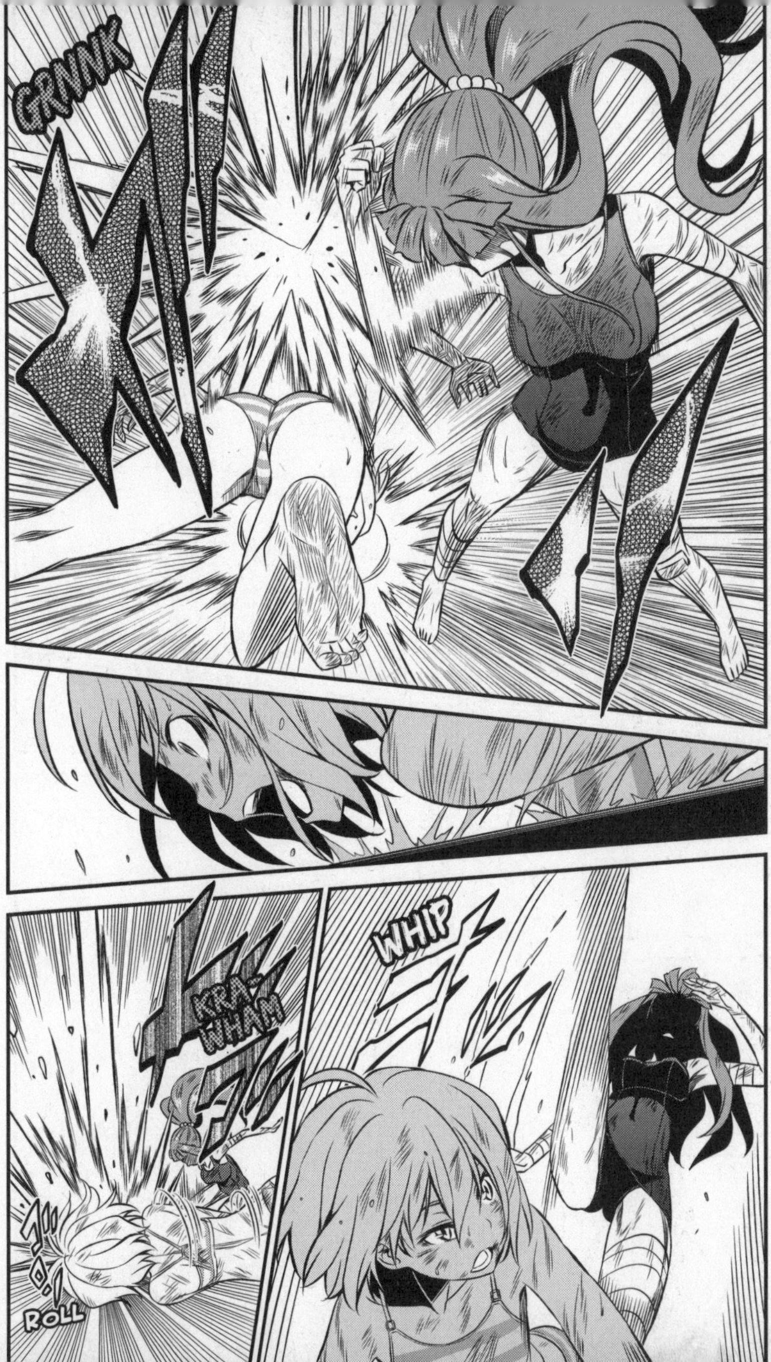
GRNNK
WHIP
KRA-WHAM
ROLL

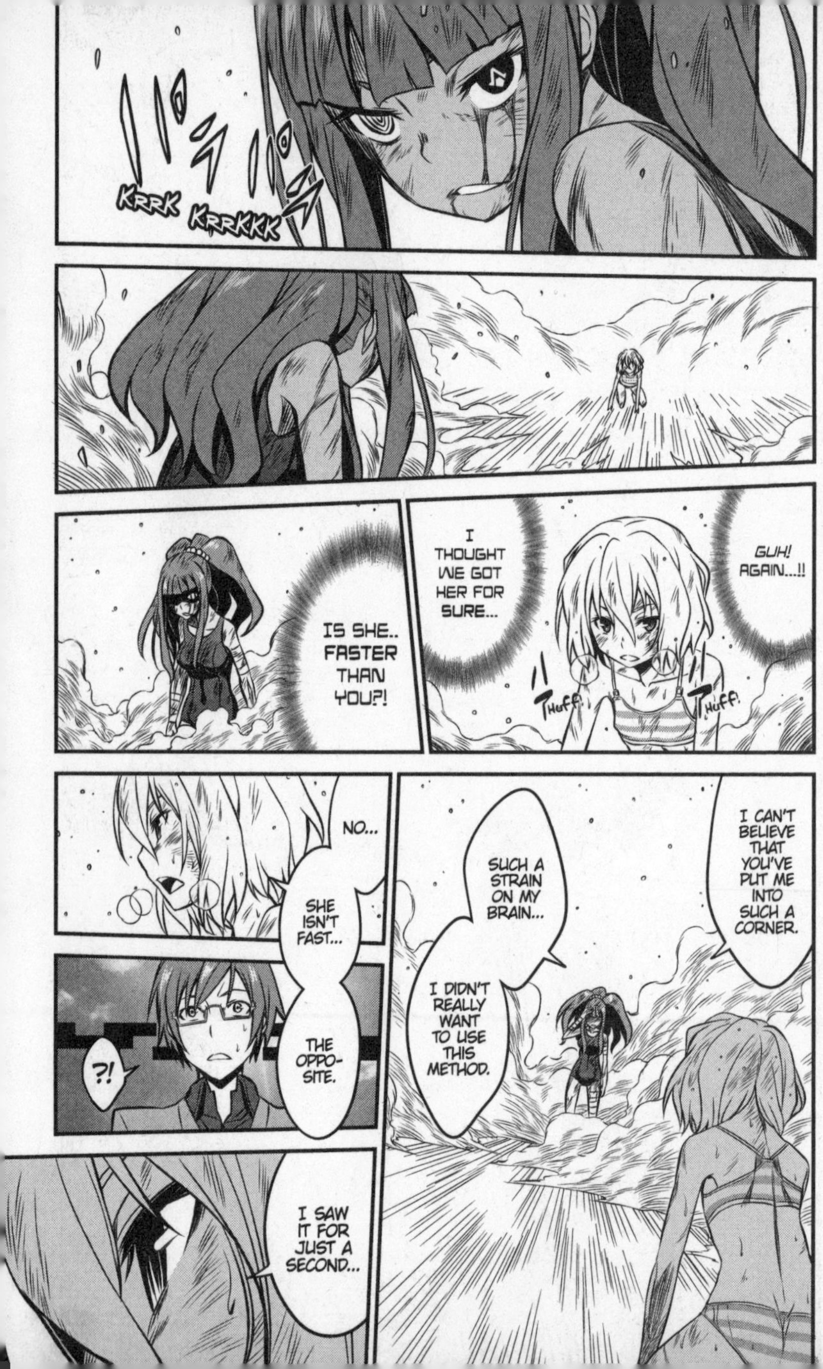
KRRK KRRKKK
GUH! AGAIN...!!
I THOUGHT WE GOT HER FOR SURE...
HUFF
HUFF
IS SHE.. FASTER THAN YOU?!
I CAN'T BELIEVE THAT YOU'VE PUT ME INTO SUCH A CORNER.
SUCH A STRAIN ON MY BRAIN...
I DIDN'T REALLY WANT TO USE THIS METHOD.
NO...
SHE ISN'T FAST...
THE OPPO-SITE.
?!
I SAW IT FOR JUST A SECOND...

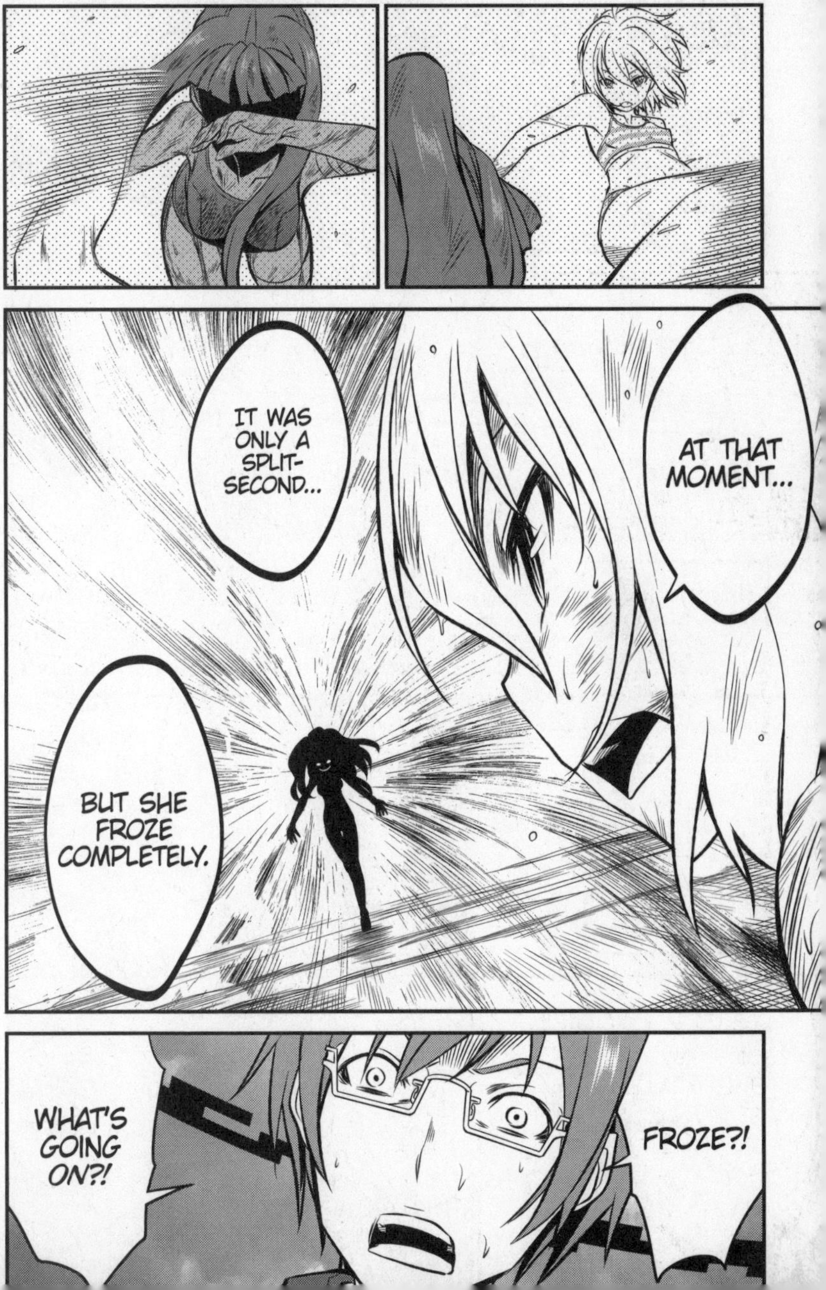
AT THAT MOMENT...
IT WAS ONLY A SPLIT-SECOND...
BUT SHE FROZE COMPLETELY.
FROZE?!
WHAT'S GOING ON?!

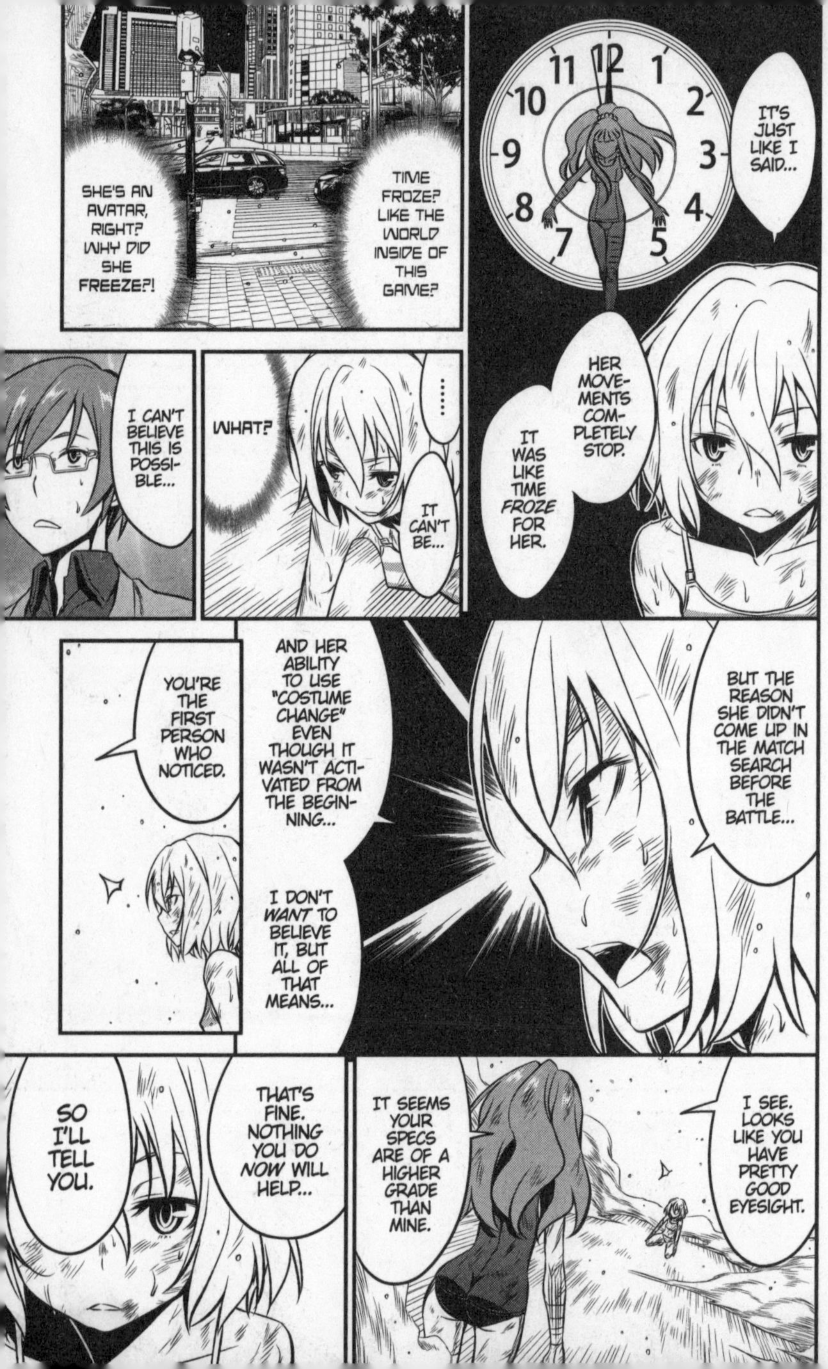
IT'S JUST LIKE I SAID...
HER MOVEMENTS COMPLETELY STOP.
IT WAS LIKE TIME *FROZE* FOR HER.
TIME FROZE? LIKE THE WORLD INSIDE OF THIS GAME?
SHE'S AN AVATAR, RIGHT? WHY DID SHE FREEZE?!
......
WHAT?
IT CAN'T BE...
I CAN'T BELIEVE THIS IS POSSIBLE...
BUT THE REASON SHE DIDN'T COME UP IN THE MATCH SEARCH BEFORE THE BATTLE...
AND HER ABILITY TO USE "COSTUME CHANGE" EVEN THOUGH IT WASN'T ACTIVATED FROM THE BEGINNING...
I DON'T *WANT* TO BELIEVE IT, BUT ALL OF THAT MEANS...
YOU'RE THE FIRST PERSON WHO NOTICED.
I SEE. LOOKS LIKE YOU HAVE PRETTY GOOD EYESIGHT.
IT SEEMS YOUR SPECS ARE OF A HIGHER GRADE THAN MINE.
THAT'S FINE. NOTHING YOU DO *NOW* WILL HELP...
SO I'LL TELL YOU.

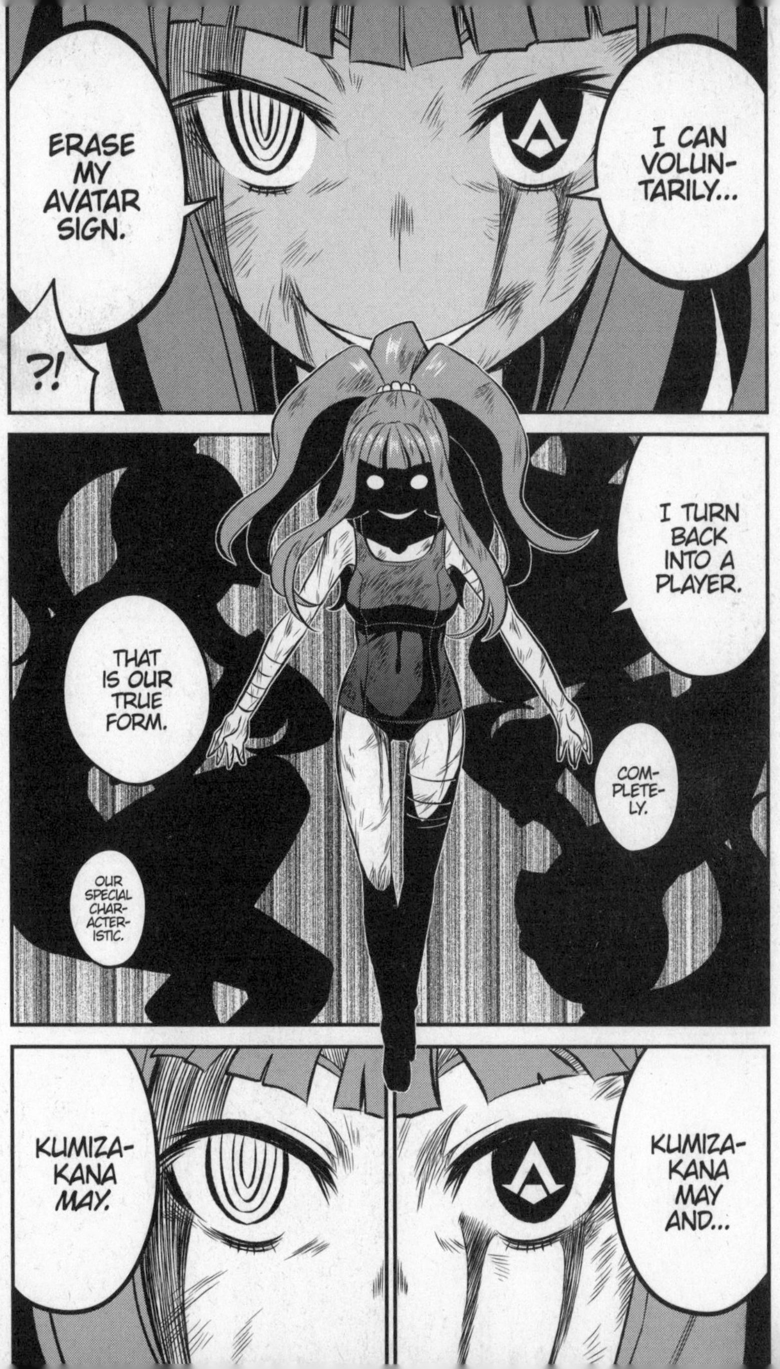

I CAN VOLUN-TARILY...
ERASE MY AVATAR SIGN.
?!
I TURN BACK INTO A PLAYER.
COM-PLETE-LY.
THAT IS OUR TRUE FORM.
OUR SPECIAL CHAR-ACTER-ISTIC.
KUMIZA-KANA MAY AND...
KUMIZA-KANA MAY.

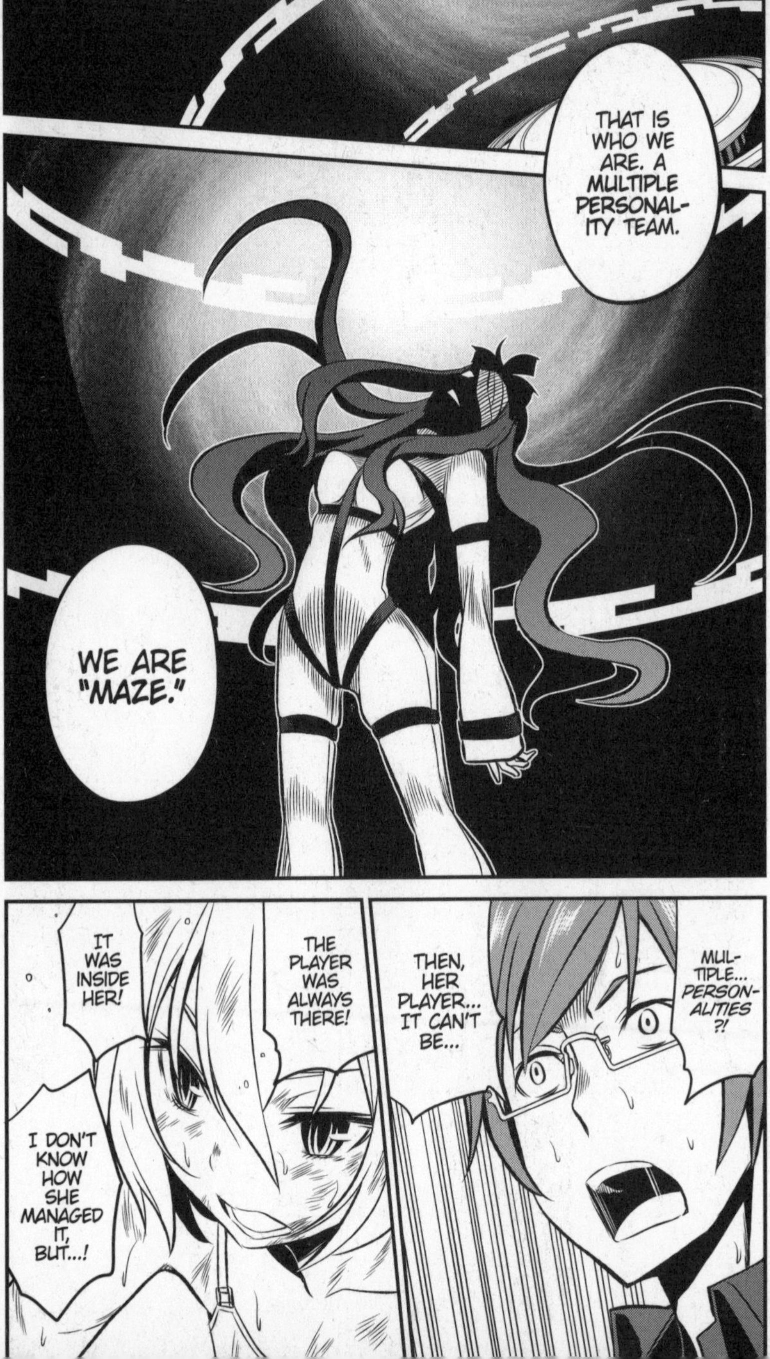
THAT IS WHO WE ARE. A MULTIPLE PERSONALITY TEAM.
WE ARE "MAZE."
MULTIPLE... PERSONALITIES?!
THEN, HER PLAYER... IT CAN'T BE...
THE PLAYER WAS ALWAYS THERE!
IT WAS INSIDE HER!
I DON'T KNOW HOW SHE MANAGED IT, BUT...!

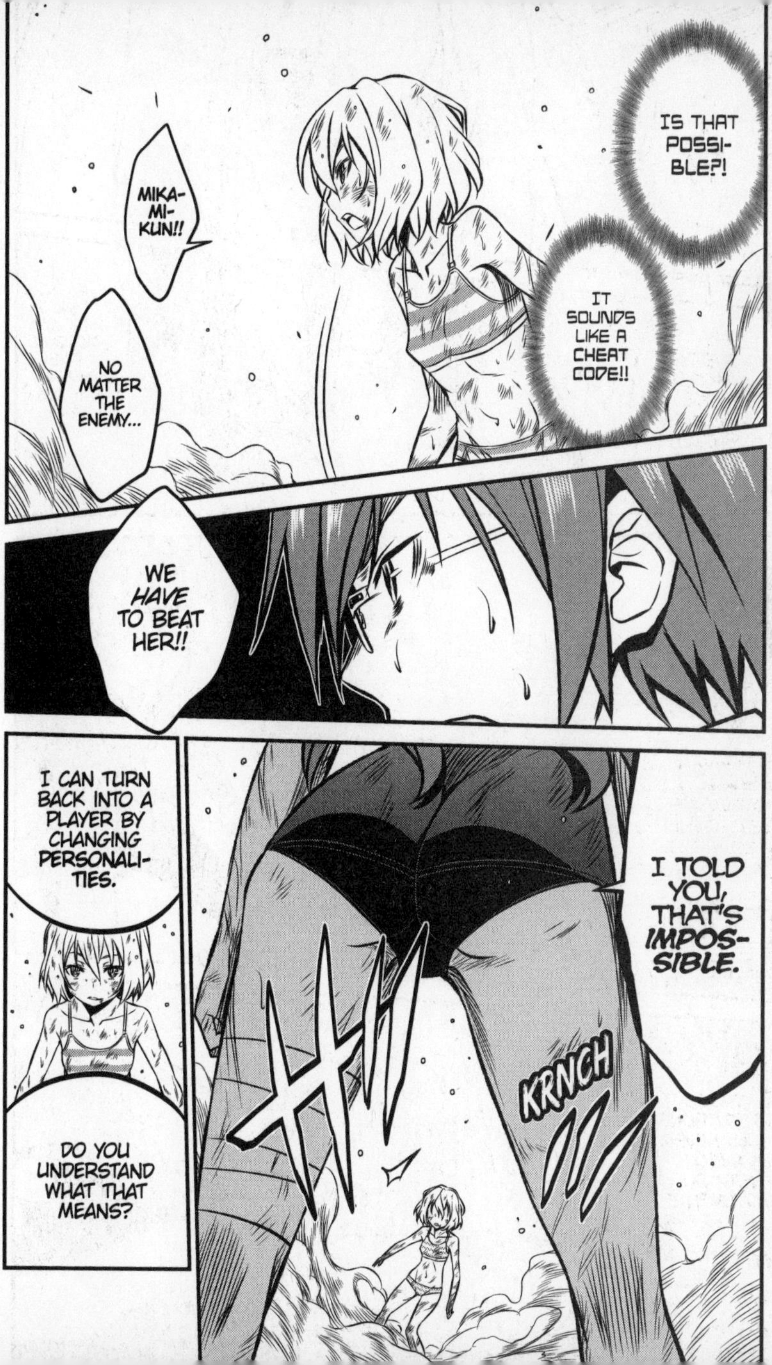
IS THAT POSSI- BLE?!
IT SOUNDS LIKE A CHEAT CODE!!
MIKA- MI- KUN!!
NO MATTER THE ENEMY...
WE *HAVE* TO BEAT HER!!
I TOLD YOU, THAT'S *IMPOS- SIBLE.*
KRNCH
I CAN TURN BACK INTO A PLAYER BY CHANGING PERSONALI- TIES.
DO YOU UNDERSTAND WHAT THAT MEANS?

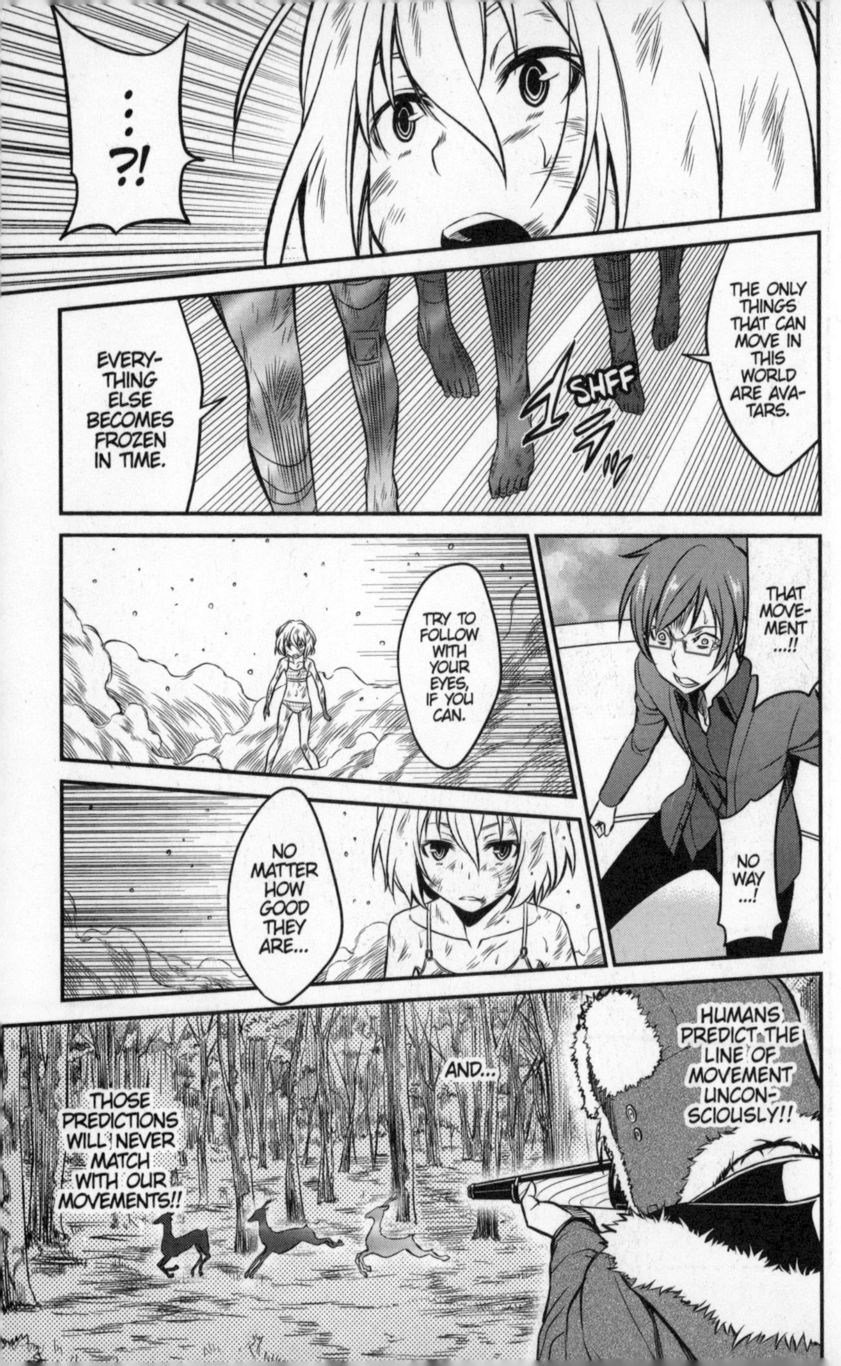
...?!
THE ONLY THINGS THAT CAN MOVE IN THIS WORLD ARE AVATARS.
SHFF
EVERYTHING ELSE BECOMES FROZEN IN TIME.
THAT MOVEMENT...!!
NO WAY...!
TRY TO FOLLOW WITH YOUR EYES, IF YOU CAN.
NO MATTER HOW GOOD THEY ARE...
HUMANS PREDICT THE LINE OF MOVEMENT UNCONSCIOUSLY!!
AND...
THOSE PREDICTIONS WILL NEVER MATCH WITH OUR MOVEMENTS!!

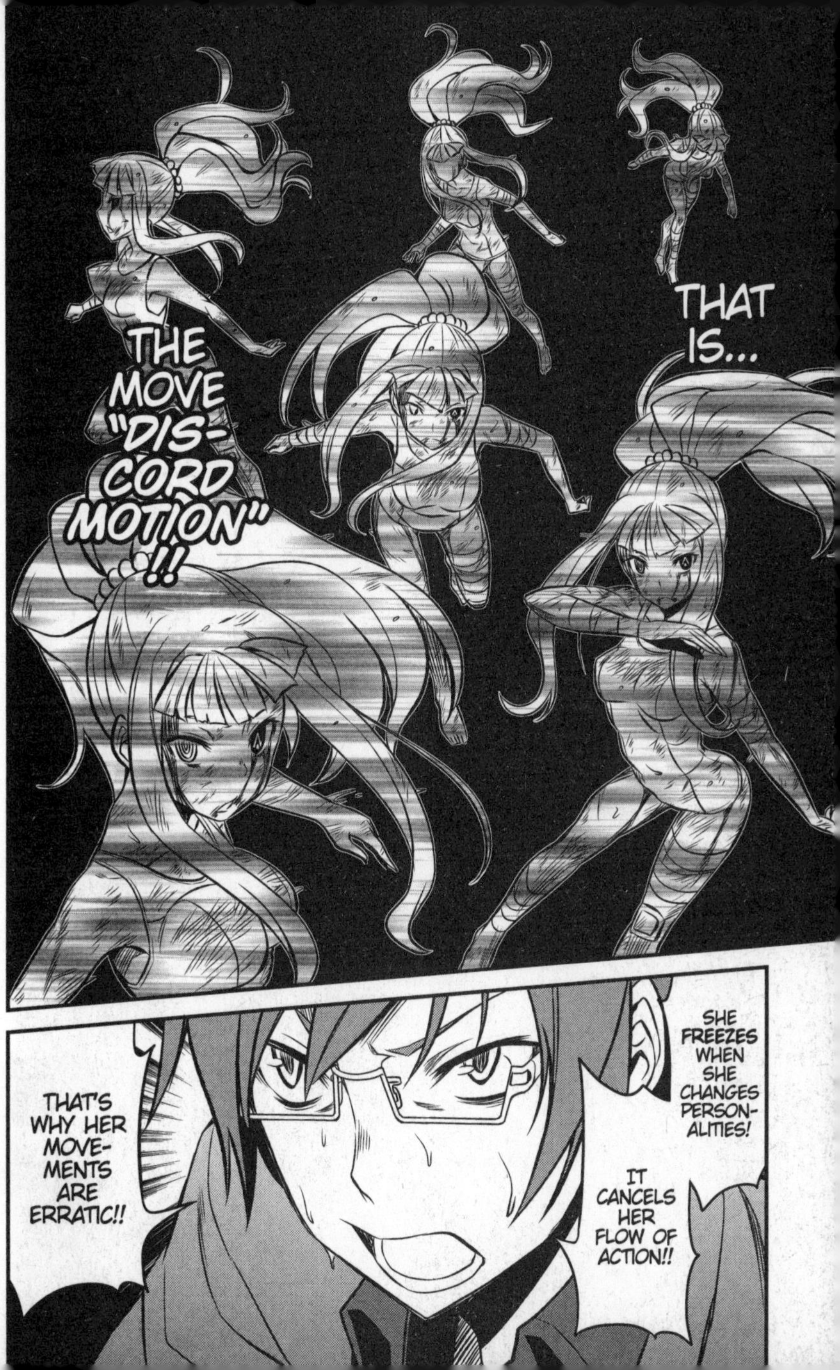
THAT IS...
THE MOVE "DIS-CORD MOTION"!!
SHE FREEZES WHEN SHE CHANGES PERSONALITIES!
IT CANCELS HER FLOW OF ACTION!!
THAT'S WHY HER MOVEMENTS ARE ERRATIC!!

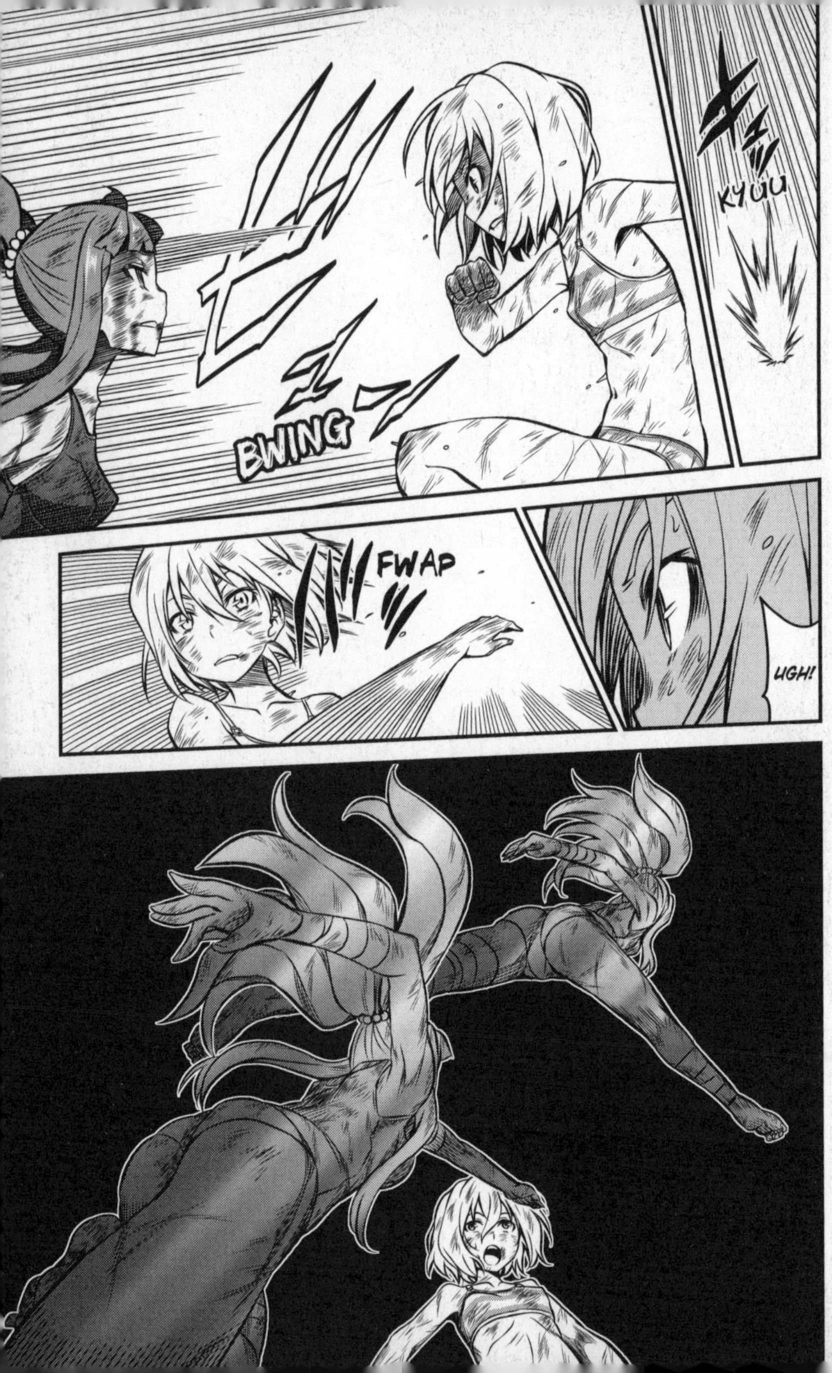
KYUU
BWING
UGH!
FWAP

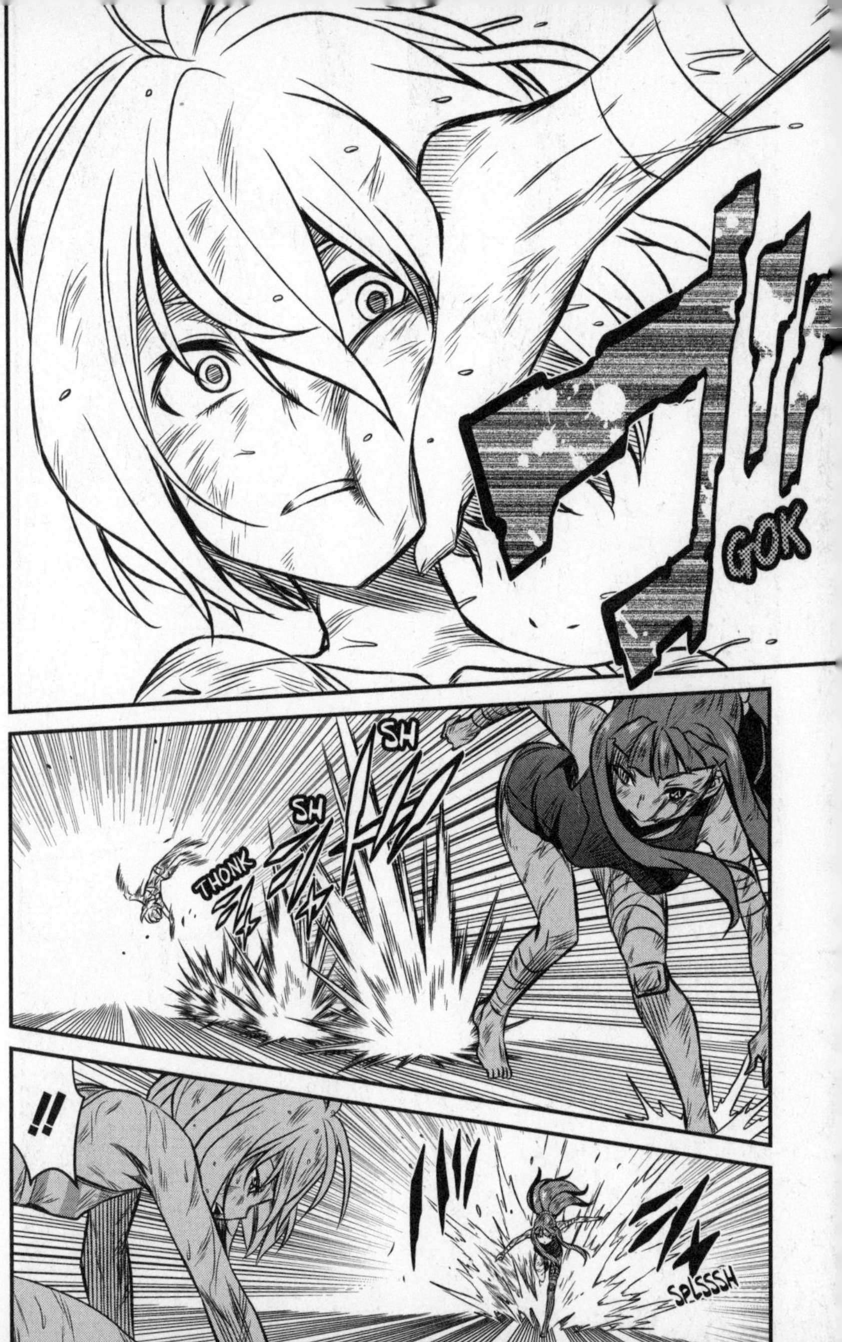
GOK
SH
SH
THONK
!!
SPLSSSH

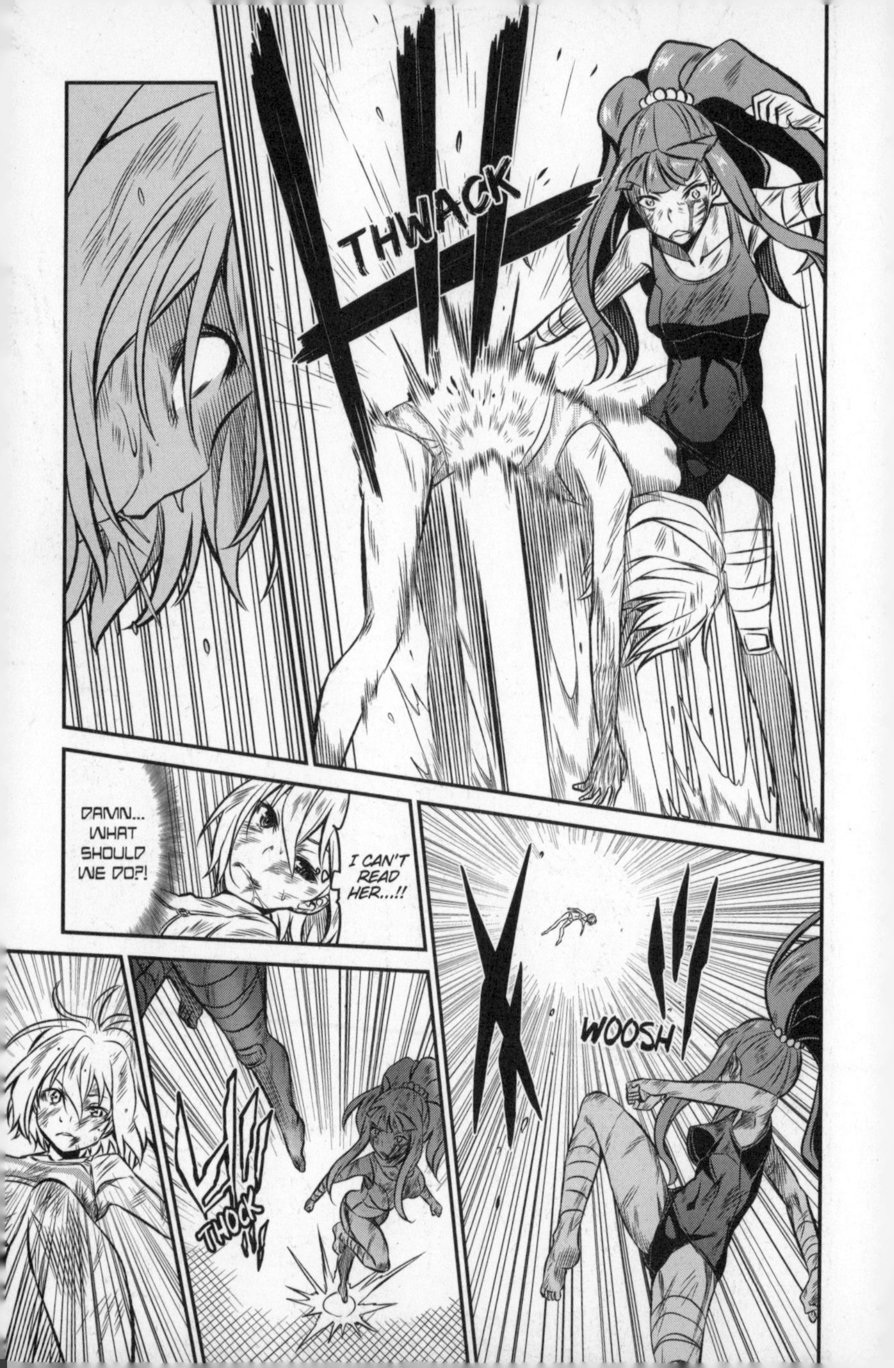
THWACK
WOOSH
I CAN'T READ HER...!!
DAMN... WHAT SHOULD WE DO?!
THOCK

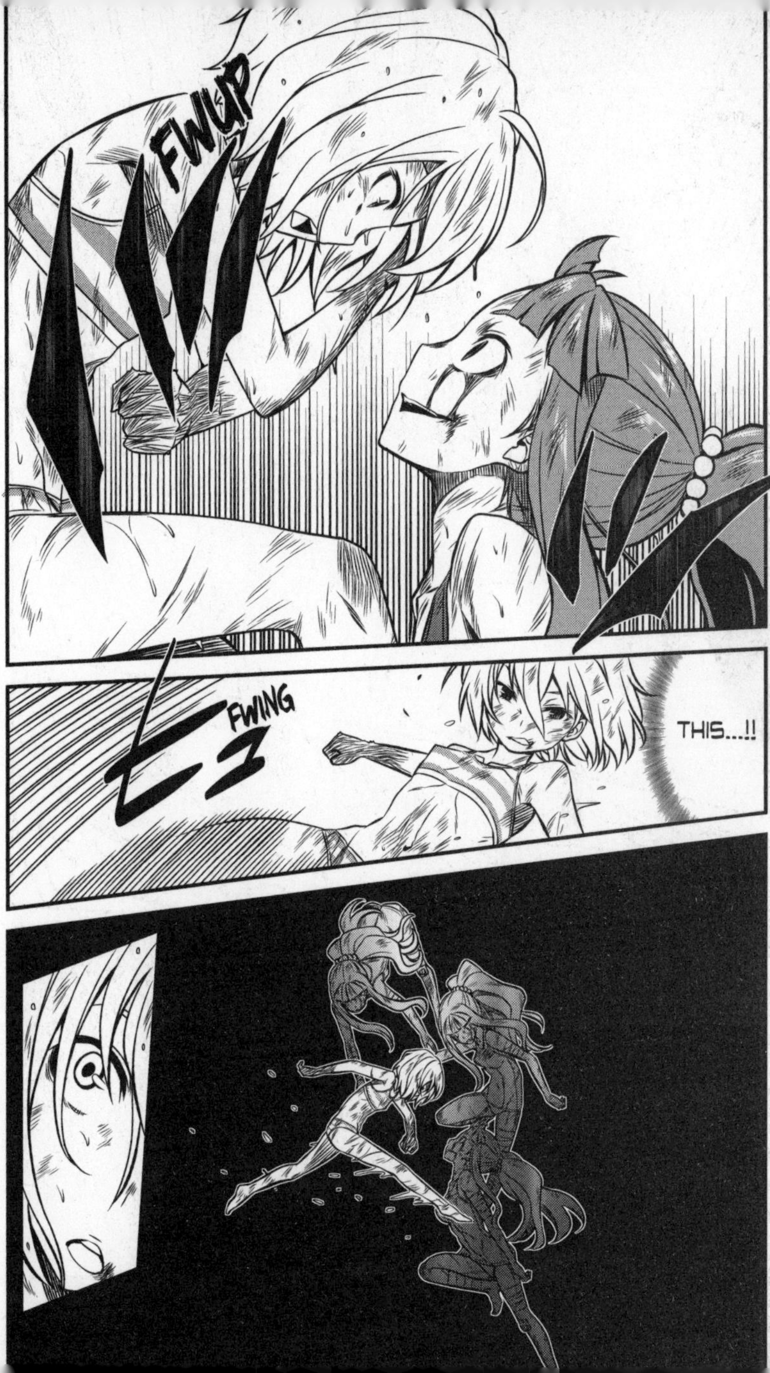
FWUP
THIS...!!
FWING

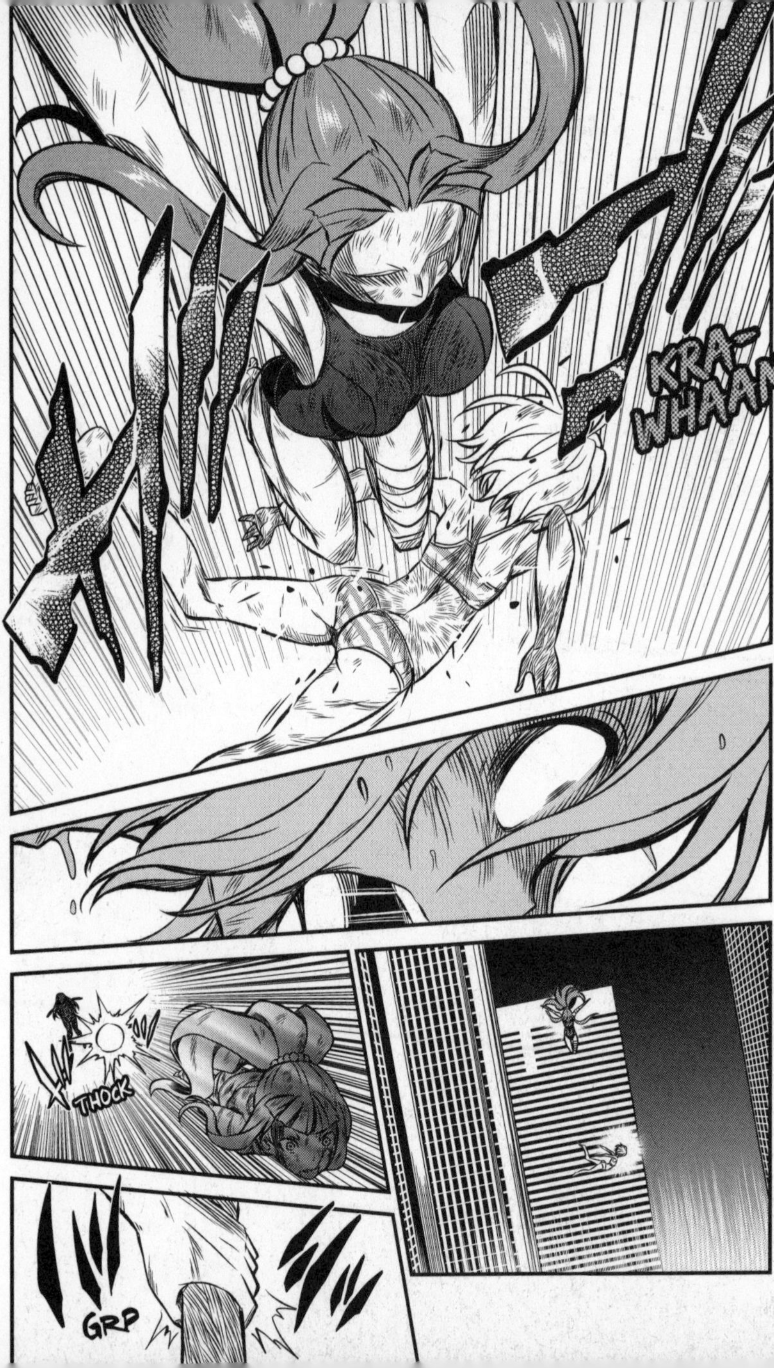
KRA-
WHAAM
THOCK
GRP

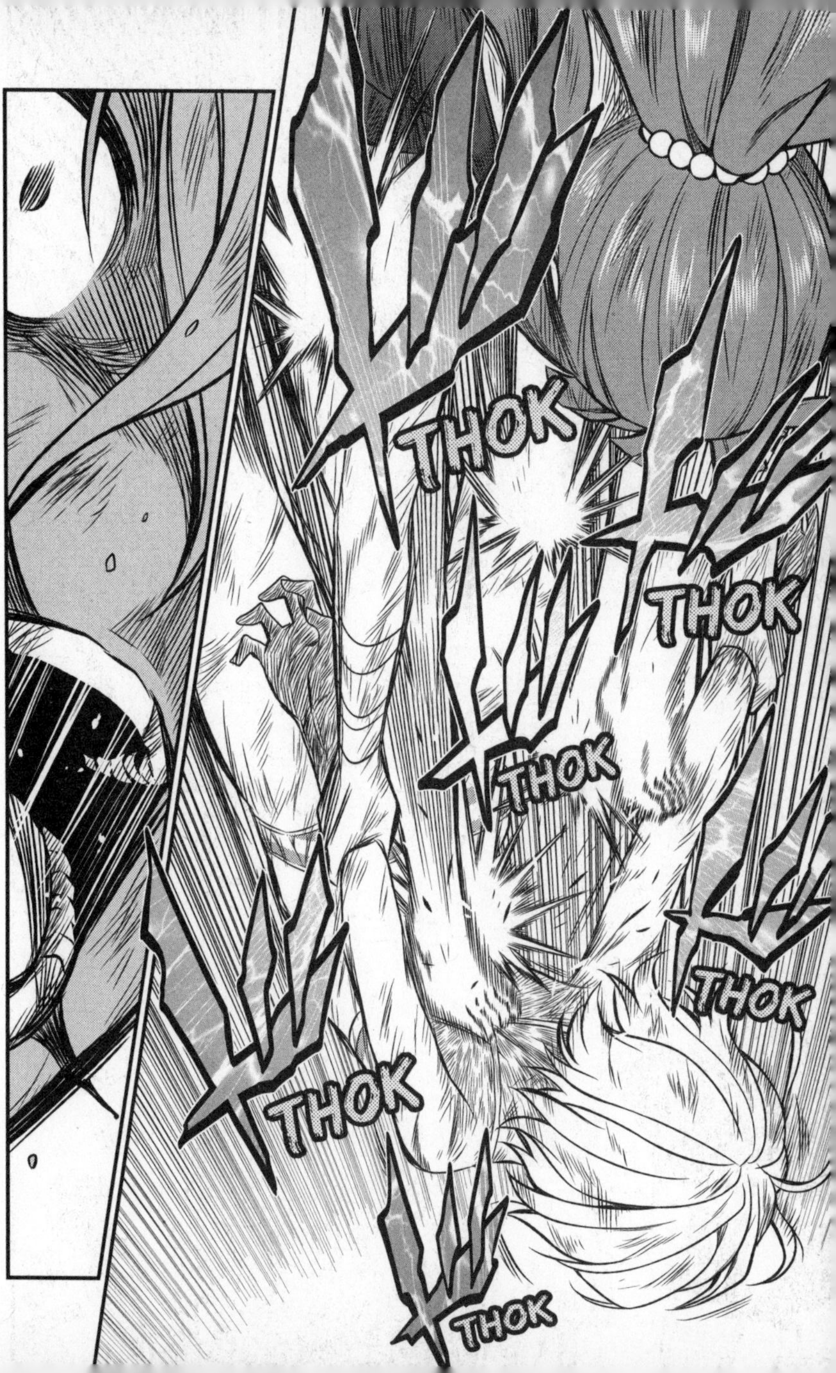
THOK
THOK
THOK
THOK
THOK
THOK

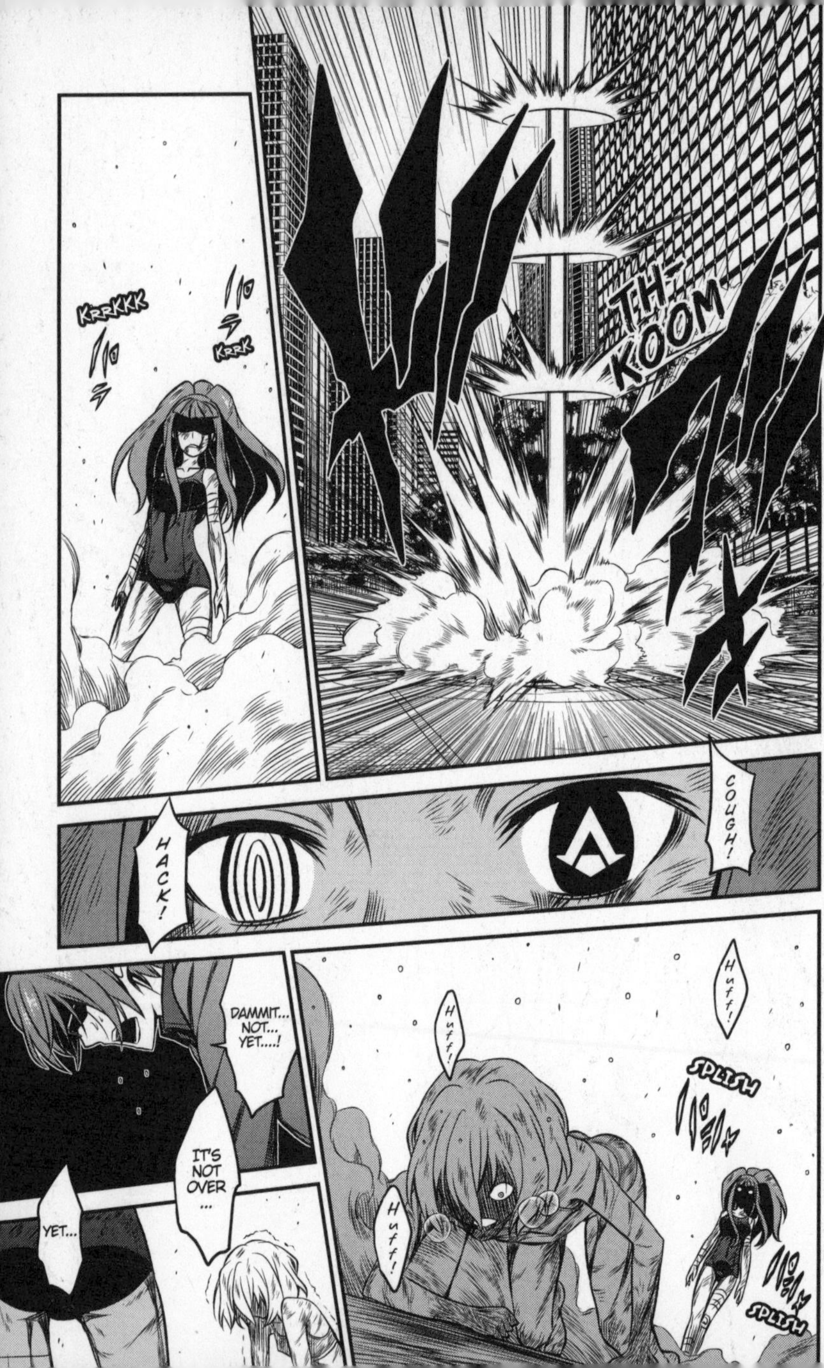
TH-KOOM
KrrKKK
KrrK
COUGH!
HACK!
Huff!
Huff!
SPLISH
Huff!
SPLISH
DAMMIT... NOT... YET....!
IT'S NOT OVER ...
YET...

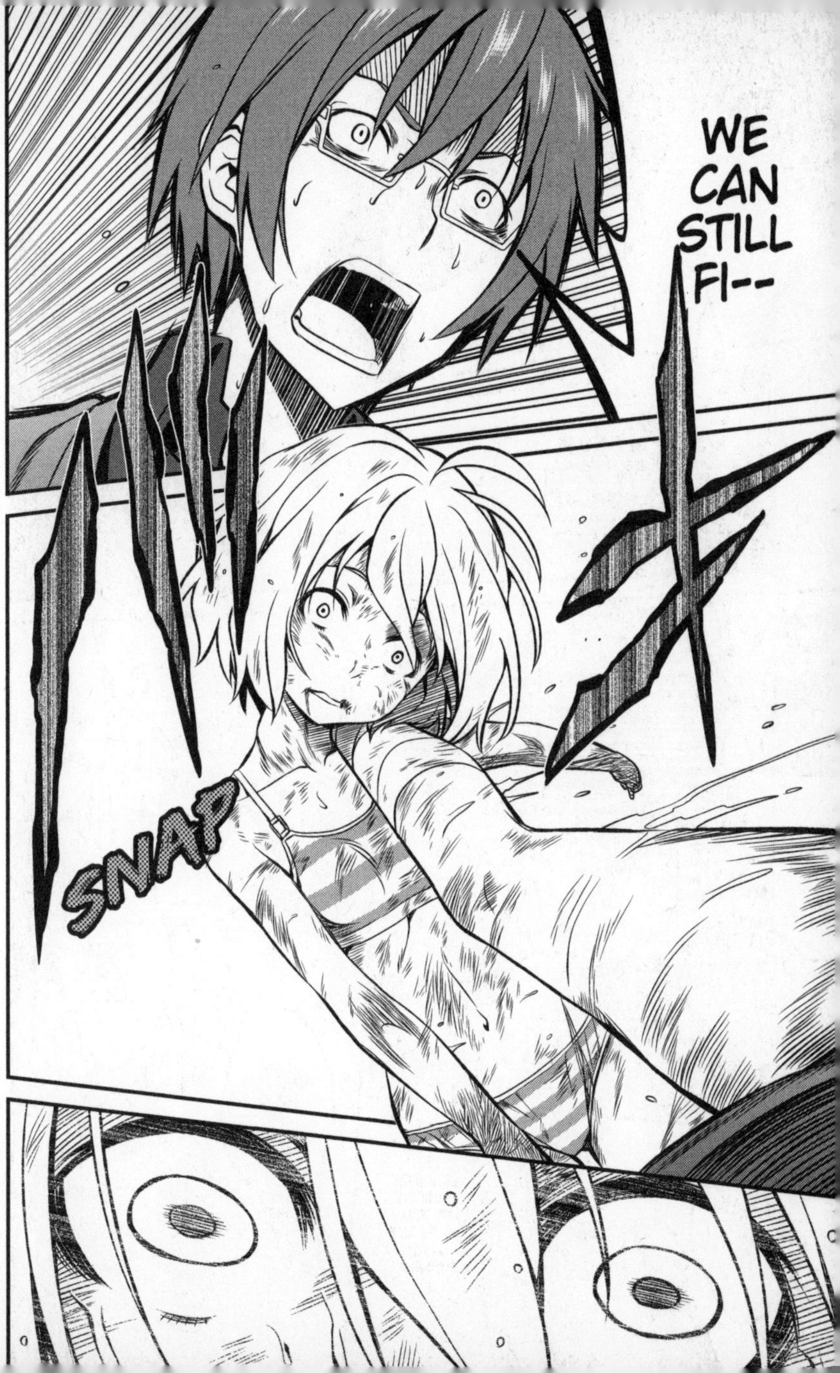
WE CAN STILL FI--
SNAP

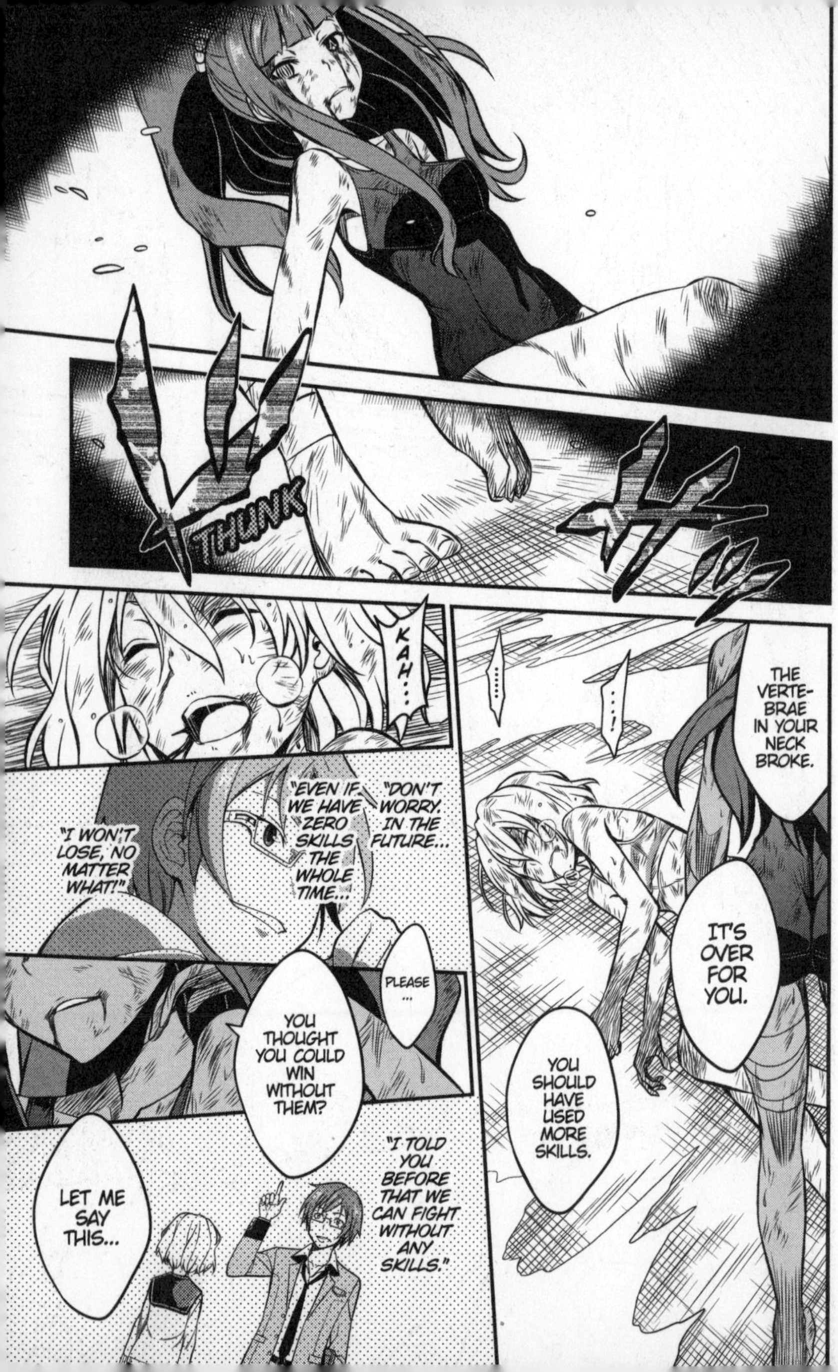
THUNK
......
...!
THE VERTE-BRAE IN YOUR NECK BROKE.
IT'S OVER FOR YOU.
YOU SHOULD HAVE USED MORE SKILLS.
KAH...
"DON'T WORRY. IN THE FUTURE...
"EVEN IF WE HAVE ZERO SKILLS THE WHOLE TIME...
"I WON'T LOSE, NO MATTER WHAT!"
PLEASE...
YOU THOUGHT YOU COULD WIN WITHOUT THEM?
"I TOLD YOU BEFORE THAT WE CAN FIGHT WITHOUT ANY SKILLS."
LET ME SAY THIS...

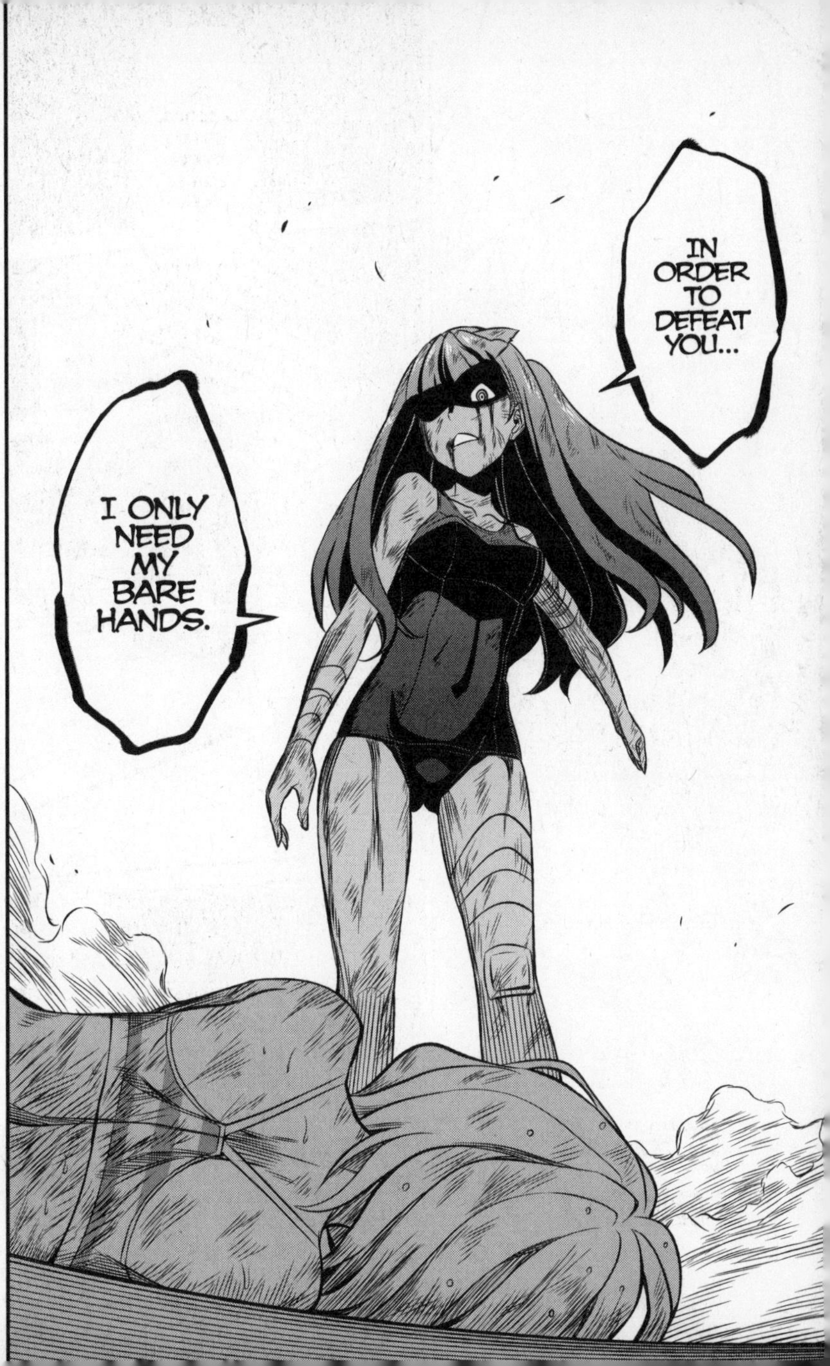
IN ORDER TO DEFEAT YOU...
I ONLY NEED MY BARE HANDS.

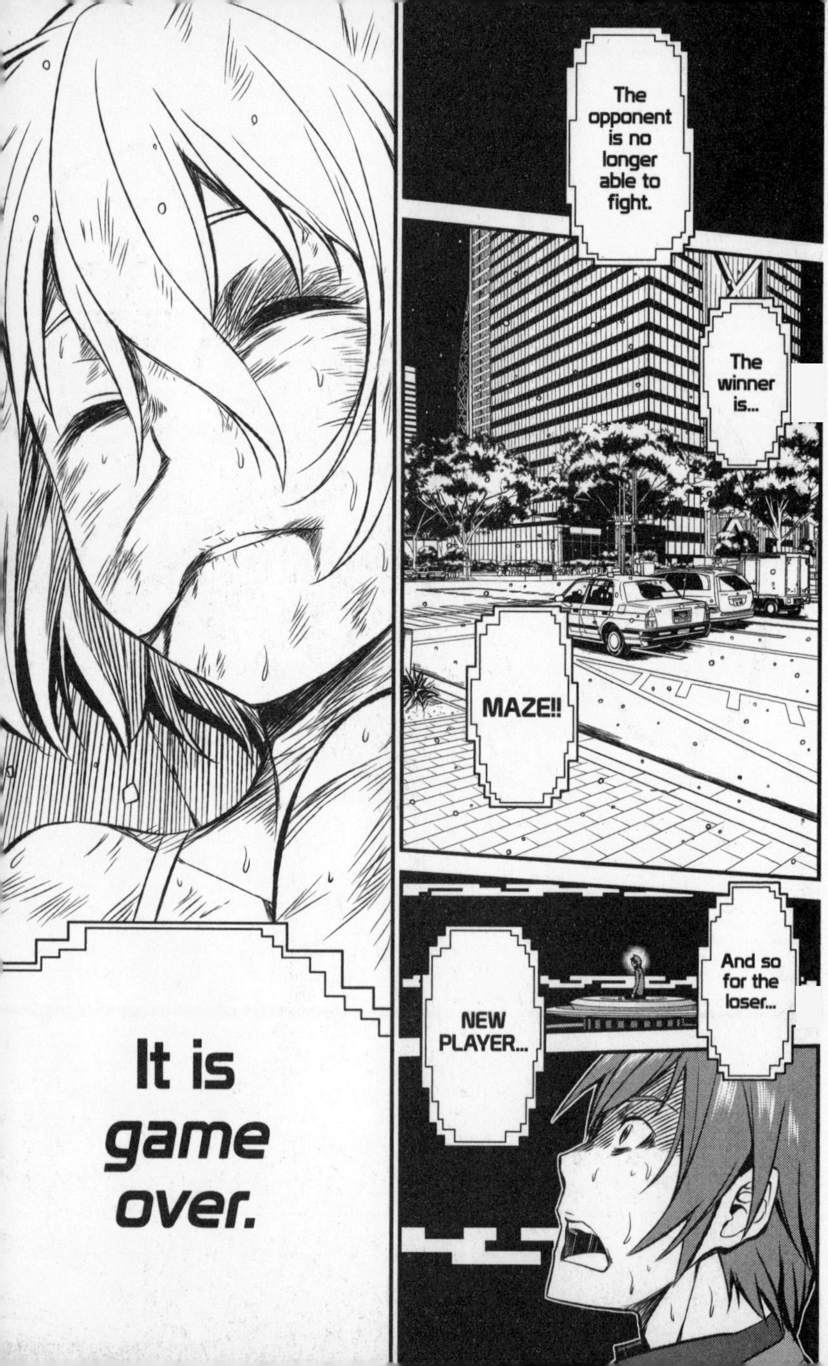
The opponent is no longer able to fight.
The winner is...
MAZE!!
And so for the loser...
NEW PLAYER...
It is game over.

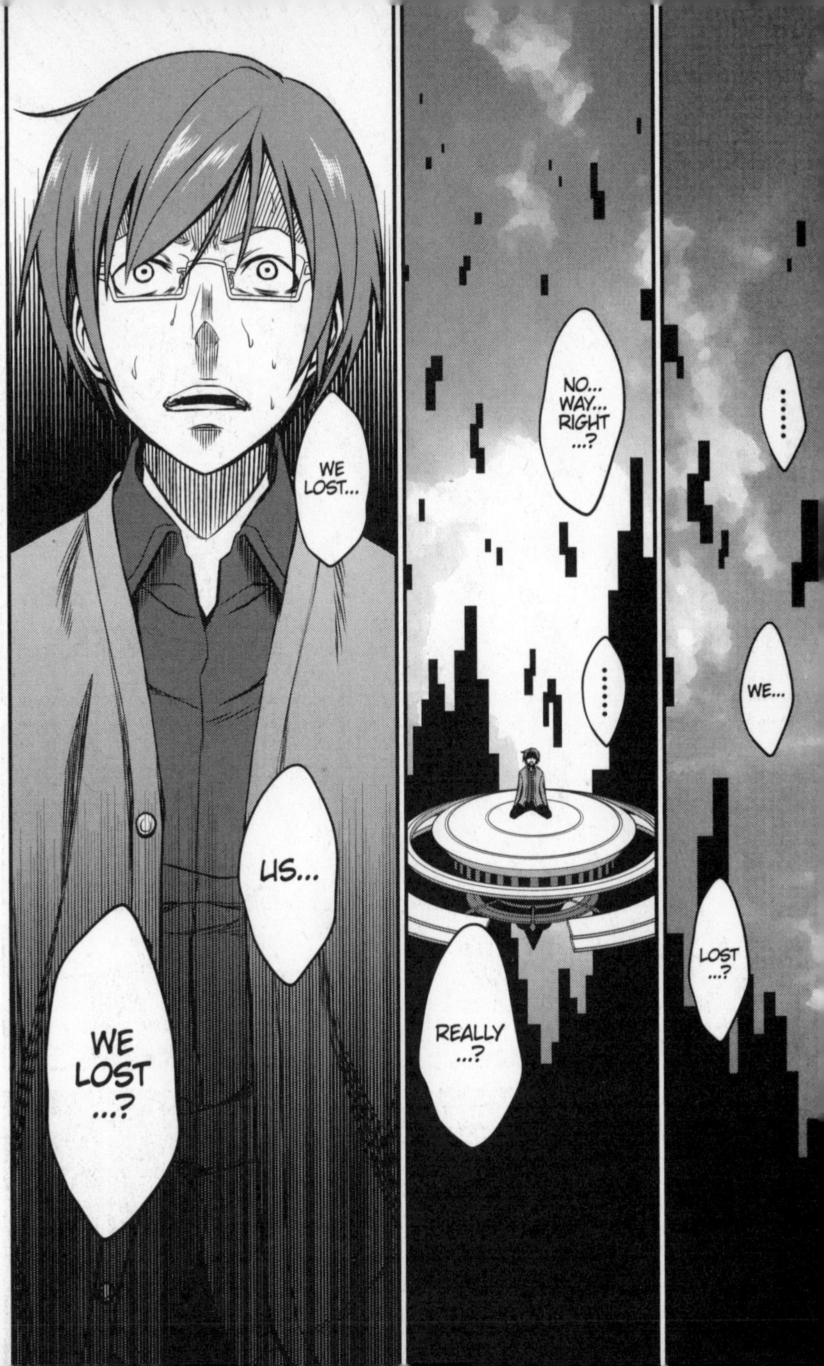
......
WE...
LOST ...?
NO... WAY... RIGHT ...?
......
REALLY ...?
WE LOST...
US...
WE LOST ...?

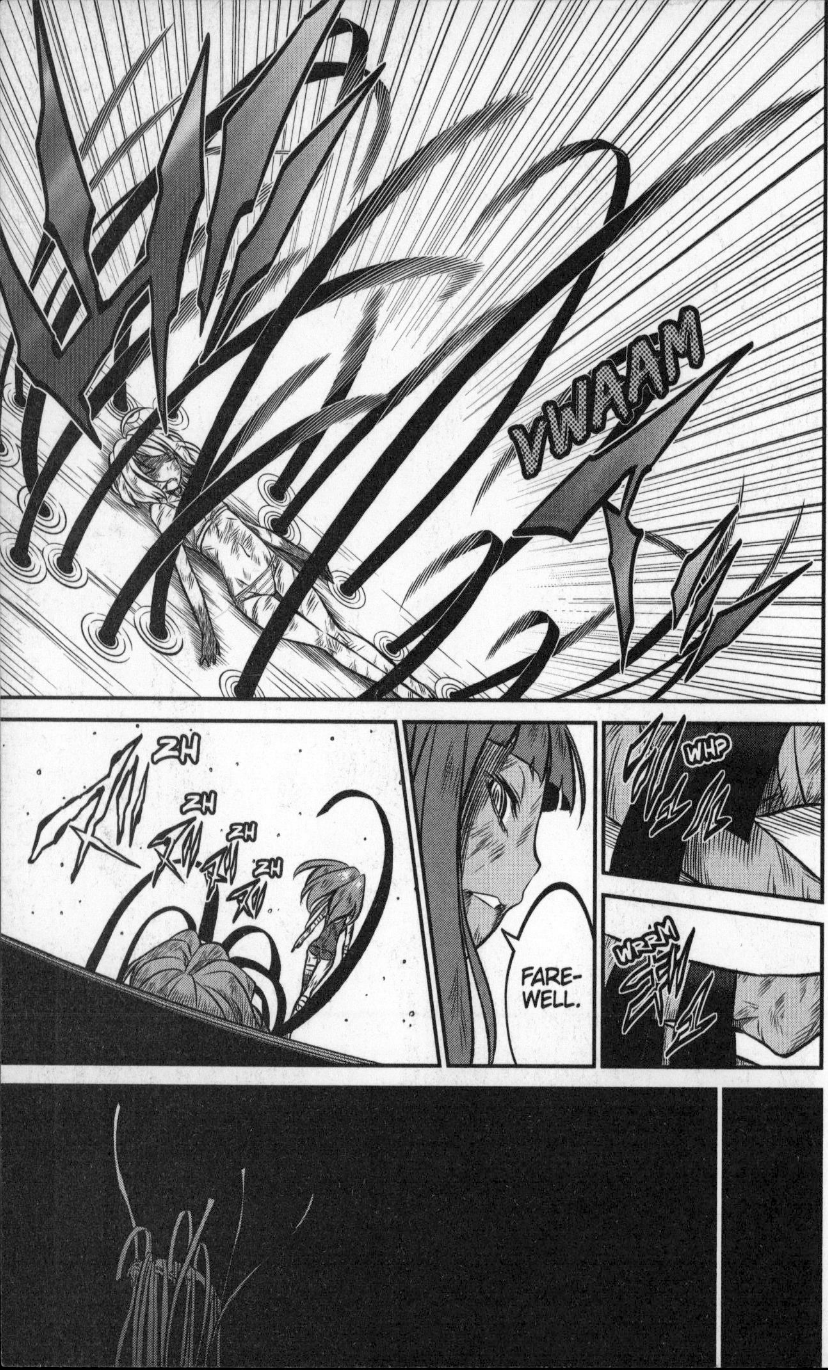
VWAAM
WHP
WRRM
FARE-
WELL.
ZH
ZH
ZH
ZH

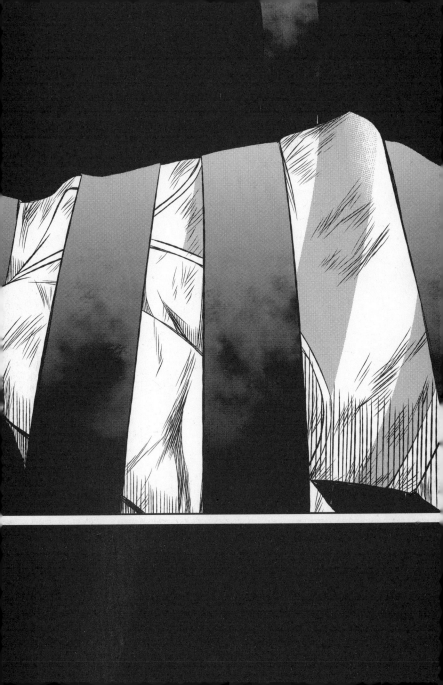

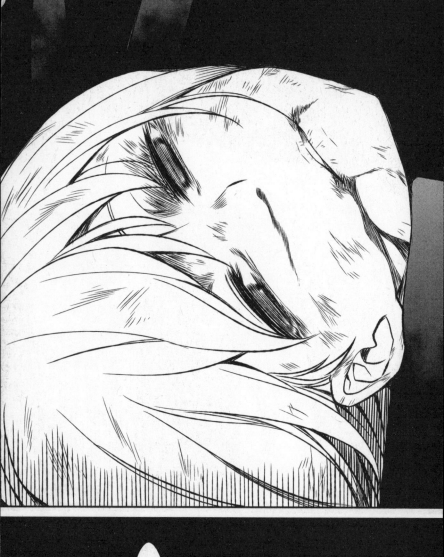

MI-
KA-
MI...

KUN...

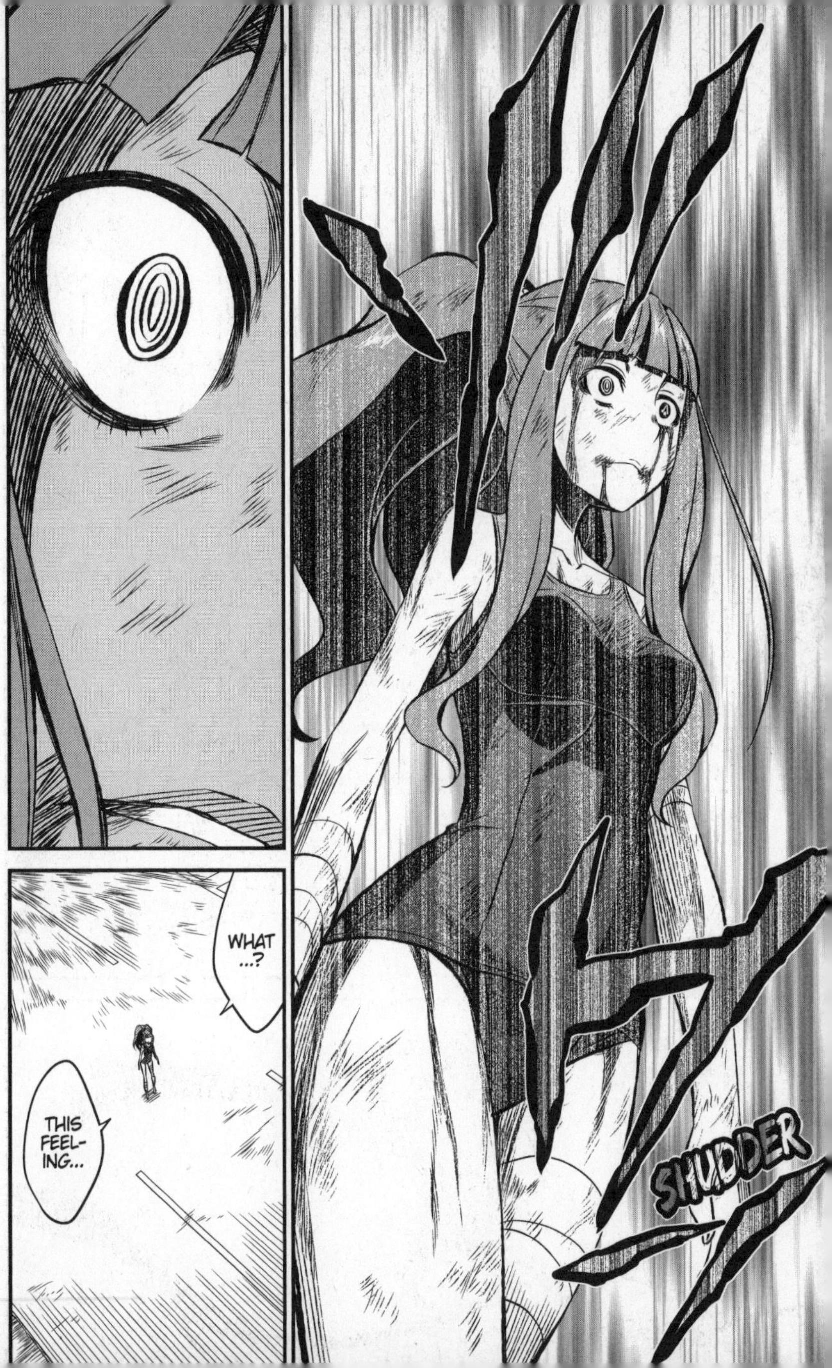
SHUDDER
WHAT ...?
THIS FEEL-ING...

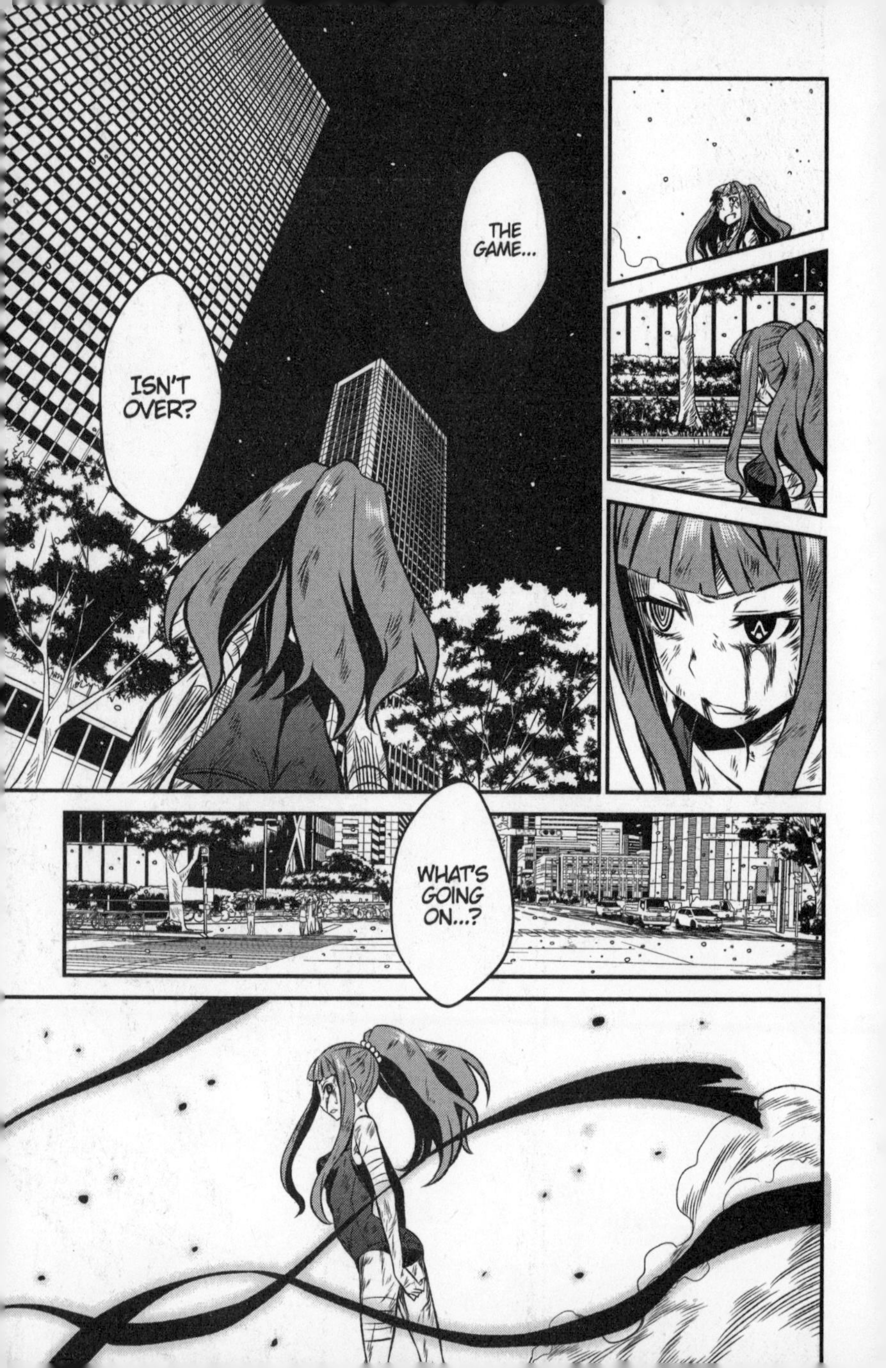
THE GAME...
ISN'T OVER?
WHAT'S GOING ON...?

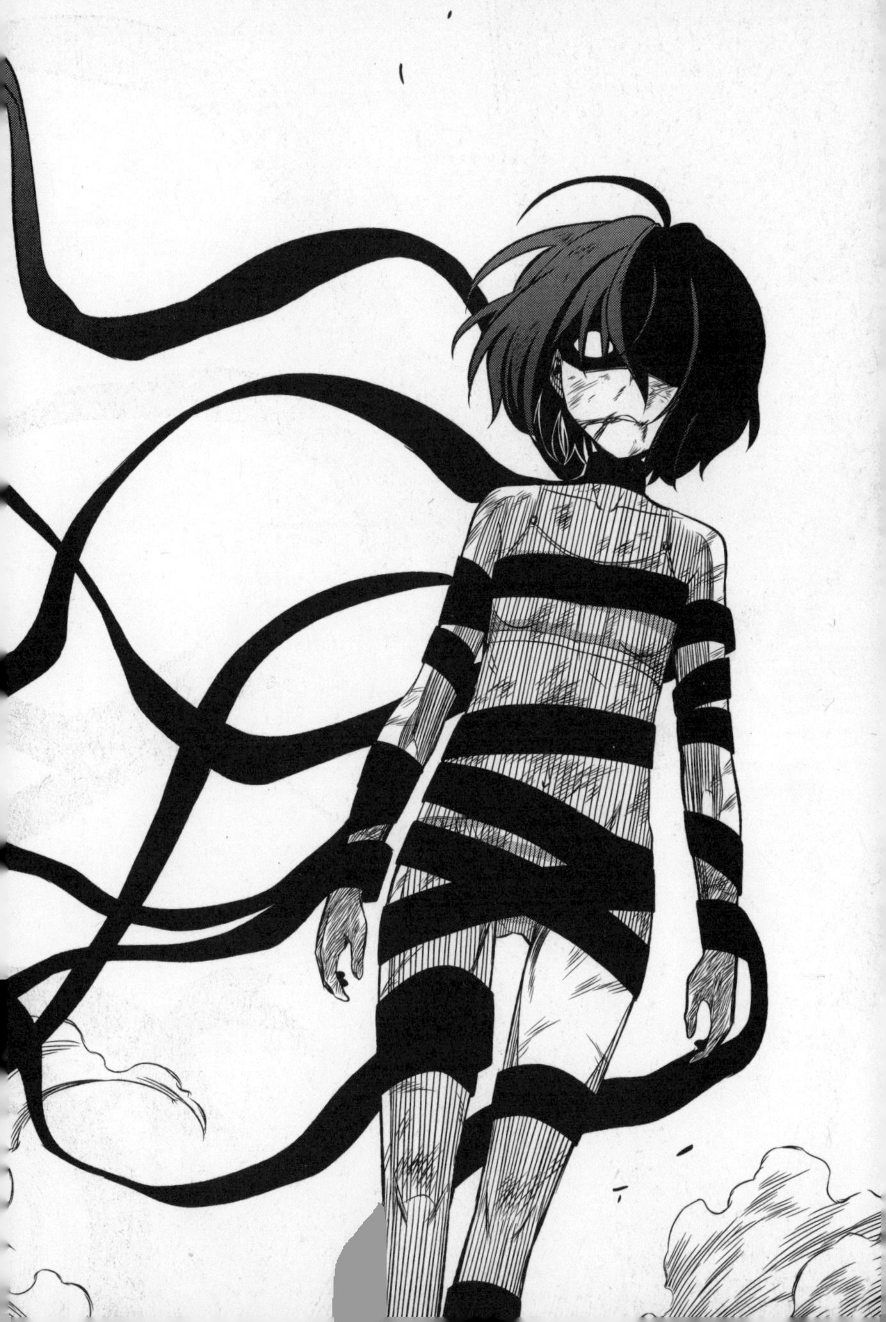

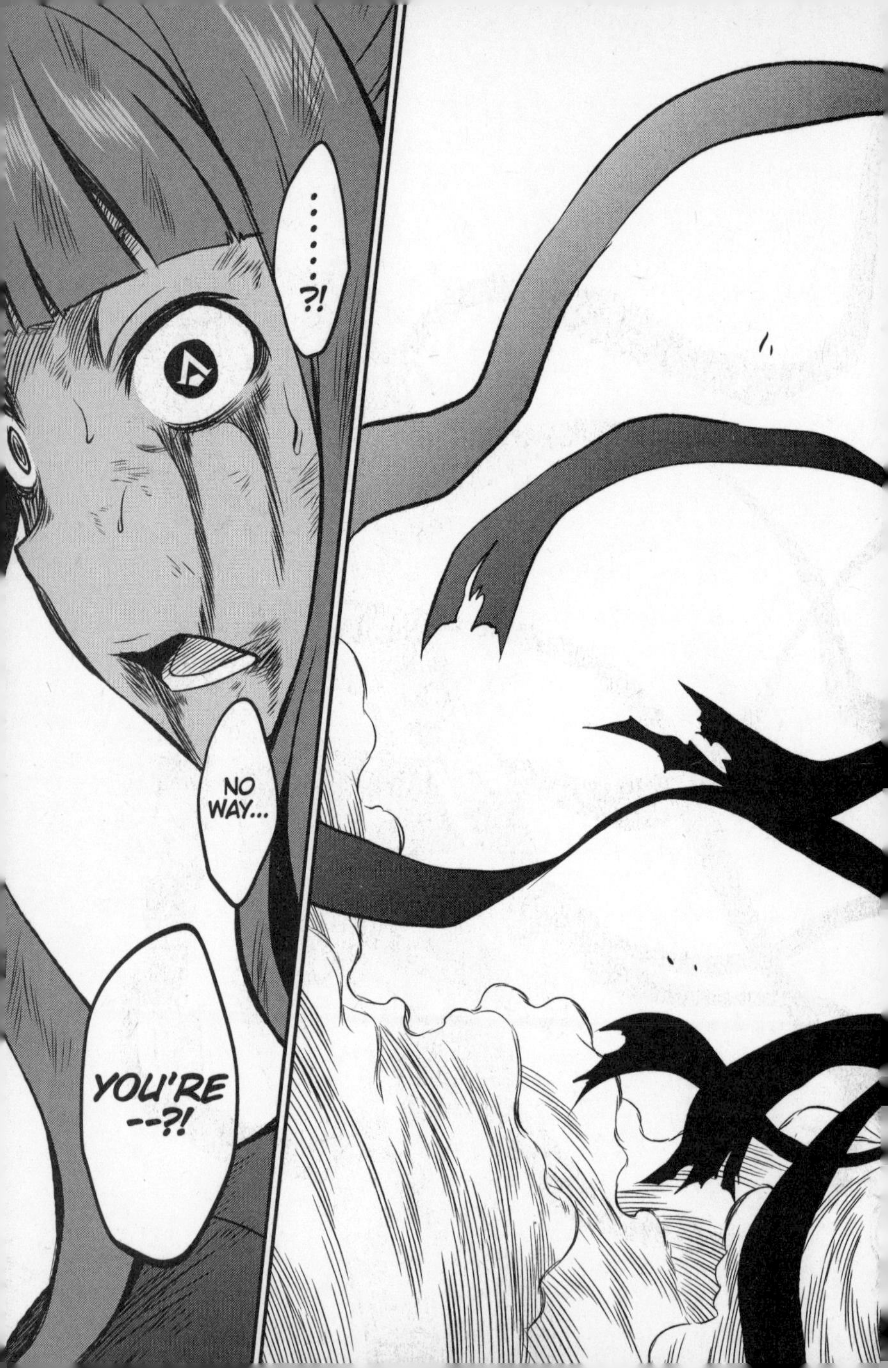
......?!
NO WAY...
YOU'RE --?!

NOT ALIVE

CHAPTER 24

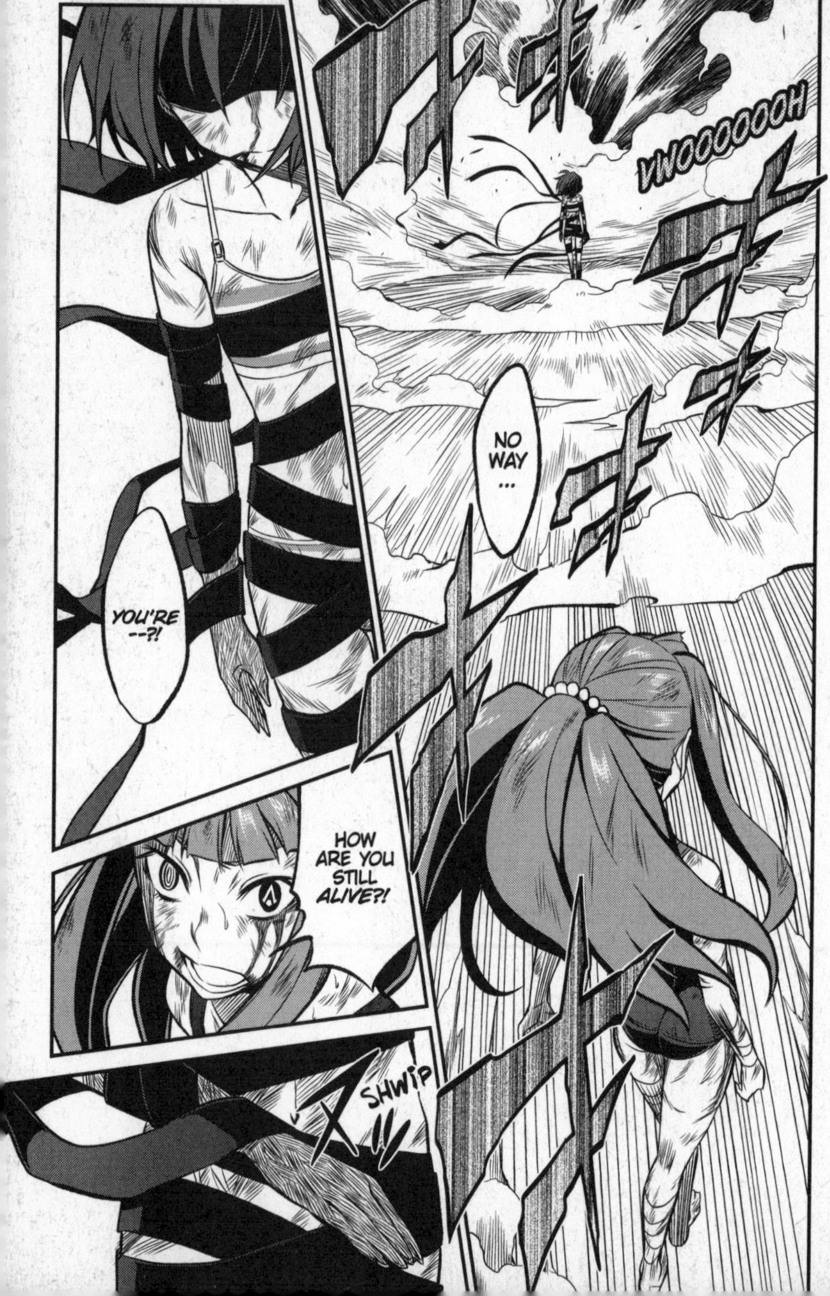
VWOOOOOOH
NO WAY ...
YOU'RE --?!
HOW ARE YOU STILL ALIVE?!
SHWIP

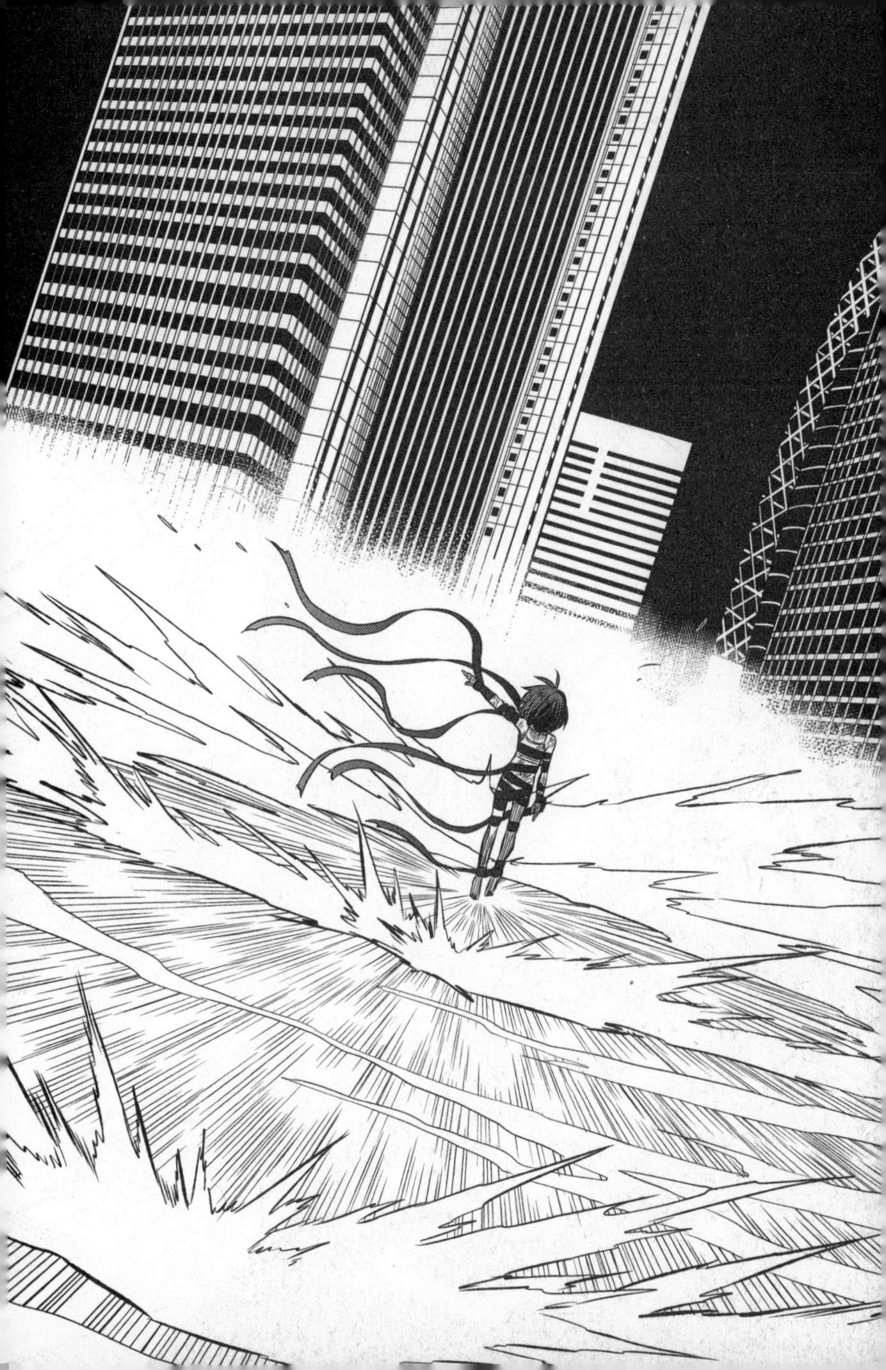

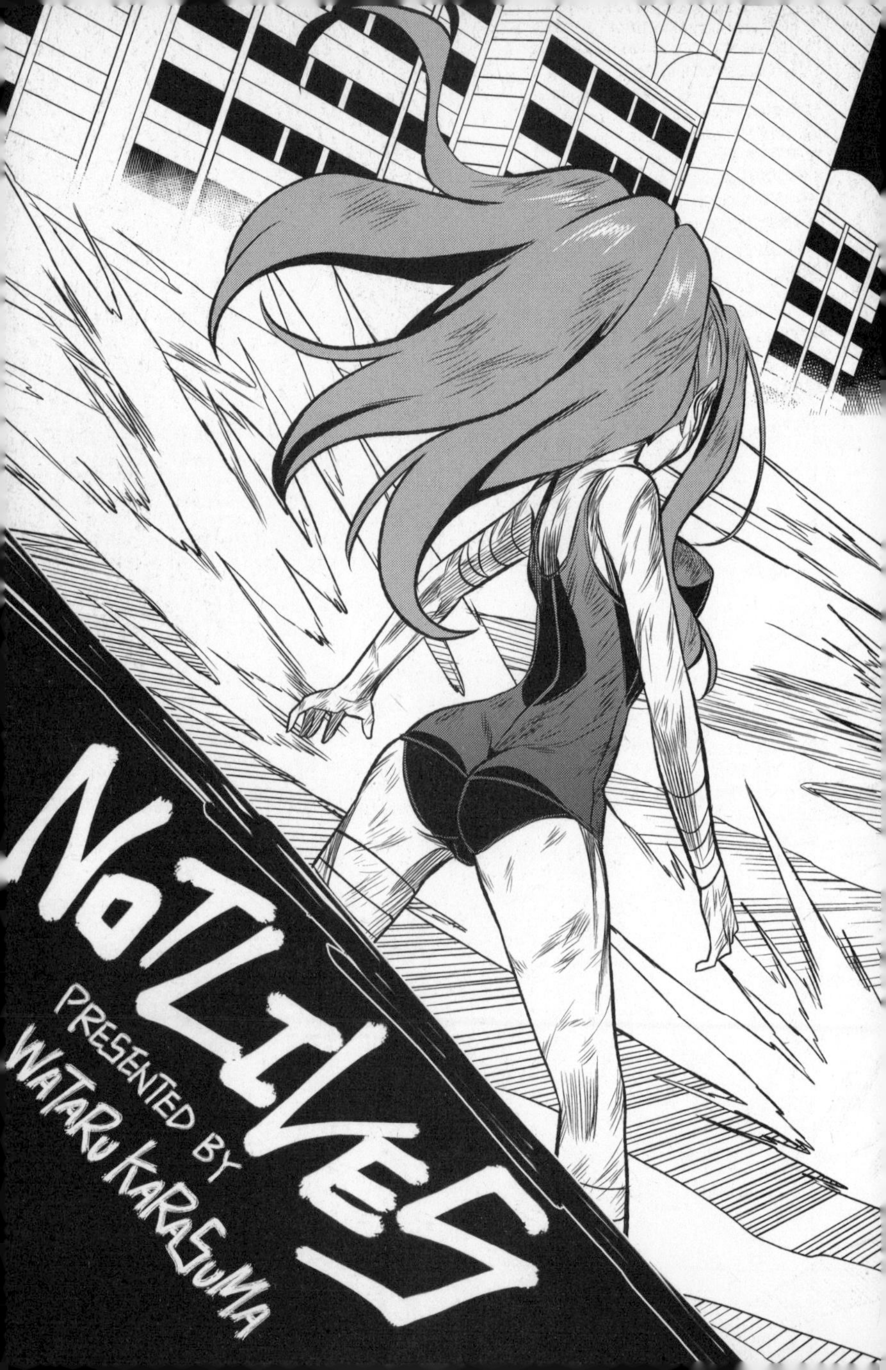
NoLIVES
PRESENTED BY
WATARU KARASUMA

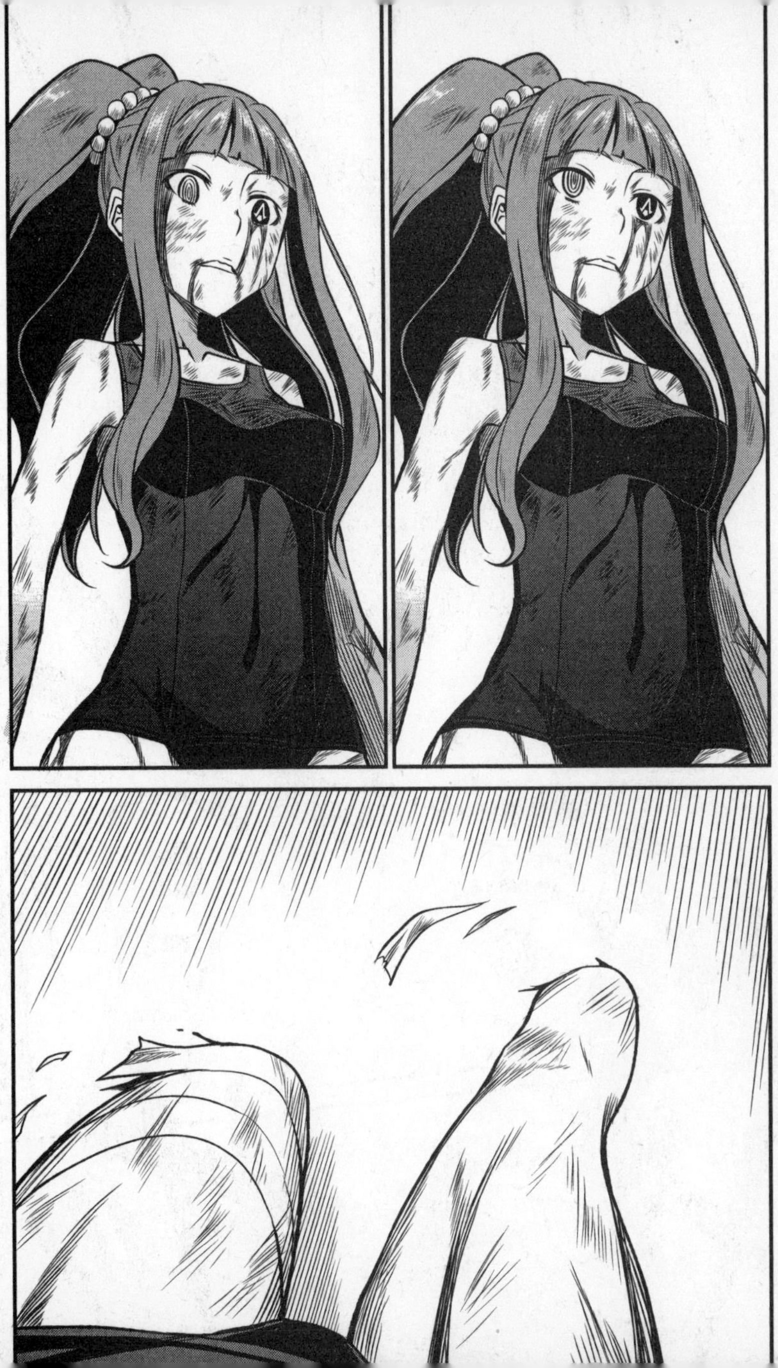

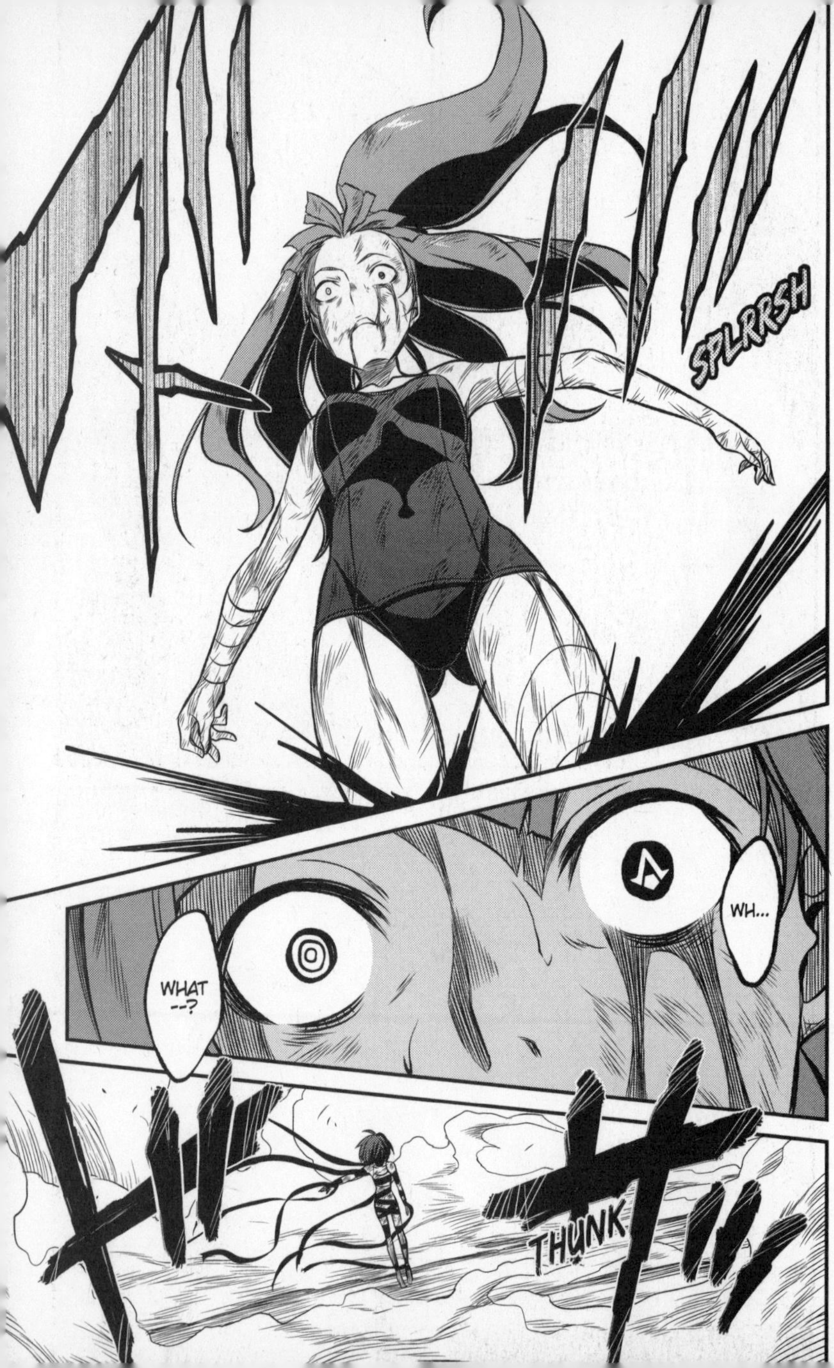
SPLRRSH
WH...
WHAT --?
THUNK

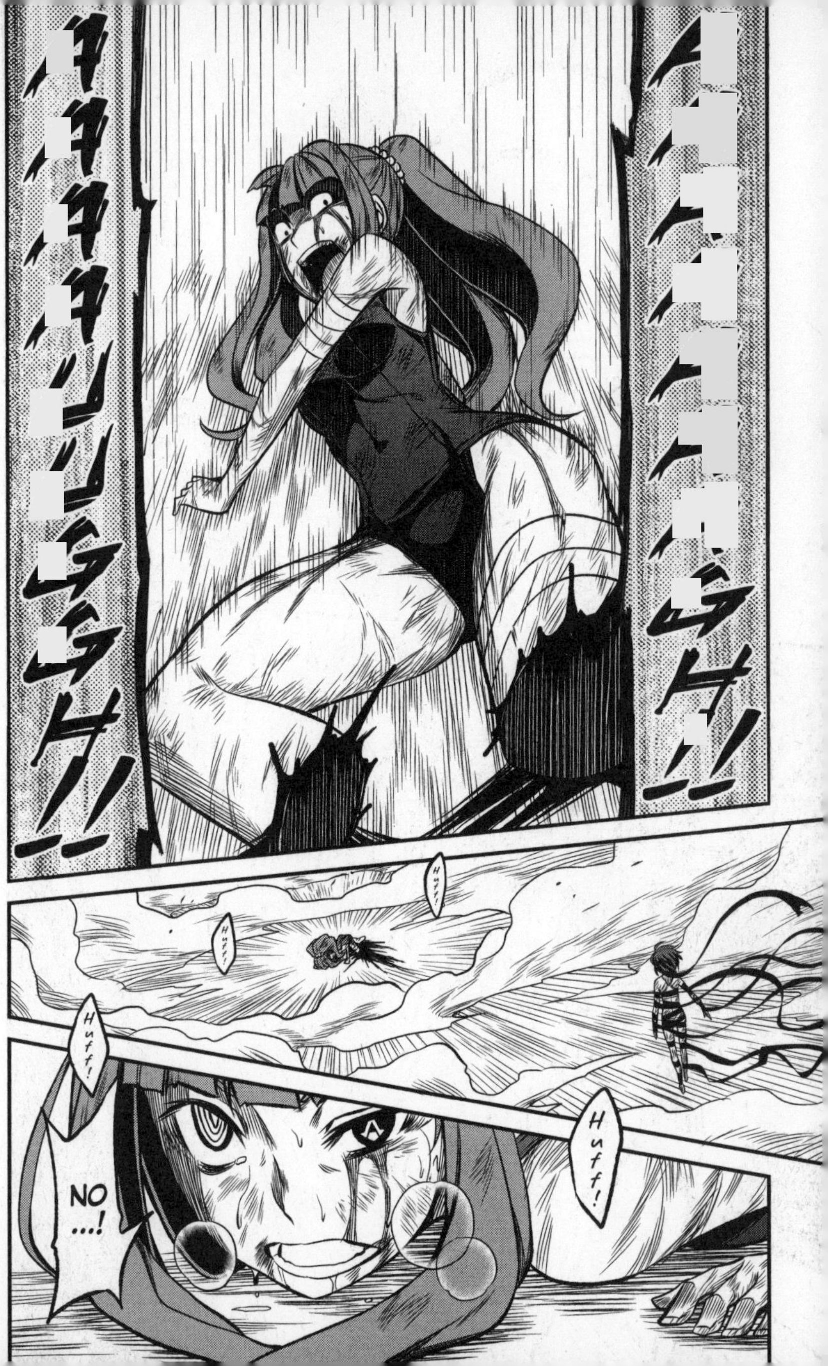
Huff!
Huff!
Huff!
NO ...!
Huff!

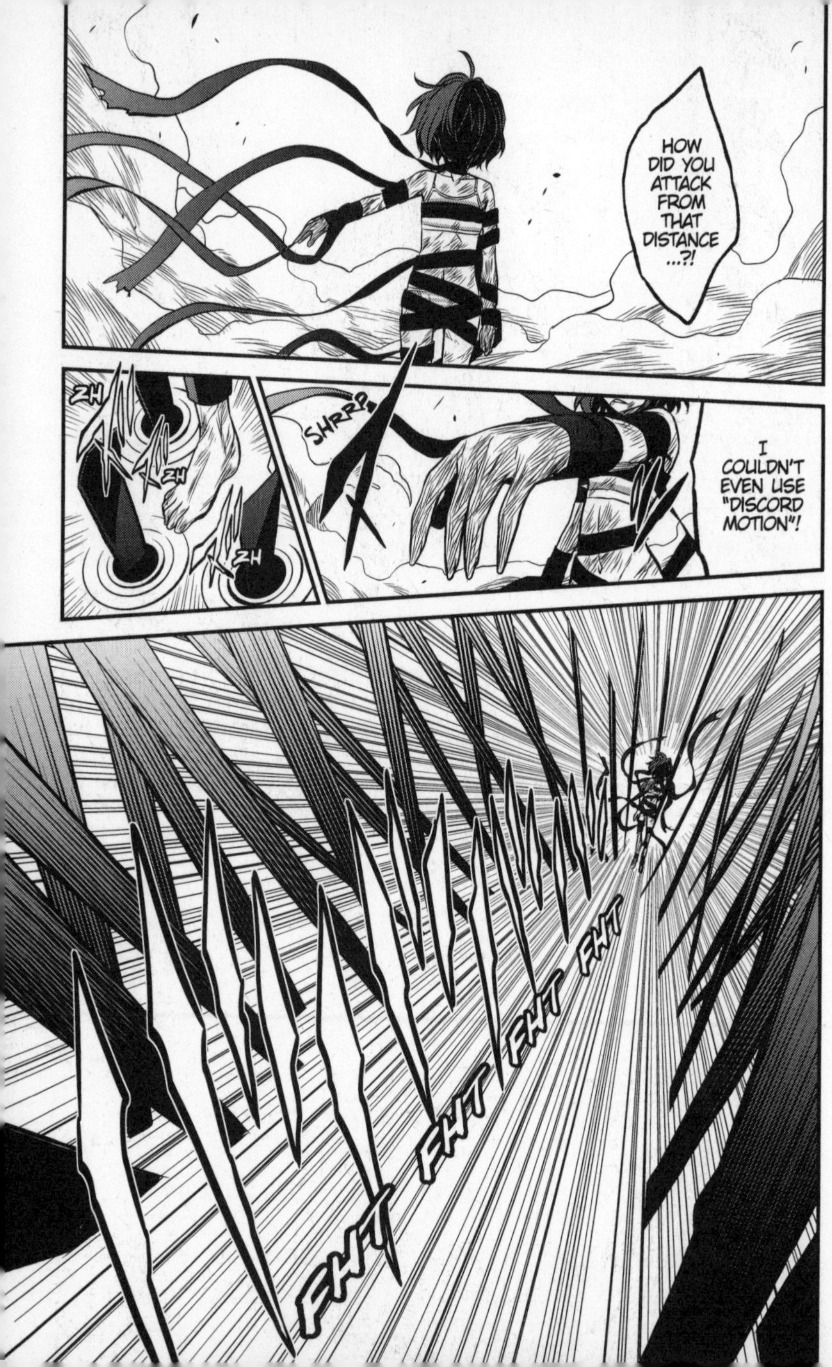
HOW DID YOU ATTACK FROM THAT DISTANCE ...?!
I COULDN'T EVEN USE "DISCORD MOTION"!
SHRRP
ZH
ZH
ZH
FHT FHT FHT FHT FHT

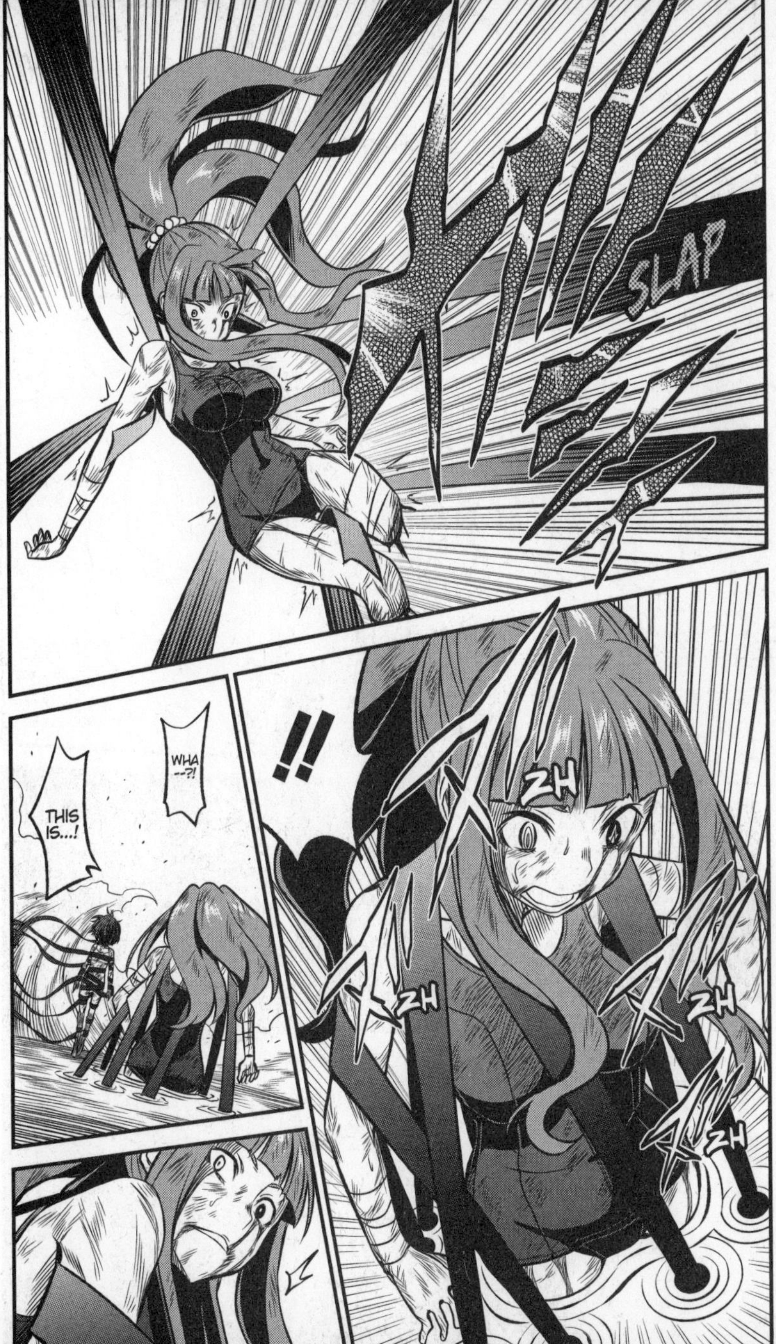
SLAP
!!
ZH
ZH
ZH
ZH
WHA --?!
THIS IS...!

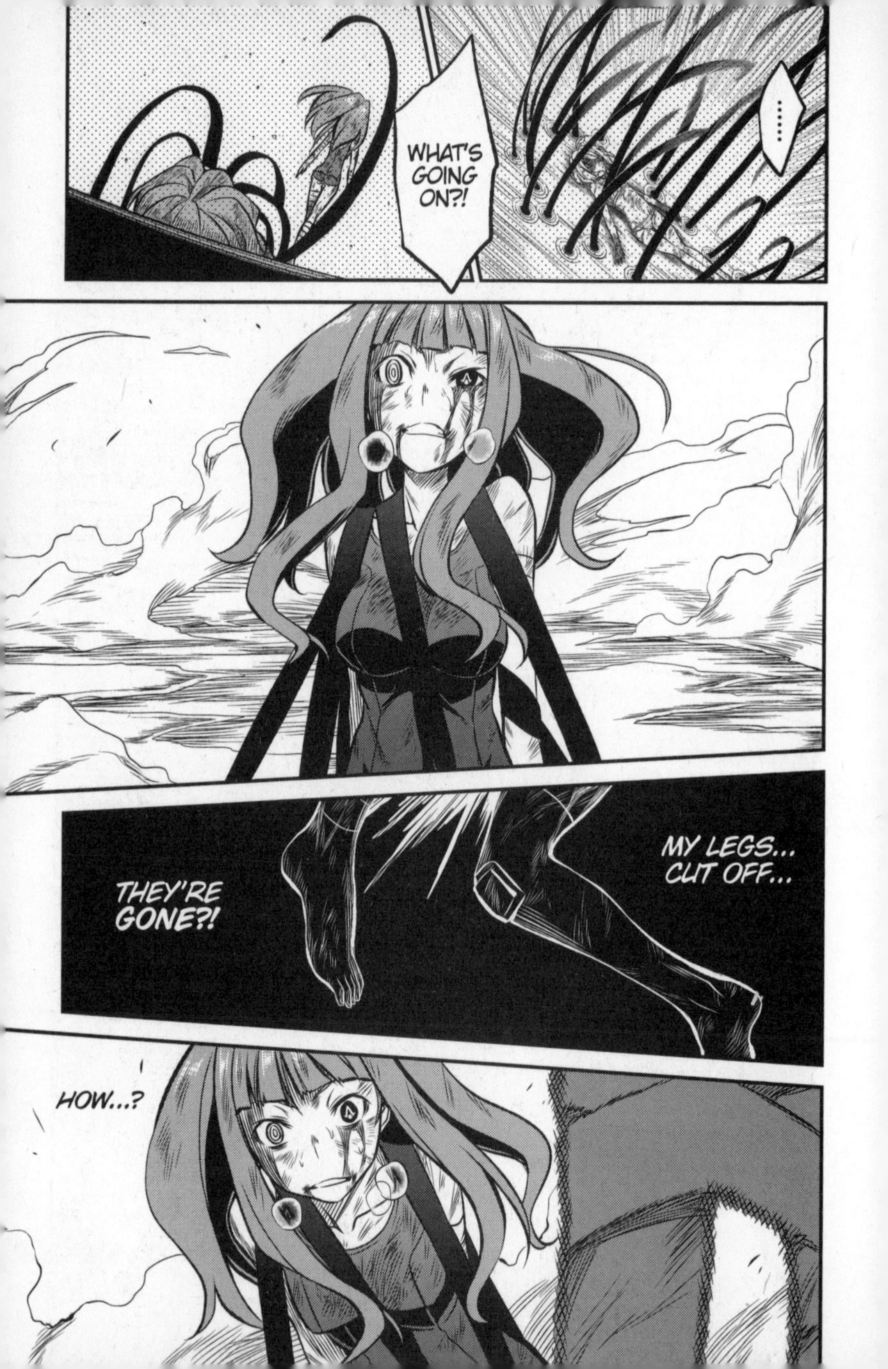
......
WHAT'S GOING ON?!
MY LEGS... CUT OFF...
THEY'RE GONE?!
HOW...?

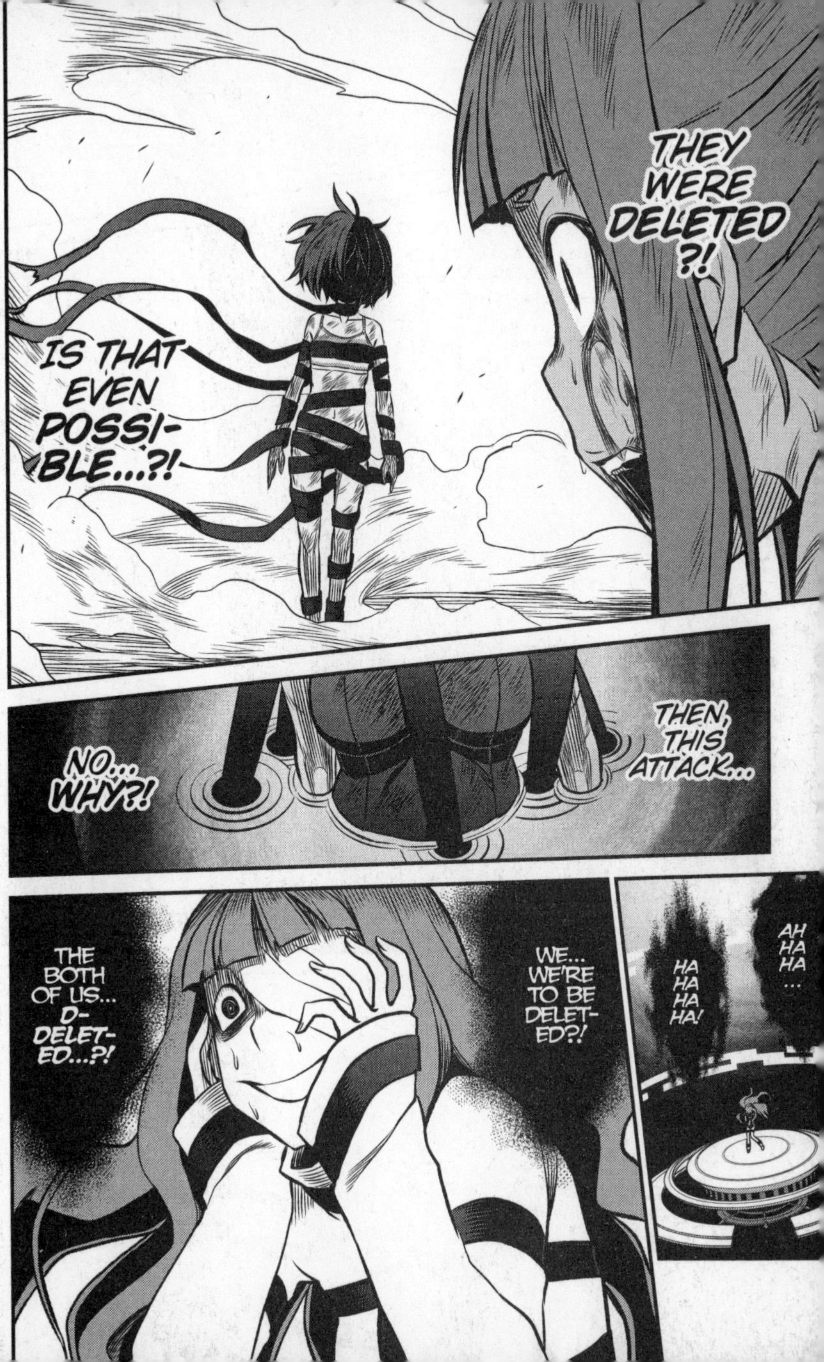
THEY WERE DELETED ?!
IS THAT EVEN POSSI-BLE...?!
THEN, THIS ATTACK...
NO... WHY?!
AH HA HA ...
HA HA HA HA!
WE... WE'RE TO BE DELET-ED?!
THE BOTH OF US... D-DELET-ED...?!

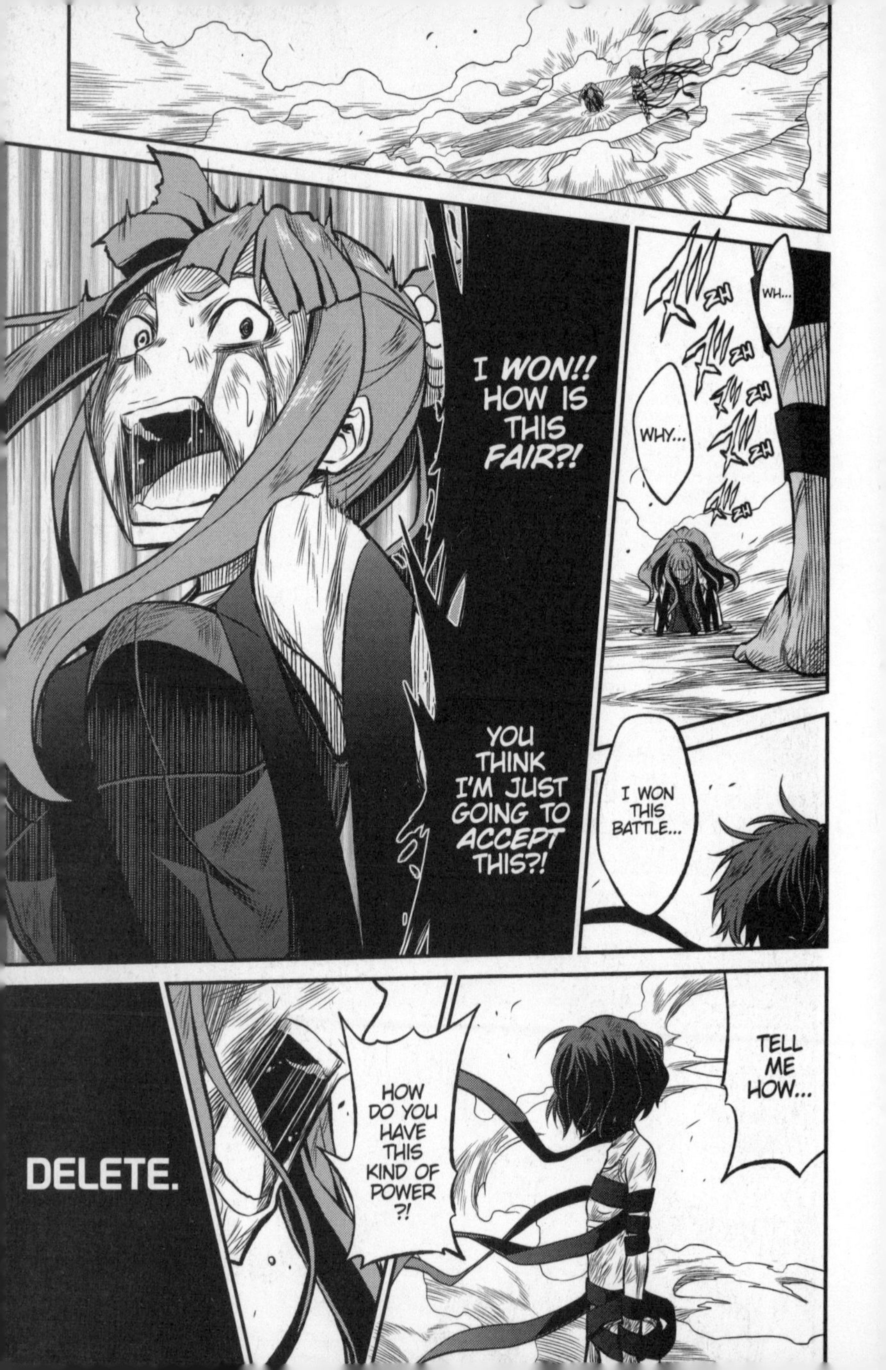

I *WON!!* HOW IS THIS *FAIR?!*
WH...
ZH
ZH
ZH
ZH
ZH
WHY...
YOU THINK I'M JUST GOING TO *ACCEPT* THIS?!
I WON THIS BATTLE...
TELL ME HOW...
HOW DO YOU HAVE THIS KIND OF POWER?!
DELETE.

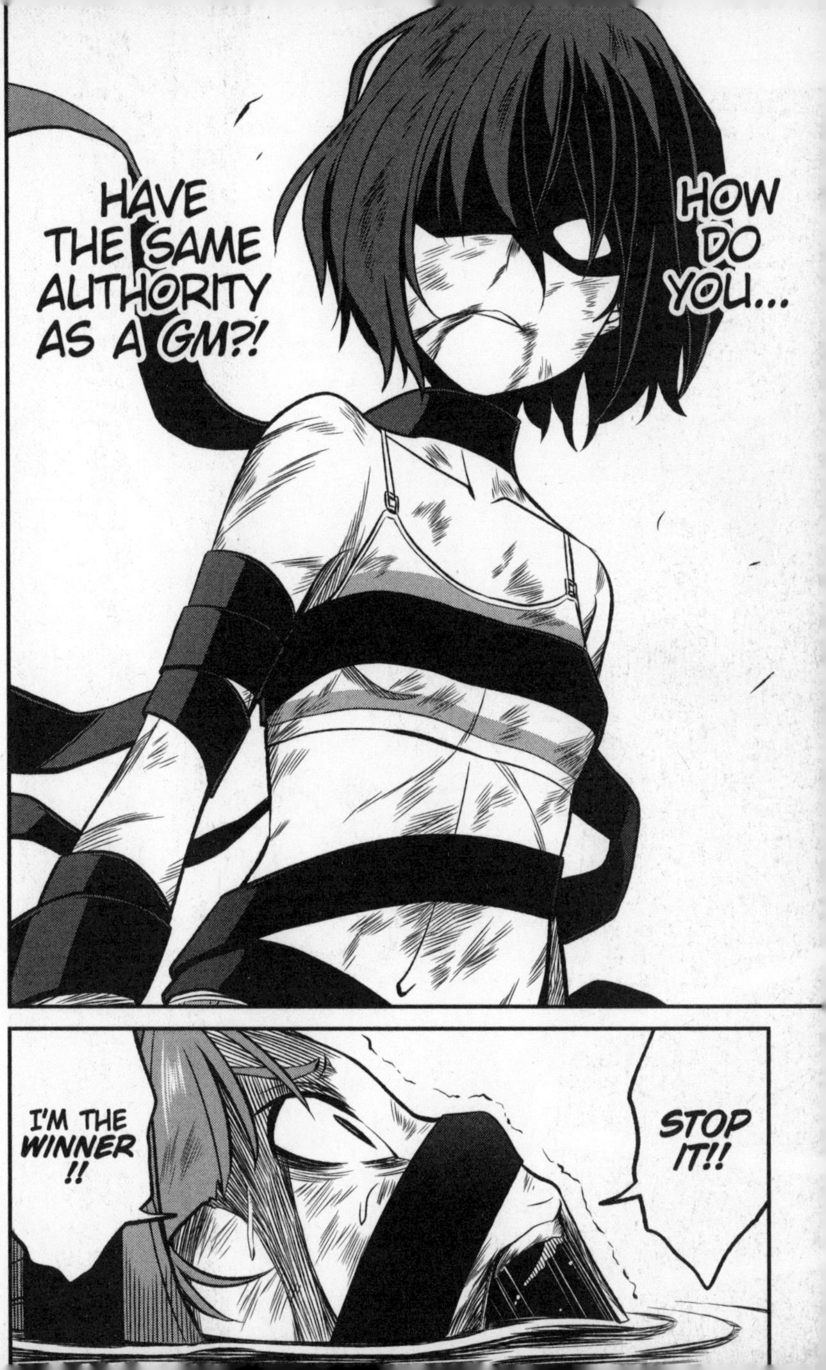
HOW DO YOU...
HAVE THE SAME AUTHORITY AS A GM?!
STOP IT!!
I'M THE WINNER!!

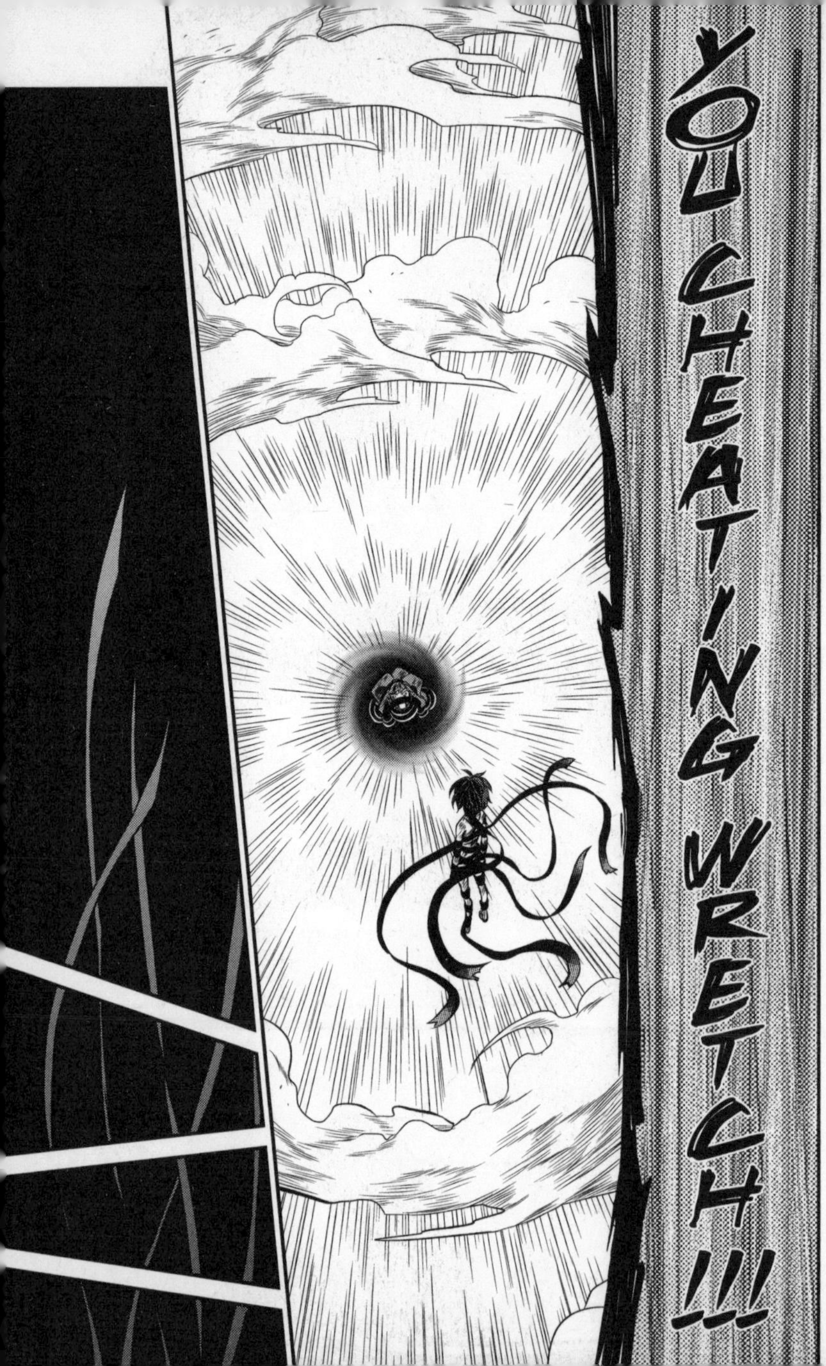
YOU CHEATING WRETCH!!!

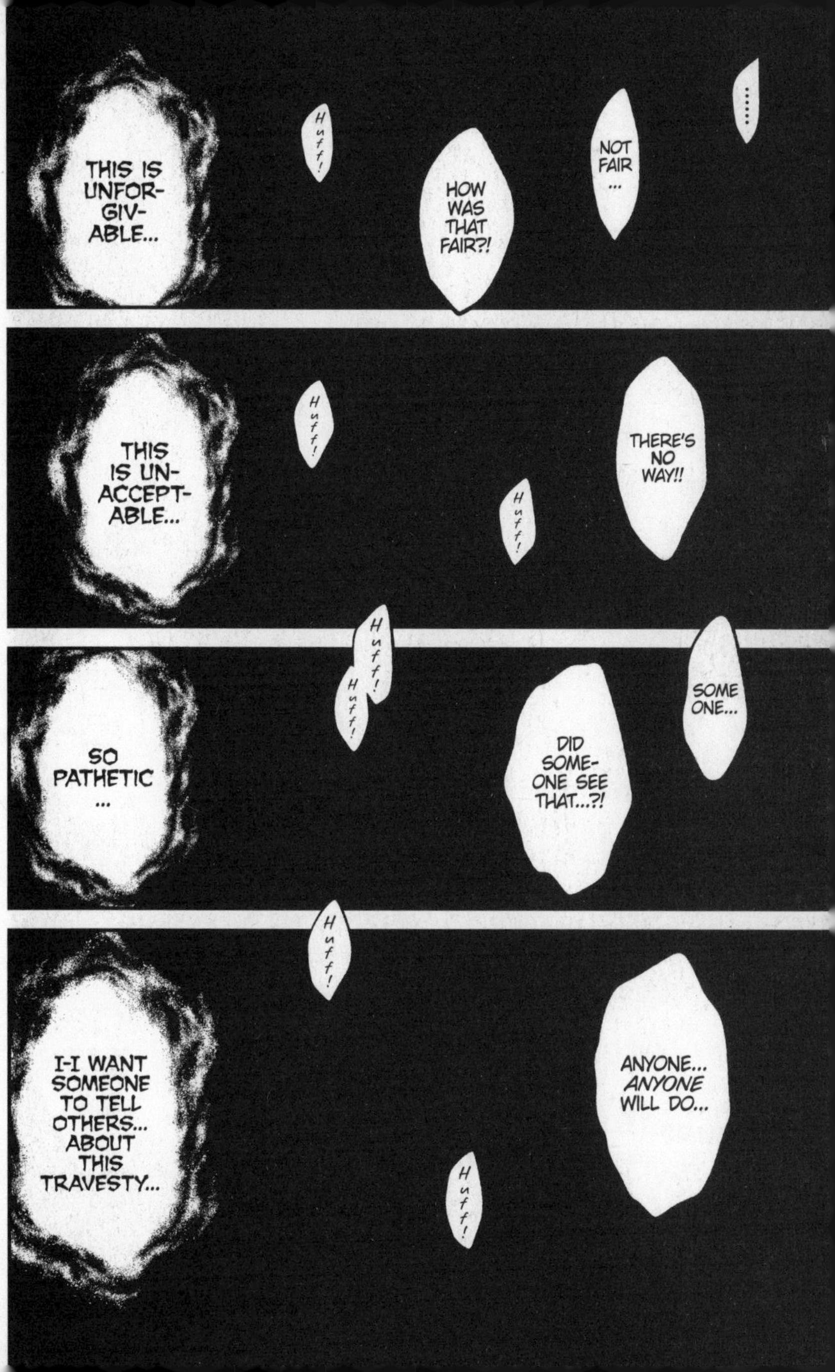
……
NOT FAIR …
HOW WAS THAT FAIR?!
Huff!
THIS IS UNFORGIVABLE...
THERE'S NO WAY!!
Huff!
Huff!
THIS IS UNACCEPTABLE...
SOME ONE...
DID SOMEONE SEE THAT...?!
Huff!
Huff!
SO PATHETIC ...
ANYONE... *ANYONE* WILL DO...
Huff!
Huff!
I-I WANT SOMEONE TO TELL OTHERS... ABOUT THIS TRAVESTY...

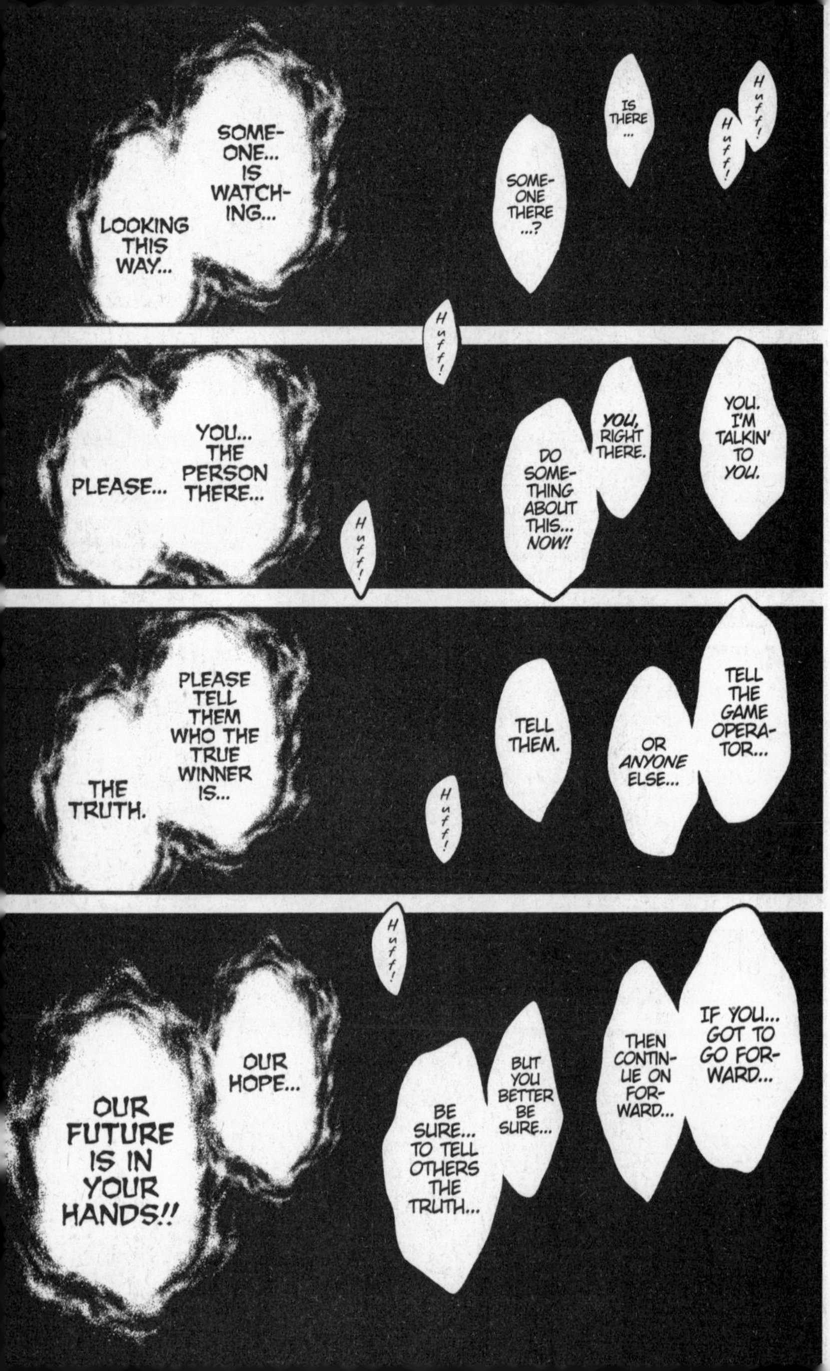
Huff!
Huff!
IS THERE...
SOMEONE THERE...?
SOMEONE... IS WATCHING...
LOOKING THIS WAY...
Huff!
YOU. I'M TALKIN' TO YOU.
YOU, RIGHT THERE.
DO SOMETHING ABOUT THIS... NOW!
Huff!
YOU... THE PERSON THERE...
PLEASE...
TELL THE GAME OPERATOR...
OR ANYONE ELSE...
TELL THEM.
Huff!
PLEASE TELL THEM WHO THE TRUE WINNER IS...
THE TRUTH.
Huff!
IF YOU... GOT TO GO FORWARD...
THEN CONTINUE ON FORWARD...
BUT YOU BETTER BE SURE...
BE SURE... TO TELL OTHERS THE TRUTH...
OUR HOPE...
OUR FUTURE IS IN YOUR HANDS!!

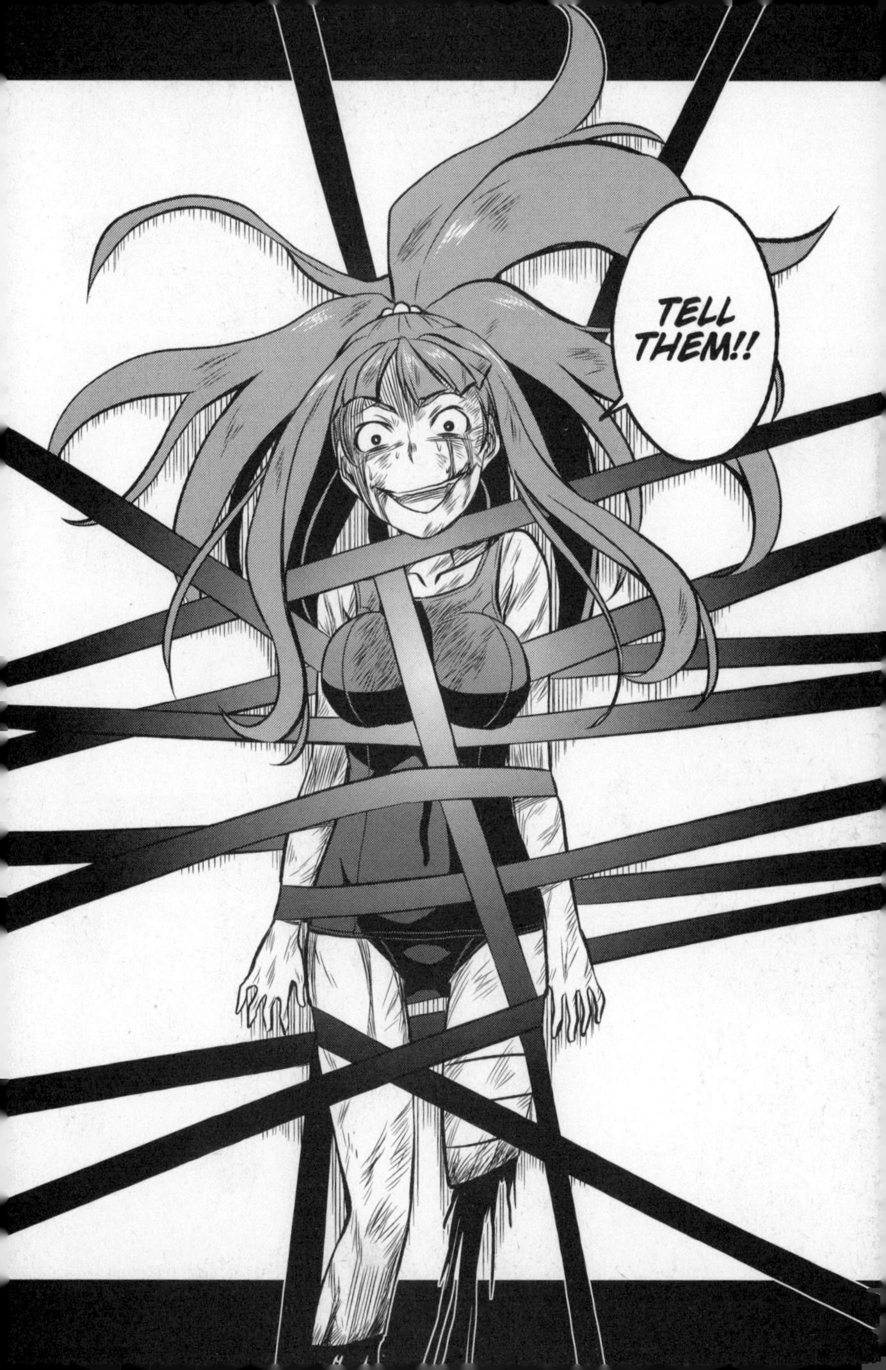
TELL THEM!!

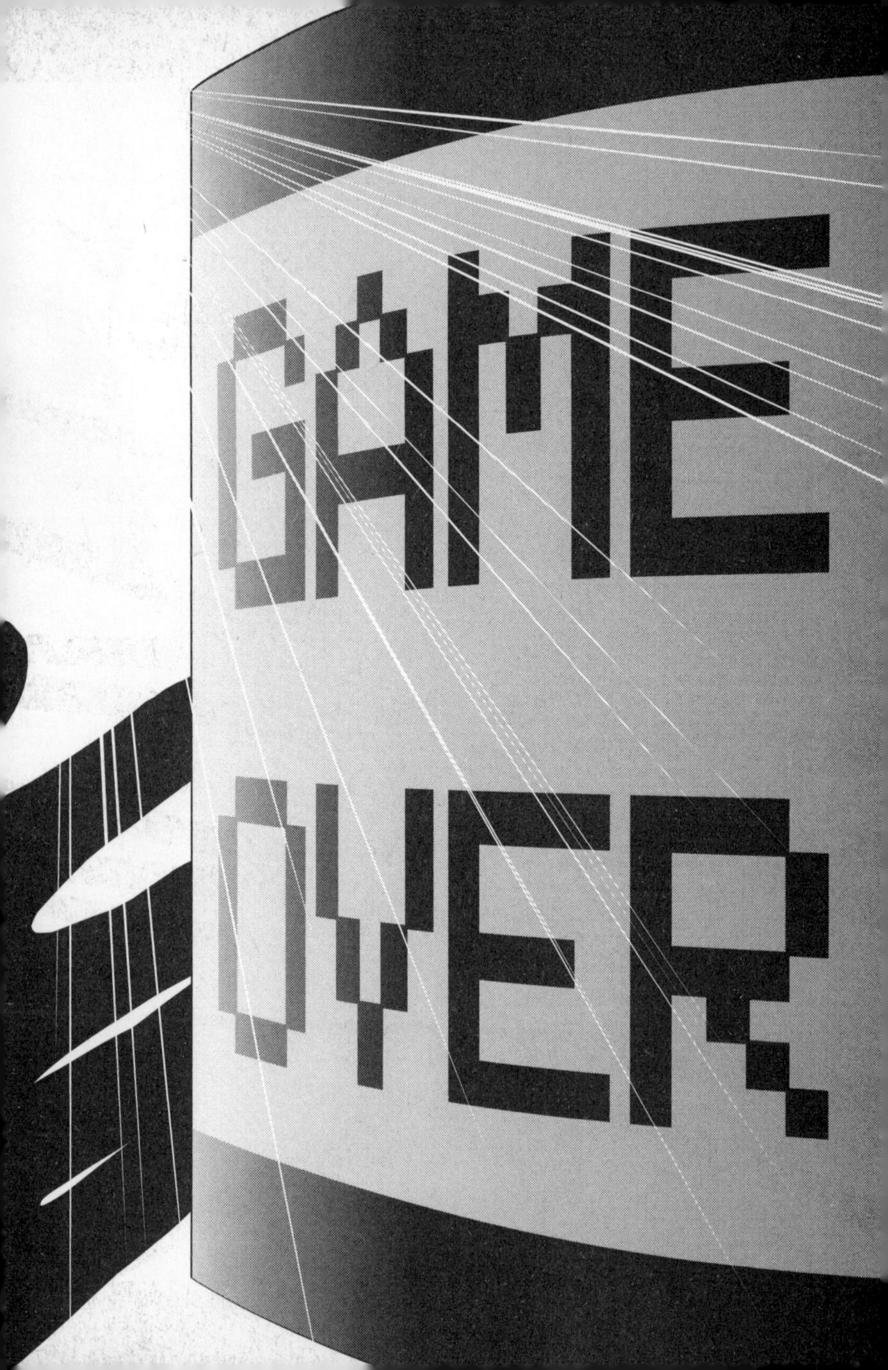
GAME
OVER

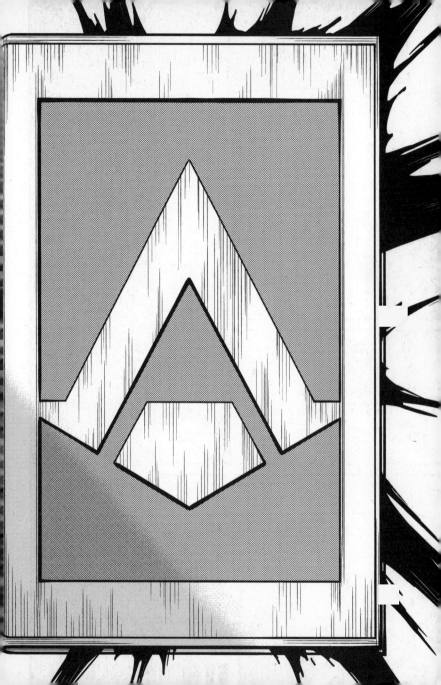

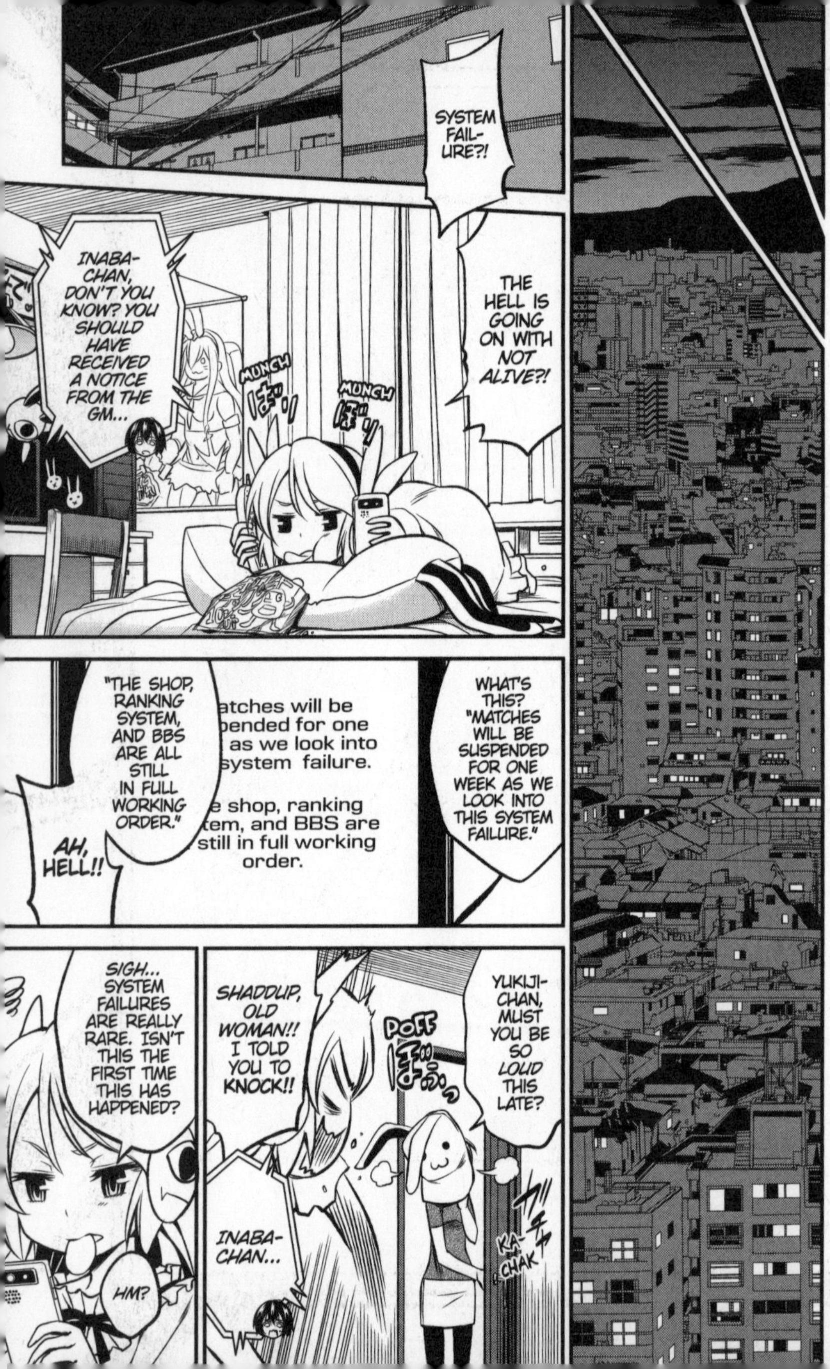
SYSTEM FAILURE?!
THE HELL IS GOING ON WITH NOT ALIVE?!
MUNCH
MUNCH
INABA-CHAN, DON'T YOU KNOW? YOU SHOULD HAVE RECEIVED A NOTICE FROM THE GM...
WHAT'S THIS? "MATCHES WILL BE SUSPENDED FOR ONE WEEK AS WE LOOK INTO THIS SYSTEM FAILURE."
atches will be pended for one as we look into system failure.
e shop, ranking tem, and BBS are still in full working order.
"THE SHOP, RANKING SYSTEM, AND BBS ARE ALL STILL IN FULL WORKING ORDER."
AH, HELL!!
YUKIJI-CHAN, MUST YOU BE SO LOUD THIS LATE?
KA-CHAK
SHADDUP, OLD WOMAN!! I TOLD YOU TO KNOCK!!
POFF
INABA-CHAN...
SIGH... SYSTEM FAILURES ARE REALLY RARE. ISN'T THIS THE FIRST TIME THIS HAS HAPPENED?
HM?

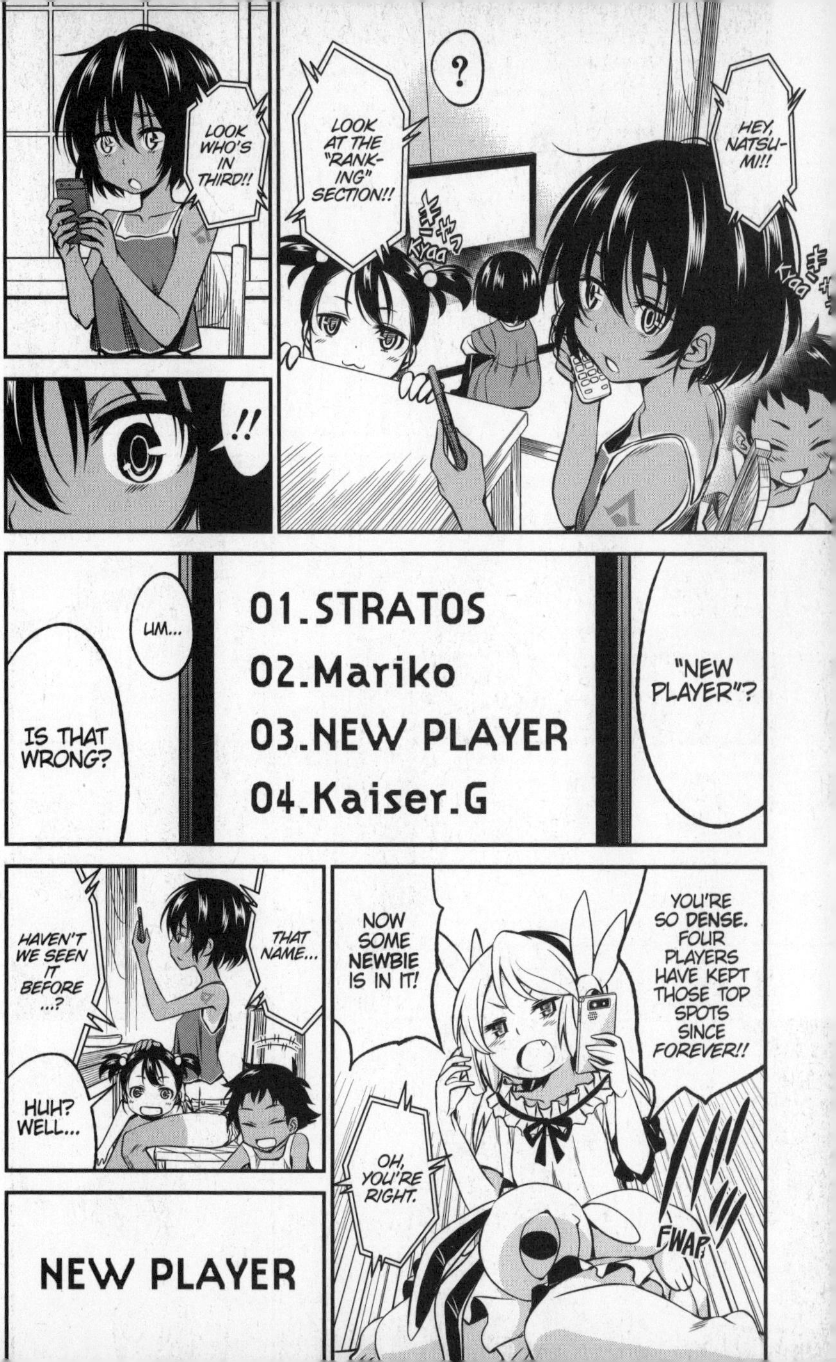

HEY, NATSUMI!!
Kyaa
?
LOOK AT THE "RANKING" SECTION!!
Kyaa
LOOK WHO'S IN THIRD!!
!!
"NEW PLAYER"?
01. STRATOS
02. Mariko
03. NEW PLAYER
04. Kaiser. G
UM...
IS THAT WRONG?
YOU'RE SO DENSE. FOUR PLAYERS HAVE KEPT THOSE TOP SPOTS SINCE FOREVER!!
NOW SOME NEWBIE IS IN IT!
OH, YOU'RE RIGHT.
FWAP
THAT NAME...
HAVEN'T WE SEEN IT BEFORE ...?
HUH? WELL...
NEW PLAYER

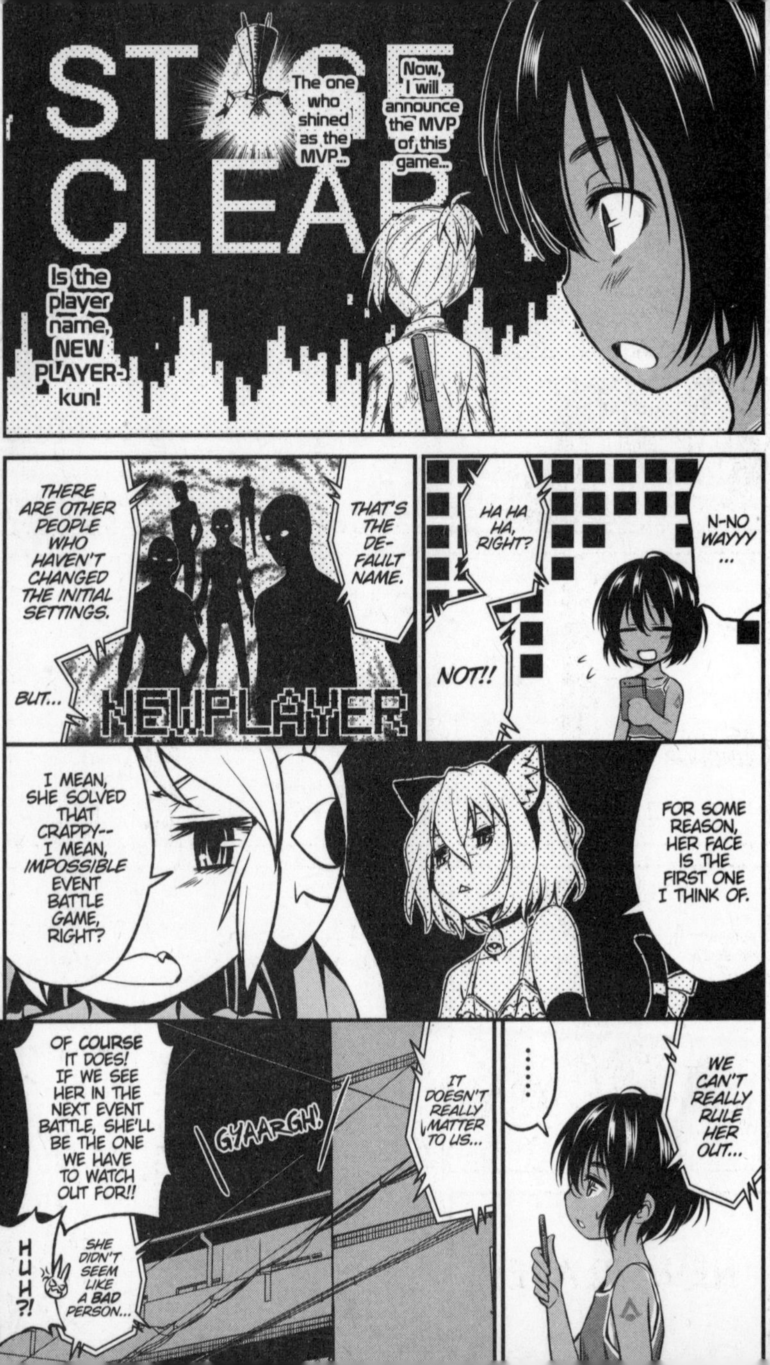

Now, I will announce the MVP of this game...
The one who shined as the MVP...
STAGE CLEAR
Is the player name, NEW PLAYER-kun!
N-NO WAYYY ...
HA HA HA, RIGHT?
NOT!!
THAT'S THE DE-FAULT NAME.
THERE ARE OTHER PEOPLE WHO HAVEN'T CHANGED THE INITIAL SETTINGS.
BUT...
NEWPLAYER
FOR SOME REASON, HER FACE IS THE FIRST ONE I THINK OF.
I MEAN, SHE SOLVED THAT CRAPPY-- I MEAN, IMPOSSIBLE EVENT BATTLE GAME, RIGHT?
WE CAN'T REALLY RULE HER OUT...
......
IT DOESN'T REALLY MATTER TO US...
OF COURSE IT DOES! IF WE SEE HER IN THE NEXT EVENT BATTLE, SHE'LL BE THE ONE WE HAVE TO WATCH OUT FOR!!
GYAARGH!
HUH?!
SHE DIDN'T SEEM LIKE A BAD PERSON...

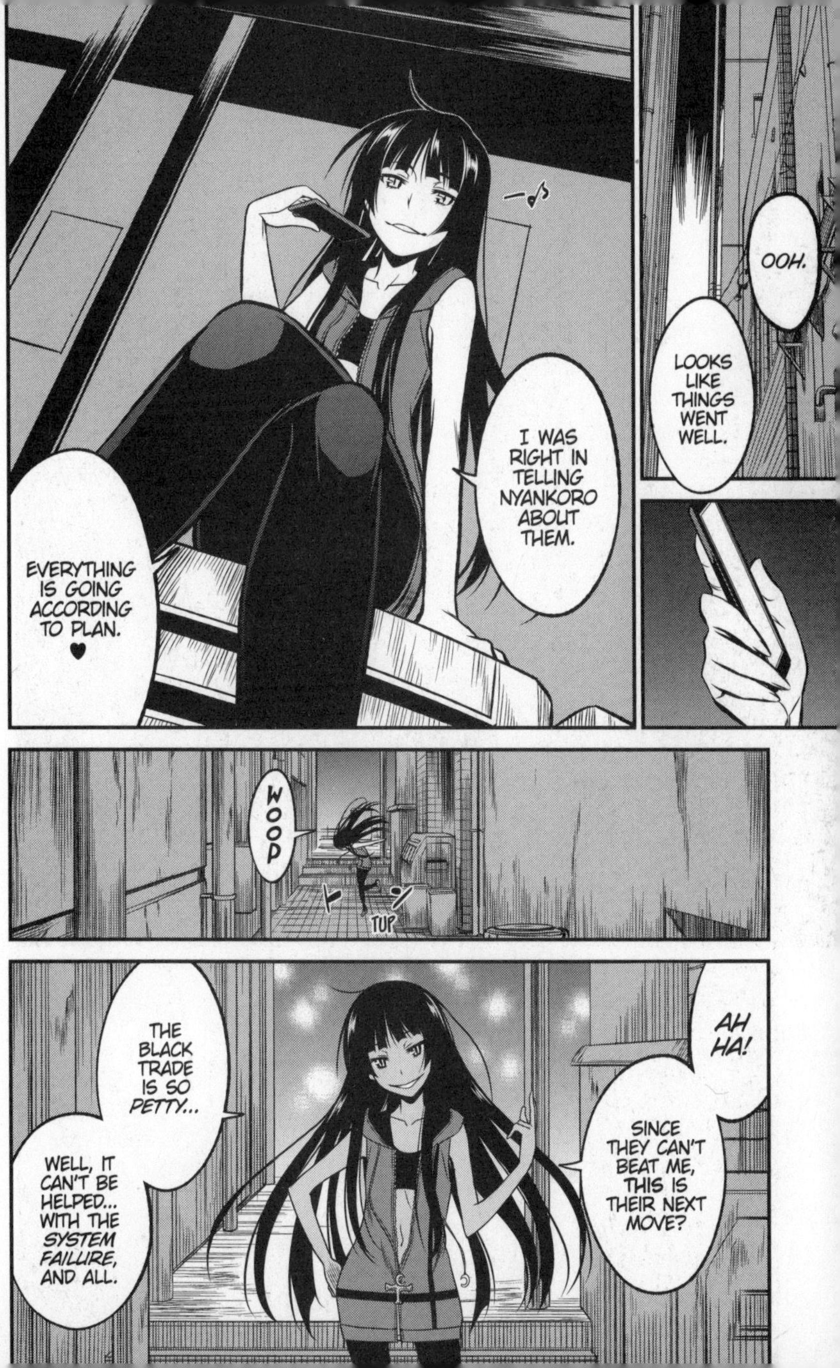

OOH.
LOOKS LIKE THINGS WENT WELL.
I WAS RIGHT IN TELLING NYANKORO ABOUT THEM.
EVERYTHING IS GOING ACCORDING TO PLAN. ♥
WOOP
TUP
AH HA!
SINCE THEY CAN'T BEAT ME, THIS IS THEIR NEXT MOVE?
THE BLACK TRADE IS SO *PETTY*...
WELL, IT CAN'T BE HELPED... WITH THE *SYSTEM FAILURE,* AND ALL.

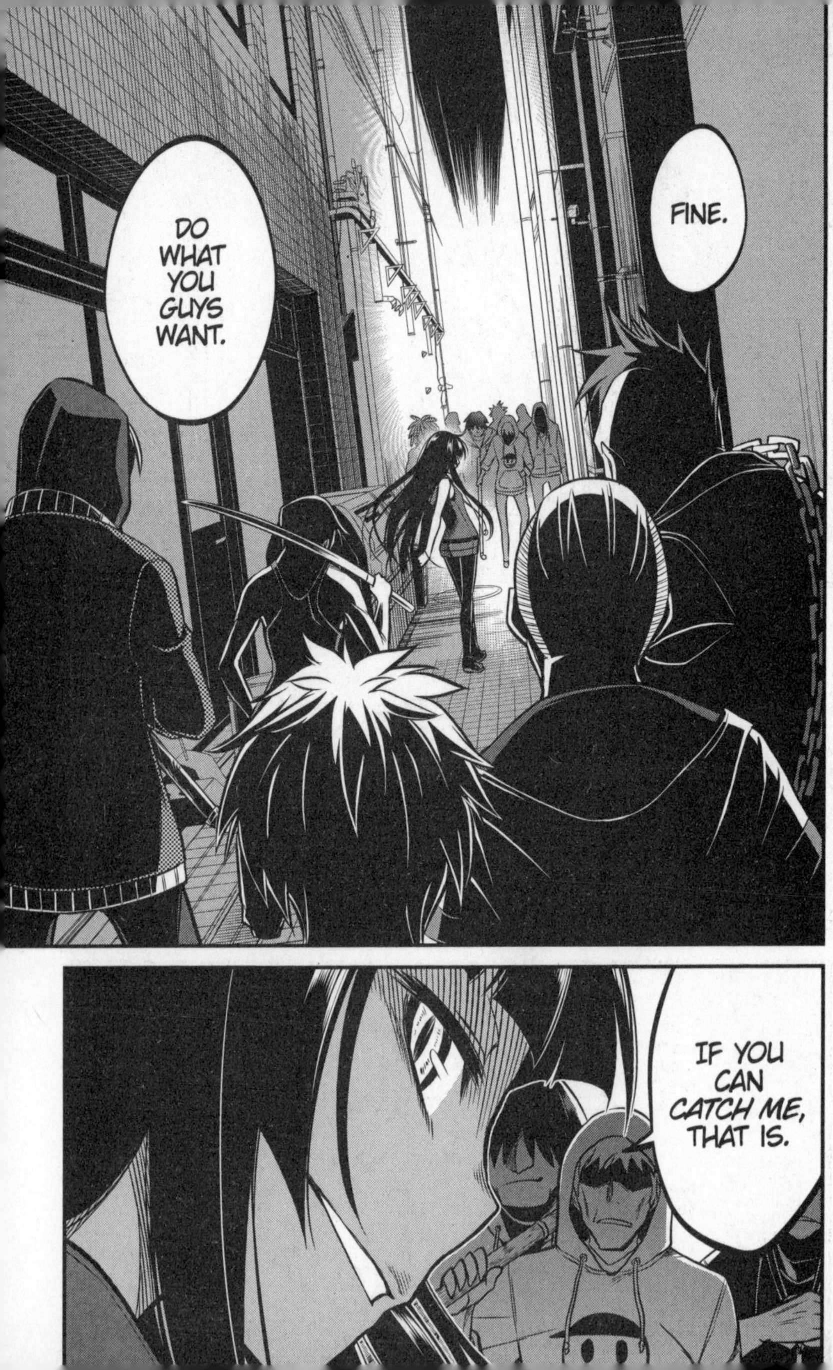
FINE.
DO WHAT YOU GUYS WANT.
IF YOU CAN CATCH ME, THAT IS.

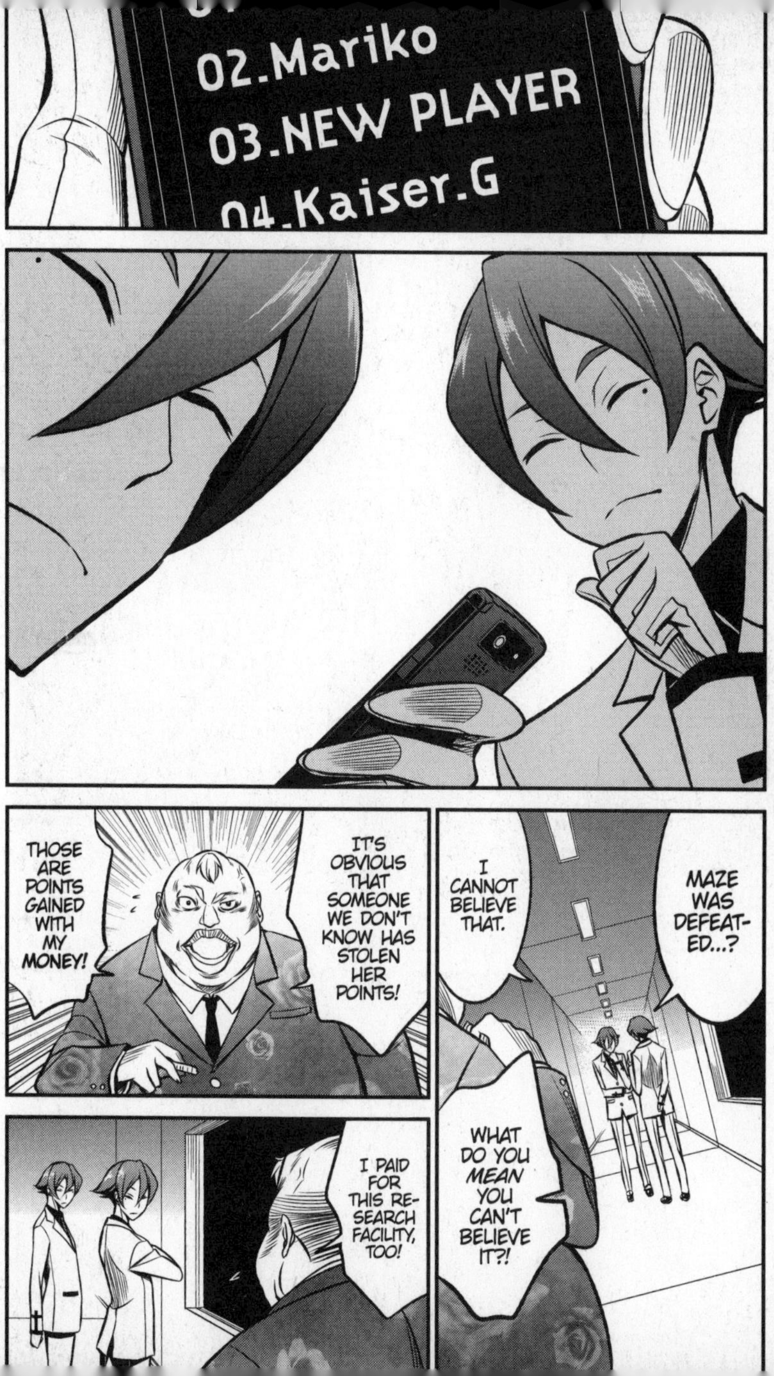
02.Mariko
03.NEW PLAYER
04.Kaiser.G
MAZE WAS DEFEAT-ED...?
I CANNOT BELIEVE THAT.
WHAT DO YOU MEAN YOU CAN'T BELIEVE IT?!
IT'S OBVIOUS THAT SOMEONE WE DON'T KNOW HAS STOLEN HER POINTS!
THOSE ARE POINTS GAINED WITH MY MONEY!
I PAID FOR THIS RE-SEARCH FACILITY, TOO!

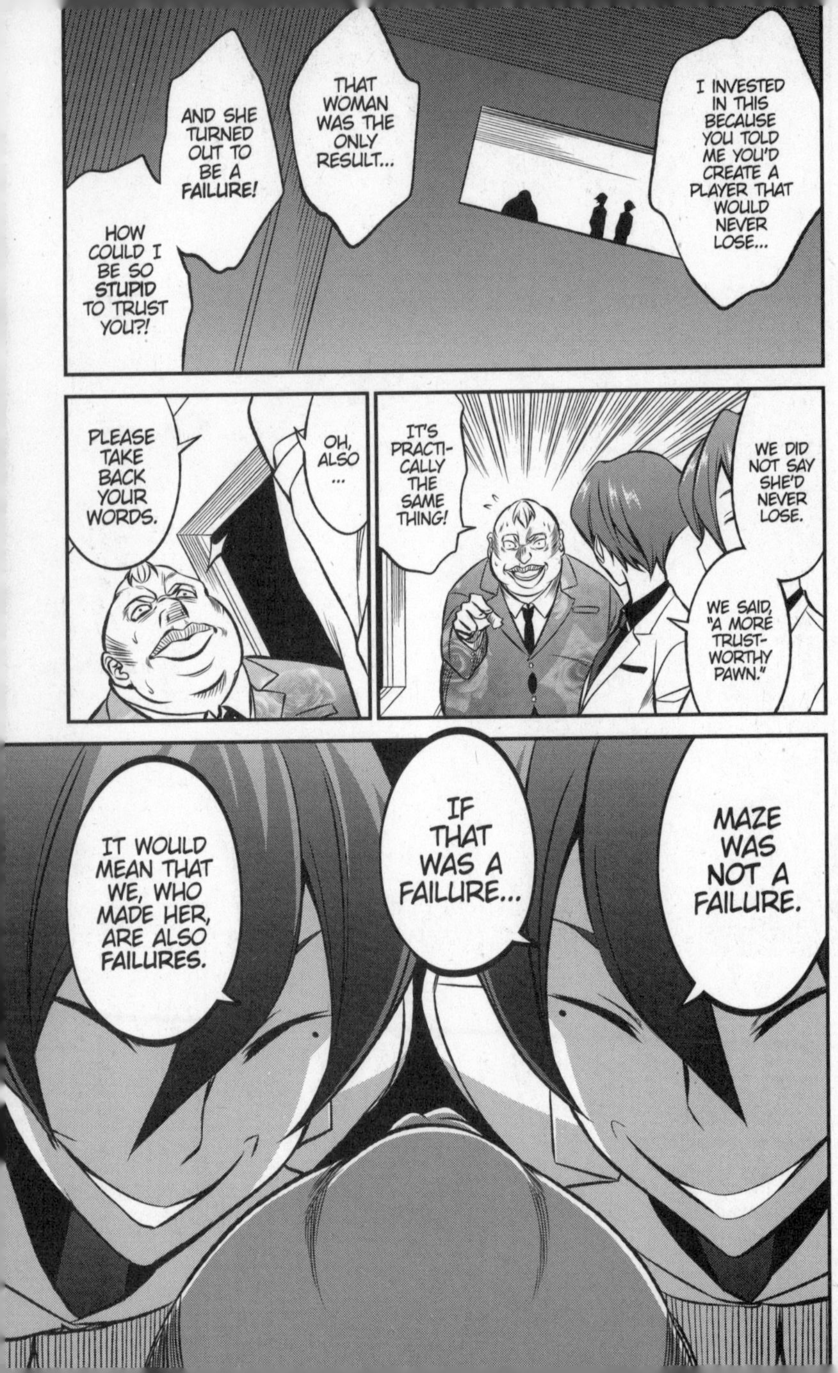
I INVESTED IN THIS BECAUSE YOU TOLD ME YOU'D CREATE A PLAYER THAT WOULD NEVER LOSE...
THAT WOMAN WAS THE ONLY RESULT...
AND SHE TURNED OUT TO BE A FAILURE!
HOW COULD I BE SO STUPID TO TRUST YOU?!
WE DID NOT SAY SHE'D NEVER LOSE.
WE SAID, "A MORE TRUST-WORTHY PAWN."
IT'S PRACTI-CALLY THE SAME THING!
OH, ALSO ...
PLEASE TAKE BACK YOUR WORDS.
MAZE WAS NOT A FAILURE.
IF THAT WAS A FAILURE...
IT WOULD MEAN THAT WE, WHO MADE HER, ARE ALSO FAILURES.

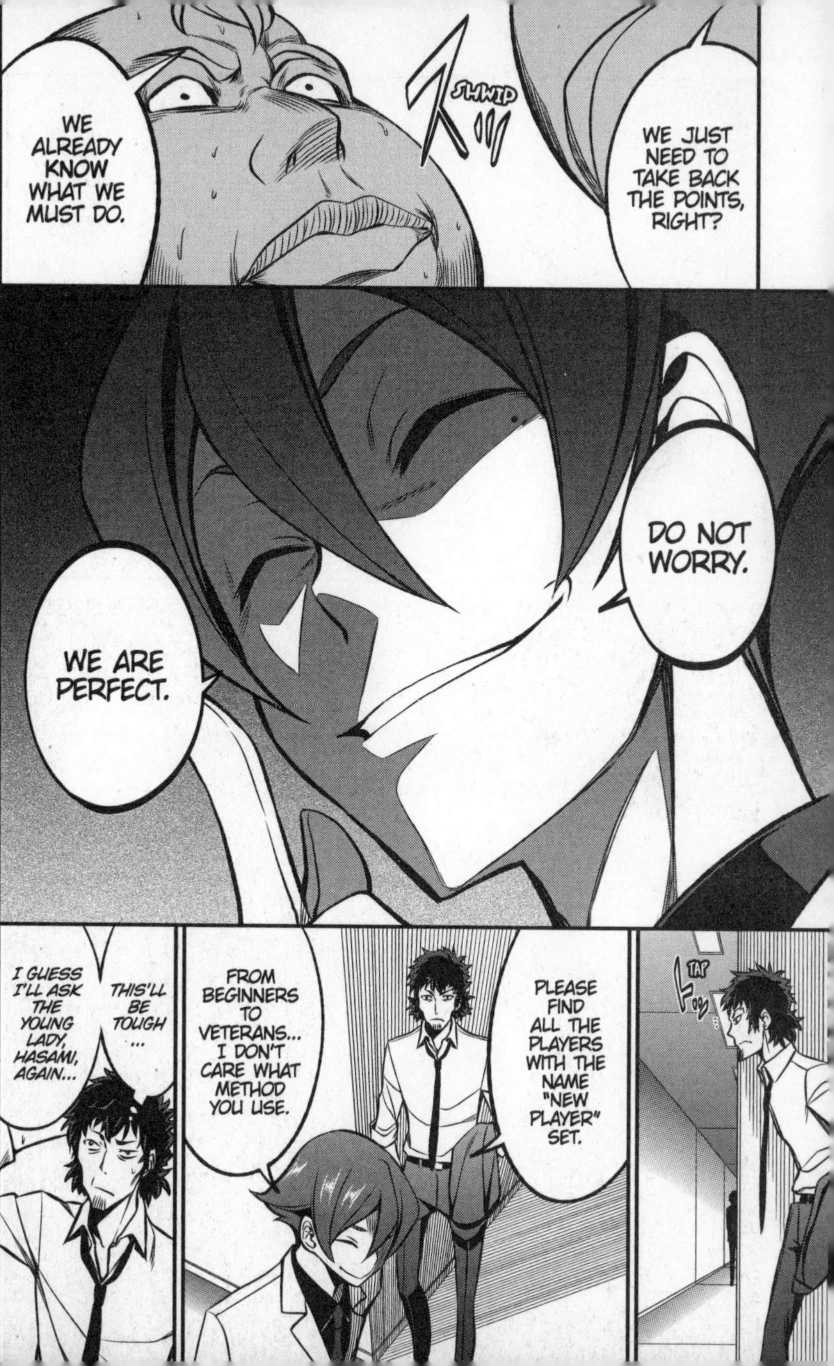
WE JUST NEED TO TAKE BACK THE POINTS, RIGHT?
SHWIP
WE ALREADY KNOW WHAT WE MUST DO.
DO NOT WORRY.
WE ARE PERFECT.
TAP
PLEASE FIND ALL THE PLAYERS WITH THE NAME "NEW PLAYER" SET.
FROM BEGINNERS TO VETERANS... I DON'T CARE WHAT METHOD YOU USE.
THIS'LL BE TOUGH...
I GUESS I'LL ASK THE YOUNG LADY, HASAMI, AGAIN...

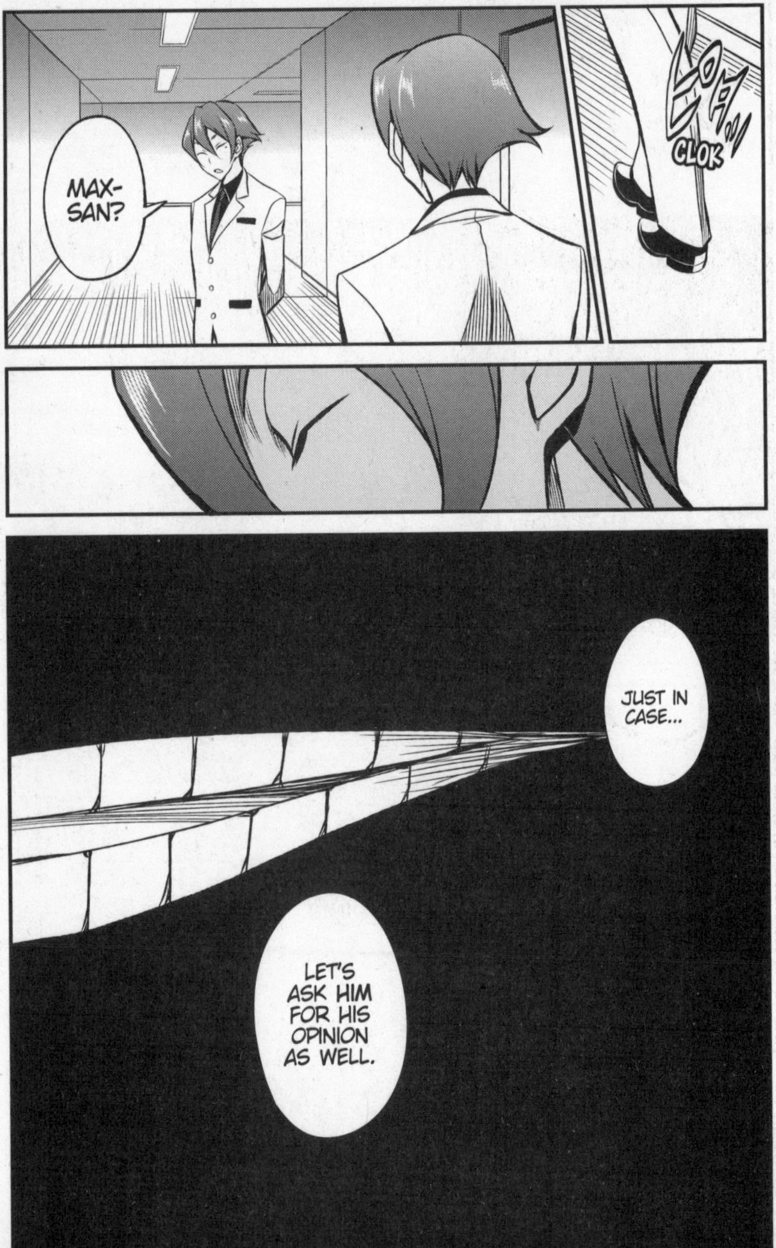
CLOK
MAX-SAN?
JUST IN CASE...
LET'S ASK HIM FOR HIS OPINION AS WELL.

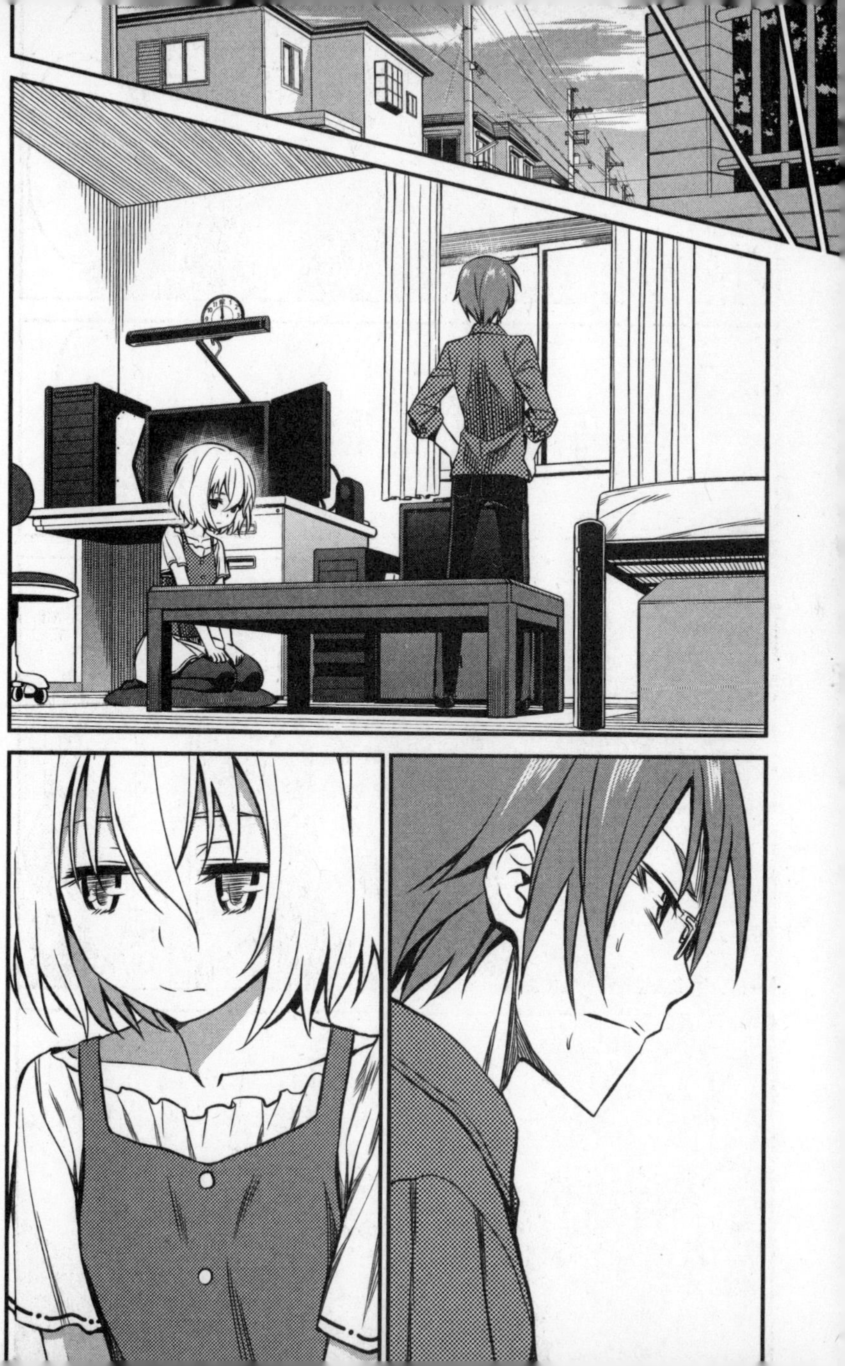

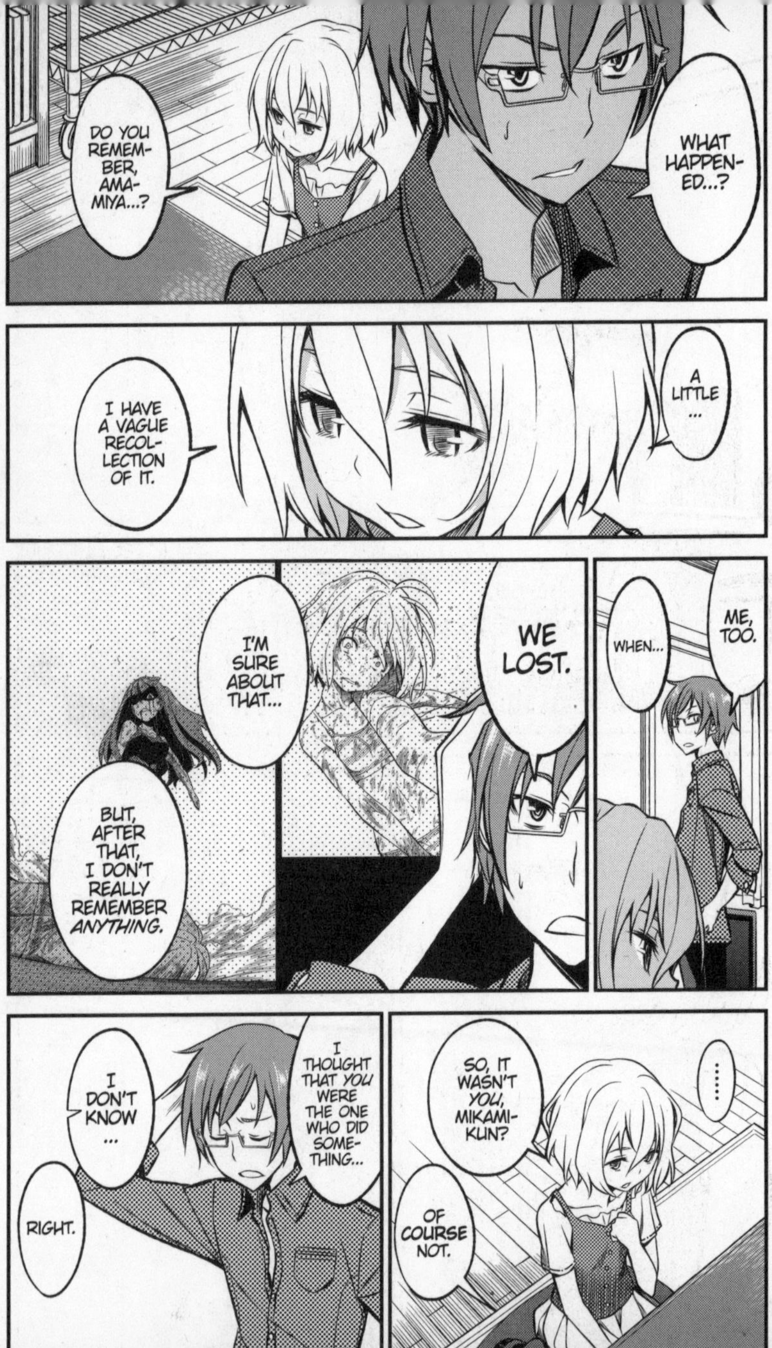
WHAT HAPPENED...?
DO YOU REMEMBER, AMAMIYA...?
A LITTLE ...
I HAVE A VAGUE RECOLLECTION OF IT.
ME, TOO.
WHEN...
WE LOST.
I'M SURE ABOUT THAT...
BUT, AFTER THAT, I DON'T REALLY REMEMBER *ANYTHING*.
......
SO, IT WASN'T *YOU*, MIKAMI-KUN?
OF COURSE NOT.
I THOUGHT THAT *YOU* WERE THE ONE WHO DID SOMETHING...
I DON'T KNOW ...
RIGHT.

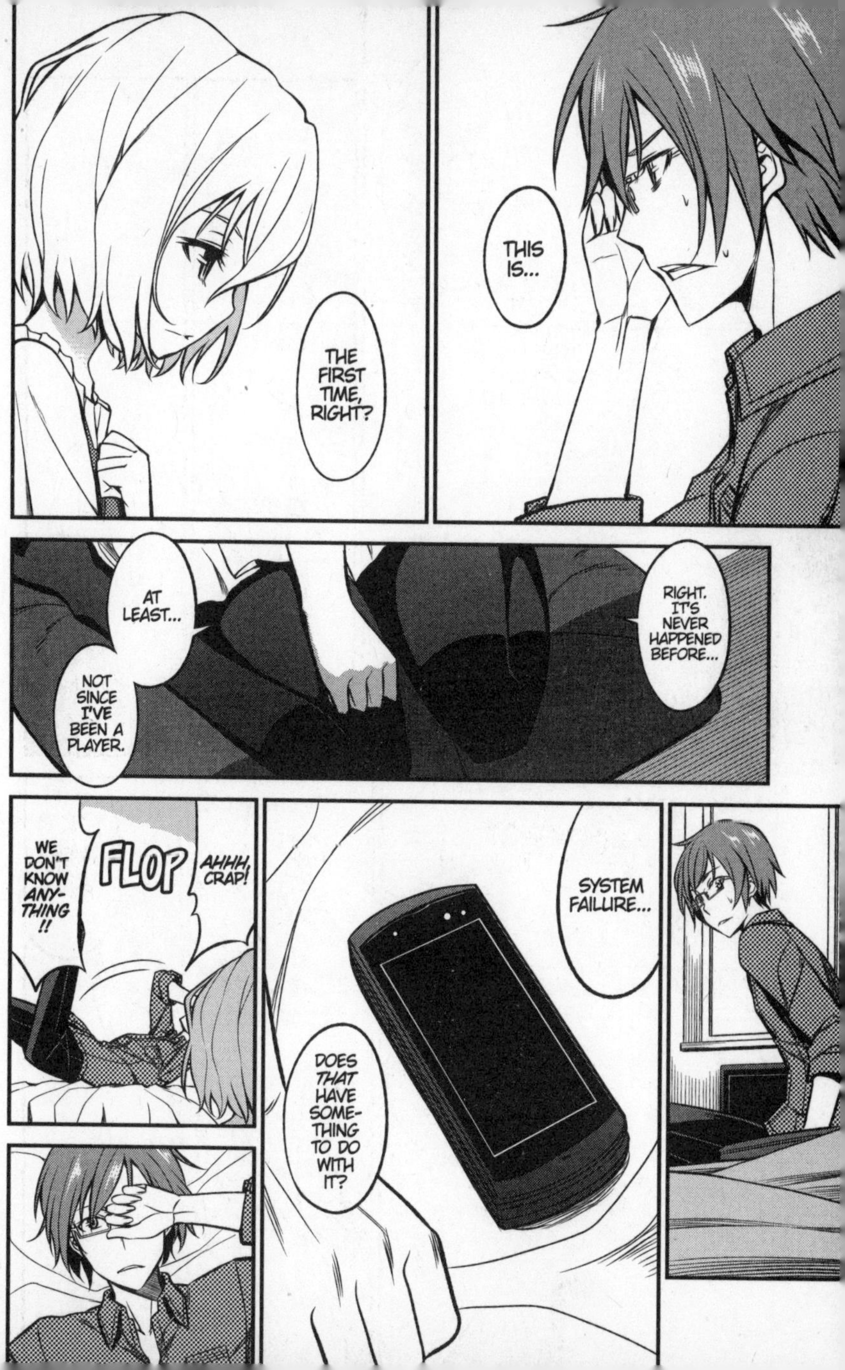
THIS IS...
THE FIRST TIME, RIGHT?
RIGHT. IT'S NEVER HAPPENED BEFORE...
AT LEAST...
NOT SINCE I'VE BEEN A PLAYER.
SYSTEM FAILURE...
DOES *THAT* HAVE SOMETHING TO DO WITH IT?
AHHH, CRAP!
FLOP
WE DON'T KNOW *ANYTHING*!!

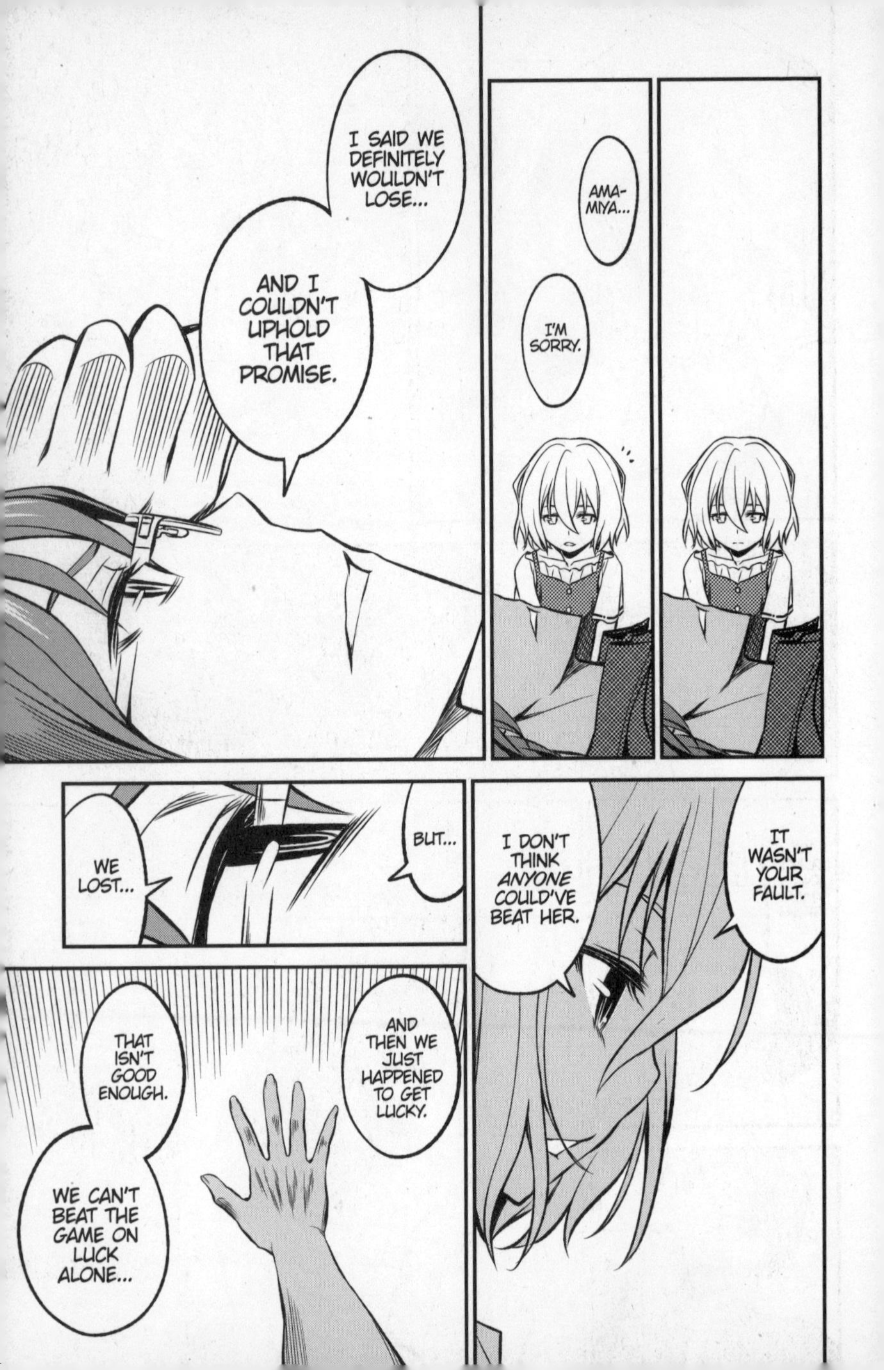
AMA-MIYA...
I'M SORRY.
I SAID WE DEFINITELY WOULDN'T LOSE...
AND I COULDN'T UPHOLD THAT PROMISE.
IT WASN'T YOUR FAULT.
I DON'T THINK *ANYONE* COULD'VE BEAT HER.
BUT...
WE LOST...
AND THEN WE JUST HAPPENED TO GET LUCKY.
THAT ISN'T GOOD ENOUGH.
WE CAN'T BEAT THE GAME ON LUCK ALONE...

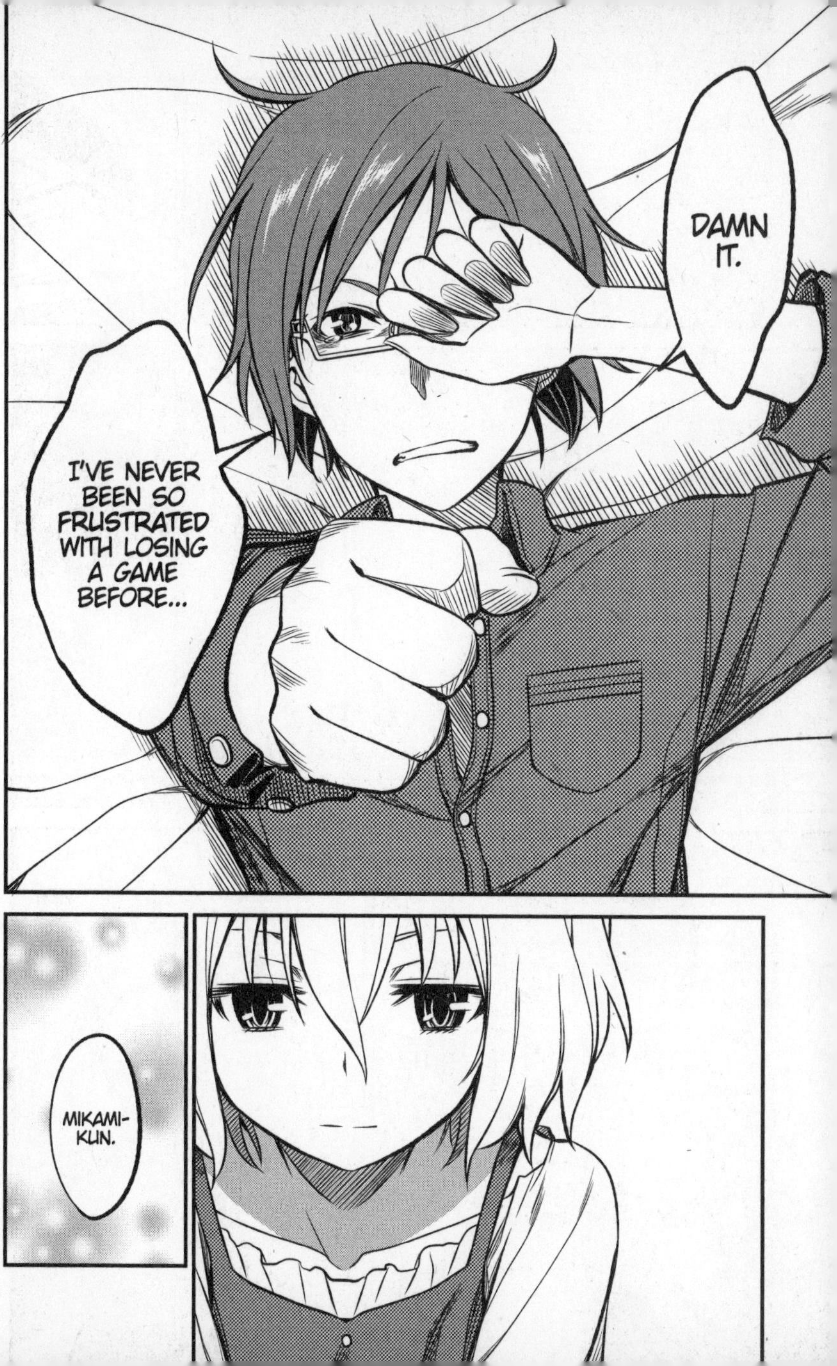
DAMN IT.
I'VE NEVER BEEN SO FRUSTRATED WITH LOSING A GAME BEFORE...
MIKAMI-KUN.

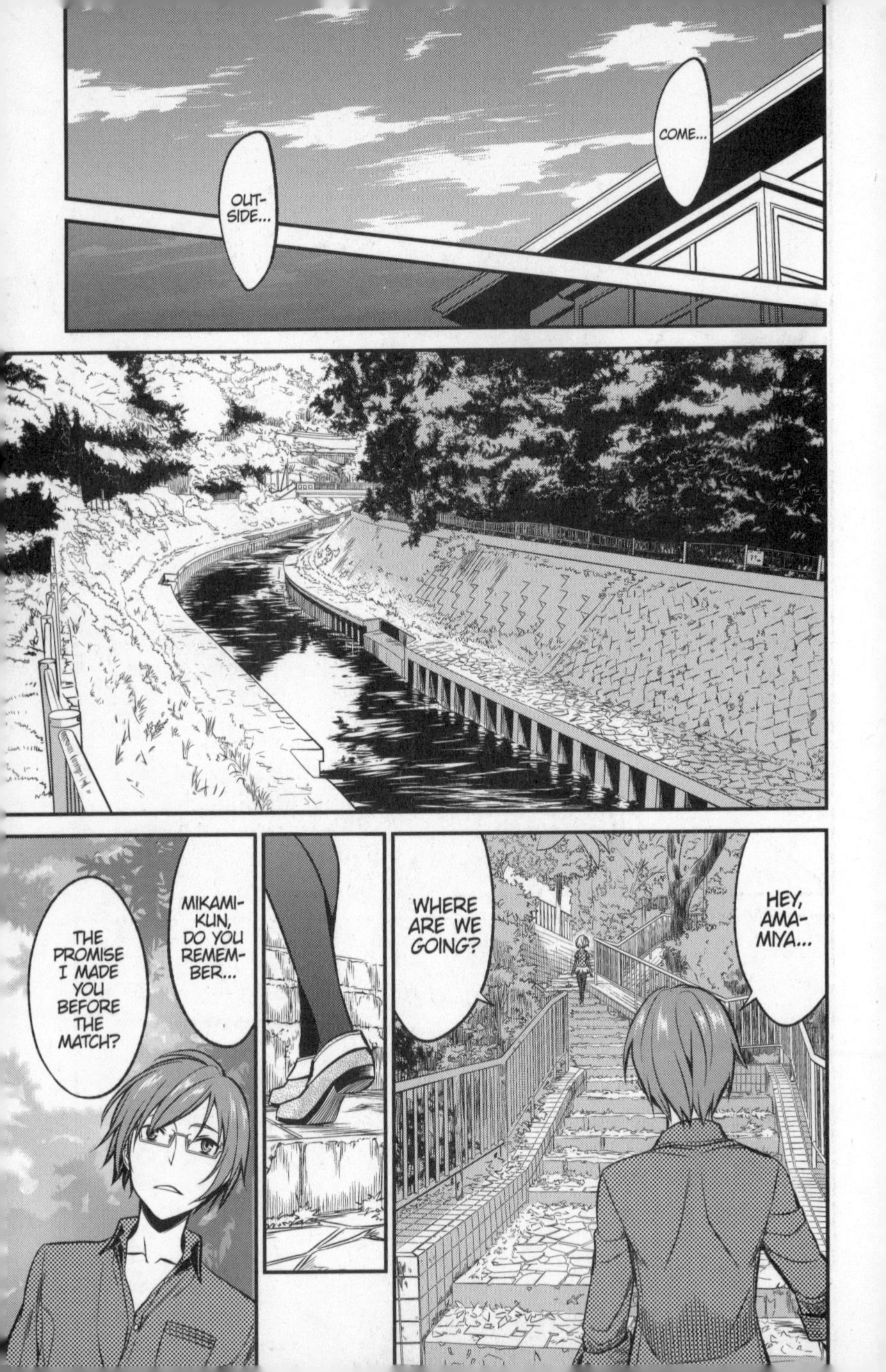
COME...
OUTSIDE...
HEY, AMAMIYA...
WHERE ARE WE GOING?
MIKAMI-KUN, DO YOU REMEMBER...
THE PROMISE I MADE YOU BEFORE THE MATCH?

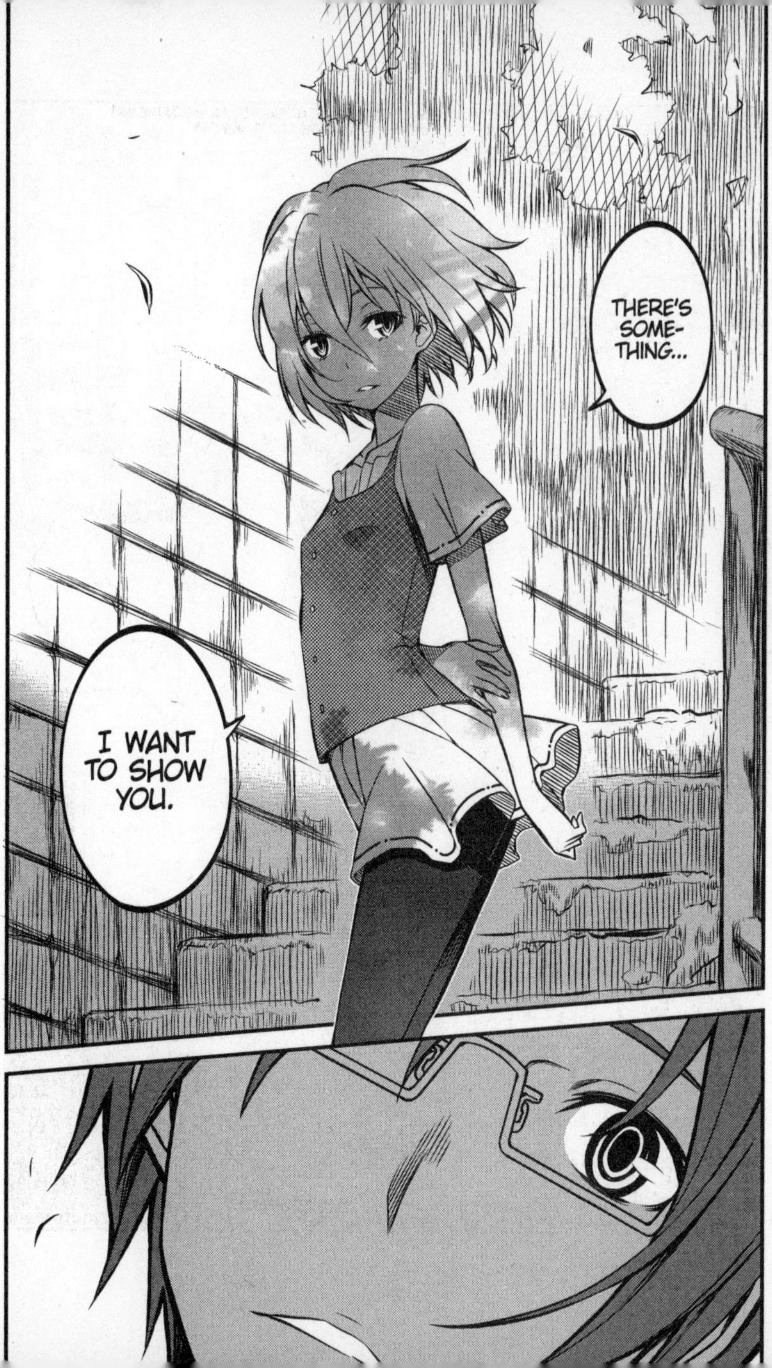
THERE'S SOME-THING...
I WANT TO SHOW YOU.

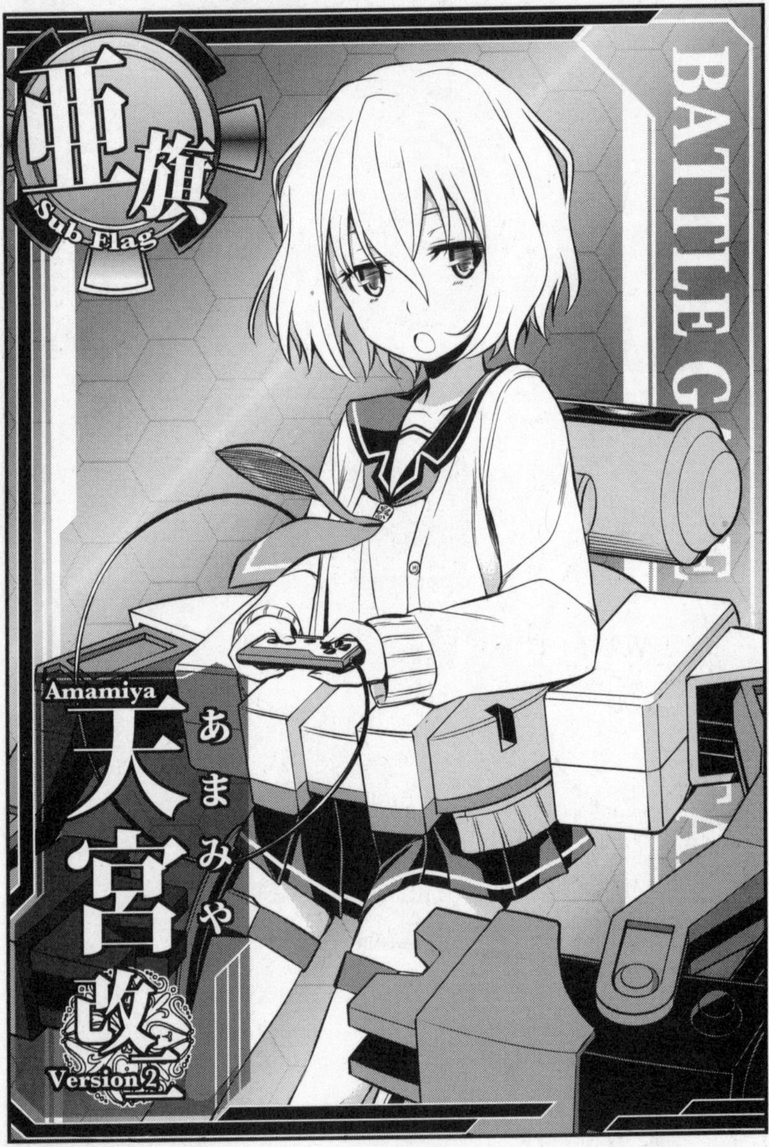
亜旗
Sub-Flag
BATTLE
Amamiya
あまみや
天宮改
Version 2

CHAPTER 25

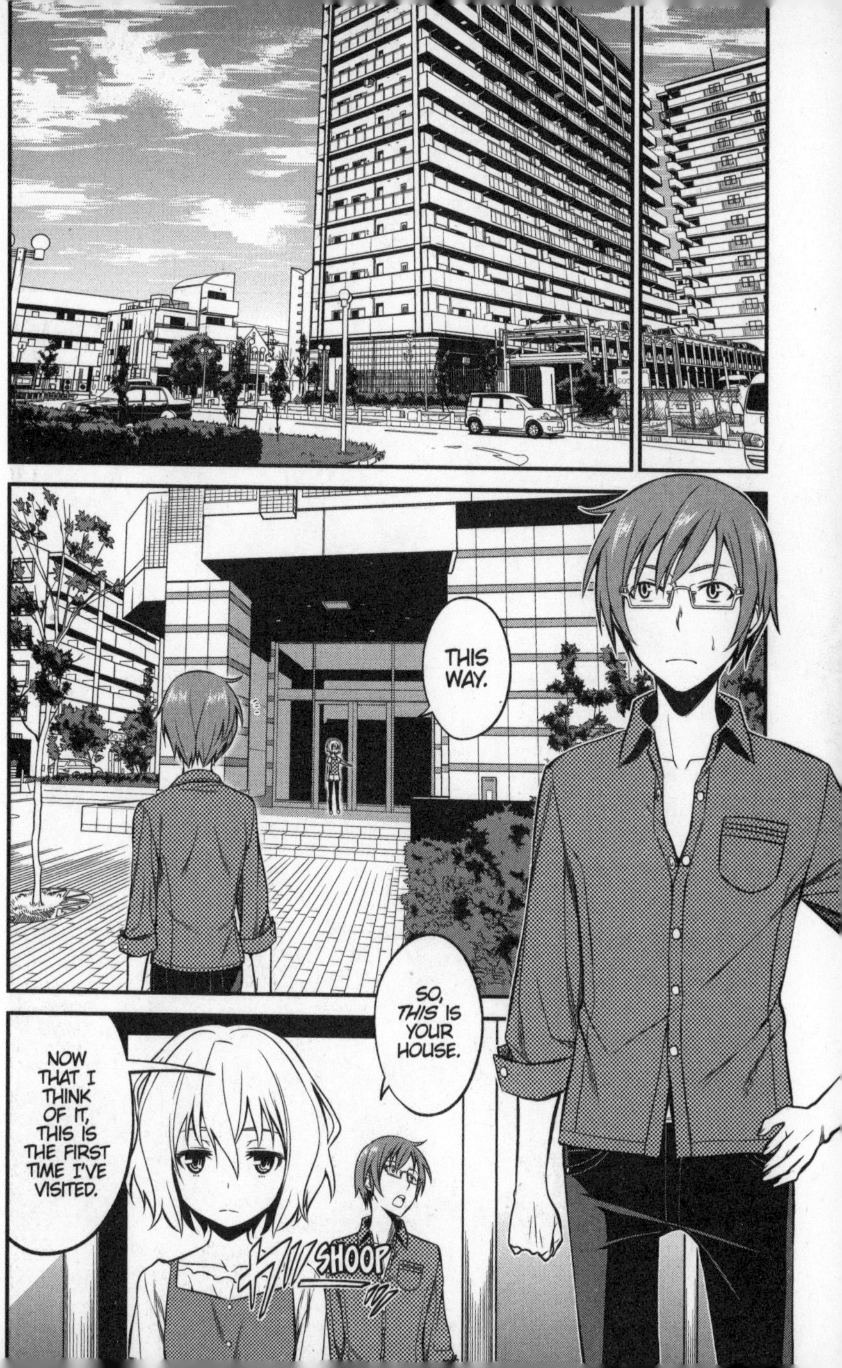
THIS WAY.
SO, *THIS* IS YOUR HOUSE.
NOW THAT I THINK OF IT, THIS IS THE FIRST TIME I'VE VISITED.
SHOOP

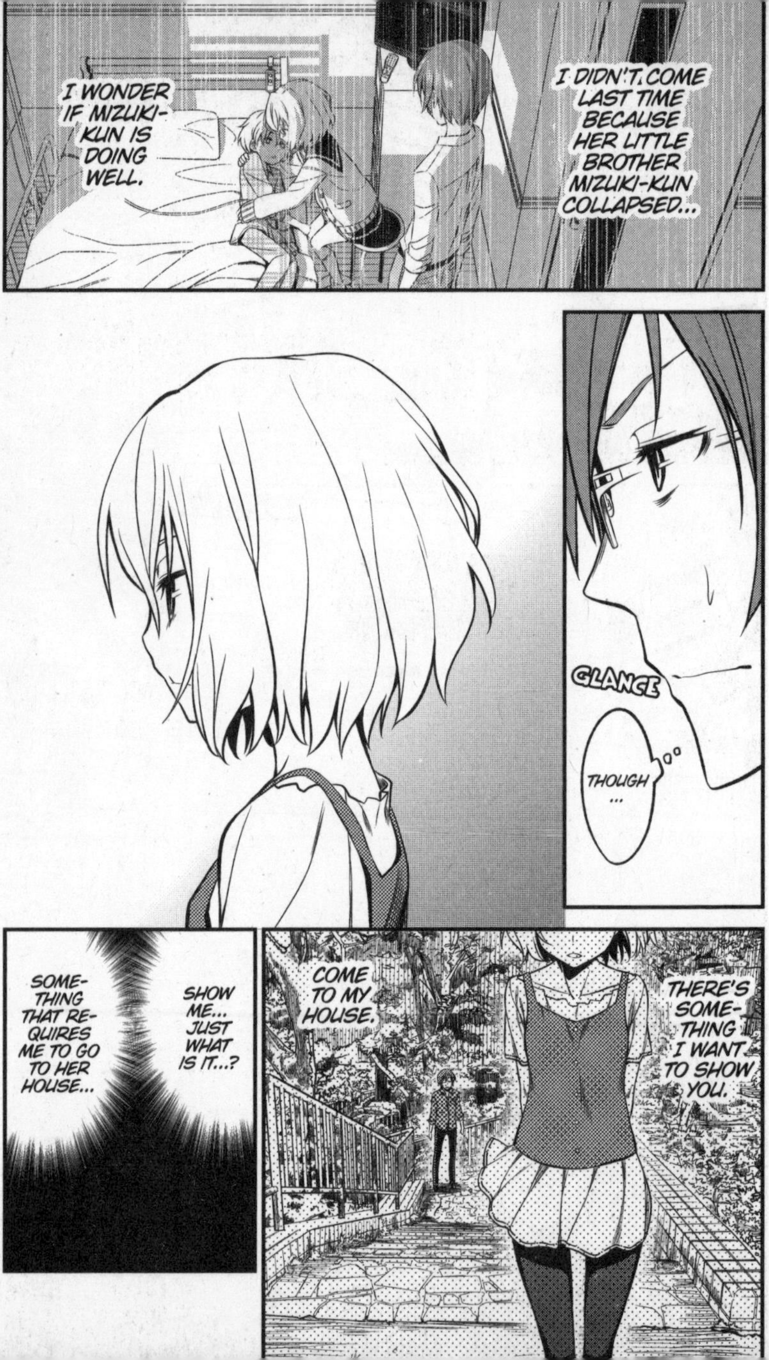
I DIDN'T COME LAST TIME BECAUSE HER LITTLE BROTHER MIZUKI-KUN COLLAPSED...
I WONDER IF MIZUKI-KUN IS DOING WELL.
GLANCE
THOUGH...
THERE'S SOME-THING I WANT TO SHOW YOU.
COME TO MY HOUSE.
SHOW ME... JUST WHAT IS IT...?
SOME-THING THAT RE-QUIRES ME TO GO TO HER HOUSE...

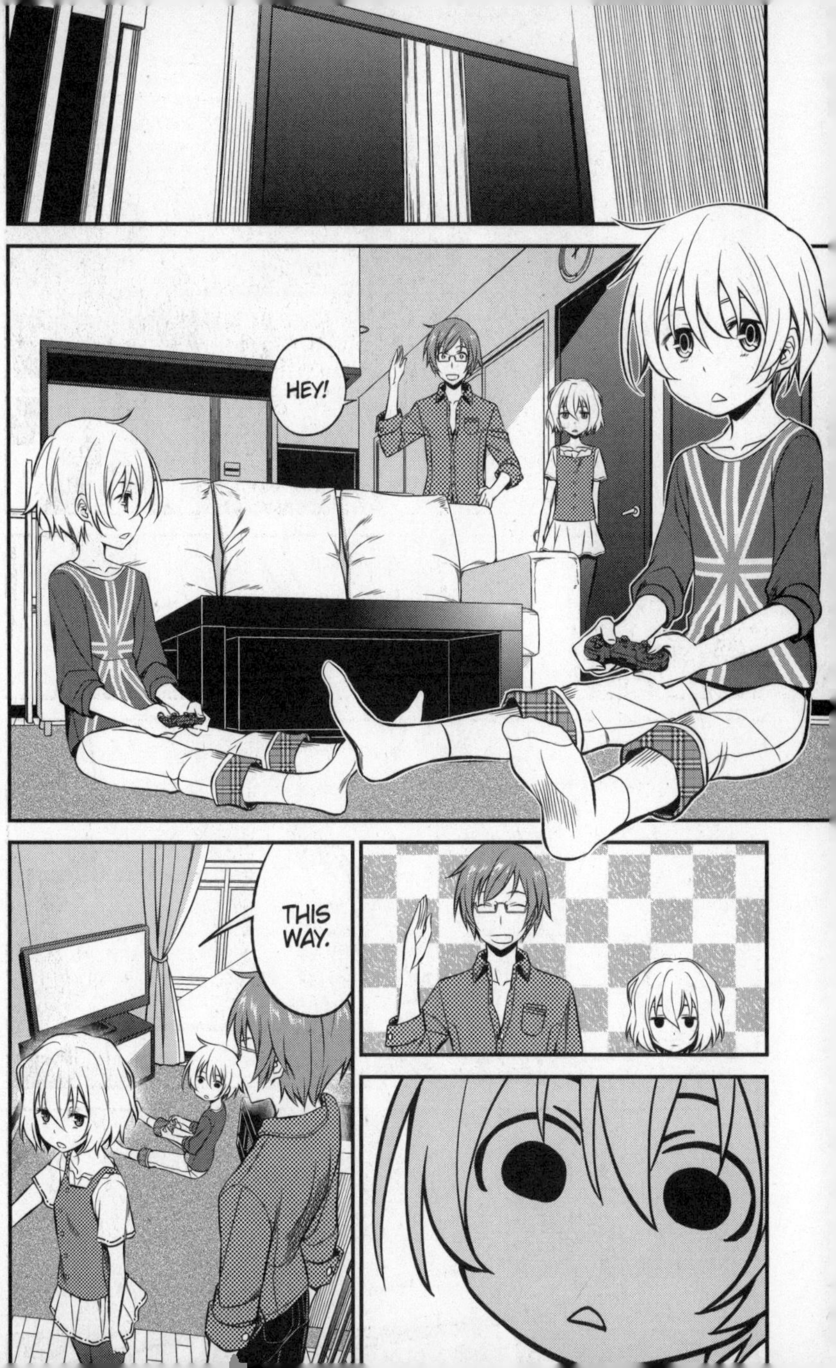
HEY!
THIS WAY.

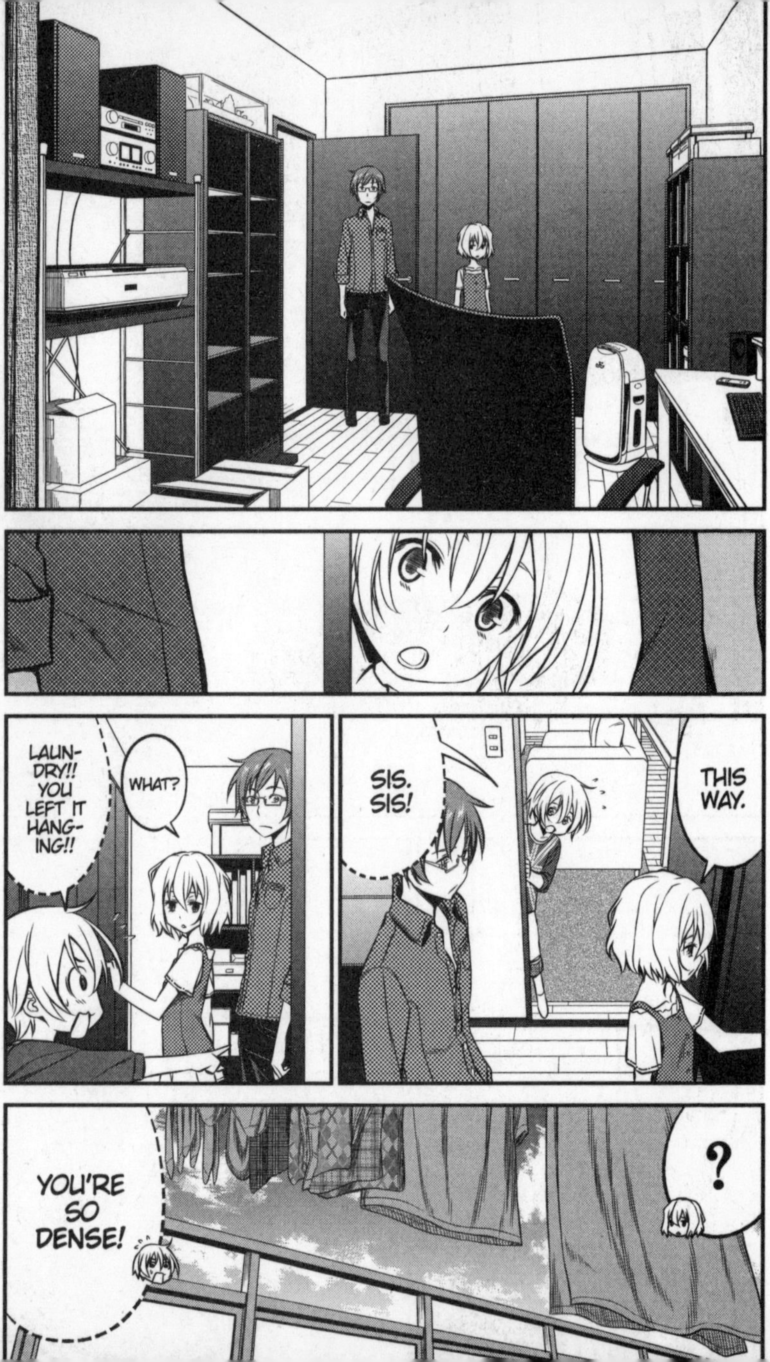
THIS WAY.
SIS. SIS!
WHAT?
LAUNDRY!! YOU LEFT IT HANGING!!
?
YOU'RE SO DENSE!

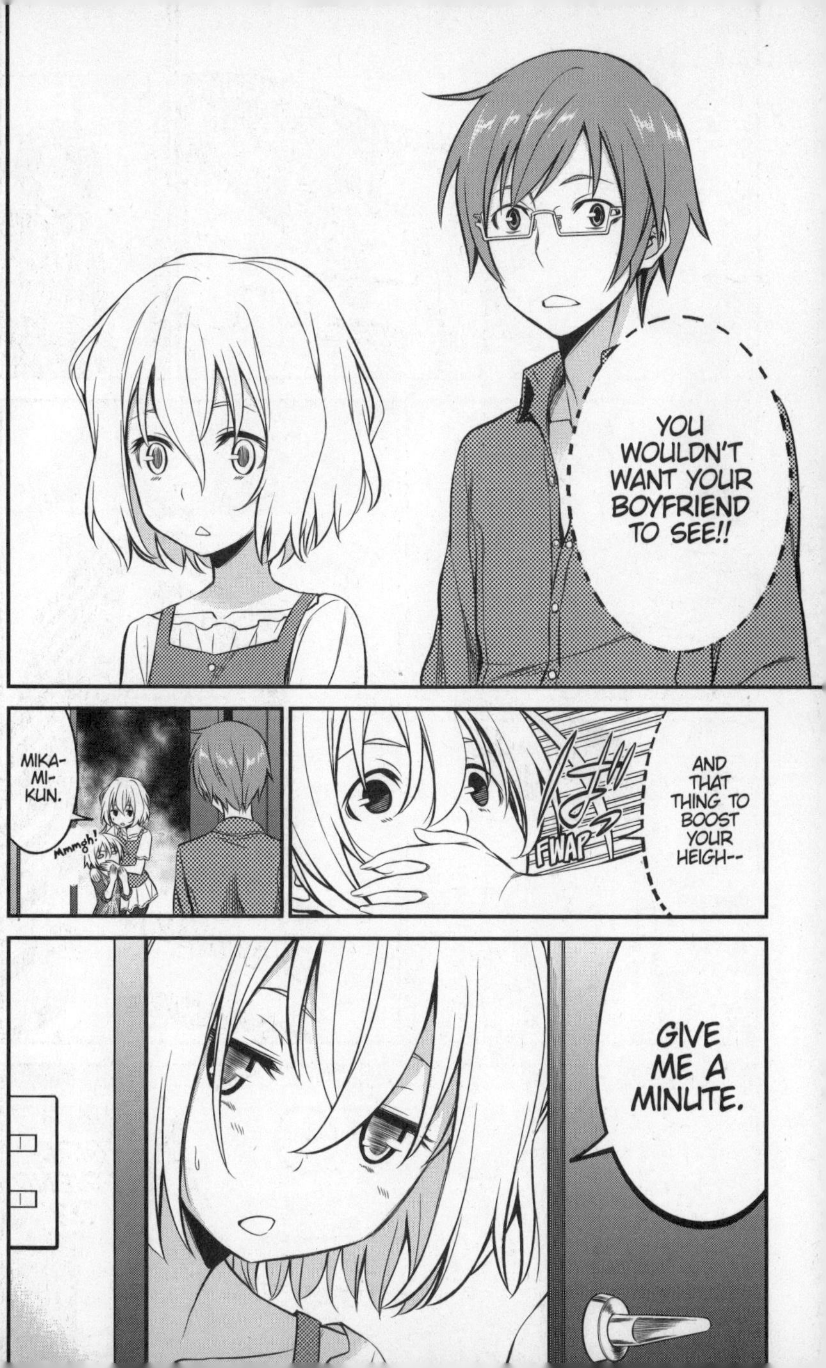
YOU WOULDN'T WANT YOUR BOYFRIEND TO SEE!!
AND THAT THING TO BOOST YOUR HEIGH--
FWAP
MIKA-MI-KUN.
Mmmgh!
GIVE ME A MINUTE.

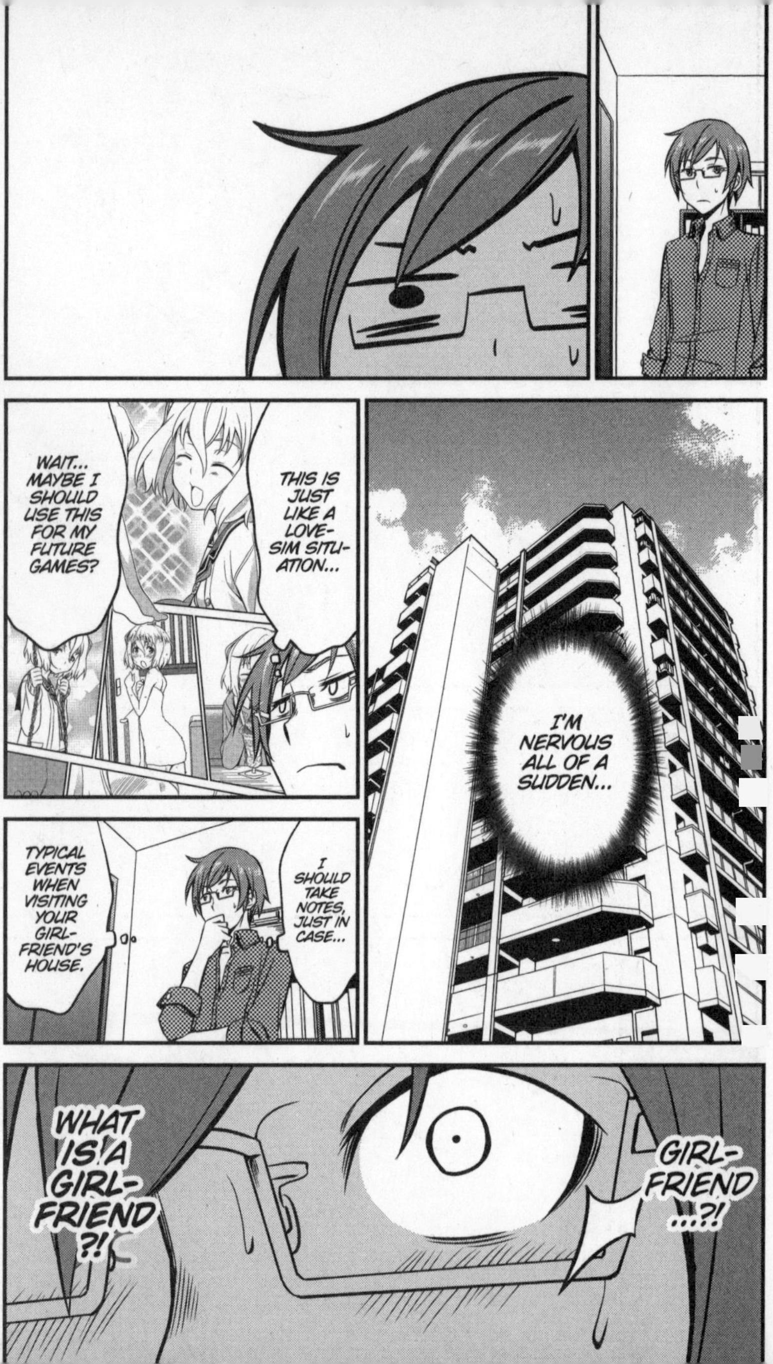
I'M NERVOUS ALL OF A SUDDEN...
THIS IS JUST LIKE A LOVE-SIM SITUATION...
WAIT... MAYBE I SHOULD USE THIS FOR MY FUTURE GAMES?
I SHOULD TAKE NOTES, JUST IN CASE...
TYPICAL EVENTS WHEN VISITING YOUR GIRLFRIEND'S HOUSE.
GIRLFRIEND...?!
WHAT IS A GIRLFRIEND?!

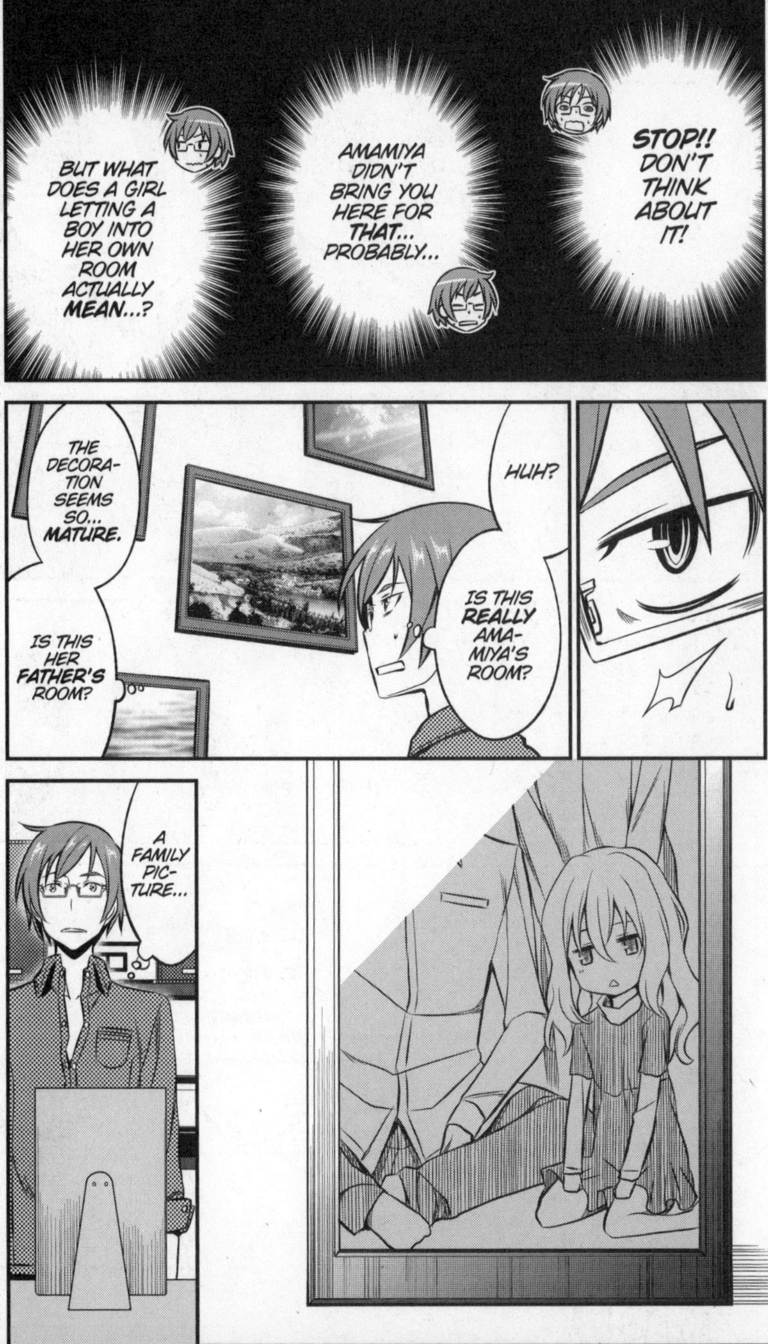
STOP!! DON'T THINK ABOUT IT!
AMAMIYA DIDN'T BRING YOU HERE FOR THAT... PROBABLY...
BUT WHAT DOES A GIRL LETTING A BOY INTO HER OWN ROOM ACTUALLY MEAN...?
HUH?
IS THIS REALLY AMA-MIYA'S ROOM?
THE DECORA-TION SEEMS SO... MATURE.
IS THIS HER FATHER'S ROOM?
A FAMILY PIC-TURE...

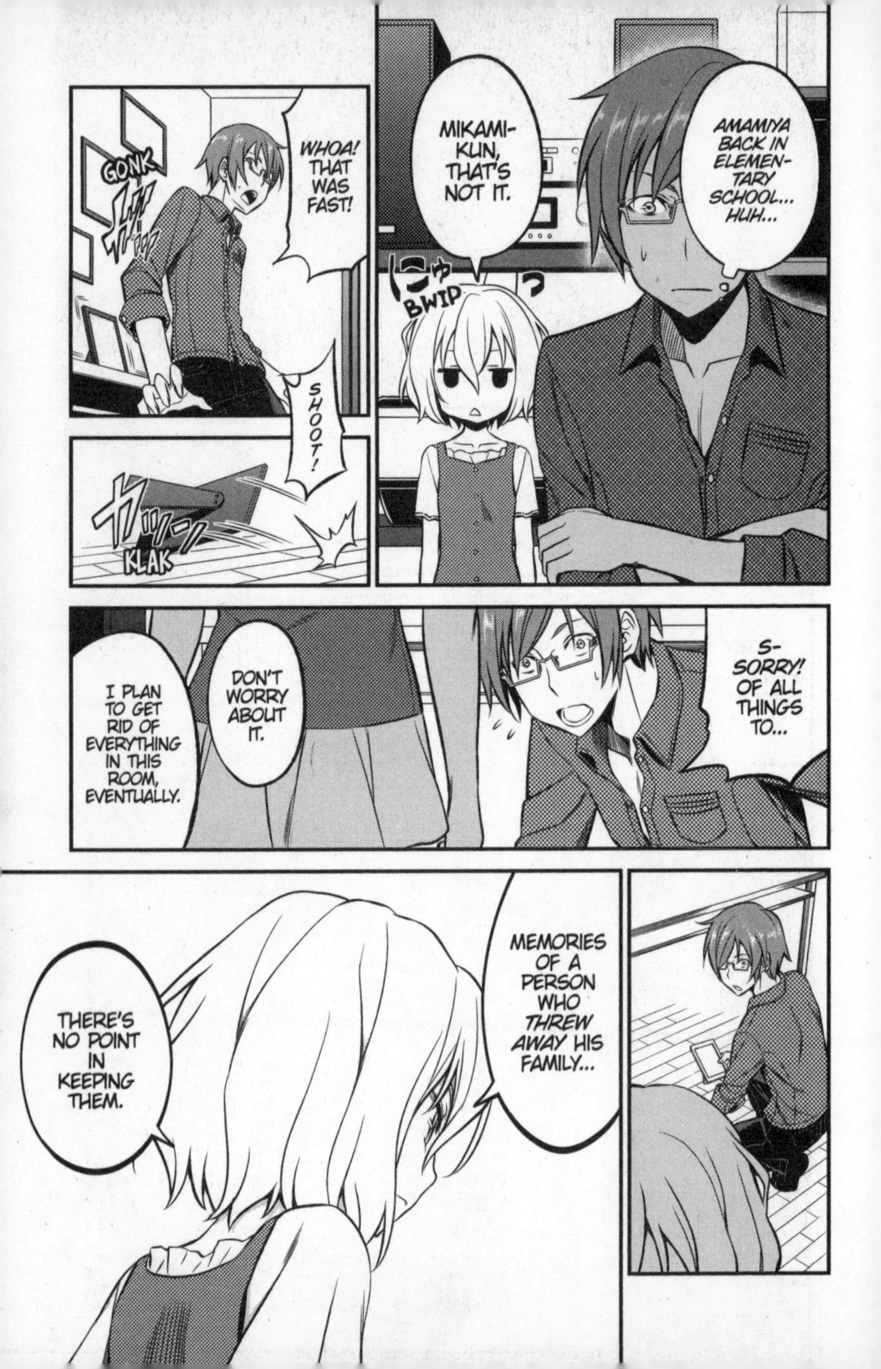
AMAMIYA BACK IN ELEMENTARY SCHOOL... HUH...
MIKAMI-KUN, THAT'S NOT IT.
BWIP
GONK
WHOA! THAT WAS FAST!
SHOOT!
KLAK
S-SORRY! OF ALL THINGS TO...
DON'T WORRY ABOUT IT.
I PLAN TO GET RID OF EVERYTHING IN THIS ROOM, EVENTUALLY.
MEMORIES OF A PERSON WHO *THREW AWAY* HIS FAMILY...
THERE'S NO POINT IN KEEPING THEM.

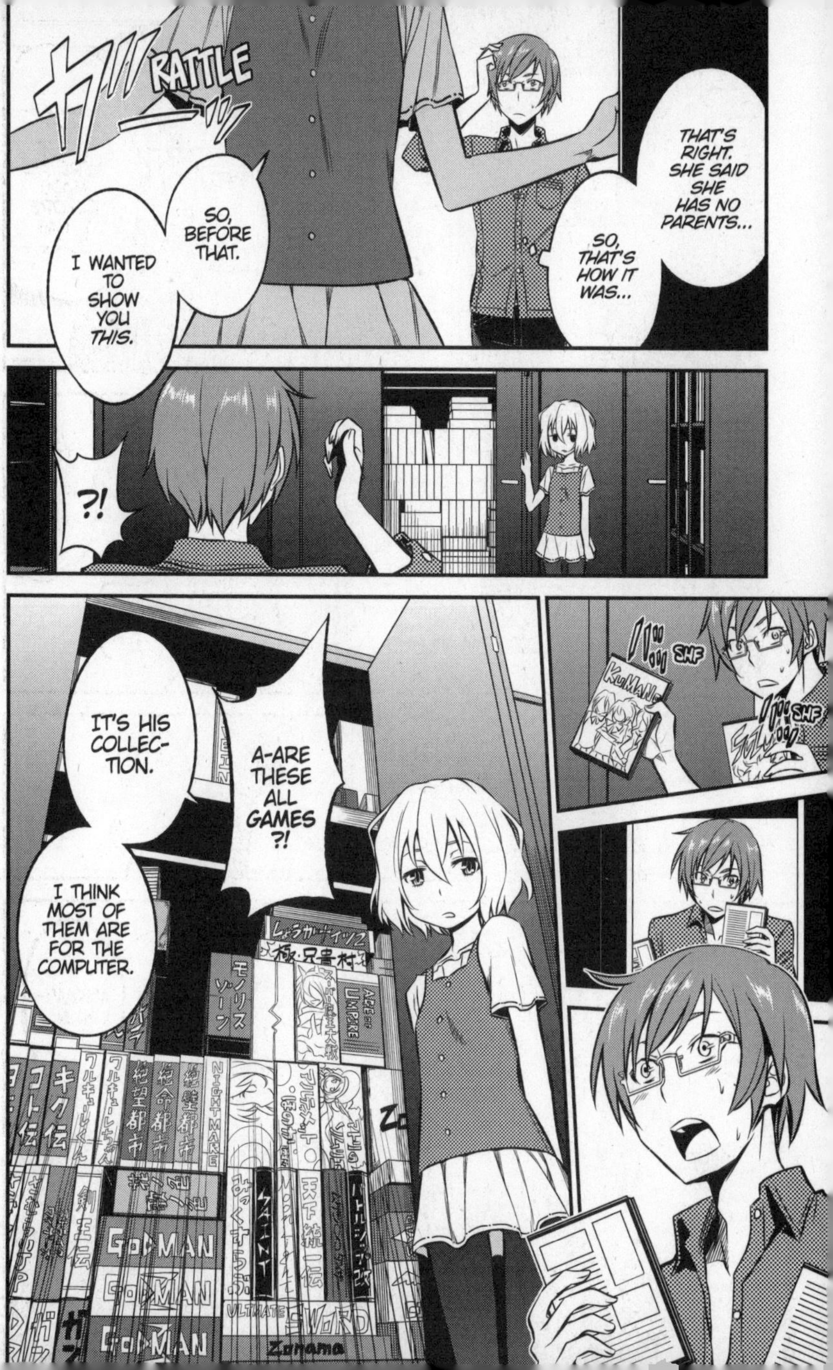
RATTLE
THAT'S RIGHT. SHE SAID SHE HAS NO PARENTS...
SO, THAT'S HOW IT WAS...
SO, BEFORE THAT.
I WANTED TO SHOW YOU THIS.
?!
SHF
SHF
A-ARE THESE ALL GAMES?!
IT'S HIS COLLECTION.
I THINK MOST OF THEM ARE FOR THE COMPUTER.
NIGHTMARE
GoDMAN
GoDMAN
GoDMAN
ULTIMATE SWORD
Zanama

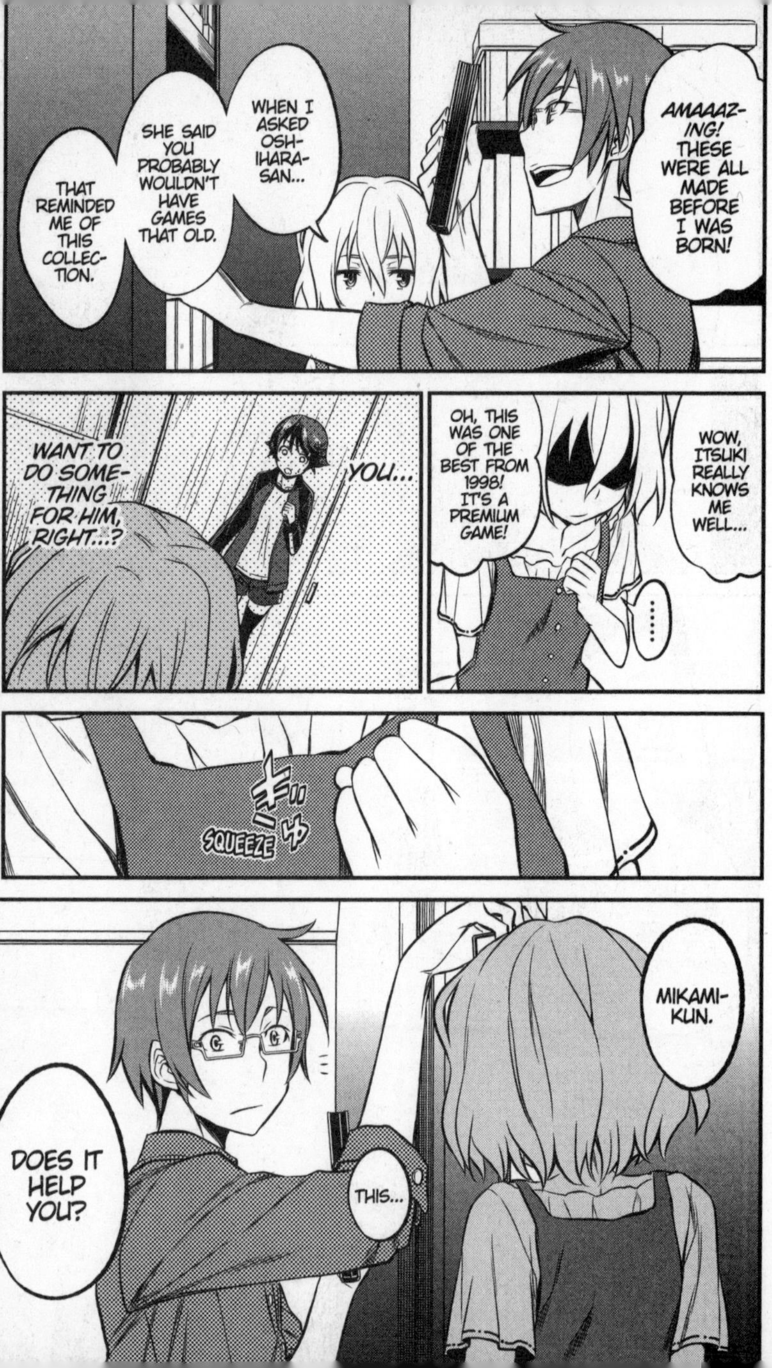
AMAAAZ-ING! THESE WERE ALL MADE BEFORE I WAS BORN!
WHEN I ASKED OSH-IHARA-SAN...
SHE SAID YOU PROBABLY WOULDN'T HAVE GAMES THAT OLD.
THAT REMINDED ME OF THIS COLLEC-TION.
WOW, ITSUKI REALLY KNOWS ME WELL...
OH, THIS WAS ONE OF THE BEST FROM 1998! IT'S A PREMIUM GAME!
......
YOU...
WANT TO DO SOME-THING FOR HIM, RIGHT...?
SQUEEZE
MIKAMI-KUN.
THIS...
DOES IT HELP YOU?

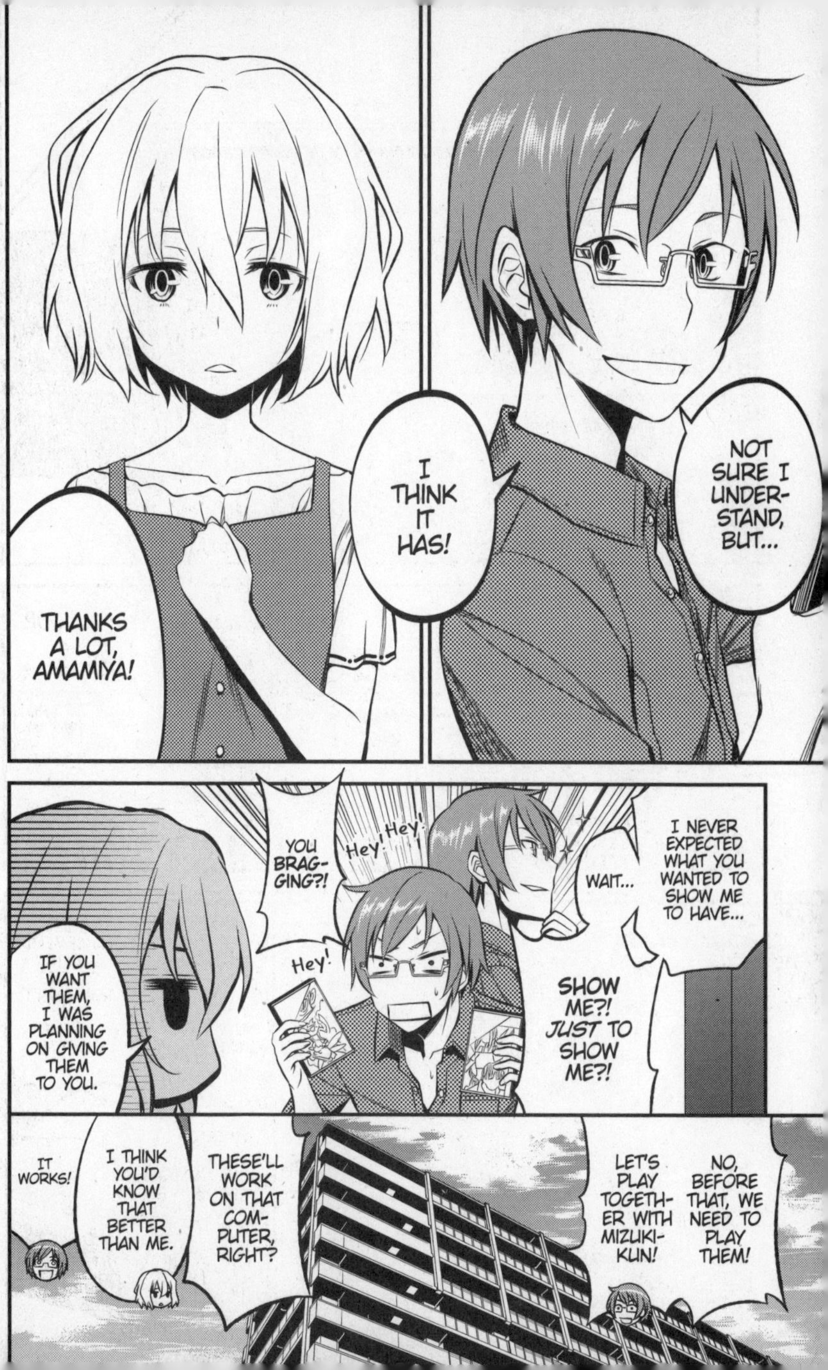
NOT SURE I UNDERSTAND, BUT...
I THINK IT HAS!
THANKS A LOT, AMAMIYA!
I NEVER EXPECTED WHAT YOU WANTED TO SHOW ME TO HAVE...
WAIT...
SHOW ME?! JUST TO SHOW ME?!
Hey! Hey!
Hey!
YOU BRAGGING?!
IF YOU WANT THEM, I WAS PLANNING ON GIVING THEM TO YOU.
NO, BEFORE THAT, WE NEED TO PLAY THEM!
LET'S PLAY TOGETHER WITH MIZUKI-KUN!
THESE'LL WORK ON THAT COMPUTER, RIGHT?
I THINK YOU'D KNOW THAT BETTER THAN ME.
IT WORKS!

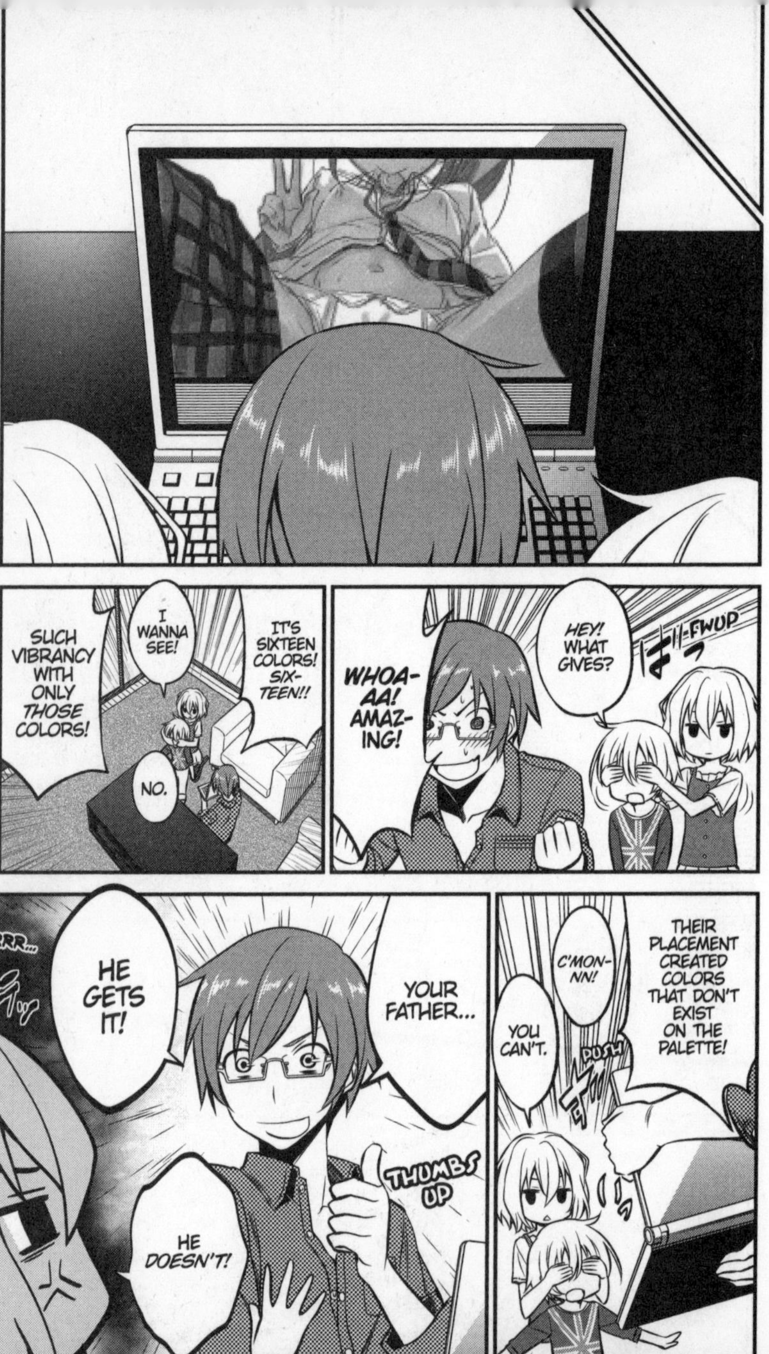
FWUP
HEY! WHAT GIVES?
WHOAA-AA! AMAZ-ING!
IT'S SIXTEEN COLORS! SIX-TEEN!!
I WANNA SEE!
SUCH VIBRANCY WITH ONLY THOSE COLORS!
NO.
THEIR PLACEMENT CREATED COLORS THAT DON'T EXIST ON THE PALETTE!
C'MON-NN!
PUSH
YOU CAN'T.
YOUR FATHER...
HE GETS IT!
GRRR...
THUMBS UP
HE DOESN'T!

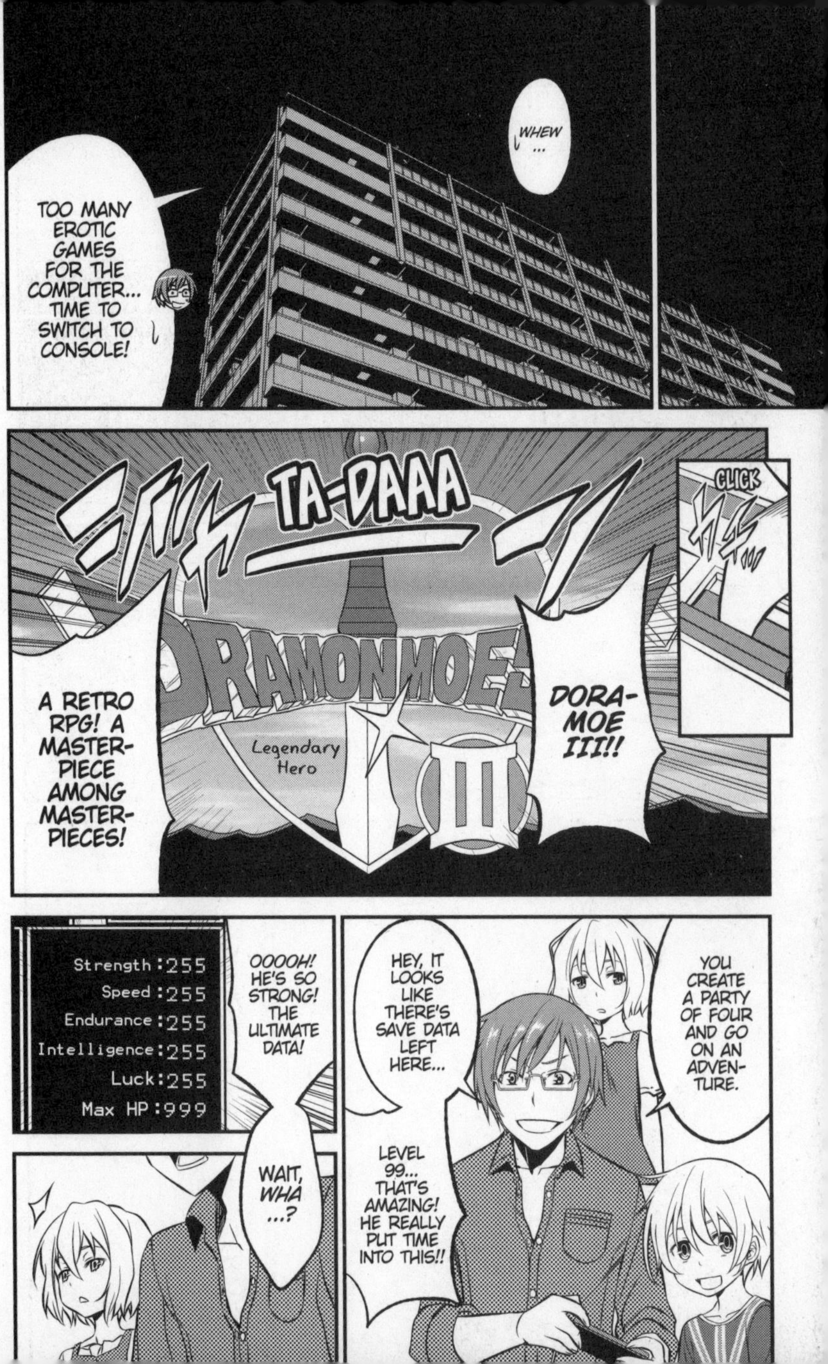
WHEW ...
TOO MANY EROTIC GAMES FOR THE COMPUTER... TIME TO SWITCH TO CONSOLE!
CLICK
TA-DAAA
DRAMONMOE
Legendary Hero
III
DORA-MOE III!!
A RETRO RPG! A MASTER-PIECE AMONG MASTER-PIECES!
YOU CREATE A PARTY OF FOUR AND GO ON AN ADVEN-TURE.
HEY, IT LOOKS LIKE THERE'S SAVE DATA LEFT HERE...
LEVEL 99... THAT'S AMAZING! HE REALLY PUT TIME INTO THIS!!
OOOOH! HE'S SO STRONG! THE ULTIMATE DATA!
Strength:255
Speed:255
Endurance:255
Intelligence:255
Luck:255
Max HP:999
WAIT, WHA ...?

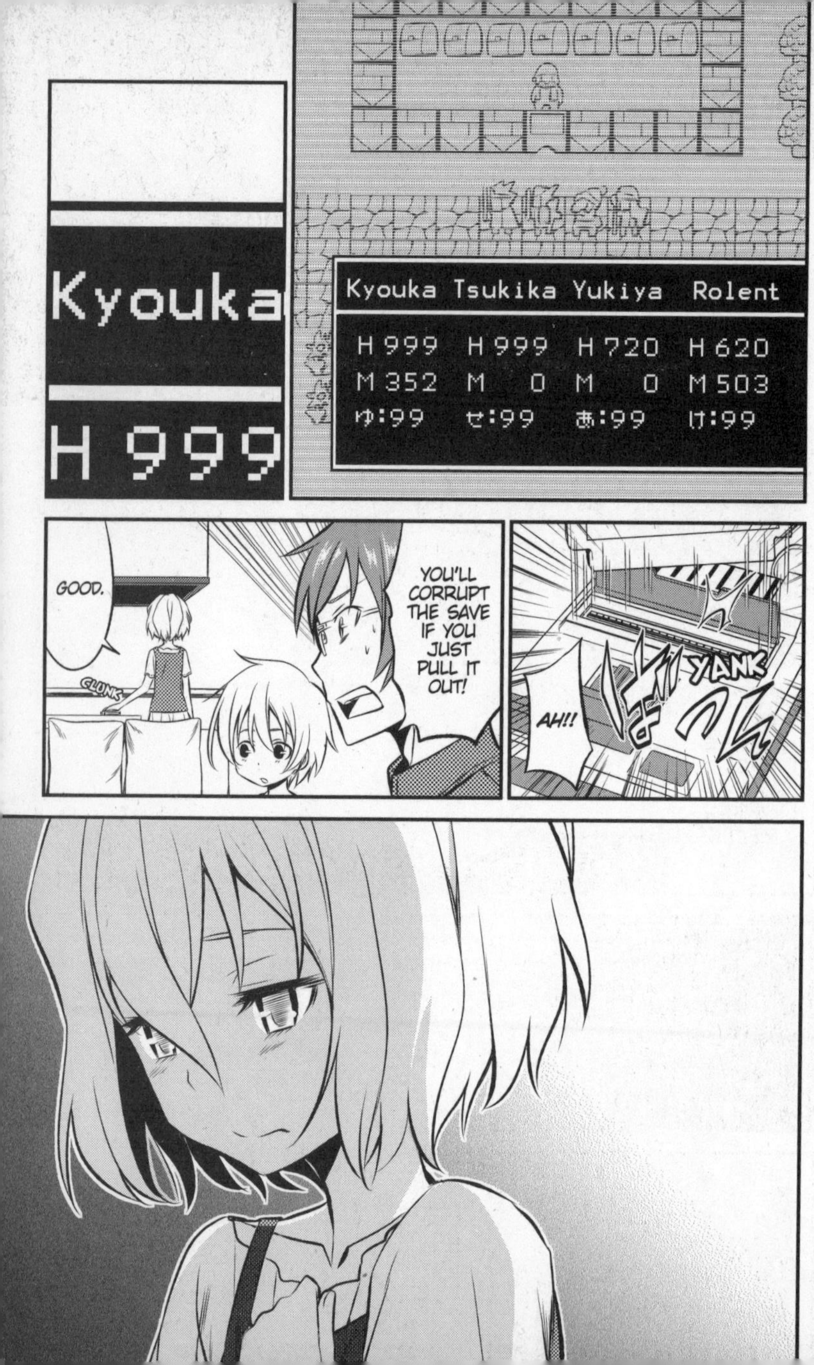
Kyouka Tsukika Yukiya Rolent
H 999 H 999 H 720 H 620
M 352 M 0 M 0 M 503
ゆ:99 せ:99 あ:99 け:99
Kyouka
H 999
AH!!
YANK
YOU'LL CORRUPT THE SAVE IF YOU JUST PULL IT OUT!
GOOD.
CLUNK

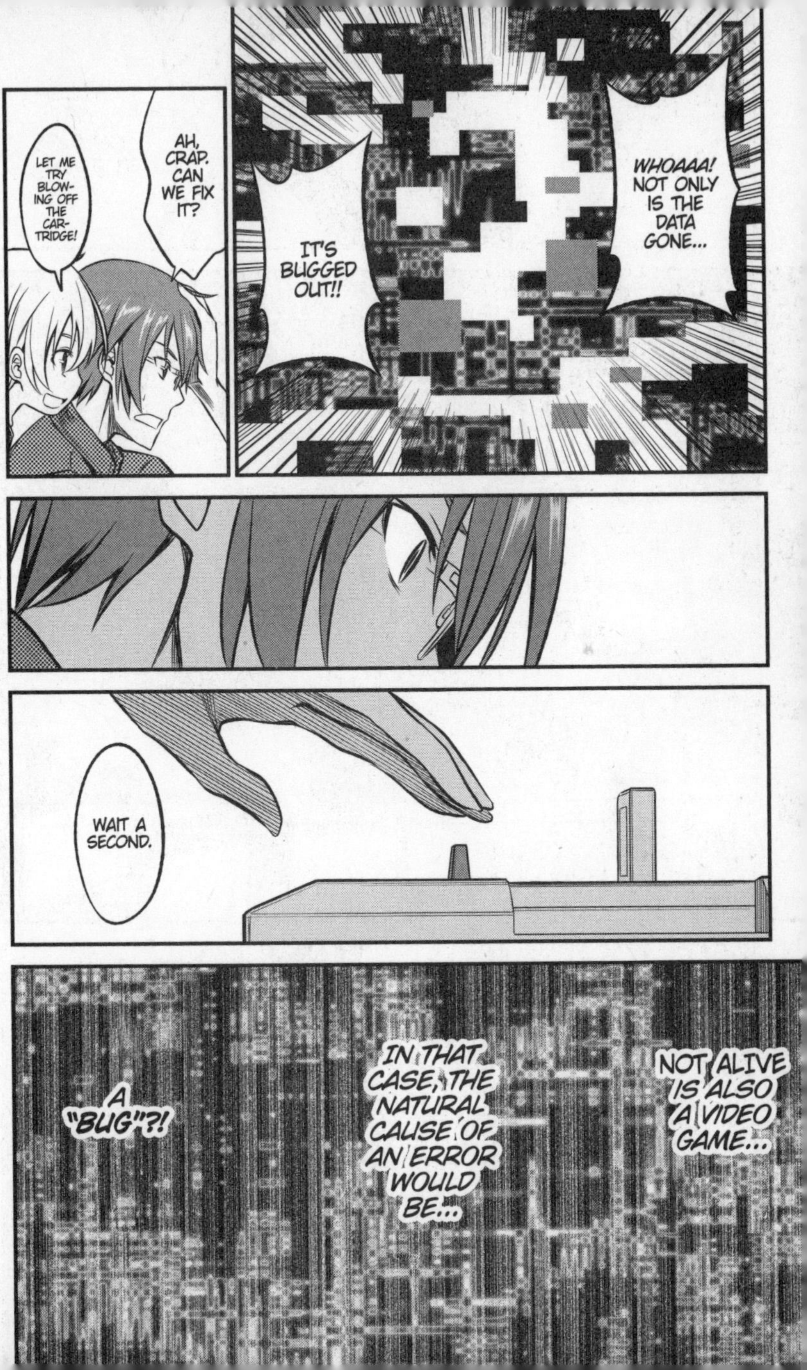
WHOAAA! NOT ONLY IS THE DATA GONE...
IT'S BUGGED OUT!!
AH, CRAP. CAN WE FIX IT?
LET ME TRY BLOW-ING OFF THE CAR-TRIDGE!
WAIT A SECOND.
NOT ALIVE IS ALSO A VIDEO GAME...
IN THAT CASE, THE NATURAL CAUSE OF AN ERROR WOULD BE...
A "BUG"?!

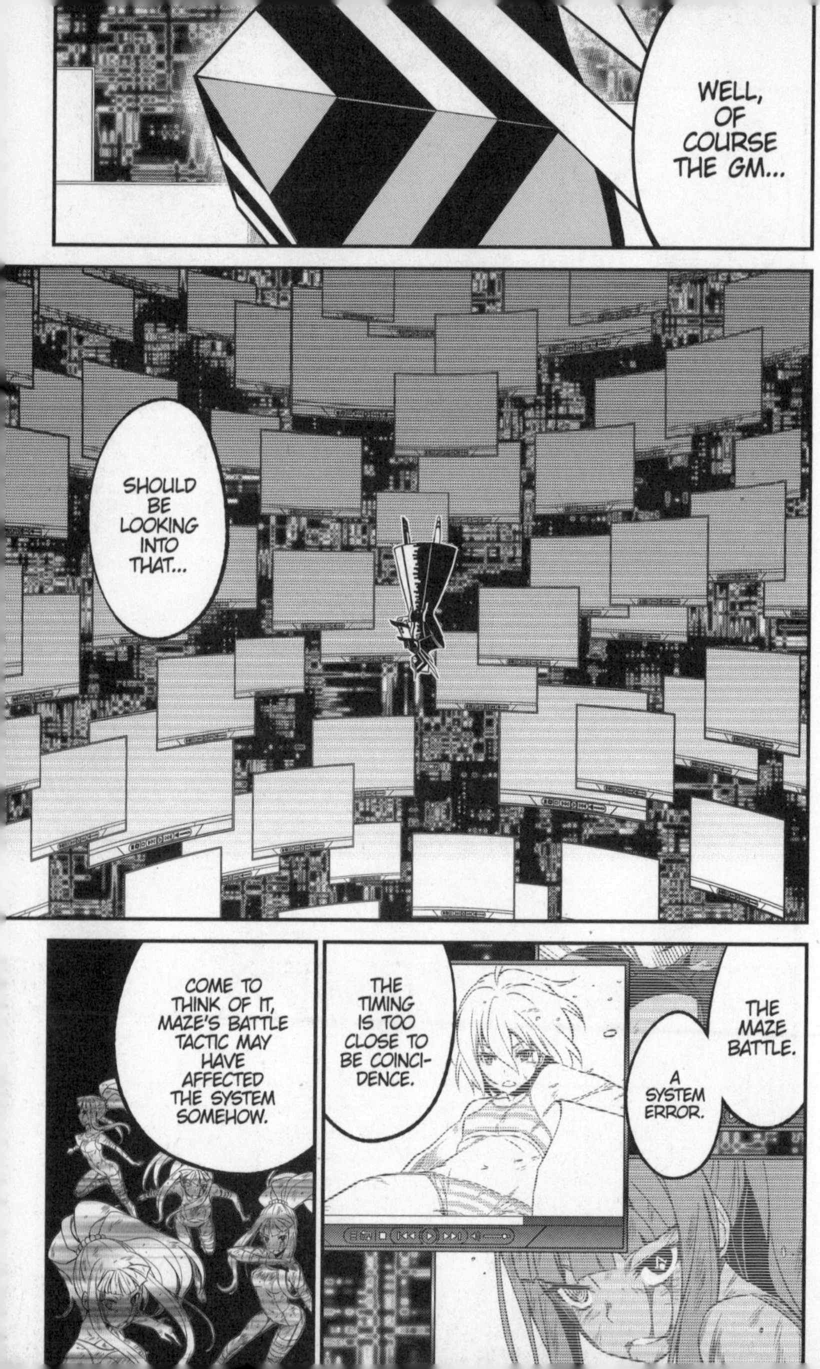
WELL, OF COURSE THE GM...
SHOULD BE LOOKING INTO THAT...
THE MAZE BATTLE.
A SYSTEM ERROR.
THE TIMING IS TOO CLOSE TO BE COINCI-DENCE.
COME TO THINK OF IT, MAZE'S BATTLE TACTIC MAY HAVE AFFECTED THE SYSTEM SOMEHOW.

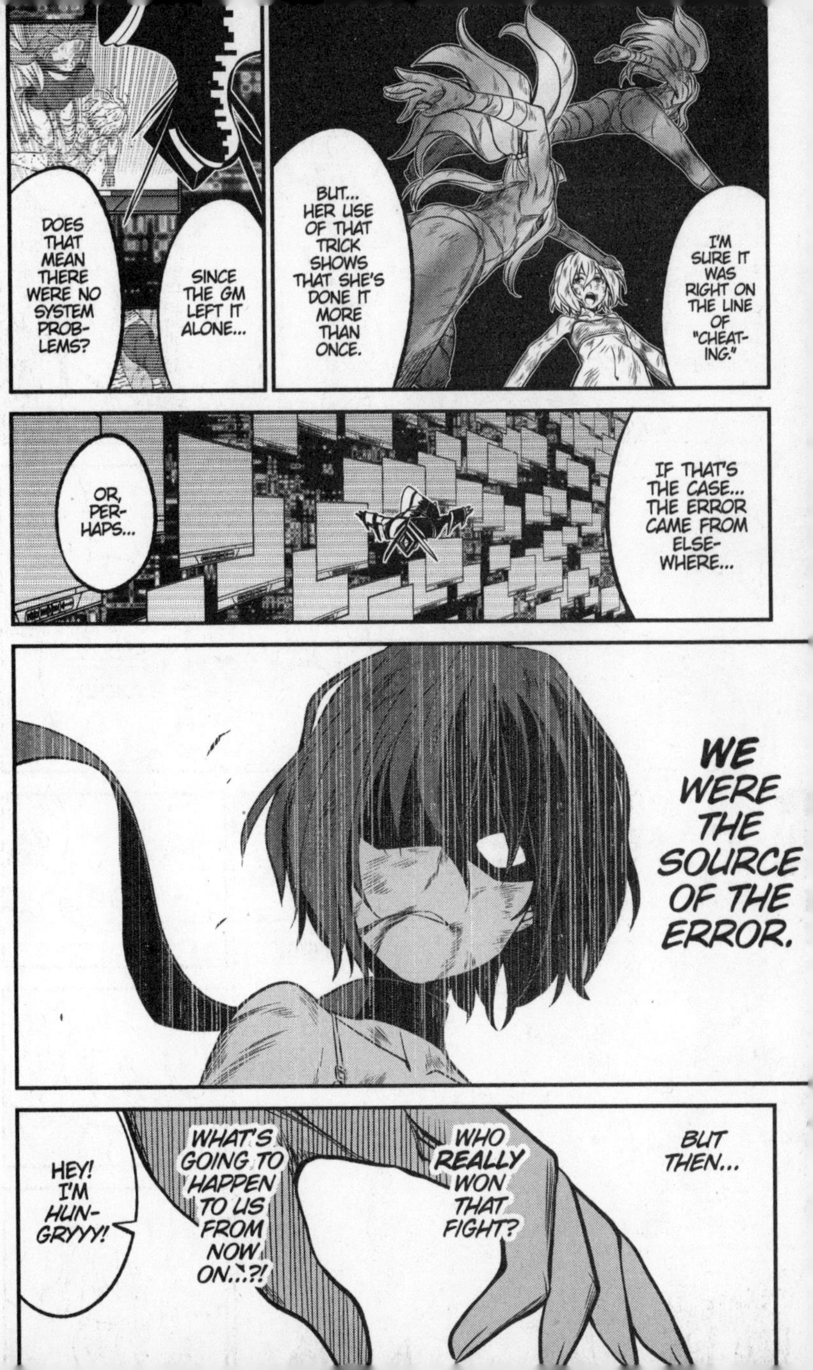
I'M SURE IT WAS RIGHT ON THE LINE OF "CHEATING."
BUT... HER USE OF THAT TRICK SHOWS THAT SHE'S DONE IT MORE THAN ONCE.
SINCE THE GM LEFT IT ALONE...
DOES THAT MEAN THERE WERE NO SYSTEM PROBLEMS?
IF THAT'S THE CASE... THE ERROR CAME FROM ELSEWHERE...
OR, PERHAPS...
WE WERE THE SOURCE OF THE ERROR.
BUT THEN...
WHO REALLY WON THAT FIGHT?
WHAT'S GOING TO HAPPEN TO US FROM NOW ON...?!
HEY! I'M HUNGRYYY!

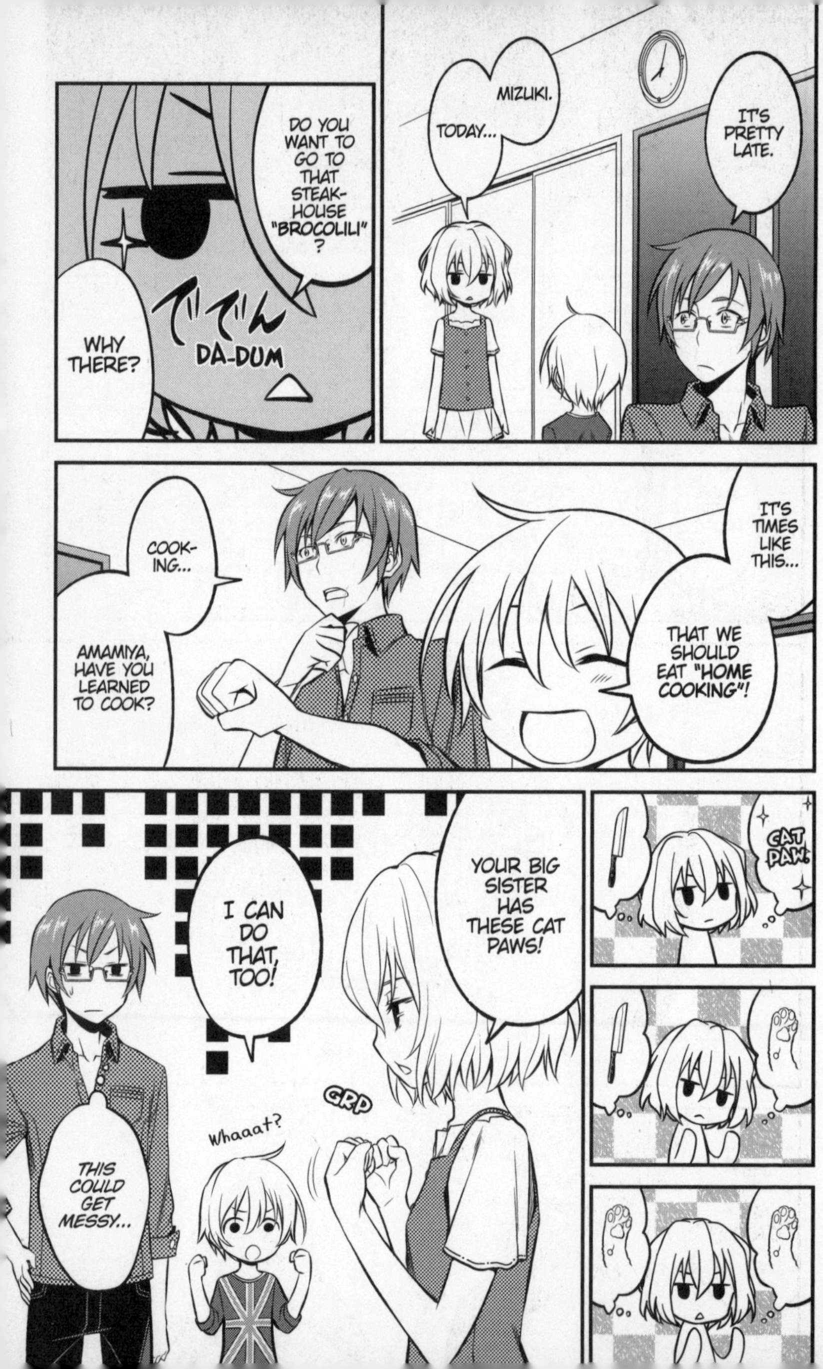
IT'S PRETTY LATE.
MIZUKI.
TODAY...
DO YOU WANT TO GO TO THAT STEAKHOUSE "BROCOLILI"?
ででん
DA-DUM
WHY THERE?
IT'S TIMES LIKE THIS...
THAT WE SHOULD EAT "HOME COOKING"!
COOKING...
AMAMIYA, HAVE YOU LEARNED TO COOK?
CAT PAW.
YOUR BIG SISTER HAS THESE CAT PAWS!
I CAN DO THAT, TOO!
GRP
Whaaat?
THIS COULD GET MESSY...

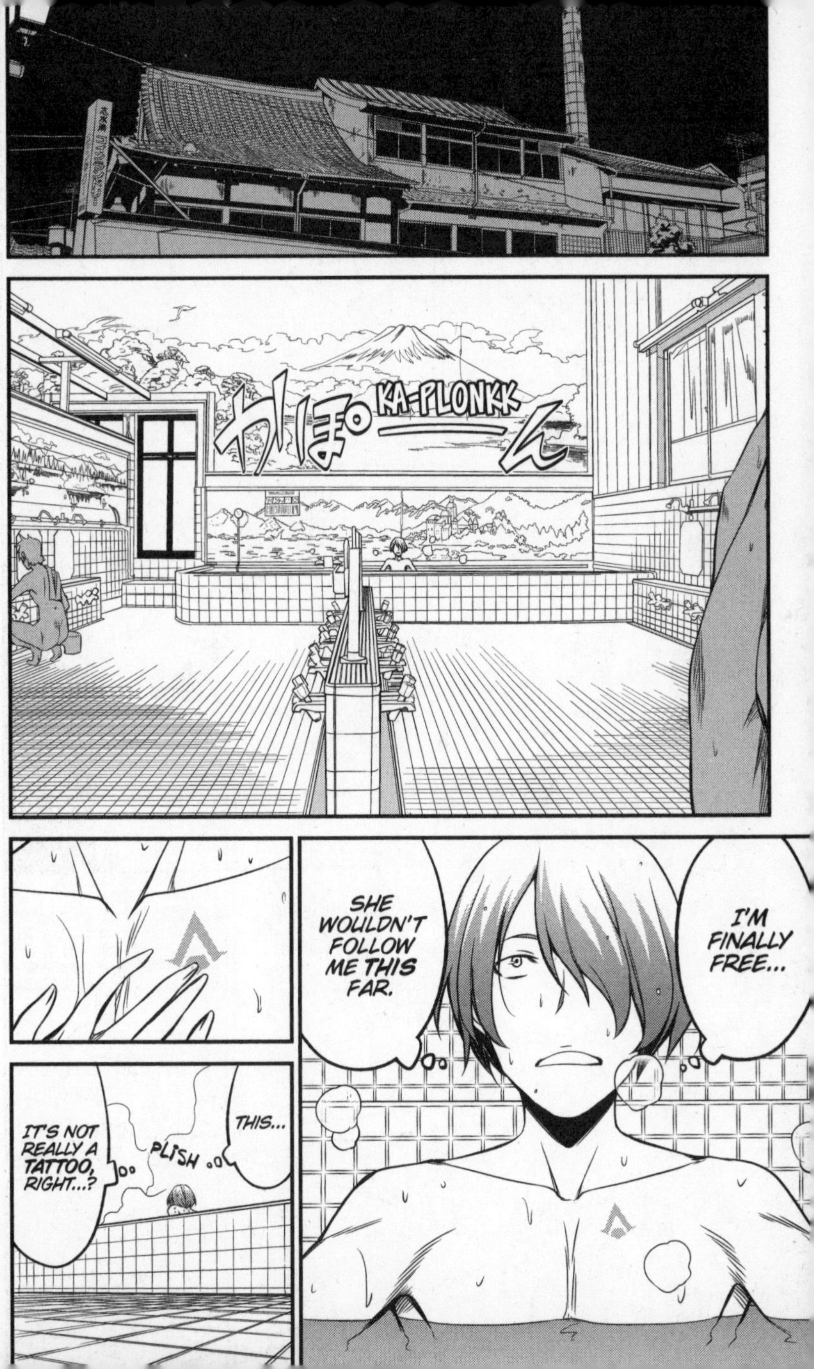
かぽーん
KA-PLONKK
I'M FINALLY FREE...
SHE WOULDN'T FOLLOW ME THIS FAR.
THIS...
PLISH
IT'S NOT REALLY A TATTOO, RIGHT...?

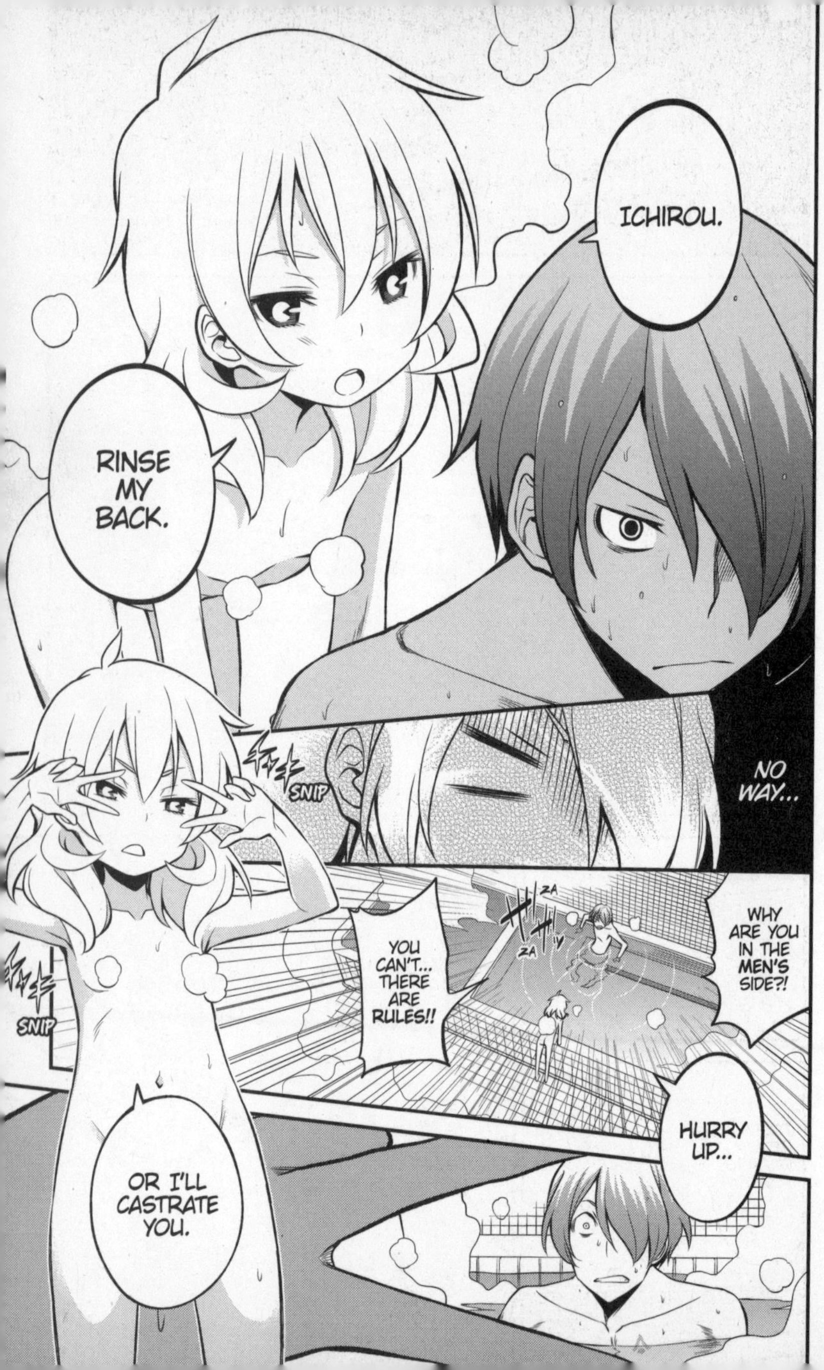
ICHIROU.
RINSE MY BACK.
NO WAY...
WHY ARE YOU IN THE MEN'S SIDE?!
ZA
ZA
YOU CAN'T... THERE ARE RULES!!
HURRY UP...
SNIP
SNIP
OR I'LL CASTRATE YOU.

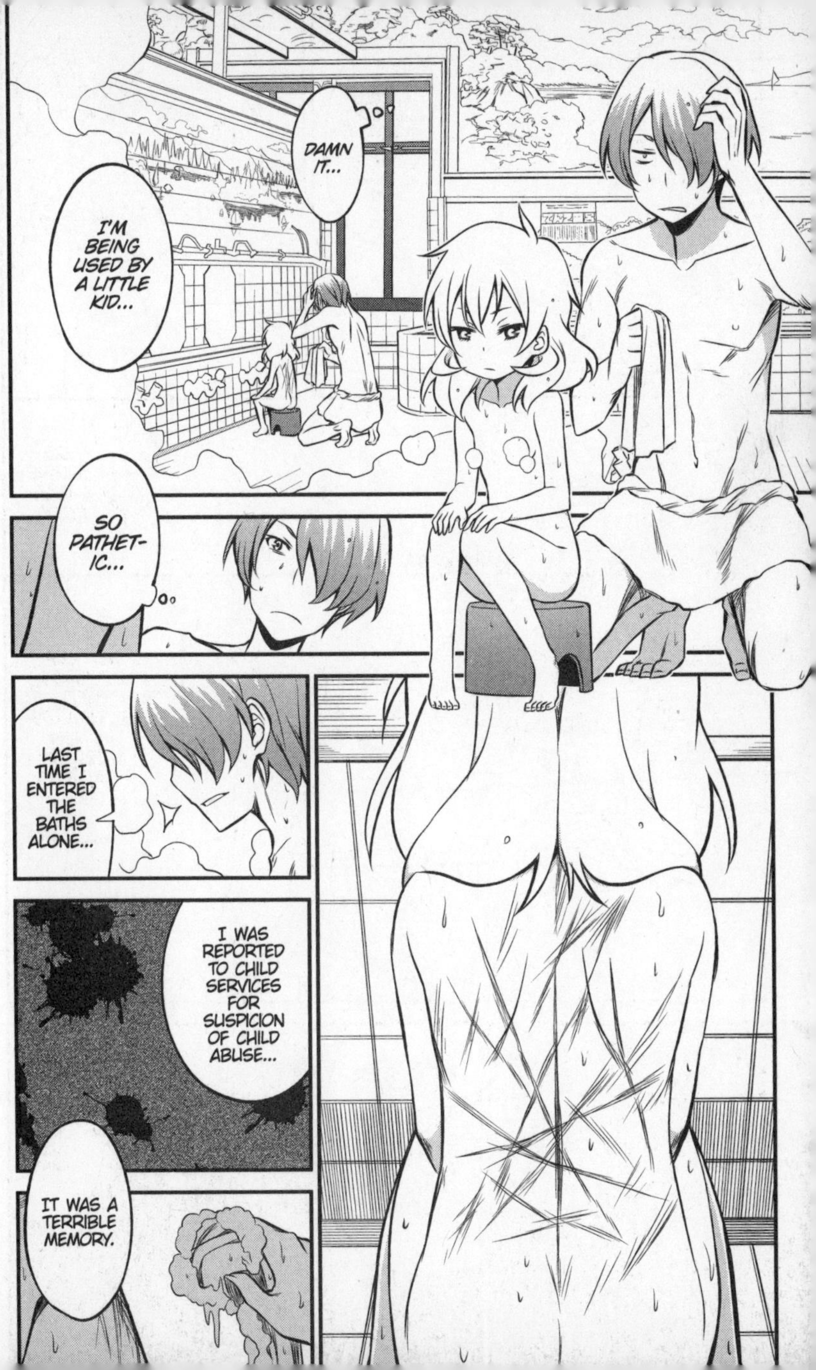
DAMN IT...
I'M BEING USED BY A LITTLE KID...
SO PATHETIC...
LAST TIME I ENTERED THE BATHS ALONE...
I WAS REPORTED TO CHILD SERVICES FOR SUSPICION OF CHILD ABUSE...
IT WAS A TERRIBLE MEMORY.

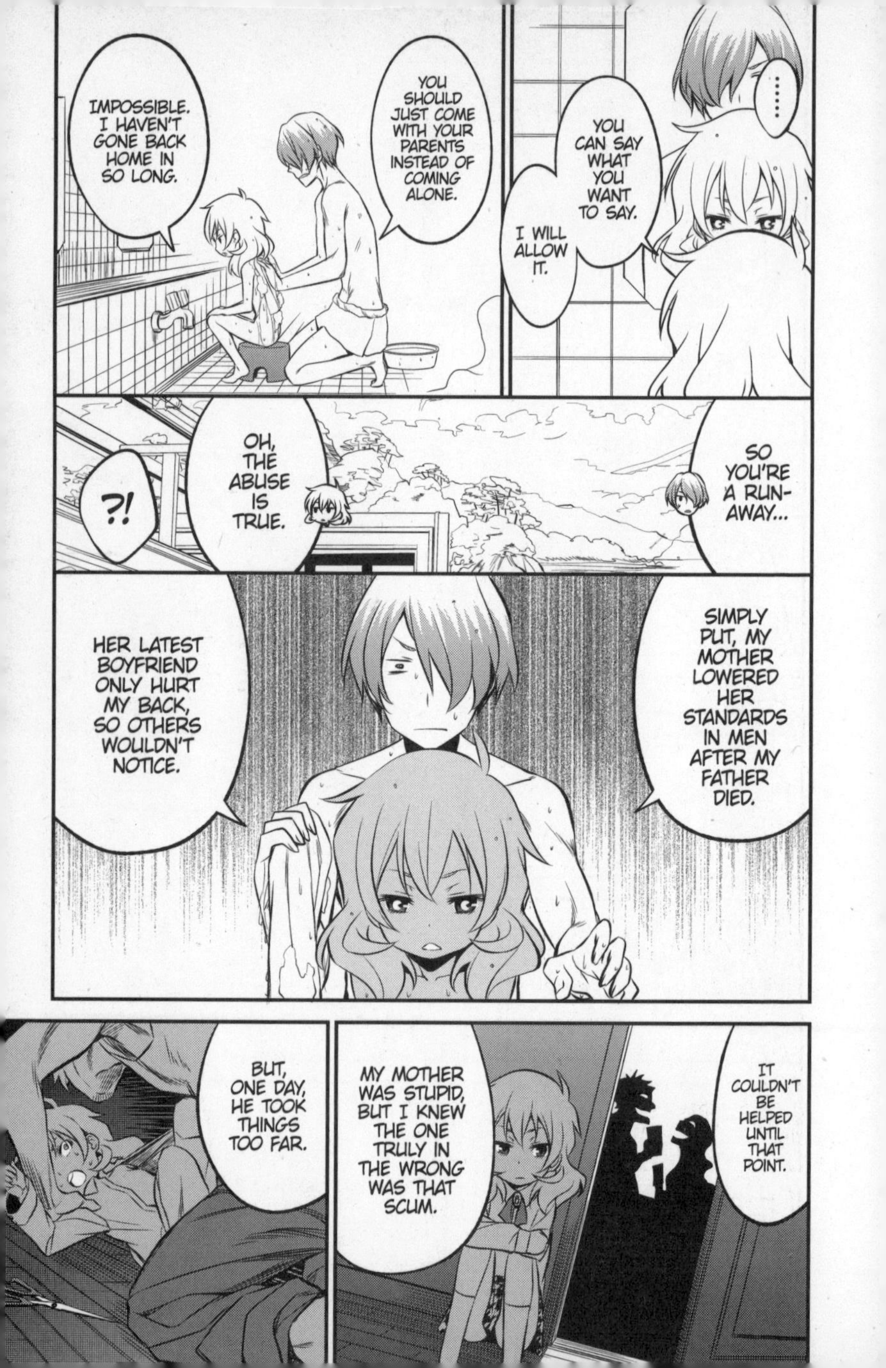
......
YOU CAN SAY WHAT YOU WANT TO SAY.
I WILL ALLOW IT.
YOU SHOULD JUST COME WITH YOUR PARENTS INSTEAD OF COMING ALONE.
IMPOSSIBLE. I HAVEN'T GONE BACK HOME IN SO LONG.
SO YOU'RE A RUN-AWAY...
OH, THE ABUSE IS TRUE.
?!
SIMPLY PUT, MY MOTHER LOWERED HER STANDARDS IN MEN AFTER MY FATHER DIED.
HER LATEST BOYFRIEND ONLY HURT MY BACK, SO OTHERS WOULDN'T NOTICE.
IT COULDN'T BE HELPED UNTIL THAT POINT.
MY MOTHER WAS STUPID, BUT I KNEW THE ONE TRULY IN THE WRONG WAS THAT SCUM.
BUT, ONE DAY, HE TOOK THINGS TOO FAR.

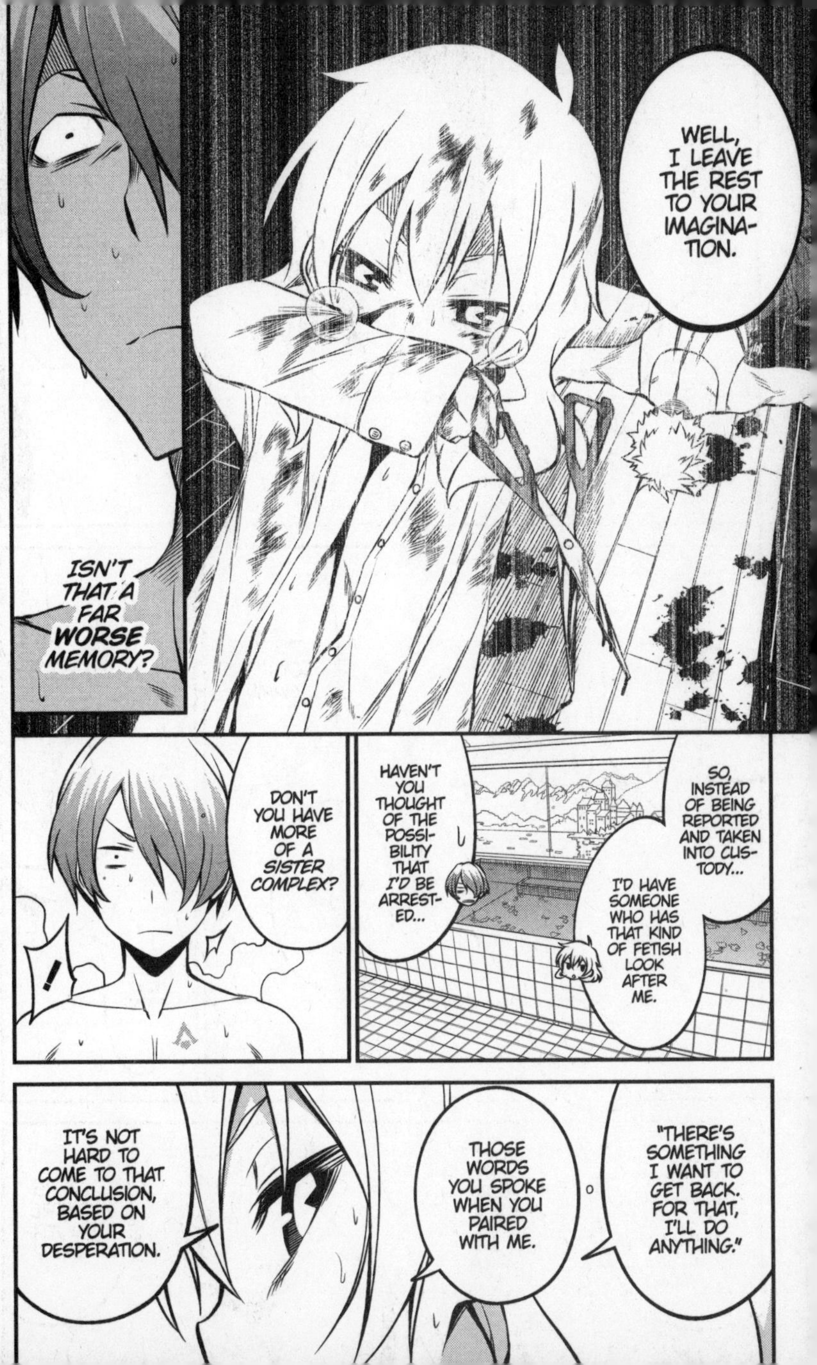
WELL, I LEAVE THE REST TO YOUR IMAGINATION.
ISN'T THAT A FAR *WORSE* MEMORY?
HAVEN'T YOU THOUGHT OF THE POSSIBILITY THAT *I'D* BE ARRESTED...
SO, INSTEAD OF BEING REPORTED AND TAKEN INTO CUSTODY...
I'D HAVE SOMEONE WHO HAS THAT KIND OF FETISH LOOK AFTER ME.
DON'T YOU HAVE MORE OF A *SISTER* COMPLEX?
!
"THERE'S SOMETHING I WANT TO GET BACK. FOR THAT, I'LL DO ANYTHING."
THOSE WORDS YOU SPOKE WHEN YOU PAIRED WITH ME.
IT'S NOT HARD TO COME TO THAT CONCLUSION, BASED ON YOUR DESPERATION.

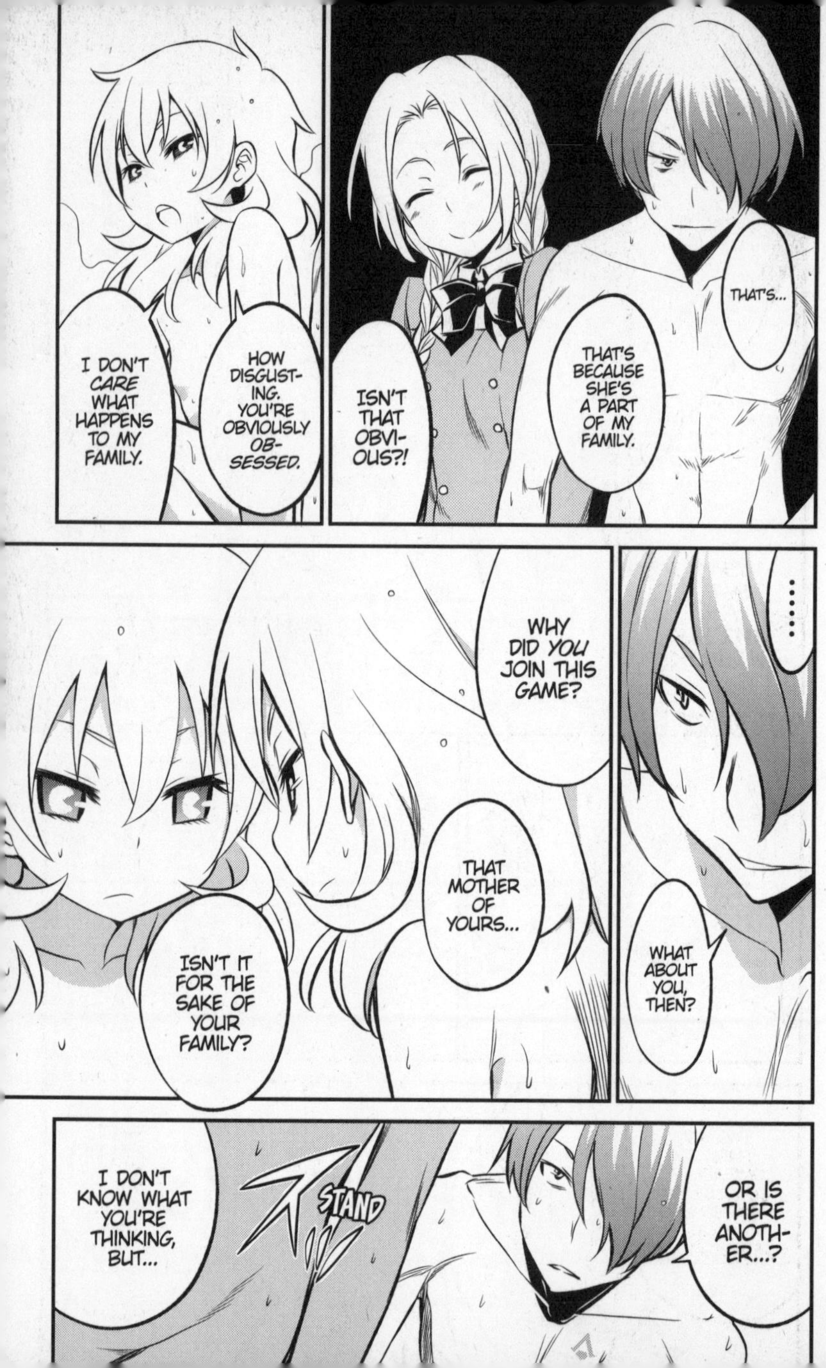
THAT'S...
THAT'S BECAUSE SHE'S A PART OF MY FAMILY.
ISN'T THAT OBVIOUS?!
HOW DISGUSTING. YOU'RE OBVIOUSLY OBSESSED.
I DON'T CARE WHAT HAPPENS TO MY FAMILY.
......
WHAT ABOUT YOU, THEN?
WHY DID YOU JOIN THIS GAME?
THAT MOTHER OF YOURS...
ISN'T IT FOR THE SAKE OF YOUR FAMILY?
OR IS THERE ANOTHER...?
STAND
I DON'T KNOW WHAT YOU'RE THINKING, BUT...

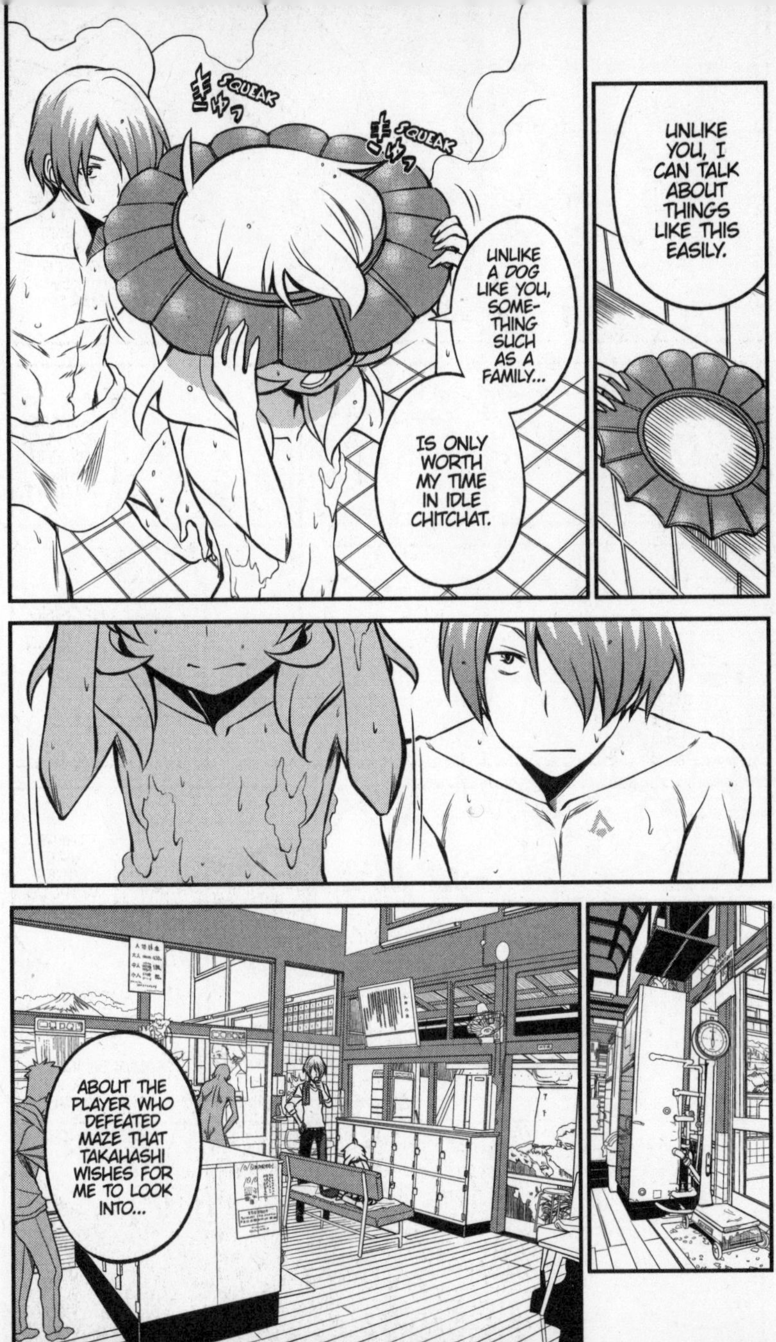
UNLIKE YOU, I CAN TALK ABOUT THINGS LIKE THIS EASILY.
SQUEAK
SQUEAK
UNLIKE A DOG LIKE YOU, SOME-THING SUCH AS A FAMILY...
IS ONLY WORTH MY TIME IN IDLE CHITCHAT.
ABOUT THE PLAYER WHO DEFEATED MAZE THAT TAKAHASHI WISHES FOR ME TO LOOK INTO...

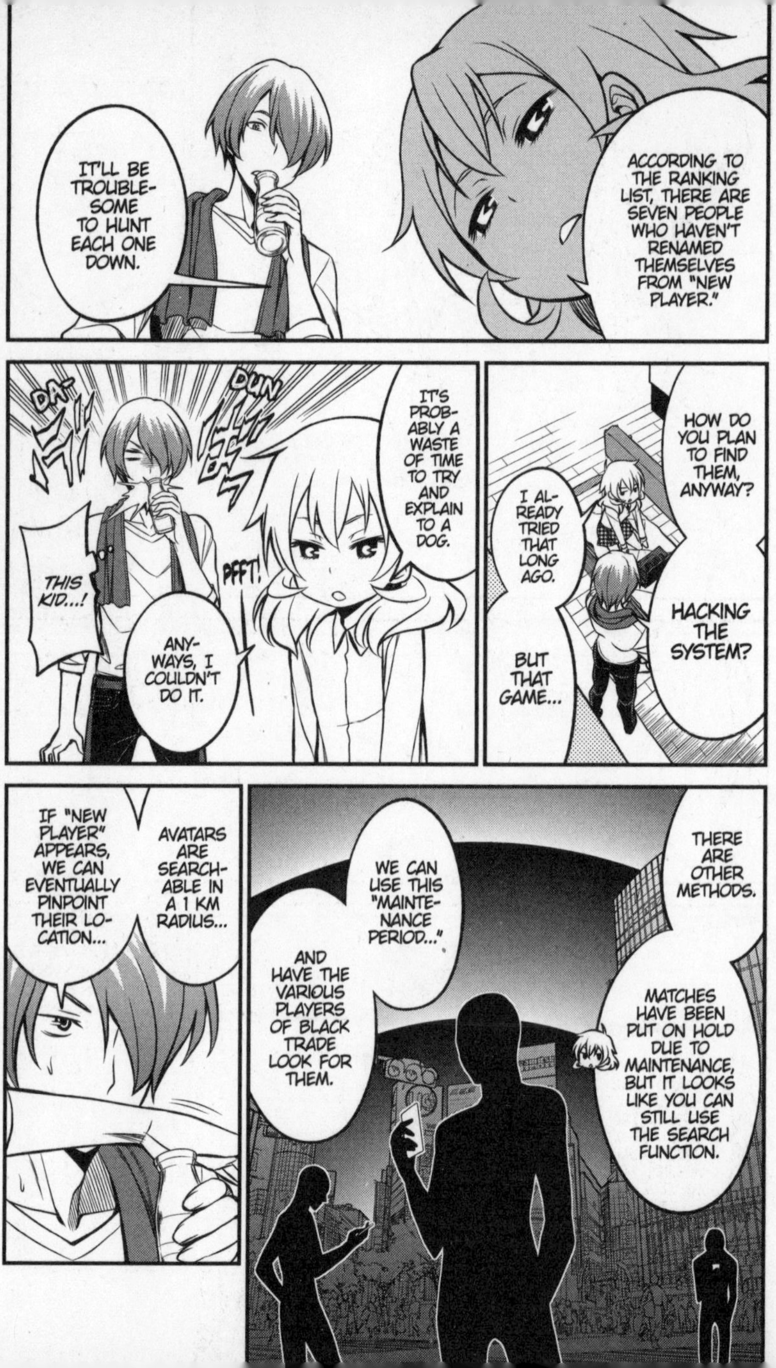
ACCORDING TO THE RANKING LIST, THERE ARE SEVEN PEOPLE WHO HAVEN'T RENAMED THEMSELVES FROM "NEW PLAYER."
IT'LL BE TROUBLESOME TO HUNT EACH ONE DOWN.
HOW DO YOU PLAN TO FIND THEM, ANYWAY?
HACKING THE SYSTEM?
I ALREADY TRIED THAT LONG AGO.
BUT THAT GAME...
IT'S PROBABLY A WASTE OF TIME TO TRY AND EXPLAIN TO A DOG.
DUN
DA-
PFFT!
ANYWAYS, I COULDN'T DO IT.
THIS KID...!
THERE ARE OTHER METHODS.
WE CAN USE THIS "MAINTENANCE PERIOD..."
MATCHES HAVE BEEN PUT ON HOLD DUE TO MAINTENANCE, BUT IT LOOKS LIKE YOU CAN STILL USE THE SEARCH FUNCTION.
AND HAVE THE VARIOUS PLAYERS OF BLACK TRADE LOOK FOR THEM.
AVATARS ARE SEARCHABLE IN A 1 KM RADIUS...
IF "NEW PLAYER" APPEARS, WE CAN EVENTUALLY PINPOINT THEIR LOCATION...

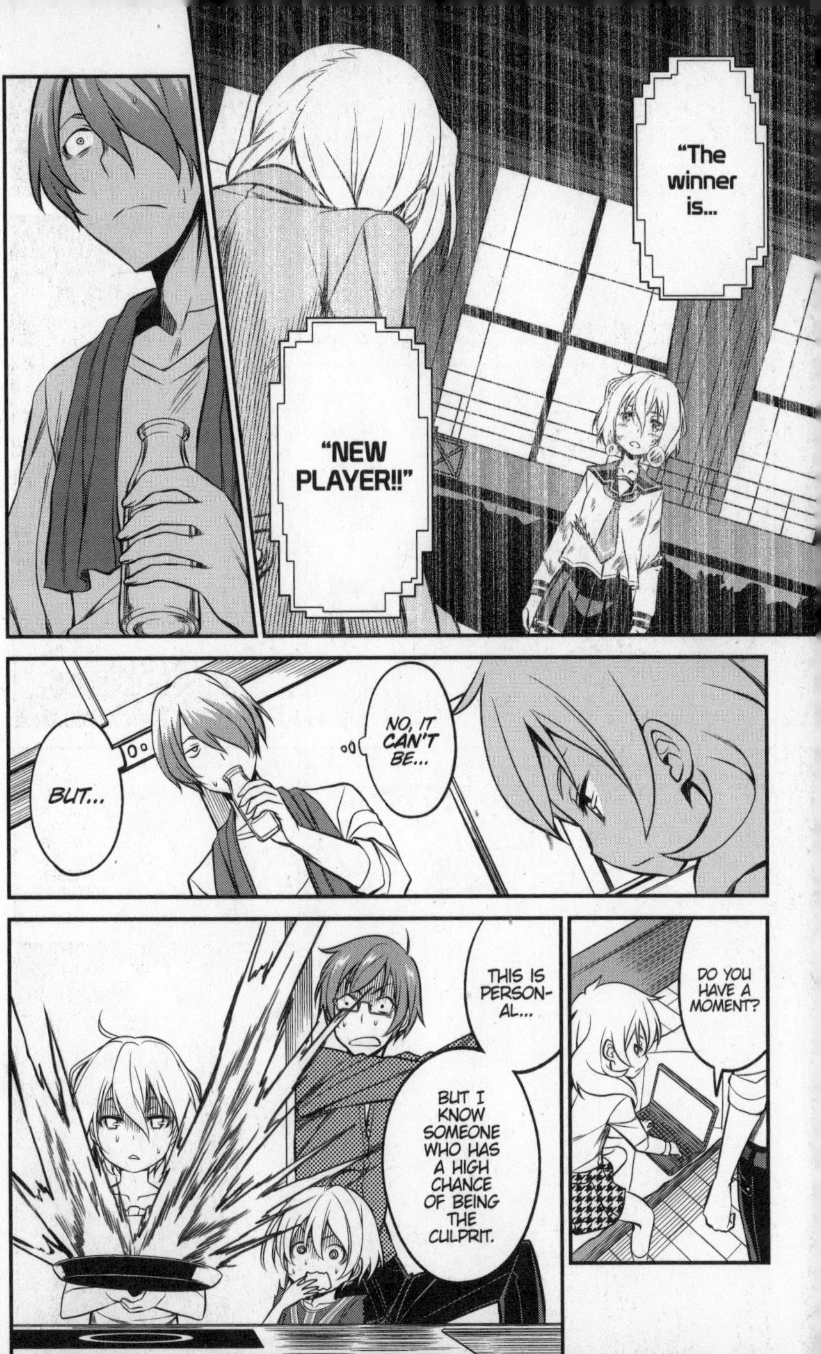
"The winner is...
"NEW PLAYER!!"
NO, IT CAN'T BE...
BUT...
DO YOU HAVE A MOMENT?
THIS IS PERSONAL...
BUT I KNOW SOMEONE WHO HAS A HIGH CHANCE OF BEING THE CULPRIT.

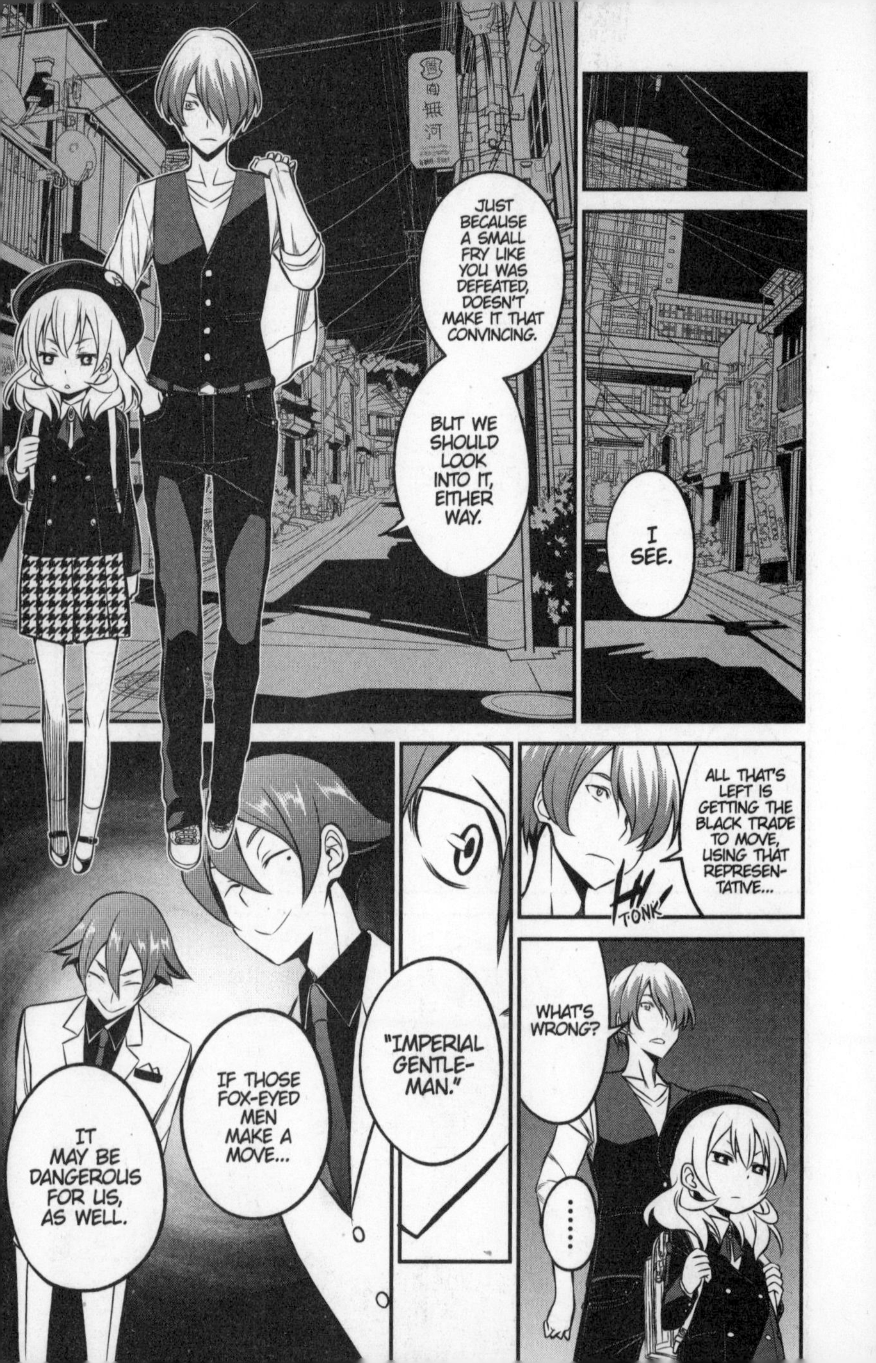
I SEE.
JUST BECAUSE A SMALL FRY LIKE YOU WAS DEFEATED, DOESN'T MAKE IT THAT CONVINCING.
BUT WE SHOULD LOOK INTO IT, EITHER WAY.
ALL THAT'S LEFT IS GETTING THE BLACK TRADE TO MOVE, USING THAT REPRESEN-TATIVE...
TONK
WHAT'S WRONG?
......
"IMPERIAL GENTLE-MAN."
IF THOSE FOX-EYED MEN MAKE A MOVE...
IT MAY BE DANGEROUS FOR US, AS WELL.

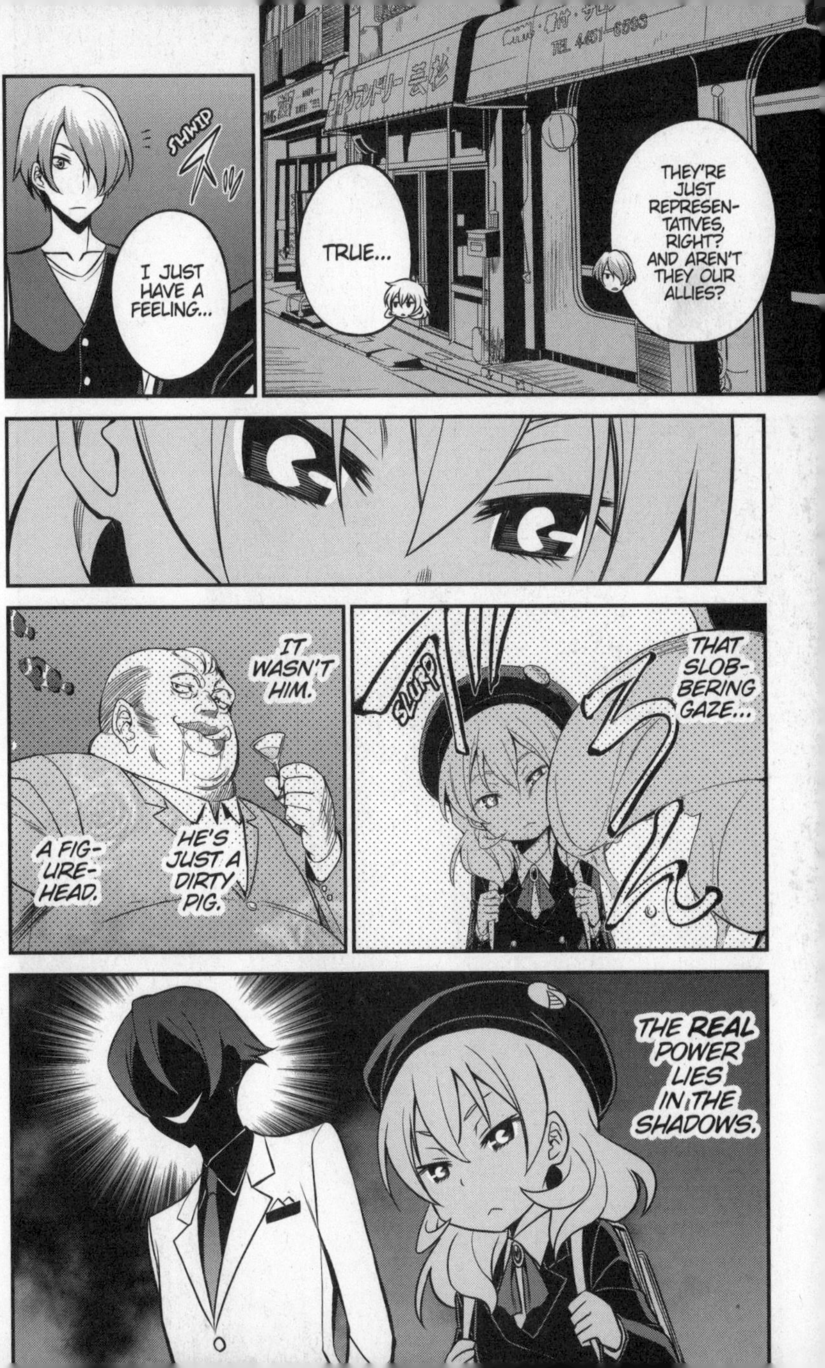
THEY'RE JUST REPRESEN-TATIVES, RIGHT? AND AREN'T THEY OUR ALLIES?
TRUE...
SHWIP
I JUST HAVE A FEELING...
THAT SLOB-BERING GAZE...
SLURP
IT WASN'T HIM.
HE'S JUST A DIRTY PIG.
A FIG-URE-HEAD.
THE REAL POWER LIES IN THE SHADOWS.

AN OVER-WHELMING POWER THAT WILL *CRUSH* THOSE WHO BETRAY THEM.

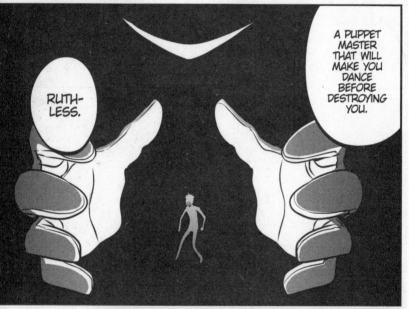

A PUPPET MASTER THAT WILL MAKE YOU DANCE BEFORE DESTROYING YOU.

RUTH-LESS.

A *TRUE* TYRANT.

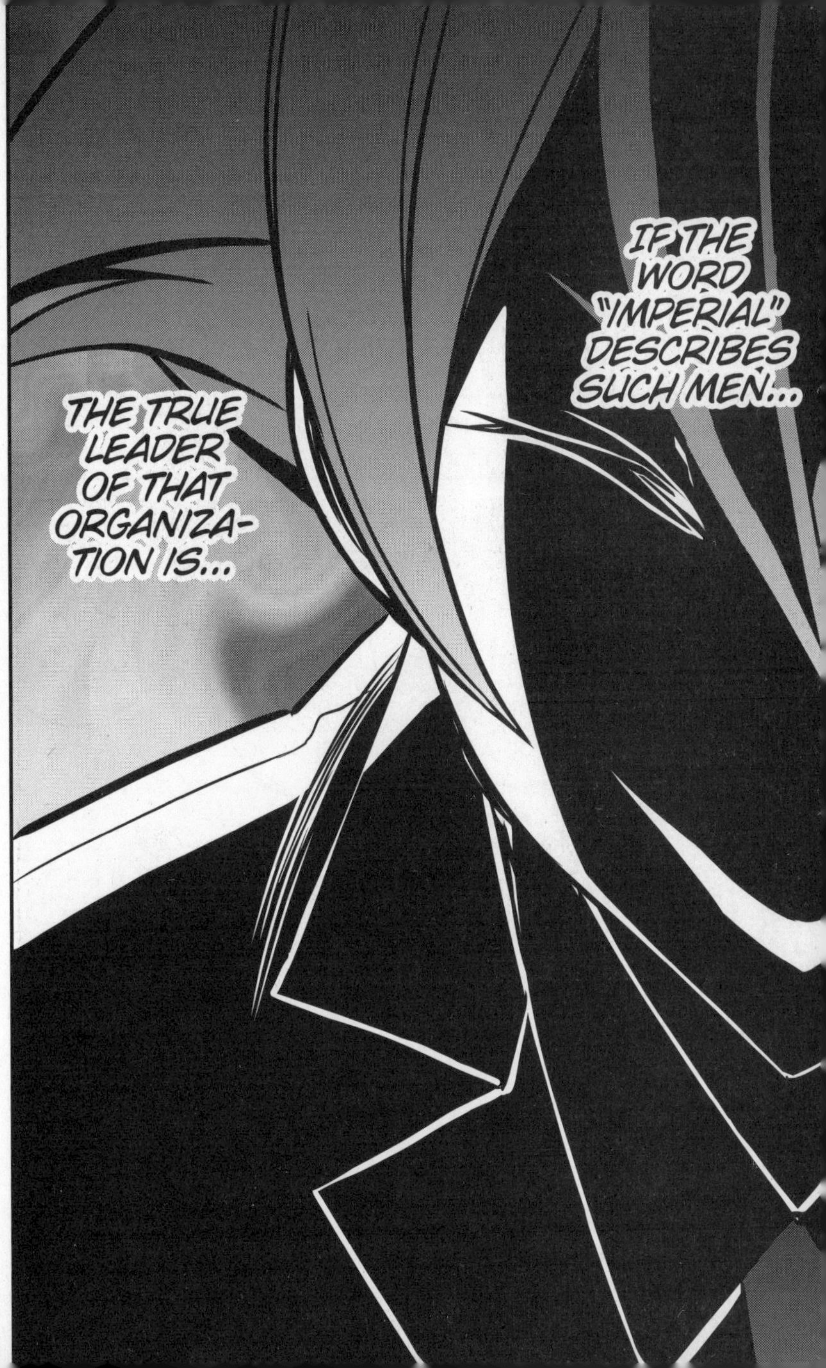
IF THE WORD "IMPERIAL" DESCRIBES SUCH MEN...
THE TRUE LEADER OF THAT ORGANIZA-TION IS...

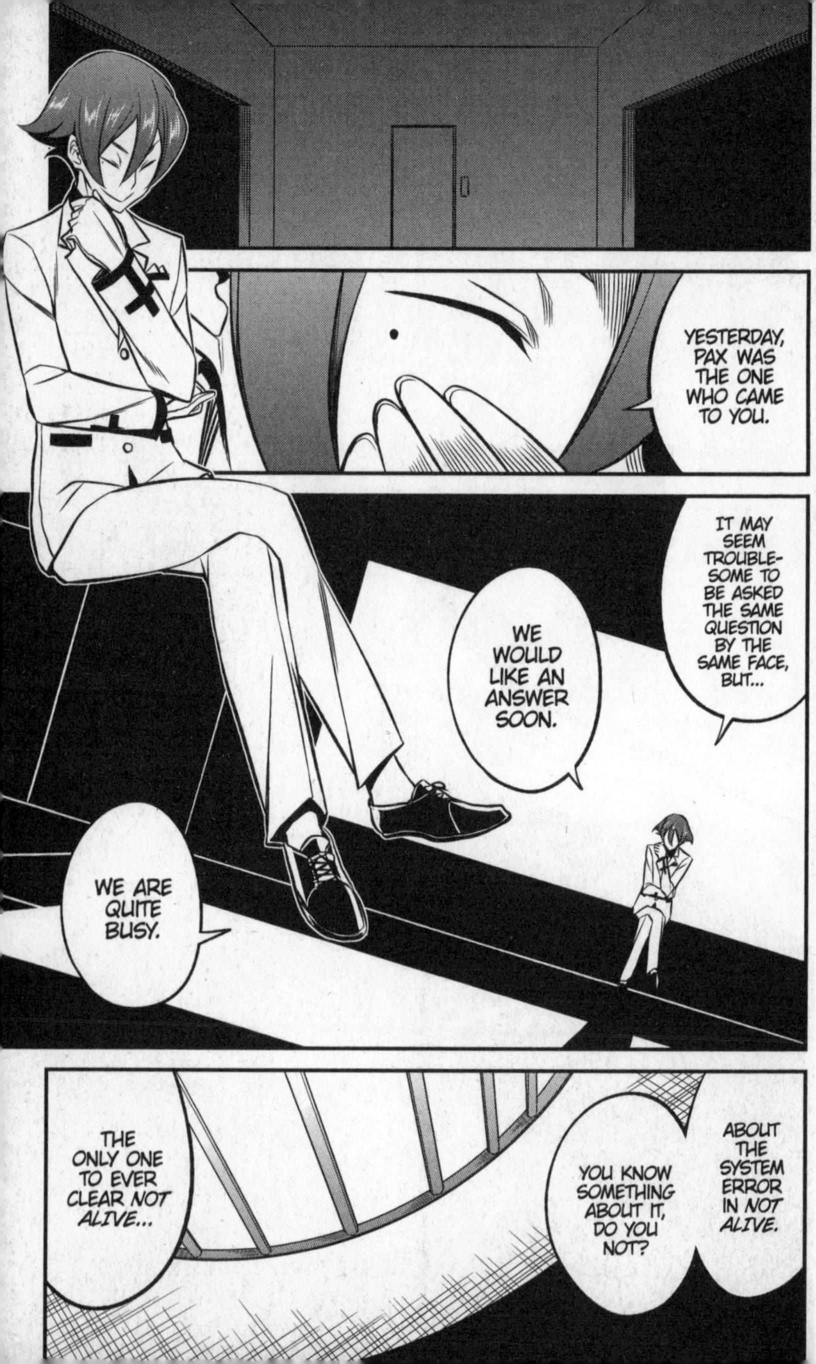
YESTERDAY, PAX WAS THE ONE WHO CAME TO YOU.
IT MAY SEEM TROUBLE-SOME TO BE ASKED THE SAME QUESTION BY THE SAME FACE, BUT...
WE WOULD LIKE AN ANSWER SOON.
WE ARE QUITE BUSY.
ABOUT THE SYSTEM ERROR IN *NOT ALIVE.*
YOU KNOW SOMETHING ABOUT IT, DO YOU NOT?
THE ONLY ONE TO EVER CLEAR *NOT ALIVE*...

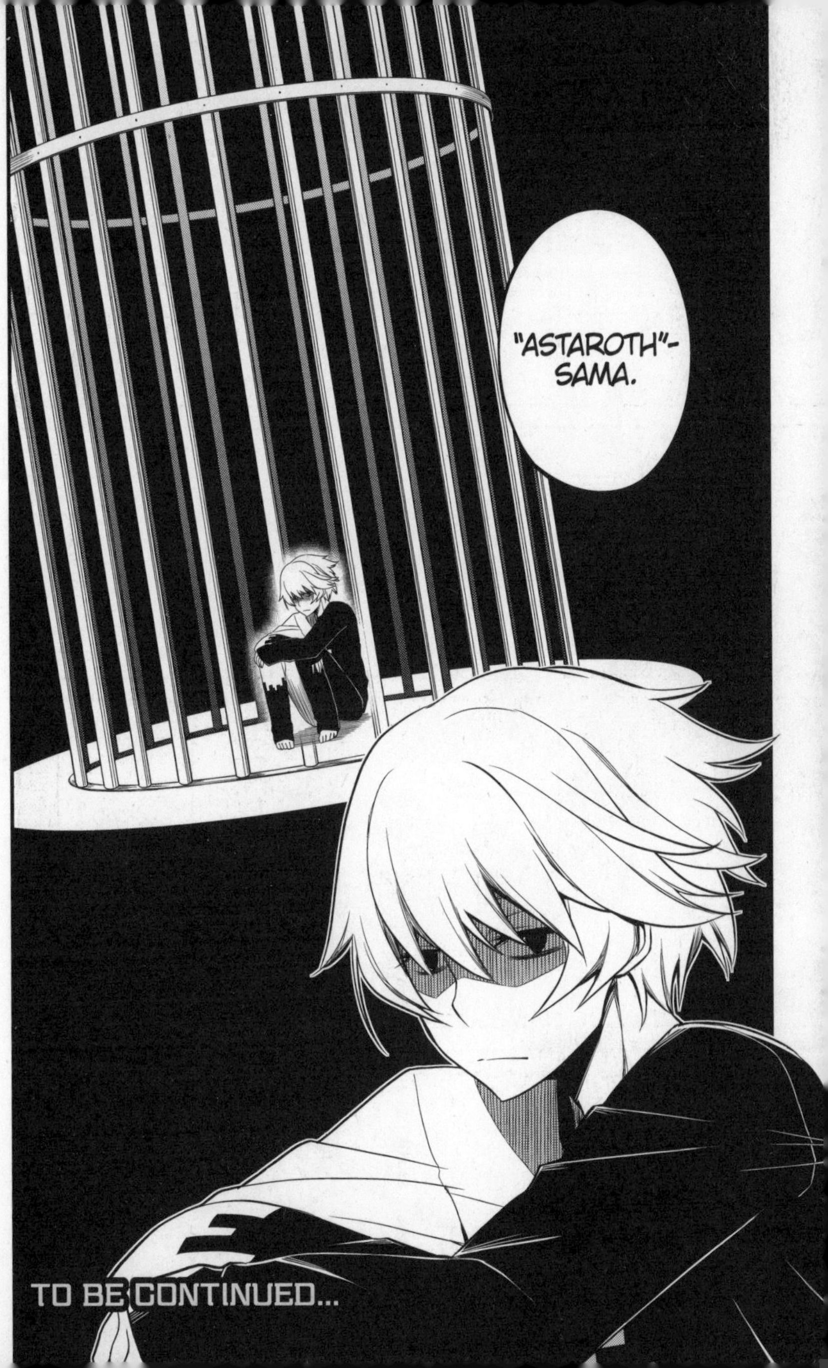
"ASTAROTH"-SAMA.
TO BE CONTINUED...

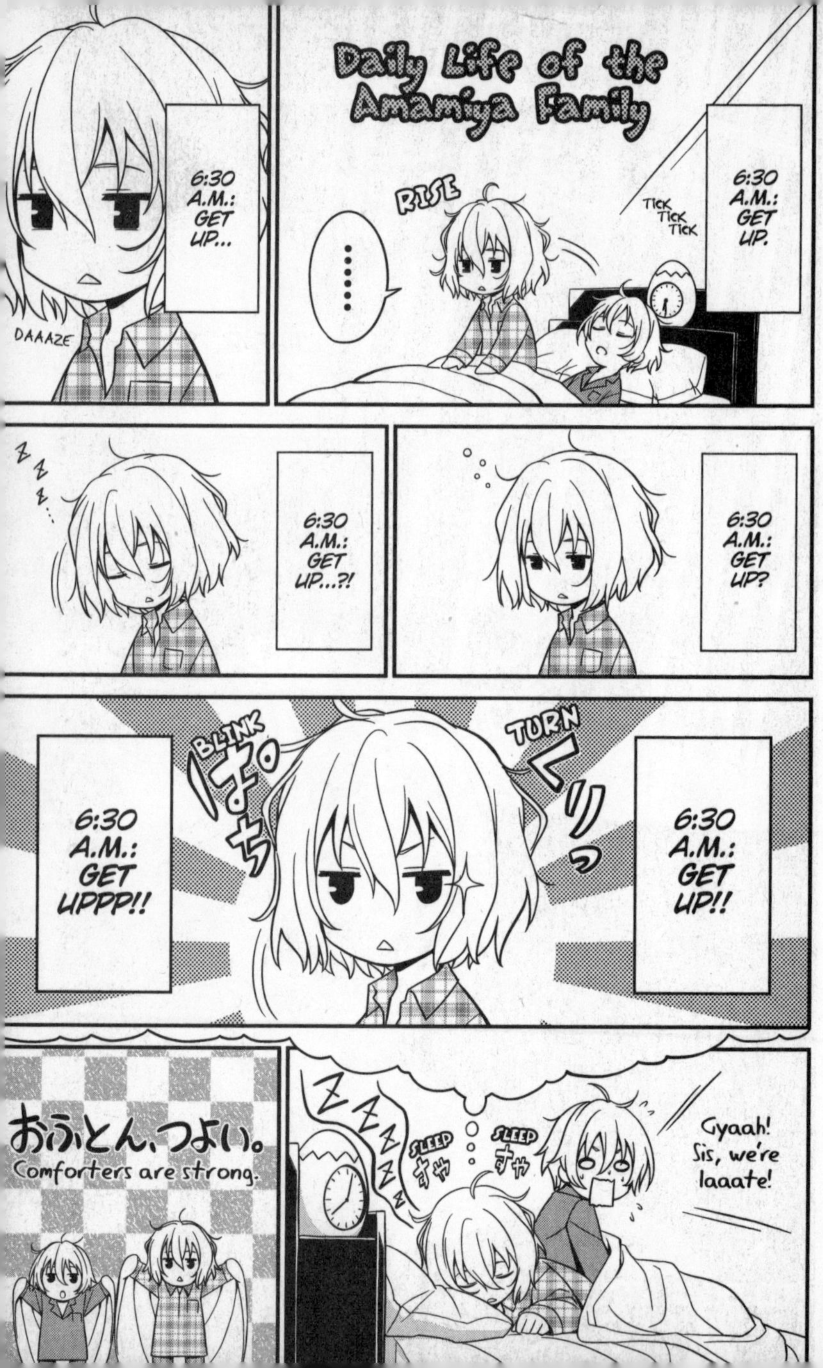
Daily Life of the Amamiya Family
6:30 A.M.: GET UP.
TICK TICK TICK
RISE
......
6:30 A.M.: GET UP...
DAAAZE
6:30 A.M.: GET UP?
6:30 A.M.: GET UP...?!
Z z z...
6:30 A.M.: GET UP!!
TURN
BLINK
6:30 A.M.: GET UPPP!!
Gyaah! Sis, we're laaate!
SLEEP
SLEEP
Z Z Z Z Z
おふとん、つよい。
Comforters are strong.

THE RELATIONSHIP BETWEEN THE TWO GETS TESTED?!

[NOT ALIVE] IS A DATING SIMULATION GAME.

IS AMAMIYA'S "LIKE" PARAMETER GOING GOOD WITH THE "STAYING OVERNIGHT EVENT"?

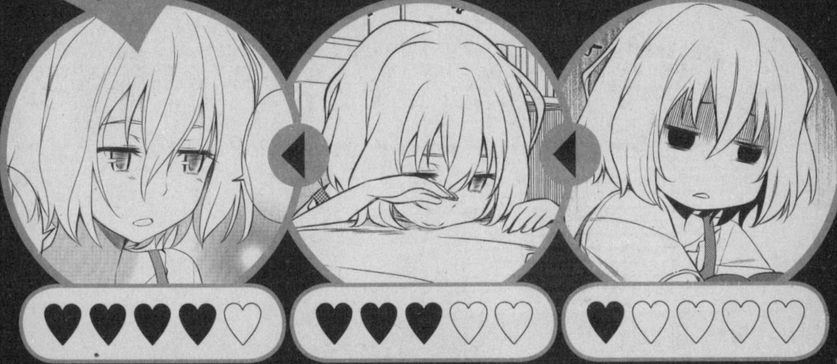

A CHANCE TO GET EVENT CGS BASED ON YOUR CHOICES!! MAYBE...?

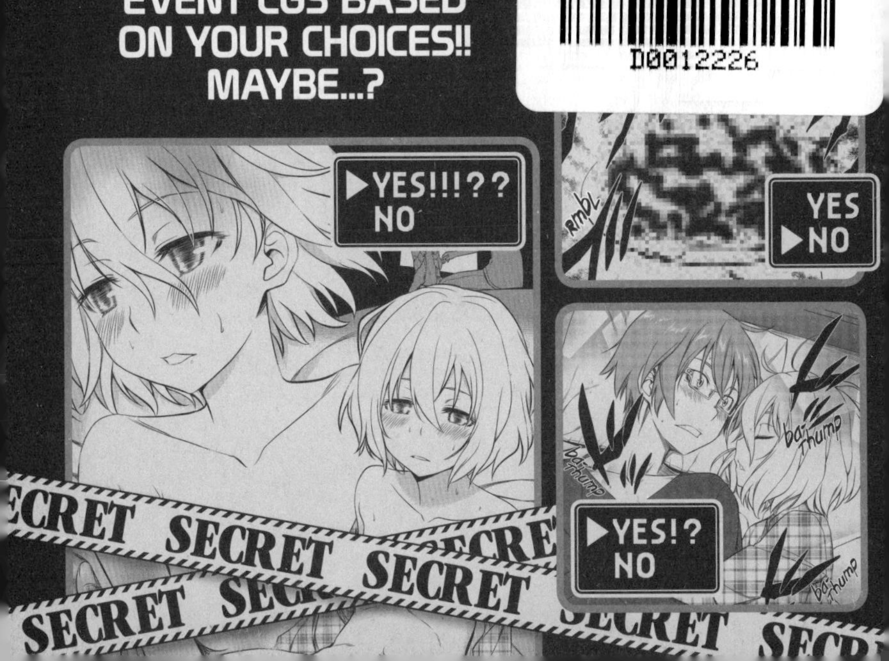
YES ▶NO
rmbl
▶YES!!!?? NO
▶YES!? NO
ba-thump
ba-thump
ba-thump
SECRET
SECRET
SECRET
SECRET